SENTENCING RAPE

This book presents an in-depth comparative study of sentencing practice for rape in six common law jurisdictions: England and Wales, Scotland, Ireland, Canada, New Zealand, and South Africa. It provides a thorough review of the medical literature on the physical and psychological effects of rape, the legal and philosophical literature on the seriousness of the offence, and the victim's role in sentencing. Given the increasingly common practice of perpetrators using mobile and online technologies to film or photograph the commission of sexual offences, the book examines recent socio-legal research on technology-facilitated sexual violence and considers the implications for sentencing.

By building on recent scholarship on judicial decision-making in sentencing and case law – comprising over 250 decisions of the relevant appellate courts – the book explores and critically analyses judicial approaches to rape sentencing. The analysis is undertaken with a view to suggesting possible reforms to rape sentencing in 'non-guideline' jurisdictions. In so doing, this book seeks to establish general principles for sentencing rape, assisting in the imposition of proportionate sentences.

This book will be of interest to judges and practising lawyers; to those researching criminal law, criminal justice, criminology, and gender studies; and to policy makers, including sentencing councils and commissions, in common law jurisdictions worldwide.

Sentencing Rape

A Comparative Analysis

Graeme Brown

•HART•
OXFORD • LONDON • NEW YORK • NEW DELHI • SYDNEY

HART PUBLISHING

Bloomsbury Publishing Plc

Kemp House, Chawley Park, Cumnor Hill, Oxford, OX2 9PH, UK

1385 Broadway, New York, NY 10018, USA

HART PUBLISHING, the Hart/Stag logo, BLOOMSBURY and the Diana logo are trademarks of Bloomsbury Publishing Plc

First published in Great Britain 2020

A catalogue record for this book is available from the British Library.

Library of Congress Cataloging-in-Publication data

Names: Brown, Graeme (Lawyer), author.

Title: Sentencing rape : a comparative analysis / Graeme Brown.

Description: Oxford ; New York : Hart, 2020. | Includes bibliographical references and index.

Identifiers: LCCN 2019053913 (print) | LCCN 2019053914 (ebook) | ISBN 9781509917570 (hardback) | ISBN 9781509917587 (Epub)

Subjects: LCSH: Rape—Law and legislation—English-speaking countries. | Sentences (Criminal procedure)—English-speaking countries.

Classification: LCC K5197 .B76 2020 (print) | LCC K5197 (ebook) | DDC 345/.02532—dc23

LC record available at https://lccn.loc.gov/2019053913

LC ebook record available at https://lccn.loc.gov/2019053914

ISBN: HB: 978-1-50991-757-0
ePDF: 978-1-50991-759-4
ePub: 978-1-50991-758-7

Typeset by Compuscript Ltd, Shannon
Printed and bound in Great Britain by TJ International Ltd, Padstow, Cornwall

To find out more about our authors and books visit www.hartpublishing.co.uk. Here you will find extracts, author information, details of forthcoming events and the option to sign up for our newsletters.

ACKNOWLEDGEMENTS

I am grateful to Mr Thomas O'Malley (NUI Galway), Professors Clare McGlynn and Thom Brooks (Durham University), Professor Jonathan Doak (Nottingham Trent University), and the anonymous reviewers at Hart Publishing for their comments on initial drafts of this book. Thank you to Bill Asquith (former Senior Commissioning Editor at Hart) and to Rosamund Jubber and Linda Staniford at Hart for their sustained support. I would also like to thank Mr Justice John Edwards of the Court of Appeal for helpful discussions on developments in sentencing law and policy in the Republic of Ireland, in particular the passing of the recent Judicial Council Bill. My friend and former colleague at the Supreme Courts in Edinburgh, Ashley Brown, gave generously of her time in checking various references at the Judges' Library, Parliament House. At Durham University, meanwhile, my thanks go to Lily Wildman for her assistance with proof reading. Any errors or omissions are mine alone. My wife, Clair Woods-Brown, continued to be a source of tremendous support and encouragement. Once again, my thanks go to Clair for her love, selflessness, and understanding during the time it has taken to research and write this book.

I have endeavoured to state the law in the various jurisdictions whose sentencing law and practice is considered in this monograph as at 1 June 2019. It has, however, been possible to take account of certain policy and legislative developments, as well as certain developments in case law, since that date.

Dr Graeme Brown
September 2019

TABLE OF CONTENTS

TABLE OF CASES

Australia

Canada

England and Wales

New Zealand

Republic of Ireland

Scotland

South Africa

TABLE OF STATUTES

Canada

England and Wales

New Zealand

Republic of Ireland

Scotland

South Africa

1

Sentencing Rape

An Introduction to the Study

On 29 April 2016 at the High Court at Aberdeen, Justinas Gubinas, Ovidijus Kavaliauskas and Nerijus Radavicius were convicted of sexually assaulting and repeatedly raping a young woman, RD, at a farmhouse near Fraserburgh, Aberdeenshire. The charge narrated that the three accused committed the offences 'while acting together, while [RD] was intoxicated and incapable of giving or withholding consent'. The parties met in a nightclub. The victim, who was heavily intoxicated, left the nightclub in a car with the three accused, thinking that she was going to a party. She was, in fact, taken to the remote farmhouse where the offences took place.

The victim gave at trial evidence that she was forced to consume more alcohol and thereafter forced to participate in various sexual acts against her will. In particular, the victim was coerced into sexual activity with two of the accused simultaneously. The accused recorded the offences on their mobile phones. Further video footage taken on mobile phones the next morning showed the first accused kicking the victim awake, before again forcing her into further sexual activity. The victim sustained bruising to her neck, lower back and buttocks, as well as vaginal injuries. Evidence was led from prosecution witnesses that, on returning home, the victim was distressed and had sobbed uncontrollably. The three accused maintained that the victim had consented to, and indeed instigated, the sexual activity. In convicting the three accused, the jury rejected their accounts.

The accused were sentenced some four weeks later, on 26 May 2016, at the High Court at Glasgow. In passing sentence, the judge made the following remarks:

> 'The crime of which you have been convicted, rape, is a grave crime against which all women should be protected. That being so, the Court will not flinch from making it plain that such crimes will attract a significant prison sentence. In the case of each of you, I consider that there is no appropriate alternative to a custodial disposal … Taking all of these factors into account and exercising such leniency as I can in all the circumstances, I sentence each of you to a period of imprisonment of four years and six months.'[1]

[1] Available at: www.scotland-judiciary.org.uk/8/1596/HMA-v-Justinas-Gubinas--Ovidijus-Kavaliauskas-And-Nerijus-Radavicius (accessed 1 September 2019).

This case, reported as *Gubinas and Radavicius v HMA*,[2] is well known to Scottish lawyers as the leading decision on how juries are to approach the assessment of video evidence. Academic and practitioner commentary has focused on this aspect of the decision (eg Gordon, 2017: 484 and Shead, 2017: 827). Yet, despite the sentences imposed on the accused being viewed as 'significant' custodial terms by the sentencing judge, sentences of four-and-a-half years' imprisonment for what amounts to the abduction and gang rape of an intoxicated victim raise important questions about how the crime of rape is sentenced. The decision in *Gubinas and Radavicius* highlights many of the key themes considered in this book. These include the seriousness of rape; the effect on the victim; the increasingly common tendency for sex offenders to film or photograph their offences; whether the sentences imposed by the courts adequately reflect the harm caused by rape and the culpability of the offender; the approach of the courts to sentencing cases featuring intoxicated or incapable victims; and how best to ensure that proportionate sentences are imposed for rape.

This book presents a comparative study of contemporary sentencing practice for the crime of rape in six common law jurisdictions: England and Wales, Scotland, Canada, the Republic of Ireland, New Zealand and South Africa. Building upon a thorough review of the medical literature on the physical and psychological effects of rape, the legal and philosophical literature on the seriousness of the offence, recent scholarship on judicial decision-making in sentencing and the sentencing case law of the various appellate courts, the book explores and critically analyses judicial approaches to sentencing rape in each jurisdiction.

The analysis is undertaken with a view to suggesting possible reforms to rape sentencing in 'non-guideline' jurisdictions, namely countries such as Scotland, the Republic of Ireland and Canada, which have traditionally eschewed numerical, prescriptive and presumptively binding sentencing guidelines, in which judges have enjoyed considerable discretion in sentencing and in which the sentencing environment has, accordingly, been relatively unstructured. In so doing, an attempt is made to establish general principles for sentencing rape in such jurisdictions to ensure that the courts impose proportionate sentences for the offence. Establishing such general principles will also achieve a level of consistency and predictability in rape sentencing, insofar as this is possible and desirable.[3]

It will be argued that reform of sentencing practice for rape in certain jurisdictions, including Scotland, is urgently required. Unlike their counterparts in jurisdictions such as New Zealand, Scottish judges, for example, do not have the benefit of guidelines when sentencing rape. Such appellate guidance that does exist, in Scotland at least, does not reflect the seriousness of the offence as measured by the physical and, in particular, the psychological harm caused to victims nor does it reflect modern societal attitudes towards the offence.

[2] [2017] HCJAC 59; 2018 JC 45 (a decision of a bench of five judges).
[3] See *HMA v Cooperwhite* [2013] HCJAC 88; 2013 SCCR 461 at [23].

Having compared sentencing practice for rape across the various jurisdictions, whether in the form of general principles, appellate guideline judgments, formal numerical guidelines issued by sentencing councils, or mandatory and minimum sentences set by the legislature, the book considers what form the proposed sentencing guidelines should take. It is argued, following O'Malley (2011), that to comply with the demands of justice, sentencing must remain discretionary and the selection of sentence in specific cases must remain exclusively a judicial task. This book argues against adopting the current system of prescriptive, numerical and presumptively binding sentencing guidelines devised by the Sentencing Council for England and Wales. It is argued that under the present English system, consistency and predictability of sentencing outcomes are achieved by standardising penal decisions (see Brown, 2017a and Cooper, 2008 and 2013). This approach, it is suggested, is contrary to the traditional focus by courts throughout the common law world on the attainment of individualised justice.

There is, however, a clear need for judicial discretion in rape sentencing to be structured by appellate guidance to allow judges to exercise *principled* discretion (O'Malley, 2001: 35). Following Harris and Gerry (2013: 241–42) this book argues that what is required is a 'behaviour-based' approach to rape sentencing: offending should be categorised by reference to the true character of the offence in question, thereby achieving consistency in sentencing (insofar as possible) while also ensuring that neither victims nor offenders are unjustly treated (2013: 242).

The Value of a Comparative Analysis of Rape Sentencing

Freiberg (2002: 237) considers that most countries tend to be 'juricentric' in their sentencing practices and their criminal justice systems 'solipsistic'. In England and Wales, this criticism has been directed at the Court of Appeal (Criminal Division), both for its apparent unwillingness to consider the sentencing jurisprudence of other jurisdictions in the course of its judgments (Brown, 2013: 676–77) and, more generally, for its refusal to engage with academic writings. Ashworth, for example, notes that:

> 'I've had a book on sentencing since 1983 [*viz. Sentencing and Criminal Justice*], publishing regular [updates] and I've never once been mentioned in any court judgment – not once … [The judges] are not interested in critical commentary' (Ashworth, 2013a).[4]

Sentencing is, however, one area of law and social policy that lends itself particularly well to comparative treatment. O'Malley (2008: 15) makes the important point that although laws and structures may vary from one country to another

[4] The address is available as a podcast. Available at: http://podcasts.ox.ac.uk/people/andrew-ashworth (accessed 1 September 2019). The relevant passage appears at one hour, 10 minutes and 30 seconds *et seq*.

and different terminology may be used, we are all struggling with the same fundamental questions: why punish? What range of penalties should be available? When is a custodial sentence appropriate? How, if at all, should judicial sentencing discretion be structured (see also Dubber, 2006: 1309)?

Michael Tonry has stressed the importance of scholars, policy makers and practitioners looking across national and jurisdictional boundaries to see what is happening elsewhere, why and with what effect (Tonry, 2002: xxvii). Comparative analyses are of particular benefit if they suggest best practice or ways in which one system may learn from another (Roberts, 2019: 231). In discussing the benefits of comparative analysis in sentencing research, Tata (2002: 10) suggests that a comparative approach places developments in one's own jurisdiction in perspective, while also allowing us to raise our eyes above the parochialism of our taken-for-granted assumptions about sentencing law and practice. In a similar vein, Lord Reed, President of the UK Supreme Court, observes that both academics and the courts open themselves to charges of parochialism if they fail to consider the approaches currently adopted in other comparable jurisdictions. His Lordship explains:

> 'I do not mean that we should reach for off-the-shelf solutions from elsewhere without considering whether they actually provide the best way forward. But we should be willing to consider the possibility that we might learn from the experience of other jurisdictions' (Lord Reed, 2015: 13; see also Lord Carloway, 2013: 10 and Lord Gill, 2016: 17–18).

Davies et al (2002: 273) remark, in a different context, upon 'the problems of cultural relativity and system difference which make life hard for the comparative scholar' and Nelken (2012: 141) highlights the difficulties caused by 'cultural variability in ideas and values'. Such concerns do not feature to any great extent in a comparative study of sentencing practice for rape, however, for the simple reason that the offence is, or ought to be, uniformly viewed with the utmost seriousness across jurisdictions. Feinberg, for example, includes rape on a shortlist of offences that are crimes 'everywhere in the civilised world', the de-criminalisation of which 'no reasonable person could advocate' (Feinberg, 1984: 10). Von Hirsch et al (2005: 210) consider rape to be one of the most demeaning impositions imaginable (see also von Hirsch and Jareborg, 1991: 26), while Gardner and Shute (2000: 193) observe that rape is arguably never excusable and is probably amongst those wrongs which are never justifiable.[5]

Similarly, while major differences in the definitions of offences between jurisdictions can cause problems in some areas of comparative sentencing research (see Freiberg, 2002: 241–42), rape is a 'universal crime' (Terblanche, 2006: 2). Rape tends to be defined in broadly similar terms across the jurisdictions examined in

[5] For a full discussion of the wrongness of rape, see Chapter 2.

this study. A legal definition of rape in each jurisdiction is provided in the relevant chapter, the focus of this book being rape broadly understood as penetration of the vagina, anus or mouth by the offender's penis, without consent.

There is accordingly a high degree of what Nelken terms 'functional equivalence' regarding the seriousness with which the courts in common law jurisdictions view, or purport to view, the offence of rape (Nelken, 2012: 149; 2002: 332; see also Örücü, 2007a: 50–53). A corollary of the seriousness with which the offence is viewed is that there is less scope in this study for falling foul of the danger of 'ethnocentricity' (see generally Nelken, 2017: 423; 2009: 291–92, 306–7; and 2000: 10). While all jurisdictions in this study regard rape as a particularly serious offence, the study seeks to compare and contrast the responses of the courts to the offence through, for example, the issuing of guideline judgments; the use of sentencing guidelines prepared by a sentencing council or commission; or the application of legislative provisions setting out mandatory and minimum sentences. Patterned differences in approaches to rape sentencing are thus considered against a background of otherwise broadly similar social conditions (see Nelken, 2002: 332 and Dubber, 2006: 1308).

This book, therefore, compares rape sentencing across the six common law jurisdictions in an attempt to learn from their practice and to challenge and improve the way in which cases of rape are sentenced (see Nelken, 2009: 291 and 2007: 3, 17–18). The aim is to compare approaches to sentencing rape for the practical purpose of suggesting reform of how the offence is sentenced in jurisdictions that do not have formal systems of sentencing guidelines (see generally Nelken, 2007: 12–13, 32; 2000: 11 and Örücü, 2007a: 44, 55 and 2007b: 413, 415–16). This is achieved through what Nelken terms a 'legal comparativist' approach: this work seeks to classify and learn from the rules, ideals and practice of sentencing in the six jurisdictions (see Nelken, 2017: 419 and 2012: 144 and 147).

The jurisdictions selected for comparison were chosen due to their having similar sentencing traditions and, broadly, similar legal cultures (see Reed, 2015: 13 and Roberts, 2009: 232). Judges in each jurisdiction have traditionally enjoyed a wide sentencing discretion. Yet to understand the way in which those convicted of rape are sentenced in each jurisdiction, it is important to clarify how the sentencing contexts differ between the various jurisdictions (see generally Davies et al, 2002: 261 and 272). In particular, one must appreciate the cultural context of the policies, procedures and practice of sentencing (Davies et al, 2002: 273–74; see also Bussani and Mattei, 2012: 3–6; Grande, 2012: 195–97; and Örücü, 2007a: 53). As Hodgson cautions, a real attempt at understanding the structure and operation of a legal process *in its own context* is required and not simply a cursory glance to see 'if they do what we do, better' (Hodgson, 2000: 152). Thus, in respect of each of the six jurisdictions considered in this book, the discussion begins by considering the sentencing landscape and methodology of the jurisdiction in question. Each chapter then proceeds to consider the nature of any general or particular sentencing guidelines used by the courts.

The Analysis of Rape Sentencing

In common with other legal comparative studies, the account presented in this book relies mainly on historical, philosophical and juridical analyses (Nelken, 2012: 148; 2002: 330; 2000: 6). Particular reliance is placed on descriptions of the activities of the courts in their reported case law and on interpretation of this case law through associated academic commentary (see Nelken, 1995: 445). As Hauffe and Porter explain, as well as being readily accessible to the researcher, founding one's analysis on case law has the advantage that one is using law reports that are themselves based on numerous sources. These include offender, victim and witness accounts, as well as forensic evidence which has already been scrutinised by the legal system in terms of its reliability (Hauffe and Porter, 2009: 474, see also Porter and Alison, 2006: 362–63). Sentencing decisions, as reported in case reports, are also one of the few points in the criminal justice system where the reasoning behind the exercise of discretion is, or ought to be, recorded in public documents. Thus, the reported sentencing decisions of the courts also provide important insights into judicial and social reasoning about rape (Chennells, 2009: 23–24).

Despite case law being a vital source for the understanding of the judicial approach to sentencing rape, the limitations of a study based purely on an analysis of case law must be recognised. As Roberts et al (2000: 1) note, only a very small percentage of sentences imposed will be captured by the reporting services. As only noteworthy cases are reported, they are not necessarily representative of the sentences imposed. Such judgments that do appear in case reports might not explain all the relevant factors considered at the time that sentence was imposed.

It must also be acknowledged that reporting rates for the crime of rape are low. It has been estimated, for example, that between 75 and 95 per cent of rapes in England and Wales are never reported to the police (see HM Crown Prosecution Service Inspectorate, 2007: 34). Various legal and extra-legal factors are identified in the research literature as increasing attrition: victims' uncertainty that their report will be taken seriously; ambivalence towards the perpetrator (especially where, as in the majority of sexual assaults, the perpetrator is known to the victim); feelings of shame, fear or humiliation; and fear of police and court procedures (see Heidensohn and Gelsthorpe, 2007: 397; Horvath and Gray, 2013: 217–18; Powell, 2015: 576; and Temkin, 2002: 1–11). Criminal justice processes such as the predominantly male-dominated adversarial trial system have, for example, been condemned by Lees as constituting a 'secondary rape' for the victims of such crime (Lees, 2002, cited in Hall, 2010: 112; see also Brooks-Hay et al, 2019: 1). Clare McGlynn explains that while feminist activism in recent years has understandably concentrated on securing public acknowledgement that rape is a serious crime that demands significant punishment through the criminal justice system, the hope that sexual violence could be eradicated by harnessing the power of the State to condemn has not been realised (McGlynn, 2011: 836; see also Campbell, 2017: 484; Godden, 2009: 25, 27–29; Lacey, 1998: 101; McGlynn et al, 2012: 239 and Powell, 2015: 580). McGlynn considers that although there has been extensive, often feminist-inspired, law reform (eg McGlynn, 2010a and Cowan, 2010), there is 'yet little evidence of any reduction in the prevalence of sexual violence, few convictions of perpetrators and a system which affords victims little justice' (McGlynn, 2011: 836; see also Larcombe, 2011: 30–31; McGlynn et al, 2012: 231; and McGlynn and Munro, 2010: 6–8). Thus, perhaps more so than with any other offence, the number of rape cases brought to appeal, either by the offender appealing his sentence or by the prosecution appealing against the sentence on the grounds of undue leniency, represent only a small fraction of the rapes committed each year (see also Godden, 2013: 105; Horvath and Gray, 2013: 229; and Porter and Alison, 2006: 363).

This is not to suggest that reported decisions of, for example, the Court of Appeal (Criminal Division) in England and Wales, of the High Court of Justiciary on appeal in Scotland[6] and of the respective Courts of Appeal in Ireland, New Zealand and South Africa concerning rape sentencing are not used daily by judges in these jurisdictions. Indeed, as we shall see, guidelines have long existed for sentencing rape in England and Wales[7] and the decisions of the Court of Appeal in appeals against sentence every year continue to shape sentencing practice (Padfield, 2016a: 235). In Scotland, the Appeal Court is now more prepared than in the past to issue guideline judgments and, in recent years, has addressed important points of principle in the sentencing of rape.[8] In the Republic of Ireland, the Supreme Court has issued certain guidance on rape sentencing,[9] while in New Zealand, a guideline judgment on rape sentencing was issued by the Court of Appeal in 2010.[10] In South Africa, meanwhile, the system of mandatory and minimum sentences for rape and the circumstances in which the courts are justified in departing from the prescribed sentences, has generated a substantial body of case law.[11] Rather than suggesting that such case law is not a valuable source of information on the sentencing practice and culture of the courts, it is simply an acknowledgement that judgments are written on only a small percentage of cases sentenced by the criminal courts.

Ideally, the use of case law as a means of understanding judicial decision-making in rape sentencing should buttress an analysis of other sources of data, such as empirical data derived from interviews with judges (eg Ashworth et al, 1984; Brown, 2017a and 2014; Mackenzie, 2005 and 2001; and Tombs, 2004). Future directions in the study of rape sentencing could incorporate a variety of different data collection methods, such as interviews with judges, prosecutors, defence counsel, victims and offenders, rather than relying solely on the reported decisions of the appellate courts. Conducting such studies may, however, prove difficult due to time, ethical and accessibility constraints (see Hauffe and Porter, 2009: 486).

[6] Hereinafter 'the Appeal Court'.
[7] See Chapter 4.
[8] See Chapter 5.
[9] See Chapter 6.
[10] See Chapter 7.
[11] Ibid.

A Note on Terminology: 'Victims', 'Survivors', 'Complainants' and 'Complainers'

The term used to describe men and women who have been raped is not uncontroversial (Horvath and Brown, 2009: 5). Terms in use include 'complainant', 'victim', 'survivor' and 'victim-survivor'. In Scottish criminal procedure, meanwhile, the term 'complainer' rather than 'complainant' is used in respect of proceedings for all criminal offences. This term may, in fact, have pejorative connotations for those unfamiliar with Scottish criminal procedure. The term 'victim' may also be used inappropriately in some contexts. As the Appeal Court noted in *Wishart v HMA*,[12] in the context of criminal proceedings it is generally the case that until guilt is admitted or proved it is inappropriate to refer to a complainer (or complainant) as being a 'victim'.[13] Thus, reference should not be made to 'the victim' until the relevant judicial determination has been made (Payne-James and Beh, 2011: 95).

In this book, the term 'victim' is used for two reasons. Firstly, the work provides a detailed examination of sentencing jurisprudence across six common law jurisdictions. The case law from these jurisdictions identifies those who have been raped as 'victims', since the sentencing stage necessarily follows from the conviction of the accused. Secondly, as fully discussed in Chapter 2, use of the term 'victim' identifies the physical and, particularly, the psychological harm caused by those who perpetrate the offence of rape.

One's status as a victim is not fixed, however, but is socially constructed, mobilised and malleable. While many prefer the term 'survivor' to 'victim', we require a word to refer to a person who has been victimised. The term 'victim' is used throughout this book in the sense of an individual having experienced a crime and having been victimised. Use of the term 'victim' is not to be taken as descriptive of that person's identity or as a categorisation of that person (Daly, 2014: 378) nor is use of the term intended to deny the agency of such persons (see Du Mont et al, 2003: 481, fn. 1).

The Scope of this Book

It is acknowledged that the sentencing of particular cases of rape is often more complex than either the leading appellate guideline judgments examined in this study or the formal system of sentencing guidelines operating in England and Wales, might suggest. In recent years there has been a significant increase in the number of cases of historic sexual abuse reported to police and far more prosecutions for historic sexual offending are now being brought than ever before

[12] [2013] HCJAC 168; 2014 JC 190.
[13] Ibid at [7]. See also *Hogan v HMA* [2012] HCJAC 12; 2012 JC 307 at [34].

(eg Inspectorate of Prosecution in Scotland, 2017: 20; Rook and Ward, 2016: Chapter 30). In Scotland, for example, sexual crimes (including historic cases) now constitute 75 per cent of the High Court's workload (Inspectorate of Prosecution in Scotland, 2017: 3). Many cases involve persistent sexual abuse of one or more victims, typically when they were children or adolescents. As a result of the increased numbers of prosecutions for historic sexual offending, elderly accused are frequently sentenced by the courts. As the Court of Appeal (Criminal Division) noted in *R v Clarke*,[14] as at 31 December 2016, the overwhelming majority of the 234 prisoners in England and Wales aged over 80 were sex offenders.[15]

The criminal courts are often faced with sentencing a multiplicity of sexual offences, often committed a very considerable time before a prosecution was initiated. In sentencing such cases, the courts balance the harm caused by sexual abuse and the offender's culpability; however the courts must also grapple with difficult issues including the weight, if any, that should be attached to factors such as the offender's old age and ill-health at the time of sentence and the prospect of the offender dying in prison. Consideration may also have to be given to the capability of the prison estate to make adequate provision for the elderly offender and perhaps to the offender's youth and relative immaturity at the time of the commission of the offences, which may have been many decades ago. In certain cases, the offender may not have committed any further offences in the intervening years and here the court may have to consider whether the offender's good character and unblemished record should have any effect on the final sentence. In England and Wales, guidance was provided on certain of these issues by the Court of Appeal (Criminal Division) in *R v H*,[16] *R v Forbes*,[17] *R v Clarke*[18] and by the Sentencing Council for England and Wales (Sentencing Council, 2013a: 155). This guidance is to the effect that an offender is to be sentenced in accordance with the regime applicable at the date of sentence (see also Rook and Ward, 2019: 9 and 349–64 and Wasik, 2014: 69–71). In Scotland, meanwhile, similar guidance on the sentencing of historic offences was provided by the Appeal Court in *Greig v HMA*.[19]

In examining the sentencing practices for rape in the UK and other common law jurisdictions, however, this book focuses primarily on what has been described in the research literature as the 'classic rape' case (eg Clay-Warner and McMahon-Howard, 2009: 725–27 and Williams, 1984: 460). To keep the discussion within a manageable length, the study examines sentencing law and practice in respect of adult rape, since the issues surrounding child sexual abuse and sentencing for such offences requires specific analysis which is beyond the scope of the present work. This book concentrates mainly, but not exclusively, on the

[14] [2017] 2 Cr App R (S) 18.
[15] Ibid at [12], citing Ministry of Justice figures.
[16] [2012] 2 Cr App R (S) 21.
[17] [2016] 2 Cr App R (S) 44.
[18] *Clarke* (n 14).
[19] [2012] HCJAC 127; 2013 JC 115.

sentencing of cases involving single instances of the rape of adult victims by adult offenders (either strangers or acquaintances).

Discussion focuses mainly on the levels of custodial sentences imposed by the courts following convictions for rape. Again, for reasons of space, certain disposals available to the courts in the jurisdictions examined in this study, such as extended sentences,[20] orders for lifelong restriction,[21] ancillary orders involving, for example, sex offender notification[22] and sexual harm prevention orders[23] are not considered in detail. Readers are referred to the relevant practitioner works and textbooks in the respective jurisdictions.[24]

Finally, it is also acknowledged that this work deals only with judicial sentencing. Nicola Padfield, however, considers that there is a mismatch between the sentences imposed by the courts and offenders' *experience* of sentencing. Padfield suggests that the time has come for a 'significant paradigm shift' requiring judges, lawyers, academic commentators and policy makers to view 'sentencing' not as a one-off event (in the sense of the task undertaken by the sentencing judge), but as an ongoing process (Padfield, 2016a: 231; see also Weitzdörfer et al, 2018: 194). In this way, a coherent sentencing 'structure' includes not only the decisions made by the sentencing judge, but also what happens to the offender throughout the sentence and at the end of the sentence (Weitzdörfer et al, 2018: 250).

For Padfield, looking at sentencing as an ongoing process, rather than simply an event, has five distinct advantages. Firstly, it can reinvigorate debate and lead to greater clarity about the different aims and values which may take priority at different times in the sentencing process. For example, while judges are concerned with imposing proportionate sentences on offenders, during the implementation stage of the sentence, the focus turns to concerns such as management of the risk posed by the offender and effective rehabilitation. While public denunciation of the offence at the initial point of sentence is clearly important, Padfield asks whether there should be more flexibility as the sentence progresses. Indeed, should the criminal justice system seek to develop more ambitious aims, such as promoting constructive citizenship and building community capacity and cohesion (Padfield, 2016a: 250–51)?

Secondly, thinking of sentencing as a process would, Padfield argues, lead to a greater understanding of the real meaning of the 'sentence'. At present, sentencing is poorly understood by the public and the media, while both judges and

[20] See, eg, s 210A of the Criminal Procedure (Scotland) Act 1995 (Scotland) and s 226A and Sch 15B to the Criminal Justice Act 2003 (England and Wales).

[21] See s 210F of the Criminal Procedure (Scotland) Act 1995.

[22] For example, under the Sexual Offences Act 2003, Pt 2 and Sch 3 (UK).

[23] See s 103A of the Sexual Offences Act 2003.

[24] In England and Wales, see, eg, Moloney, 2016 (re notification and notification orders); Freer, 2019: Chapters 9 and 21, and Picton, 2016 (re sexual harm prevention orders) and Wasik, 2014: 99–101 (re extended sentences) and 297–99 (re sex offender notification). For a discussion of sex offender notification orders in the Republic of Ireland under Pt 2 of the Sex Offenders Act 2001, see Leahy and Fitzgerald O'Reilly, 2018: 243–49 and O'Malley, 2016: 397–403.

practitioners often struggle to understand the real meaning of the sentence imposed (Padfield, 2016a: 251–52). Thirdly, Padfield contends that thinking of sentencing in terms of a process would result in a more credible, orderly and efficient system. This, it is argued, would lead to the fourth advantage, namely greater fairness, with increased public confidence in the penal system and the credibility of sentences. Fifthly, Padfield suggests that a greater focus on the process of sentencing might provoke significant sentencing reform, perhaps leading to a radical overhaul of the law on sentencing and the enforcement of sentences (Padfield, 2016a: 252). Padfield concludes:

> 'Since sentencing is in effect a whole series of inter-connected decisions, the processes which link them need review … Sentencing in practice is a string of decisions taken by very many different players, often over a number of years … There are strong arguments for suggesting that the 'front door' sentence imposes only a provisional sentence, which can and should be regularly reviewed by a judicial authority. The extent to which a judicial body should coordinate a sentence, monitor progress and seek to ensure compliance should be the subject of further debate, with much more focus being given in that debate to sentencing as an on-going process' (2016a: 252, 254).

A full discussion of issues raised by Padfield surrounding the shift in our view and understanding of sentencing is not possible in this work. Nevertheless, in the context of rape sentencing, Padfield's thesis may have important implications regarding the treatment of sex offenders, particularly those sentenced to lengthy terms of imprisonment. The 'paradigm shift' that Padfield advocates is intriguing and this concept could be usefully explored in future research on sentencing law and practice.

An Outline of the Chapters

This book examines the physical and psychological effect of rape on the victim, the wrongness of the offence and the way in which new technologies, such as smartphones, are used as tools to blackmail, control, coerce, harass, humiliate, objectify and further violate the victims of sexual offences. Chapter 2 considers the nature of the offence of rape. It considers the medical and psychological effects of the offence on victims through a comprehensive survey of legal, medical and social science research on the impact of rape. The chapter proceeds to examine the wrongness of rape from a philosophical perspective and concludes with an examination of the victim's role in sentencing. In so doing, the chapter sets the scene and provides the necessary context, for the remainder of the study. Chapter 3, meanwhile, explores the trend in recent years for perpetrators of rape to record the commission of their offences or to photograph their victims, using mobile phones. This behaviour, seen by the courts in several jurisdictions as constituting a serious aggravation for sentencing purposes, is considered through Nicola Henry and Anastasia Powell's concept of 'technology-facilitated sexual violence' (Henry and Powell, 2016a and

2016b; Powell and Henry, 2017a) and Clare McGlynn and Erika Rackley's concept of 'image-based sexual abuse' (McGlynn and Rackley, 2017a and 2017b). Offenders' motivations in filming rape and sexual assault are examined through the work of Sandberg and Ugelvik (2017). The psychological effect of such filming on victims of rape is reviewed and the implications for sentencing practice is explored through an examination of recent appellate decisions.

As Maguire (2016: 300) observes, understanding the sentencing framework underpinning a particular sentencing system is an important starting point for appreciating how a system works in theory and practice. For this reason, Chapters 4 to 7, which examine the key themes and developments in rape sentencing in England and Wales, Scotland, Canada, Ireland, New Zealand and South Africa, each begin with a discussion of the law of rape and the key features of the sentencing framework in the jurisdiction in question.

Chapter 4 examines the development of sentencing guidelines for rape in England and Wales. The chapter begins by considering the traditional approach to sentencing by the English courts. The various forms of sentencing guideline are then considered by reference to each of the four stages in the evolution of English sentencing guidelines. Firstly, the Court of Appeal's narrative guidelines in *R v Billam and others*[25] and their subsequent development by the Court, are considered. Secondly, the advice of the Sentencing Advisory Panel and the subsequent guideline case of *R v Millberry and others*[26] is explored. Thirdly, discussion turns to the Sentencing Guidelines Council's Definitive Guideline on the Sexual Offences Act 2003. Finally, an analysis of the Sentencing Council's Definitive Guideline on the 2003 Act is provided. The question of whether to allow a reduction in sentence to an offender who pleads guilty (a common issue at every stage of the development of English rape guidelines) is then considered.

In Chapter 5, sentencing practice in Scotland is examined. The chapter begins by situating Scottish sentencing through an exploration of judicial sentencing methodology, in particular, appellate guidance on the manner in which Scottish judges should undertake the sentencing task. The Appeal Court's increased willingness to issue guideline judgments is noted, along with its recent acknowledgement that Scottish judges may have recourse to English sentencing guidelines in certain cases. This section concludes with a discussion of the recently established Scottish Sentencing Council and its own, very limited, output in terms of sentencing guidance.

In the absence of specific guidelines for sentencing rape, Chapter 5 proceeds by considering certain early appellate sentencing guidance provided by the Appeal Court in *HMA v Shearer*.[27] In particular, the chapter examines the way in which the sentence of three-and-a-half years' imprisonment set by the Appeal Court in

[25] [1986] 8 Cr App R (S) 48.
[26] [2003] 2 Cr App R (S) 31.
[27] 2003 SCCR 657.

that case has come to be used by the Scottish courts as a 'benchmark' or 'starting point' in sentencing rape. The Scottish approach is contrasted with sentencing practice in Canada, through a discussion of *R v Sandercock*,[28] an influential decision in which the Alberta Court of Appeal set a similar starting point of three years' imprisonment for so-called 'major sexual assault'.[29] The development of the approach towards sentencing relationship or acquaintance rape in Scotland is then analysed by reference to a series of appellate decisions, culminating in *HMA v SSK*.[30] Through an analysis of recent case law, the range of sentences imposed by the Scottish courts in rape cases is considered. The chapter concludes by exploring the practice of guilty plea discounting and the problems this raises in cases of rape.

Rape sentencing law and practice in the Republic of Ireland is considered in Chapter 6. The traditional, discretionary-based approach to sentencing is examined, along with two important recent developments in Irish sentencing: the issuing of guideline judgments in respect of certain offences by the appellate courts and the recent steps taken towards the creation of a Sentencing Guidelines and Information Committee. Judicial sentencing methodology, in the form of a two-tiered or two-step approach, is then considered. The final part of this chapter considers how rape is sentenced by the Irish courts. In particular, an analysis is provided of the decision in *People (DPP) v Tiernan*,[31] in which the Supreme Court set out certain principles to guide judges in sentencing rape; the decision of Charleton J sitting at first instance in *People (DPP) v Drought (sub nom People (DPP) v D(W))*;[32] and academic reviews of contemporary sentencing practice. As in Chapters 4 and 5, the issue of plea-based reductions, or discounts, in rape sentencing is also considered.

In Chapter 7, the discussion turns to two very different ways of structuring judicial sentencing discretion and the implications this has for sentencing rape. Firstly, through a study of sentencing practice for rape in New Zealand, it is shown that judges in this jurisdiction have long had the benefit of guidelines to guide their discretion. It is demonstrated, however, that the current guideline judgment on rape sentencing in New Zealand, the decision of the Court of Appeal in *R v AM*,[33] is very different in both form and operation to the sentencing guidelines presently operating in England and Wales. The Court of Appeal's guidelines in *AM* are considered in detail against the background, firstly, of the New Zealand Parliament's incursion into the common law of sentencing in the form of the Sentencing Act 2002 and, secondly, the aborted proposals to establish a New Zealand Sentencing Council.

The chapter proceeds to contrast the guideline-based approach in New Zealand with the South African approach to sentencing rape through mandatory and

[28] 1985 ABCA 218; (1985) 22 CCC (3d) 79.
[29] Ibid at [17].
[30] [2015] HCJAC 114; 2016 SCCR 74.
[31] *People (DPP) v Tiernan* [1988] IR 250.
[32] [2007] IEHC 310; [2008] 1 IR 308.
[33] [2010] NZCA 114; [2010] 2 NZLR 750.

minimum sentences. The traditional, discretionary-based approach to sentencing in South Africa, epitomised by the decision in *S v Zinn*[34] in which judges were directed to consider a 'triad' consisting of the crime, the offender and the interests of society,[35] is examined. The Criminal Law Amendment Act 105 of 1997, which introduced mandatory life sentences for rapes featuring certain aggravating factors and lengthy minimum terms of imprisonment for rapes in which such factors are absent, is then considered. The operation of the statutory departure, or escape, clause (by which the court can impose a lesser sentence if it is satisfied that 'substantial and compelling circumstances' exist) is explored by reference to case law and academic commentary. This leads to a discussion of certain systemic problems with prescribed sentences for rape, in particular the imposition of disproportionate sentences and the absence of any gradation in levels of sentence to reflect increasing offence severity. The chapter also explores the reasons why the South African courts are perceived as being lenient in their sentencing of rape, despite the minimum sentence legislation. It is shown that, in a continued attempt to impose proportionate sentences, South African judges frequently apply the statutory departure clause and, in so doing, seek to justify sentences of less than life imprisonment through an informal 'grading' of offences. The chapter concludes by comparing the New Zealand guideline-based system with the South African system of mandatory and minimum sentences. The shortcomings of the South African legislation are highlighted and suggestions for reform are made, focusing on a guideline judgment modelled on the decision of the New Zealand Court of Appeal in *R v AM*.[36]

The concluding chapter, Chapter 8, considers the desirability of the appellate courts in 'non-guideline' jurisdictions issuing sentencing guidelines for the offence of rape and the form that such guidelines should take. In particular, the chapter considers whether sentencing should be the 'human process' advocated by commentators such as Cooper (2008) and Harris and Gerry (2013) or whether sentencing guidance should take the form of the 'algorithmic' process preferred by commentators such as Roberts (2019, 2011) and exemplified in the guidelines issued by the Sentencing Council for England and Wales.

[34] 1969 (2) SA 537.
[35] Ibid at 540G–H.
[36] *R v AM* (n 33).

2

The Seriousness of Rape and the Victim's Role in Sentencing

Introduction

Rape is one offence whose known profile has changed considerably in the last 35 years (Ashworth, 2015: 143). Mason and Lodrick report that British Crime Survey data from 2000 indicates that 0.4 per cent of female respondents aged between 16 and 59 disclosed that they had been raped in the preceding year. Assuming that the findings would be generalisable to other years, this would equate to one in every 250 women in the UK being raped each year (Mason and Lodrick, 2013: 28). A recent government report which analyses sexual offending from the Crime Survey for England and Wales documents that an estimated 3.4 per cent of adults aged 16 to 59 have been victims of rape or sexual assault by penetration since the age of 16, equivalent to an estimated 1.1 million victims (Office for National Statistics, 2018: 5). The joint publication by the Ministry of Justice, Home Office and the Office for National Statistics in 2013, meanwhile, reviewed the data from the previous three years' Crime Surveys for England and Wales. It found that, on average, 85,000 women and 12,000 men report being raped every year in the UK (Ministry of Justice et al, 2013: 6).

Most rapes are committed by someone known to the victim, such as current or ex-partners or husbands, or recent acquaintances.[1] The joint report found that the most commonly reported victim–offender relationship amongst victims of the most serious sexual offences, including rape, was that of partner or former partner (56% of victims). In about a third of all sexual offences the offender was found to be somebody known to the victim, other than a partner or family member (Ministry of Justice et al, 2013: 16). Thus, around 90 per cent of victims of the most serious sexual offences knew the perpetrator. For other sexual offences, the perpetrator was known to less than half of the victims (Ministry of Justice et al, 2013: 6). Similar figures are reported in the recent analysis undertaken by the

[1] See Avegno et al, 2009: 331–32; Ingemann-Hansen et al, 2009: 185; Jones et al, 2004: 455, 457; McCall-Hosenfeld et al, 2009: 595; McGregor, 2005: 89; Martin et al, 2007: 336; Mason and Lodrick, 2013: 28; Ministry of Justice et al, 2013: 16; Petrak et al, 1997: 342; Riggs et al, 2000: 360–61; Stermac et al, 2001: 1218; Warner, 2005: 235.

Office for National Statistics (Office for National Statistics, 2018: 16–19). The fact that, in the UK, around 90 per cent of victims of the most serious sexual offences know the perpetrator contradicts the commonly held belief that rapes are most frequently committed by strangers (see Mason, 2014: 537; Mason and Murphy, 2016: 1318–19).

A particularly troublesome aspect of the social context in which rape is committed is the impact of negative societal attitudes about the offence. Rape myths, identified by feminist theorists from the 1970s onwards, comprise 'prejudicial, stereotyped, or false beliefs about rape, rape victims and rapists' (Burt, 1980: 217). Such rape myths maintain, for example, that so-called 'real rapes' are committed by strangers, usually in public places and result in significant physical injury (Estrich, 1986: 1092). In terms of such rape myths, 'real victims' are respectable individuals who neither drink alcohol to excess nor engage in other forms of behaviour that put them at risk of being assaulted. While these stereotypes are at odds with the realities of sexual offending, there is nevertheless extensive evidence of rape-myth acceptance within society (Bohner et al, 2009; Chennells, 2009: 25–26; Leahy, 2019: 4–9 and 2014: 19–20).

The Physical Effects of Rape

Payne-James et al (2011: 132) report that while many incorrectly assume that sexual assaults will result in injury to the victim, in the majority of cases no such injuries are seen.[2] The study by McLean et al (2011), for example, sought to obtain reliable normative data concerning the prevalence of genital injuries resulting from consensual and non-consensual intercourse (2011: 27–28). The authors recruited 500 adult participants from a sexual assault referral centre in Manchester, along with 68 comparison participants (2011: 28–29). It was found that less than a quarter of adult complainants of rape by a single assailant sustained injuries to the genitalia that were visible within 48 hours of the offence. While this was approximately three times more than women who sustained genital injuries during consensual intercourse, the authors stress the importance of recognising that over three-quarters of all rape complainants do not sustain any genital injuries (2011: 32).

McLean et al report that their findings are consistent with those of an earlier study by Bowyer and Dalton (1997). That study, which comprised an analysis of the case notes of 83 rape complainants, found that only 27 per cent of complainants sustained visible genital injuries, most of which comprised minor bruises,

[2] See also Bassindale and Rahuf, 2014: 67; Crane, 2013: 103; Cybulska, 2014a: 73; Hilden et al, 2005: 205; Mason and Lodrick, 2013: 28; Mason and Murphy, 2016: 1319; McLean et al, 2004: 169; Möller et al, 2012: 3142; Nardello et al, 2013: 766; Rogers, 2009: 149; Rogers and McBride, 2011: 86; Rogers and Newton, 2005: 73; Shepherd, 2003: 132; Walker, 2015: 175–76; Warner, 2005: 235; White, 2013: 114, 123 and 2016: 1280; Whitwell et al, 2015: 254–56; and Wyatt et al, 2011: 370

scratches and grazes (1997: 618–19). This led Bowyer and Dalton to conclude that the examining doctor will usually find no genital injuries upon examining rape complainants (1997: 620).

Certain North American studies suggest that rapes and other sexual assaults committed by strangers tend to be more violent (see Avegno et al, 2009, Jones et al, 2004 and Stermac et al, 1995).[3] In more recent studies from the UK and Europe, however, several report a higher incidence of physical violence in sexual assaults committed either by partners or by acquaintances. A study of 164 cases of sexual assault between 2002 and 2006 in Belfast, for example, found that victims assaulted by acquaintances were more likely to sustain genital injuries than those assaulted by strangers (Maguire et al, 2009: 151). These findings were consistent with the earlier study by Hilden et al, 2005 (cited in Maguire et al, 152). Similarly, the study by McLean et al found that the probability of a complainant sustaining genital injuries in the course of a rape was greater when the assailant was known to her than when the assault was committed by a stranger (McLean et al, 2011: 32).

Most recently, Möller et al explored differences in the extent of violence and physical injury sustained by victims of sexual assault committed by intimate partners compared with sexual assaults by strangers and acquaintances (Möller et al, 2012: 3142). Having examined the medical and forensic records of 503 women attending a sexual assault centre in Stockholm, the authors found that women sexually assaulted by their intimate partners were more likely to report physical violence than women assaulted by strangers and acquaintances (Möller et al, 2012: 3139–40). In particular, the violence used by intimate partners (present in 90% of cases) was found to be more severe than that used by strangers and acquaintances (2012: 3144). While violence used by the latter groups tended to consist solely of holding the victim, the violence used by intimate partners was more variable and included a higher prevalence of kicks, punches and attempts to strangle the victim (2012: 3139–40, 3144). Victims of intimate partner or acquaintance assault were also more likely to sustain a combination of vaginal and anal injuries than victims assaulted by strangers (2012: 3140, 3145). The authors conclude that sexual assaults committed by intimate partners are more violent than assaults committed by strangers (2012: 3144). A recent Australian study undertaken by Zilkens et al (2016), meanwhile, found non-fatal strangulation to be a common feature of sexual assaults committed by intimate partners (2016: 2–3; see also White, 2019: 256).

These studies are consistent with certain other US and Canadian studies, all of which challenge the stereotypes which suggest that rapes committed within established relationships are less serious and less violent, than rapes committed by strangers. McCall-Hosenfeld et al (2009), for example, examined the medical records of 478 sexual assault victims who attended hospitals in Massachusetts

[3] *Cf* the studies by Bergen (1996), Finkelhor and Yllo (1985), McCall-Hosenfeld et al (2009) and Stermac et al (2001) discussed later in the chapter.

between 2003 and 2005. Fifty-five per cent of those who reported being assaulted by a known assailant also reported having been subjected to severe violence (McCall-Hosenfeld et al, 2009: 593–94). Stermac et al (2001), meanwhile, studied the medical records of patients reporting to a hospital-based sexual assault centre in Ontario between 1992 and 1999 who had been sexually assaulted by either current or previous spouses (97 patients), partners (256 patients), or acquaintances (194 patients). The authors report that boyfriends and spouses were most likely to use physical violence and restraint in the course of the sexual assault (Stermac et al, 2001: 1226–27, 1230), with boyfriends being significantly more likely to use weapons (2001: 1227, 1230). Victims of sexual assault by partners and spouses were significantly more likely than victims of acquaintance assault to present with physical injuries (including both soft tissue and internal injuries), the injuries also being more severe than in acquaintance assault (2001: 1228–29, 1231).

The earlier study by Finkelhor and Yllo, which examined 326 cases of marital rape in the Boston area, found that 48 per cent of all cases of marital rape were characterised by verbal and physical abuse. In these cases (classified by the authors as 'battering rape') marital rape was found to be an extension of general violence in the relationship (Finkelhor and Yllo, 1985, cited in Martin et al, 2007: 333). Similarly, Bergen found battering rape to be the most common form of marital rape in her sample of 40 rape victims (Bergen, 1996 cited in Martin et al, 2007: 333).

In cases of either stranger rape or relationship rape where genital injuries are present, their degree and extent may be influenced by the victim's age, the type of sexual activity and the degree of intoxication of either or both of the parties (Payne-James et al, 2011: 132; Wyatt et al, 2011: 371). Genital injuries typically include bruising and/or lacerations. Non-genital injuries in sexual assault (which may be more common – see Sugar et al, 2004: 75 and Welch and Mason, 2007: 1154) may include marks of blunt contact (such as punches or kicks), restraint (such as ties around the victim's wrists or ankles and grip marks) and bite marks (Cattaneo et al, 2014: 694; Cowan and Hunt, 2008: 324–25; Crane, 2013: 106–7; Knight, 1992: 233; Payne-James et al, 2011: 132–33; Rogers, 2009: 149–50; Walker, 2015: 173; Wall, 2014: 56–58). In their study of 95 adult victims of oral rape, Brew-Graves and Morgan (2015: 156–58) report that minor oral injury, comprising mainly abrasions to the lips, occurred in just under a fifth of patients. Even if no genital injuries are sustained in cases of vaginal rape, victims may still suffer other gynaecological complaints including bleeding, infection, irritation or chronic pelvic pain (Jina and Thomas, 2013: 18).

Emergency contraception may be required (Piegsa, 2014: 82–83; White, 2016: 1284). A US study into rape-related pregnancy estimated the rate of pregnancy at 5 per cent per rape among women of reproductive age (Holmes et al, 1996, cited in Piegsa, 2014: 81). Given the potential risk of sexually transmitted infections (typically gonorrhoea, chlamydia, syphilis, HIV and hepatitis B) appropriate prescribed medication will also be necessary (Cattaneo et al, 2014: 696; Cybulska, 2014a: 74–77 and 2014b: 516–18; Jina and Thomas, 2013: 16, 21; Kerr et al, 2003: 269;

Rogers, 2009: 150–51; Welch and Mason, 2007: 1154–56; White, 2013: 113, 124). It is standard practice to discuss antibacterial prophylaxis with victims of sexual assault and to screen for bacterial infections at a genitourinary clinic 10 to 14 days after the assault (Girardin et al, 2003: 427, 434; Rogers and McBride, 2011: 121–22; Rogers and Newton, 2005: 113–15; Wyatt et al, 2011: 375). Treatment and longer-term management of any physical health problems experienced by the victim are best managed by genitourinary medicine specialists, who can provide the most appropriate and current post-assault treatment and advice (Payne-James and Beh, 2011: 117).

Physical Injury and Multiple Perpetrator Rape

Although in the majority of cases rape victims are unlikely to sustain physical injury, rapes involving two or more perpetrators appear to involve more aggression and use of physical assault and restraint (Kelly, 2013: xvi; Lambine, 2013: 70; Ullman, 2007: 48–49 and 2013: 202–5; Woodhams, 2013: 182; Woodhams and Horvath, 2013: 2; Woodhams et al, 2012: 729). The study by Bijleveld et al (2007) of group sex offending by 42 juveniles aged 17 and under in the Netherlands, for example, found that victims were often repeatedly assaulted, threatened and humiliated (2007: 22–23, 26).

Porter and Alison (2006), meanwhile, examined the details of 223 group rape offences involving 739 separate offenders. The details were collated from UK and US law reports and media reports between 1945 and 2001 (Porter and Alison, 2006: 362–64). Offenders and victims were found to be predominantly young persons: 60 per cent of offenders were under 21 with the most frequent age being 16 (2006: 364); all but three of the victims were female, 68 per cent of whom were under 21 (2006: 366). Groups most frequently comprised two or three offenders (2006: 366). While 93 per cent of cases involved vaginal penetration of the victim (2006: 367), in almost a third of cases the victim was repeatedly raped by at least one of the perpetrators (2006: 368). The offences typically revealed a degree of violence above that necessary to control the victim: 36 per cent of offences involved single acts of violence while multiple acts of violence occurred in 28 per cent of cases. While extreme forms of violence often led to the victim's death, lesser forms of violence included punching (26%), slapping (7%), kicking (6%) and biting (3%). The authors report that verbal violence in the form of insulting or demeaning the victim occurred in 9 per cent of cases. At least one type of weapon was used in 43 per cent of cases (most often a knife) and several different weapons were used in a further 9 per cent of cases. While weapons were most often used to control the victim, they were used to harm them in a quarter of cases (2006: 368–70). The authors suggest that:

> '[T]he level of violence in group rape could be a function of the number of offenders involved in the attack. The presence of others can cause an escalation in violence through

> processes such as a diffusion of responsibility, feelings of relative anonymity and also individuals modelling the aggressive behaviour of each other […]' (2006: 377–78; see also Lambine, 2013: 70–71; Morgan et al, 2012: 2417 and Woodhams, 2013: 188–89).

While such assaults had previously been described in both the academic literature and the media as 'gang rapes' and 'group rapes' (the international variations in definition being discussed by da Silva et al, 2013: 10–12), these terms had their own criminological and sociological connotations. Neither term satisfactorily encapsulated the variety of offenders involved nor the contexts in which such offences take place; in particular, the term 'gang rape' conflated the use of sexual violence by street gangs and sexual violence by other groups (Firmin, 2013: 97–100). Horvath and Kelly thus propose the term 'multiple perpetrator rape' ('MPR') as an alternative overarching term for any sexual assault involving two or more perpetrators (Horvath and Kelly, 2009: 94).

Horvath and Kelly analysed the details of 101 rape allegations recorded in a six-month period in a large, predominantly urban, police force in England (2009: 84–85). The authors found that the majority of victims and perpetrators were of secondary school age or were young adults (2009: 86). Most incidents involved two perpetrators (2009: 87). Just under half of the victims were injured in the course of the offences. The authors categorise the majority of injuries in the study (70%) as 'minor', involving bruising or abrasions; just under a quarter (24%) are categorised as 'moderate', involving extensive bruising or cuts, or internal bleeding; and six per cent of injuries are categorised by the authors as 'severe', involving a combination of internal and external extensive bruising, lacerations, or fractures (2009: 89).

The contemporaneous study by Hauffe and Porter (2009), which compared cases of single perpetrator rapes and MPR, also found that victims were subjected to more violence in cases of MPR. The authors examined 60 cases of sexual assault by a single offender and 60 cases of MPR reported in various, predominantly UK, law reports between 1964 and 2006 (2009: 473). The offenders involved in MPR were found to be younger than those involved in lone rape; they were typically males in groups of three and evidenced more hostile and violent behaviour toward the victim (2009: 483). In particular, the authors found that cases of MPR are more likely to feature acts of multiple violence including violence to restrain the victim, the use of multiple weapons and perpetrators pushing and dragging the victim. Multiple perpetrator rapes are also significantly more likely than lone assaults to involve multiple rape by the same offender (2009: 479–81). Multiple acts of violence were reported in 78 per cent of cases of MPR. Group offenders typically removed the victim's clothing themselves (70%); they often held the victim down (57%) and used violence to restrain the victim (58%) (2009: 482).

Subsequent studies have also found that victims of MPR tend to be teenage girls or young women; that victims are subjected to multiple and repeated acts of sexual abuse; that MPR involves more violence and aggression and that there is a greater likelihood of the victim sustaining bodily and ano-genital injuries than in cases of rape by a single perpetrator (see Chambers et al, 2013; da Silva et al, 2014; Morgan et al, 2012; and Woodhams and Cooke, 2013).

The Psychological Effects of Rape

Arguably, a focus purely on the physical harm caused by rape is too narrow (see Statman, 2012: 107 and Stanton–Ife, 2010: 160–61). Wertheimer, for example, suggests that the harm of rape is rooted in the distress and psychological damage to which it gives rise (Wertheimer, 2003: 102–12). Regard must be had also to victims' experiences of rape and the ways in which their lives are changed by the fact of their having been raped (Gardner and Shute, 2000: 195–96). Ripstein, for example, contends that sexual assault violates the victim's independence. On Ripstein's account, the rapist violates the victim's independence by using her powers for his own purposes. As Ripstein argues: 'The trespass against [the victim's] person is *primary* and any consequent injury *secondary* to it' (Ripstein, 2006: 235, emphasis added). Apart from physical injury, any harm to the victim depends on her own evaluation of what has been done to her (Gardner and Shute, 2000: 197; see also Lodrick and Hosier, 2014: 90). While it has long been considered important to consider the psychological as well as the physical harm experienced by the victim (see, eg, Kift, 1995: 78 and Lacey, 1998: 115), the greater focus in certain jurisdictions' sentencing guidelines on the psychological harm caused by sexual offending makes such a consideration essential in sentencing rape (see Harris, 2013: 847).

Many factors will affect an individual's response to trauma and psychological reactions vary greatly between individuals (Mason and Murphy, 2016: 1324; see also Mason and Lodrick, 2013: 30 and McGregor, 2005: 17). As Campbell argues, victims should not be viewed as a homogeneous class and their experiences, reactions and interests are not uniform or necessarily consistent (Campbell, 2017: 483). The personal 'meaning' that a victim ascribes to an incident is likely to be very significant and this is illustrated by the differences between stranger and acquaintance rape (Mason and Murphy, 2016; Mason and Lodrick, 2013). While it might be assumed that stranger rape would be far more traumatic, this is often not the case. Victims of acquaintance rape suffer similar levels of depression and experience greater difficulty in re-establishing intimate relationships than victims of stranger rape (Mason and Murphy, 2016; Mason and Lodrick, 2013; see also Rogers, 2009: 151 and Ullman and Siegel, 1993: 128–31).

Immediate psychological consequences of rape can include feelings of shock, denial, fear, confusion, anxiety, withdrawal, guilt or nervousness (Jina and Thomas, 2013: 19; Mason and Murphy, 2016: 1324; Maw et al, 2008: 126–27; Rothbaum et al, 1992: 456, 471). Research commissioned by the Sentencing Council for England and Wales[4] found that victims of sexual offences repeatedly stress their long-term psychological impact (Nicholls et al, 2012: 21). A victim's mental health difficulties may persist for years and into later life (Maw et al, 2008: 124–25; Sachs-Ericsson et al, 2014: 724–26).

[4] On the Sentencing Council's guidelines for rape, see Chapter 4.

Post-traumatic stress disorder ('PTSD') has been found to be a prominent, although not universal, response to rape (Rothbaum et al, 1992: 473). There are four broad symptom groups in PTSD: (i) persistent re-experiencing of the traumatic event; (ii) persistent avoidance of stimuli associated with the traumatic event and numbing of general responsiveness; (iii) negative alterations in cognitions and mood; and (iv) persistent symptoms of increased arousal, such as difficulty sleeping, poor concentration, anger and irritability (Mason and Murphy, 2016: 1325; see also Mason and Lodrick, 2013: 31; Möller et al, 2014: 1; Rothbaum et al, 1992: 456; and Whittington and Wykes, 2000: 465). For a formal diagnosis to be made, the symptoms must last for more than a month and lead to clinically significant distress or impairment in social, occupational or other important areas of functioning (Rogers, 2009: 151).

Symptoms such as flashbacks or recurrent nightmares can occur immediately after the assault and have been reported up to 12 months after an attack, especially if not treated (Jina and Thomas, 2013: 19; Lodrick and Hosier, 2014: 90; Mason and Lodrick, 2013: 31). A US study by Kilpatrick et al (1987), for example, found that 51 per cent of rape victims developed PTSD sometime after the assault and the symptoms persisted in 16.5 per cent of victims when they were re-assessed some years later (Kilpatrick et al, 1987: 487). A later study by Dahl of 55 victims of rape and attempted rape in Oslo found that the majority displayed symptoms of PTSD within the first two weeks after the assault, although the duration criterion was not fulfilled (Dahl, 1989: 59). A contemporaneous, unpublished study by Resnick et al (1989) found that 76 per cent of rape victims met the diagnostic criteria for PTSD at some point within a year of the assault (cited in Rothbaum et al, 1992: 456). In their study of 51 rape victims, Bownes et al (1991) found that 70 per cent suffered from PTSD, leading the authors to conclude that PTSD is likely to be a long-term problem for a significant proportion of rape victims (Bownes et al, 1991: 28–29). Most recently, in their study of 317 victims of rape and attempted rape who attended an emergency sexual assault clinic in Stockholm over a 34-month period, Möller et al (2014) found that just under 39 per cent of victims developed PTSD six months after the assault. Fifty-one per cent of victims reported significant impairment in their daily lives and almost half of all victims suffered from moderate or severe depression six months after the assault, regardless of PTSD status (Möller et al, 2014: 5).

A victim's risk of developing PTSD will depend upon factors such as his or her previous background and support systems, the circumstances of the assault and the response that the victim receives from others (including professionals such as physicians and police) upon reporting the offence (White, 2016: 1286). Rape victims who experience PTSD may avoid engaging with the investigative and criminal processes, which may result in re-traumatisation (Cybulska, 2014b: 513).

While in no way seeking to minimise or understate the serious psychological effects of stranger rape, it must also be noted that marital, relationship and acquaintance rape has a profound emotional effect on the victim (Martin et al, 2007: 343). This is principally due to the abuse of trust involved in the commission of the offence (see Gardner and Shute, 2000: 212; Temkin, 2002: 44; and Warner, 2000: 601). Mason and Lodrick explain:

> 'A woman raped by an acquaintance potentially has to question everything she ever held 'true'. If she cannot trust her own judgement … and of how she would respond if faced with sexual threat, how can she go about her daily life? The world is suddenly a malevolent place where sex offenders are people she knows and not strangers 'out there' to be mistrusted and avoided' (Mason and Lodrick, 2013: 31; see also Kift, 1995: 84 and Russell, 1982: 798–99).

Certain segments of society (and indeed, certain professionals within the medical and criminal justice fields) appear to consider that marital rape is somehow less traumatic than stranger rape, perhaps because one's partner is a 'known quantity'.[5] The reality, however, is that victims of marital rape appear to suffer even more traumatic consequences than victims of stranger rape (Bergen, 1996: 59; Rumney, 2003: 874). By reference to the literature on rape trauma, including the study by Lees (2002), Rumney notes that acquaintance rape tends to be more traumatic and has longer-term psychological effects than stranger rape. Victims find it more difficult to come to terms with acquaintance rape. They frequently feel betrayed, both by the offender and, importantly, by their own judgement; it generally makes them more fearful of men, since they no longer know whom to trust (Lees, 2002: 17, cited in Rumney, 2003: 882; see also Koss et al, 1994; Larcombe, 2011: 35–36; McGregor, 2005: 67–68, 71; Temkin, 2002: 51–52; and Warner, 2005: 244).

Studies have also shown that women who have been sexually assaulted by their partners are at a higher risk of experiencing mental health problems than those who have suffered only physical abuse (Bennice et al, 2003; Cole et al, 2005; McFarlane et al, 2005a; Stermac et al, 2001: 1220–21). Victims who have been raped by a spouse or partner are likely to experience long-term psychological effects such as significant depression and PTSD (Martin et al, 2007: 345; McGregor, 2005: 68; Möller et al, 2014: 7; Temple et al, 2007: 293, 295). In a study conducted with women suffering intimate partner violence, McFarlane et al found that women who reported sexual violence by a partner were over five times more likely to threaten or attempt suicide within three months compared with women who were physically, rather than sexually, abused (McFarlane et al, 2005b).

The psychological trauma sustained in any case of rape will have the secondary effect of reducing the victim's ability to work or study, to forge new relationships or maintain positive relationships with family and friends (Martin et al, 2007: 341; Nicholls et al, 2012: 21). For example, in a small-scale study Connop and Petrak interviewed six men about their experiences following their partner's disclosure of rape and interviewed three rape victims who discussed the impact of their own assault on their partner (Connop and Petrak, 2004: 31). All but one of the relationships had either broken down or appeared to be on the verge of doing so (2004: 33).

[5] See, eg, the guideline judgment of the Court of Appeal (Criminal Division) in *R v Millberry* [2003] 2 Cr App R (S) 31 at [13], discussed in Chapter 4.

Most respondents described difficulties with their sexual relationships (2004: 34–35). The authors report that there was a tendency for rape victims to experience anger and blame from their partners, as well as support and understanding, as they struggled to come to terms with the assault (2004: 35, 37).

Longer-term consequences include the use of alcohol or drugs as a coping mechanism (Lodrick and Hosier, 2014: 90; Mason and Lodrick, 2013: 31; Mason and Murphy, 2016: 1326). This may itself render the victim more likely to experience further sexual assault (Avegno et al, 2009: 330; Hall and Moore, 2008: 296; Jones et al, 2004: 457; Najdowski and Ullman, 2011: 218, 220). Victims may also engage in self-harming behaviour and experience panic disorders and suicidal thoughts (Dahl, 1989: 58–59; Jina and Thomas, 2013: 19; Martin et al, 2007: 341).

Victims of rape and sexual assault may require counselling or psychological support following the offence (Brooker and Tocque, 2016: 30–33; Kerr et al, 2003: 269; Payne-James et al, 2011: 133; Rogers and McBride, 2011: 122; Rogers and Newton, 2005: 115; Wyatt et al, 2011: 375). As victims may experience mental health problems at any time following the offence, either at the point of the assault or many months or years later, appropriate care may be required over a long period (Jina and Thomas, 2013: 16, 21). Rape victims suffering PTSD should be offered a course of trauma-focused psychological treatment with subsequent pharmacological treatment if symptoms persist (Mason and Lodrick, 2013: 34; Mason and Murphy, 2016: 1340–41).

The Physical and Psychological Effects of Male-on-Male Rape

As with rape and sexual assault committed against women, the prevalence of sexual violence against men is difficult to determine. While there is evidence that the extent of the problem is underestimated (White, 2016: 1273), it has been suggested that in the UK rapes committed against men account for between 5 and 10 per cent of the total of reported rapes (King et al, 2000: 2; McLean, 2013: 40; McLean et al, 2005: 2). Thus, a substantial minority of adult sexual assault victims is male (Payne-James and Beh, 2011: 1000).

McLean et al report a study which sought to identify differences between comparable aspects of sexual assault on males and females (2004 and 2005). The authors note that the gendered term 'male rape' erroneously emphasises the supposed separateness of male rape from female rape. In so doing, it reinforces the idea that male rape is a rarity. The result, the authors suggest, is that men will remain less likely to report their experiences and that public services will continue to be designed for female clients. For these reasons, the authors prefer the term 'male-on-male rape' for offences that involve a male perpetrator and a male victim (McLean et al, 2005: 2; see also McLean, 2013: 40–41 and McLean et al, 2004: 166).

Although certain studies suggest that, statistically, homosexual men are more likely to be victims of male-on-male rape and that they are more likely to report sexual assault by other men than are heterosexual men, it is important to appreciate that heterosexual and bisexual men are routinely victimised.[6] While research on victims of male-on-male rape clearly demonstrates the negative effects of the offence, it should be noted that the research data are typically derived from very specific (and sometimes relatively small) samples of men, such as victims contacting counselling services or emergency departments in hospitals. Much of the research on the effects of male-on-male rape draws on the experiences of clinical patients, such as those referred to psychiatric services or of men who have presented for treatment at their GP practices or at genitourinary medicine clinics. Assessing the effects of male-on-male rape in only clinical, or very specific, samples means that victims who do not belong to these populations have rarely been investigated (see Walker et al, 2005a: 71).[7] Thus male-on-male rape is arguably 'the most overlooked form of rape' (Heger, 2000: 177).

It appears that offences of male-on-male rape may be more violent, may be more likely to involve the use of a weapon by the perpetrator and involve a greater likelihood of the victim sustaining bodily injury than rapes committed against women.[8] The study by Walker et al, for example, sought to provide a detailed descriptive analysis of the nature and effects of rape on a non-clinical sample of 40 men who had been raped as adults (Walker et al, 2005a: 71–72). The authors found that physical force, such as punching, kicking and slapping, was used in more than half the cases and violent force was used in over a quarter of cases. While all cases involved penile penetration of the victim's anus, in 15 per cent of cases the victim was also anally penetrated by one or more objects and perpetrators subjected victims to sadomasochistic practices in over 17 per cent of cases. The majority of victims experienced physical injuries during the assault, including anal lacerations and bleeding, bruising, broken bones, knife wounds and burns (Walker et al, 2005a: 72–73, 78). It was also common for perpetrators to verbally abuse the victim during the rape, using misogynistic or homophobic language (2005a 74; see also King et al, 2000: 2).

Studies also suggest that males are more likely to be victims of multiple perpetrator rape.[9] McLean et al, for example, examined the records of 7,773 clients (7,403 women and 370 men) who attended a sexual assault referral centre in Manchester between 1986 and 2003 (McLean et al, 2005: 3–4). The authors found that two assailants were involved in 11.6 per cent of male cases and in 7.3 per cent of female cases (2005: 5). In the study by Walker et al of 40 male-on-male rape victims, a

[6] See Coxell et al, 1999: 849; Davies, 2002: 207–8; Hillman et al, 1990: 249; Huckle, 1995: 189; King et al, 2000: 12; Mezey and King, 1989: 206; Rentoul and Appleboom, 1997: 272; Reeves et al, 2004: 524; Walker et al, 2005a: 72, 77.

[7] See also Graham, 2006: 189; Hillman et al, 1990: 249; Light and Monk-Turner, 2009: 1852–53; Peterson et al, 2011: 22; Stermac et al, 2004: 902; Vearnals and Campbell, 2001: 283; and Whitwell et al, 2015: 256.

[8] See Graham, 2006: 190; Hillman et al, 1990: 249; Mezey and King, 1989: 206; Reeves et al, 2004: 524–25; Rentoul and Appleboom, 1997: 270; Stermac et al, 2004: 913; Tewksbury, 2007: 26; *cf* Kimerling et al, 2002: 531; Larsen and Hilden, 2016: 10 and McLean et al, 2005: 7.

[9] For a full discussion of multiple perpetrator rape, or 'MPR', see above.

quarter of cases involved two perpetrators and three or more perpetrators were involved in 12.5 per cent of cases (Walker et al, 2005a: 73). Reeves et al found that 26 out of 92 males attending a sexual assault referral centre in London between 2000 and 2003 reported being assaulted by more than one assailant (Reeves et al, 2004: 524). The study by Nesvold et al, meanwhile, involved a comparison of the records of 380 individuals (358 women and 22 men) who attended sexual assault support centres in four Nordic capital cities over a 12-month period. It was found that 38 per cent of male victims and just over 13 per cent of female victims reported being assaulted by multiple perpetrators (Nesvold et al, 2005: 180).[10]

Victims of male-on-male rape may experience the same psychological sequela as female victims.[11] In the study by Walker et al, all 40 respondents experienced long-term negative psychological and behavioural effects after the assault. Almost every respondent reported depression and some form of anxiety in the weeks and months following their assault (Walker et al, 2005a: 75–76). Nearly every respondent in the study reported feeling a loss of self-respect or self-worth. Over 80 per cent of respondents reported that they experienced profound feelings of guilt and self-blame; these feelings typically focused on their failure to prevent the assault or their inability to fight back. Many respondents reported partaking in behaviours such as self-harm or the abuse of alcohol or drugs; eating problems and disorders were also reported. Over half of the respondents in the study reported suicidal ideation and just under half had actually attempted to end their own lives (Walker et al, 2005a: 77, 79; see also Walker et al, 2005b: 448–449 and the studies by Kalichman et al, 2001: 6 and Ratner et al, 2003: 71–72). The small-scale study by Huckle of 22 victims of male-on-male rape referred to a forensic psychiatric service in South Wales found that nine victims fulfilled the criteria for a diagnosis of post-traumatic stress disorder (Huckle, 1995: 189).

Victims may suffer from sexual dysfunction. In their small-scale study of 22 men who suffered sexual assault, Mezey and King report that sexual dysfunction was an almost universal theme, as was interference in the ability to form close, trusting relationships (Mezey and King, 1989: 207). These difficulties can continue for years after the assault and may cause problems with existing relationships (Walker et al, 2005a: 71, 76). In addition, heterosexual victims may become confused about their sexual orientation.[12] Homosexual victims may also experience problems with their sexual orientation. When behaviour that was formerly associated with consensual sexual activity becomes associated with violence, homosexual men can experience

[10] See also Hillman et al, 1990: 249; Huckle, 1995: 189; Kimerling et al, 2002: 529; Larsen and Hilden, 2016: 11; Rentoul and Appleboom, 1997: 270; and Stermac et al, 2004: 913.

[11] See Davies, 2002: 211; Davies and Rogers, 2006: 368; Elliott et al, 2004: 210; Hillman et al, 1990: 249–50; Huckle, 1995: 191; Kimerling et al, 2002: 531; Mezey and King, 1989: 207–8; Peterson et al, 2011: 19; Rentoul and Appleboom, 1997: 270–271; Tewksbury, 2007: 29; Whittington and Wykes, 2000: 470.

[12] See Ben-David and Silfen, 1993: 184; Davies, 2002: 208; Bullock and Beckson, 2011: 202–4; King, 1990: 1345; King et al, 2000: 3; Mezey and King, 1989: 207; Peterson et al, 2011: 20; Tewksbury, 2007: 30–31; Whittington and Wykes, 2000: 470.

difficulty in defining their sexuality in a positive way; they may lose trust in their partners or in men in general (Walker et al, 2005a: 70–71). Seventy per cent of respondents in the study by Walker et al reported experiencing long-term crises with their sexual orientation and 69 per cent with their sense of masculinity after the assault (Walker et al, 2005a: 76).

As with female victims of rape, appropriate prescribed medication will be required given the potential risk of sexually transmitted infections. In particular, screening for rectal and pharyngeal gonorrhoea is suggested for victims of male-on-male rape. Male-on-male rape may carry a particularly high risk of HIV transmission (Reeves et al, 2004: 525). Victims should be screened for HIV at examination, with a follow-up examination six months later (Hillman et al, 1990: 249; McLean, 2013: 44; Rentoul and Appleboom, 1997: 271). The general principles of offering support and treatment to men who have suffered sexual assault are similar to those described for women (Mezey and King, 2000: 142). As with female victims of rape, medical professionals dealing with the physical trauma of male-on-male rape should be aware of the high risk of victims developing psychiatric symptoms. Referrals for counselling and specific interventions such as cognitive behavioural therapy may be required (King, 1990: 1345; Mezey and King, 2000: 147–50; Rentoul and Appleboom, 1997: 271; Vearnals and Campbell, 2001: 282).

A 'Unique Violation' – The Wrongness of Rape

In September 2009, the Home Office invited Baroness Vivien Stern to undertake a review into how rape complaints were handled by public authorities in England and Wales (Stern, 2010). The review began by considering the crime of rape and the framework within which the law operates. On the nature of the offence, Stern explains:

> 'It is a unique violation that often leaves its victims with deep traumas that last for many years, sometimes forever … [It is] a crime that strikes at the whole concept of human dignity and bodily integrity' (2010: 28, 118).

Similarly, Kelly observes:

> 'Unlike other forms of assault, rape violates personal, intimate and psychological boundaries – what in human rights language is designated human dignity and bodily integrity and in feminist and critical theory is termed sexual autonomy or sexual sovereignty. The meaning of rape for women, within gender and generational relations and cultural contexts, underlies its emotional, psychological and social impacts and consequences' (Kelly, 2008: 256, references omitted; see also McGovern, 2014: 250–51).

While, as Gardner and Shute (2000) observe, rape is amongst those wrongs which can never be excused or justified, the authors pose the question of what exactly makes the crime of rape worse than other crimes that can be defined in terms of absence of consent, such as vandalism, theft and assault? In what dimension is rape worse and wherein does its 'worseness' lie (Gardner and Shute, 2000: 193–95)?[13]

For Gardner and Shute, the act of rape involves the objectification of the victim. While the victim's autonomy and choice in sexual matters are violated by the act of rape, Gardner and Shute place particular emphasis on what they describe as the 'instrumentalisation' of the victim: rape involves the conversion of an autonomous individual with his or her own feelings and experiences into a mere instrument or tool for the sexual gratification of the rapist (2000: 203–4). An assault may also be motivated by the rapist seeking to exert power, domination and control over the victim (see McGregor, 2005: 225; Stern, 2010: 31; 33; and Welch and Mason, 2007: 1154; *cf* Palmer, 1988). Ripstein, for example, conceptualises all criminal wrongdoing as 'domination', in the sense of violation of the victim's independence (Ripstein, 2006: 231). Ripstein explains:

> 'If I use force … to get you to do something for me that you would not otherwise do, I wrong you … I have used you and in so doing, made your choice subject to mine and deprived you of the ability to decide what to do' (2006: 234).

As Ashworth observes, it is not just that rape victims are wronged by the invasion of their right to respect for private life, of which sexual autonomy is a central feature, because the distinctly sexual element of the offence brings in other considerations such as shame, humiliation, exploitation and objectification (Ashworth, 2015: 144–45; see also Lacey, 1998: 106; McGregor, 2005: 226–32; and Warner, 2005: 236). Gardner and Shute explain that the rapist treats his victim as a *thing* and not a *person*:

> 'Rape … is the sheer use of a person [often] accompanied by violence, terror, humiliation etc. … Rape is humiliating even when unaccompanied by further affronts, because the sheer use of a person and in that sense the objectification of a person, is a denial of their personhood. It is literally dehumanizing … [A]ll sheer use of human beings, all treatment of them merely as means, is *ab*use; and rape is the central case of such abuse' (Gardner and Shute, 2000: 205, emphasis per original; see also Gardner, 2018: 49–50 and 2012: 127–28 and Sangiovanni, 2017: 83).

For Gardner and Shute (2000: 205), this line of thought generates the basic distinction between rape and most non-sexual offences against the person. Non-consensual sexual intercourse is a wrong against the person raped because it is a violation of their right to sexual autonomy (Gardner and Shute, 2000: 208; see also Brooks, 2012: 200, 203; Childs, 2001: 311; Fenwick, 1992: 871; McGregor, 2005: 68; and Munro, 2014: 747). More particularly, as McGregor explains, it comprises a violation of the victim's *negative* sexual autonomy in the sense that the victim is no longer free from unwanted sexual access and no longer has control over their sexual

[13] Gardner and Shute's essay is reproduced (with only 'a few stylistic changes and some added cross-referencing in the footnotes' – Gardner, 2007a: vii), in Gardner, 2007b: 1–32.

borders (McGregor, 2005: 112, 226; see also Martín Alcoff, 2018: 4–5, 111–12). On this account, rape amounts to the *sheer use* of the victim (Gardner and Shute, 2000: 211–12; see also Gardner, 2007c: 242; *cf* Gardner, 2017: 13).[14]

In a similar vein, Brudner argues that the core part of criminal law concerns the protection of rights, understood as the unimpeded exercise of individual choice (Brudner, 2009: 31; see also Lavi, 2011: 440). Core offences, or 'true crimes' (Brudner, 2009: 8–9), comprise violations of individual rights, the most important of which for present purposes is the violation of the victim's bodily integrity (Brudner, 2009: 9, 171; Lavi, 2011: 440). Brudner develops a rights-based notion of 'legal retributivism' (19–20, 38–55). For Brudner, punishment is not justified solely on the basis of the harm caused by a criminal act, but rather on the extent to which the criminal act interferes with the autonomous choice of the victim (2009: 136; see also Brooks, 2011: 430–31). As different crimes can be distinguished 'according to the importance to liberty of the interest harmed' (Brudner, 2009: 54), the seriousness of rape hinges on the fact that, as Archard (2007) argues, sex is central to our identity as human beings. We thus have a central interest in the non-violation of our sexual integrity (Archard, 2007: 391–92; see also Sangiovanni, 2017: 85 and Statman, 2012: 109). Hampton elaborates:

> 'Our humanity is deeply engaged in the sexual experience. Sexuality and humanity are deeply entangled … Our sexuality is deeply important to each of us and in certain ways central to our sense of self' (Hampton, 1999: 147; 151, cited in Archard, 2007: 390; see also Gardner, 2018: 49; McGregor, 2005: 221–22, 224; and Stanton–Ife, 2010: 143).

The rapist, however, treats his victim as something less than a self-respecting human being able to decide and speak for themselves when it comes to their own sexuality; he treats the victim, in essence, as 'just a sex-aid for [his] gratification' – the clearest imaginable objectification of the victim (Gardner and Shute, 2000: 213; see also Archard, 2007: 390, 393; McGregor, 2005: 222, 225 and Stanton–Ife, 2010: 148–49). As one respondent in the study by Walker et al (2005a) of male-on-male rape[15] explained: 'The loss of dignity can be quite overwhelming. The very essence of one's character and being has been invaded and treated as worthless, just there for the taking' (Walker et al, 2005a: 77). In a similar vein, Jordan notes that:

> 'In the act of rape the rapist seizes control of the victim's body, violating the victim's sense of autonomy. The sense of disempowerment is immense. Another person has taken charge of one's body, manipulating it like a puppet, reducing the victim to an object, a prop in that man's world' (Jordan, 2008: 180).

[14] For criticism of this aspect of Gardner and Shute's thesis, see Stanton–Ife (2010), who argues that rape is destructive of personality itself and that *consent* should be the key explanation of the wrongness of rape (2010: 149–57, especially at 155–57). See also Statman (2012), who argues that rape's wrongness lies in the fact that it is a *humiliation* and claims that there is no need to seek further reasons as to why this is the case and Watt (2014), who contends that Gardner and Shute take insufficient account of the emotional significance of rape. For replies, see respectively Gardner (2012: 123–28) and Gardner (2017).

[15] Discussed above.

A particular instance of rape may be aggravated by the physical and psychological harm caused to the victim. Nevertheless, the wrongfulness of the rape itself remains even in the absence of such harms, for example, in cases where the victim is raped while unconscious due to the ingestion of alcohol or drugs (Gardner and Shute, 2000: 196–98, 212, 217; see also Gardner, 2007c: 242). Rape, Gardner and Shute conclude, amounts to the most straightforward breach of another's right to sexual autonomy: it is 'morally unlicensed objectification' (2000: 215), a 'timeless ritual of humiliation, degradation and dehumanisation' (Gardner, 2018: 50).

The Court's 'Duty to Understand' in Sentencing Rape

> 'An understanding of the character of a victim's attendant and consequent suffering is indispensable … to our understanding of the wrongness … of rape. The testimony of victims must remain a very strong consideration in our understanding of the wrongness, badness and gravity of rape. This fits naturally into the idea that horrific violations typically involve damage … [b]ut our sense of the horrific must in general be informed by testimony of how certain suffering feels from the inside' (Stanton–Ife, 2010: 160).

In a useful discussion that draws on the work of Runciman (1983), Bottoms (2010) develops a model of sentencing theory that highlights the importance of the court being fully appraised of both the physical and psychological effects of an offence on the victim. For Bottoms, the essence of what he terms the court's 'duty to understand' in imposing sentence is that it requires the judge to consider fully all the factual matters relevant to the sentencing decision before proceeding to make that decision (Bottoms, 2010: 27).

Bottoms explains that Runciman argues, firstly, that social theory consists of both 'evaluation' (involving value-choices) and 'understanding' and, secondly, that there are three separate strands within the generic concept of 'understanding': *reportage*, *explanation* and *description* (Bottoms, 2010: 23). Insofar as sentencing is concerned, the end point of the judge's work in a specific case is a *decision*, namely the imposition of an appropriate sentence. In Runciman's language, in imposing sentence the judge necessarily engages in 'evaluation'. Bottoms notes that a key subsequent question then becomes: how can 'understanding', in its various senses, help the judge towards a good solution to her evaluative task (2010: 23)?

In elaborating Runciman's thesis, Bottoms explains that the first strand of 'understanding' – *reportage* – is the provision of an accurate factual account of what has happened on a given occasion or over a given period of time (Bottoms, 2010: 23–24). In the context of Scottish sentencing procedure, for example, reportage is provided by the Crown narrative (AN Brown, 2010: 160); the agreed narrative delivered by the Crown in the event of the accused having pleaded guilty (Chalmers et al, 2007a: 62–63; McPherson, 2013: 141–47); or, in appropriate cases, by a proof (or hearing) in mitigation (AN Brown, 2010: 161; Kelly, 1993: 15; Nicholson, 1992: 114). In the other common law jurisdictions considered in this work, reportage is also provided by the Crown or by the State in similar procedures. In England and Wales, for example, the prosecutor will provide the court with a statement of the facts (Ashworth, 2015: 423–25 and 430–31; Wasik, 2014: 17–18). In order to establish the facts in cases where the accused has pleaded guilty, the court may require to hold a special hearing following the procedure set out in *R v Newton*[16] and elaborated upon in *R v Cairns*[17] (a so-called '*Newton* hearing', see Ashworth, 2015: 425–27 and Wasik, 2014: 18–21). Similar provisions exist for the prosecution to provide the court with statements of facts in the Republic of Ireland (see O'Malley, 2016: 793–96 and 2013a: 713–19); New Zealand (see Hall, 2007a: 250–51); and South Africa (see Terblanche, 2016: 95, 98–99, 100–5).

On Runciman's account, the second strand of 'understanding' is *explanation* – where reportage asks the 'what' question, explanation asks the 'why' question (Runciman, 1983: 19, cited in Bottoms, 2010: 24). At the sentencing stage, such 'explanation' is provided by reports prepared at the request of the judge to provide additional factual information about the circumstances of the offence and the character of the offender. In English criminal procedure the relevant 'explanation' may be provided by a pre-sentence report[18] (see Ashworth, 2015: 432–34; Bottoms, 2010: 30; Wasik, 2014: 30–32), or a medical report[19] (see Wasik, 2014: 32–33). In Scotland, such 'explanation' may be provided by a criminal justice social work report,[20] a psychiatric report, or a risk assessment,[21] while in the Republic of Ireland, probation or other pre-sentence reports may be ordered by the sentencing judge (see O'Malley, 2016: 800–1).

In all three jurisdictions, counsel for the accused will deliver a plea in mitigation (in England and Wales, see Ashworth, 2015: 434–35; Solley, 2002: 320; Thomas, 2002: 481; and Wasik, 2014: 36–39; in Scotland, see AN Brown, 2010: 161; Nicholson, 1992: 118–19; and Stewart, 1997: 186; and, in the Republic of Ireland, see O'Malley, 2016: 802–4, 811–12). In addition to providing, in Runciman's terms, the requisite 'explanation', the importance of the plea in mitigation in sentencing is highlighted by Jacobson and Hough's empirical study into mitigation and the role of personal factors in sentencing. The authors found that counsel's plea in mitigation can often, if done effectively, be influential in the determination of sentence (Jacobson and Hough, 2007: 45; see also Ashworth et al, 1984: 43–45; Tombs, 2004: 43; 48; Millie et al, 2007: 256; and Roberts, 2010: 21).

The third strand within the generic concept of 'understanding' – *description* or, as Bottoms prefers, 'appreciative description' – meanwhile asks the question 'what like'? (Runciman, 1983: 19, cited in Bottoms, 2010: 24). For Bottoms, 'appreciative description' better refers to the 'internal view of the subject' (2010: 25). Bottoms

[16] (1982) 4 Cr App R (S) 388.
[17] [2013] 2 Cr App R (S) 73.
[18] See the Criminal Justice Act 2003 ('the 2003 Act'), s 158.
[19] Ibid, s 157.
[20] See the Criminal Procedure (Scotland) Act 1995 ('the 1995 Act') ss 204(2A) and 207(4).
[21] A risk assessment is required if consideration is being given to the imposition of an extended sentence (see s 210A(4) of the 1995 Act and the decision in *Robertson v HMA*, 2004 SCCR 180 at [26]).

observes that, as noted by Homans (1984), Runciman's *description* – or Bottoms' own *appreciative description* – can itself be divided into two sub-categories: *individual (appreciative) description* and *general (appreciative) description* (Bottoms, 2010). For Runciman, appreciative description is an identifiably different task for the social scientist (or, for our purposes, for the judge) than either reportage or explanation (Bottoms, 2010: 25).

Insofar as sentencing an offence of rape is concerned, the *general appreciative description* of the offence may, for example, be contained within a guideline judgment or set of sentencing guidelines which identify 'standard' aggravating factors (see Bottoms, 2010: 32).[22] The *individual appreciative description*, meanwhile, can be supplied through a victim personal statement in England and Wales, a victim statement in Scotland, victim impact evidence in the Republic of Ireland and victim impact statements in New Zealand and South Africa.[23] For Bottoms, the court will, in certain cases, need to receive such personalised and victim-orientated appreciative descriptions to maximise its understanding prior to imposing sentence (2010: 33).

Bottoms explains that such evidence can add a valuable further dimension to the total evidence before the court and that, crucially, in the absence of such information, the court might misread other (more 'standardised') evidence before it (Bottoms, 2010: 34). For example, the Crown narrative or prosecutor's statement of the facts in a case of rape might contain information to the effect that, having been medically examined and having received medical treatment, the victim did not suffer any great physical trauma. While, as we have seen,[24] this may well be true in the majority of cases, such an account fails to consider the long-term psychological trauma sustained by many rape victims and may well give an inaccurate impression of the harm caused by the particular offence.

Thus, for Bottoms, the absence of *appreciative description* can significantly distort the judge's overall understanding of the seriousness of a particular offence. Even accurate *reportage* (of the facts of the case) and *explanation* (in the sense of the offender's motivation, background and personal circumstances) can be misleading if the judge has no adequate *appreciative-descriptive* understanding of the nature of the offence and its effects on the victim (Bottoms, 2010: 35). Bottoms, in fact, illustrates this point by reference to the offence of rape:

> 'Would it be reasonable … to say that a sentencing court that sentences a rapist while not fully appreciating, in the appreciative-descriptive sense, what it is like to be the victim of such a crime, 'may fairly be told that it is acting on behalf of society while knowing little or nothing about what it is called upon to judge'? The answer, I think, has to be in the affirmative' (Bottoms, 2010: 35, citing Runciman, 1983: 34).

At the sentencing stage, *reportage* remains important but *explanation* and, especially in sentencing rape, *appreciative description* are of generally enhanced

[22] See Chapters 4 to 7.
[23] Discussed later in this chapter.
[24] See the discussion above.

significance (Bottoms, 2010: 39–40). Bottoms thus concludes that in appropriate cases, including those of particular complexity or seriousness, such as rape, the sentencing court has a duty to consider evidence relating to a victim-orientated appreciative description, principally as part of its overall 'duty to understand' (2010: 36–37). As Shapland and Hall (2010: 186) argue, proportionality in sentencing requires adequate information concerning the seriousness of the offence, including information about the effects on the victim and the short or long-term psychological harm done to victims (2010: 182). For Shapland and Hall, as for Bottoms, victim input is necessary for proper sentencing; sentencing without such victim input is 'impoverished sentencing' (2010: 186; see also Edwards, 2004: 976, 978).

Hearing the Victim: The Use of Victim Statements in Sentencing Rape

The principal way in which judges are provided with victim-orientated appreciative descriptions of the physical and psychological effects of rape is through victim impact evidence, in the form of victim personal statements or victim impact statements. The English victim personal statement ('VPS') scheme, for example, was introduced in October 2001 as 'a means of providing victims with a voice at sentencing' (Roberts and Erez, 2010: 248). A VPS gives the victim a formal opportunity to say how a crime has affected them physically, psychologically and financially. The VPS will be taken into account by the judge when determining the sentence (Ashworth, 2015: 440; Hall, 2010: 156 and 2009: 106–7; Miller, 2014: 797; Shapland and Hall, 2010: 177).

Victim personal statements generated considerable controversy when they were first introduced. Debate focused on the propriety of allowing victims input into the sentencing process and the way in which such input should be structured. Some commentators argued that victim input could be detrimental to procedural and substantive justice, while also eroding defendants' rights (see Doak et al, 2009: 652–58; Erez and Rogers, 1999: 218–19; Hoyle, 2012: 411; Roberts and Erez, 2010: 232–33; in particular, compare Ashworth, 2015: 438–39 and 1993 and Sanders et al, 2001, with Erez, 2000 and 1999; Roberts and Erez, 2004; and Chalmers et al, 2007b).

Much of the controversy that accompanied the introduction of the VPS scheme has died away although, despite certain guidance from the Court of Appeal (Criminal Division) on their use,[25] these statements still present challenges for the courts at the stage of sentencing (Roberts and Azmeh, 2019: 701–2). How and to what extent should a VPS influence sentencing (Edwards, 2013: 79–80)? The Court of Appeal (Criminal Division) has stressed the importance of the VPS in sentencing cases of rape and sexual assault. In *R v Ismail*,[26] a case involving the rape of a

[25] See *R v Perkins* [2013] 2 Cr App R (S) 72 and *R v Chall* [2019] EWCA Crim 865.
[26] [2005] 2 Cr App R (S) 88.

16-year-old girl by forcible oral penetration, Lord Woolf CJ criticised the fact that no such statement was available to the sentencing judge and continued:

> 'In a case of this sort we consider that it should be routine to obtain a victim impact statement. It is most important that the sentencing judge has information as to that matter … A victim impact statement, particularly when the victim is as young as 16, is absolutely essential … [The impact on the victim] is an important factor which the courts must take into account in deciding the appropriate sentence.'[27]

Provision is also made for the court to receive victim impact evidence in the Republic of Ireland[28] (see Kilcommins et al, 2018: 37–38, 61; Leahy and Fitzgerald O'Reilly, 2018: 239–41; and O'Malley, 2016: 291–300); New Zealand (see Hall, 2014: 474–75, 591–605 and 2007a: 252–53); South Africa (see Müller and van der Merwe, 2006; Terblanche, 2016: 123–24; van der Merwe, 2008; and van der Merwe and Skelton, 2015); and Scotland[29] (see Chalmers et al, 2007a, 2007b, 2007c; Ferguson and McDiarmid, 2014: 26; and Munro, 2016: 158).

In South Africa, the Supreme Court of Appeal has stressed the importance of obtaining victim impact reports in rape cases.[30] In Scotland, meanwhile, while the prosecutor is obliged to lay any victim statement before the court,[31] unlike practice in England and Wales[32] there is currently no duty on the court to ensure that, if possible, a victim statement is available prior to the judge passing sentence in a case of rape. The study by Chalmers et al (2007b) found that, generally, few victims take the opportunity to make victim statements in Scotland (2007b: 367–69). The authors report that respondents were more likely to make victim statements in cases involving serious offences; however, the study still found that only 46 per cent of rape victims in the sample made a victim statement (2007b: 368).

Thus, in many rape cases in the Scottish courts, the sentencing judge will have no information from the victim about what her experience of victimisation and its aftermath felt like (see Bottoms, 2010: 29). On Bottoms' account,[33] this means that while Scottish judges will be provided with suitable *reportage* (in the form of the Crown narrative) and suitable *explanation* (in the form of a criminal justice social work report, perhaps also a formal risk assessment and the plea in mitigation), they will frequently lack an adequate victim-focused *appreciative description* of the physical and psychological trauma sustained by the particular victim (Bottoms, 2010; *cf HMA v AB*[34]).

[27] Ibid at [8]. See also *R v Black* [2006] EWCA Crim 2306 at [28] and [29].
[28] Under the Criminal Justice Act 1993, s 5 as amended by the Criminal Procedure Act 2010.
[29] Under the Criminal Justice (Scotland) Act 2003, s14.
[30] See *DPP v Thabethe* [2011] ZASCA 186; 2011 (2) SACR 567 (SCA) at [21] and *S v Mudau (sub nom S v SMM)* [2013] ZASCA 56; 2013 (2) SACR 292 (SCA) at [25].
[31] Section 14(5) of the 2003 Act.
[32] See *Ismail* (n 26).
[33] See above.
[34] [2015] HCJAC 106; 2016 SCCR 47 at [14].

3

Technology-Facilitated Sexual Violence and Image-Based Sexual Abuse

The Filming of Rape and Sexual Assault

Introduction

In March 2011, the English Court of Appeal (Criminal Division) issued its judgment in *Attorney General's Reference (Nos 3, 73 and 75 of 2010).*[1] The Court took this opportunity to highlight a concerning new trend in sexual offending and in cases of rape in particular. In two of the three cases of rape referred to the Court by the Attorney General as being unduly lenient, the offenders had used mobile phones to photograph the victims. Both victims were bound and in states of undress following the rapes. In one case, the offender had threatened to post the images of the victim on the internet if she told anyone about the offence. In delivering the judgment of the Court, the Lord Chief Justice (Judge) said this:

> 'A pernicious new habit has developed by which criminals take photographs of their victims – often just to show off to their friends; often just to add something to the humiliation which the victim is already suffering; and sometimes … either as a form of pressure to discourage any complaint … but also possibly for the purposes of blackmail … Anyone can understand what a powerful lever may be given to the criminal by his possession of photographs taken of the victim when, as in these cases, she has been subjected to degrading treatment … We make it clear that from now onwards the taking of photographs should always be treated as an aggravating feature of any case and in particular of any sexual cases. Photography in these circumstances usually constitutes a very serious aggravating feature of the case.'[2]

At the time the Court issued its judgment, there was already a Definitive Guideline in place for the sentencing of sexual offences. That guideline had been issued four years earlier by the Sentencing Guidelines Council (see SGC, 2007a);[3] however, the Definitive Guideline was silent on the issue of whether the English courts were entitled to regard the photographing or video recording of an offence as an

[1] [2011] 2 Cr App R (S) 100.
[2] Ibid at [7](2).
[3] For a full discussion of the development of English sentencing guidelines for the crime of rape, see Chapter 4.

aggravating factor. The Court of Appeal thus took the opportunity to amplify the terms of the guideline then in force (Thomas, 2011: 583). The decision in *Attorney General's Reference (Nos 3, 73 and 75 of 2010)* illustrates the importance of empowering courts to establish or recognise new aggravating factors when the need to do so becomes obvious (O'Malley, 2016: 209).

Filming the rape or other sexual abuse of a child or young person may amount to the production of child sexual abuse images or so-called 'child pornography'. This may be charged as a separate offence[4] and, in certain jurisdictions, sentencing guidelines exist for offences involving the production, possession and distribution of child sexual abuse images. In England and Wales, for example, the present Definitive Guideline on sexual offences issued by the Sentencing Council for England and Wales sets out a starting point of six years' imprisonment, with a range of four to nine years' imprisonment, for the most serious offences involving the production of child sexual abuse images (Sentencing Council, 2013a: 77; Rook and Ward, 2016: 646–66). In Scotland, the High Court of Justiciary on appeal ('the Appeal Court') broadly accepted the current English sentencing guidelines in its decision in *Wood v HMA*.[5] The Appeal Court had earlier approved and, indeed, expanded upon, the previous set of English sentencing guidelines for child pornography offences in its decision in *HMA v Graham*[6] (see Brown, 2010 and Gillespie, 2010). In *Wood*, the Appeal Court noted that the English guidelines should be used as framework by Scottish judges but that they should not be applied too rigidly, sentencing being 'a matter of judgment and discretion in the particular circumstances of the case'.[7]

Insofar as adult victimisation is concerned, a growing body of research has started to explore the complex motivations behind offenders' actions in recording or photographing acts of sexual assault. An emerging scholarly literature, particularly in Australia and in England and Wales, has also started to focus on the impact of these practices on adult victims.

Technology-Facilitated Sexual Violence and Image-Based Sexual Abuse

In Australia, the phenomenon identified by the Court of Appeal in the *Attorney General's Reference*[8] case is conceptualised as 'technology-facilitated sexual violence'

[4] For example, in England and Wales see s 1(1)(a) of the Protection of Children Act 1978 ('Indecent photographs of children'); in Scotland see s 52(1)(a) of the Civic Government (Scotland) Act 1982 ('Indecent photographs etc. of children'); in the Republic of Ireland see s 5(1)(a) of the Child Trafficking and Pornography Act 1998 ('Producing, distributing etc, child pornography'); and, in South Africa, see s 20 of the Criminal Law (Sexual Offences and Related Matters) Amendment Act 2007 ('Using children for or benefitting from child pornography').

[5] [2017] HCJAC 2; 2017 JC 185.

[6] [2010] HCJAC 50; 2011 JC 1 at [21] to [50].

[7] *Wood* (n 5) at [28].

[8] *Attorney General's Reference (Nos. 3, 73 and 75 of 2010)* (n 1).

by Nicola Henry and Anastasia Powell (Henry and Powell, 2016a and 2016b; Powell and Henry, 2017a). In England and Wales, meanwhile, Clare McGlynn and Erika Rackley term this form of offending 'image-based sexual abuse' (McGlynn and Rackley, 2017a and 2017b). McGlynn et al argue that the term 'abuse' more accurately captures the extent and nature of the harms experienced by victims. They suggest that conceptualising the issue in terms of 'violence' may signal physical violence to many. They also consider the term 'abuse' to have greater breadth and resonance in public, policy and legislative debates (McGlynn et al, 2017: 38–39; see also McGlynn and Rackley, 2016 and 2017b: 43–44).

The concepts of technology-facilitated sexual violence and image-based sexual abuse encompass a broad range of phenomena that have at their core the non-consensual creation and/or distribution of private sexual images (McGlynn and Rackley, 2017a: 11). For present purposes, however, technology-facilitated sexual violence and image-based sexual abuse are taken as ways of conceptualising offences in which mobile and online technologies are used as tools to blackmail, control, coerce, harass, humiliate, objectify or violate the victim of a sexual offence (Henry and Powell, 2016a: 398, 400; Henry and Powell, 2015a: 759 and 2016b: 1–2; McGlynn and Rackley, 2017a: 4–7 and 2017b: 42; McGlynn et al, 2017: 35; Powell and Henry, 2017a: 4–6 and 2015: 3). The offending can take the form, amongst other things, of the unauthorised, non-consensual creation and distribution of sexual images and the creation and distribution (actual or threatened) of sexual assault images (Henry and Powell, 2015a: 759 and 2014: 85; McGlynn and Rackley, 2017a: 1, 6–7; 2015a; and 2015b: 2; Powell and Henry, 2017b: 208; Powell et al 2018a: 306–7). The concepts of technology-facilitated sexual violence and image-based sexual abuse seek to recognise that rather than existing in a distinct 'offline/online dualism', contemporary manifestations of sexual violence are increasingly mediated, facilitated or extended through the internet, social media and other digital communication technologies (Henry and Powell, 2014: 88 and 92; McGlynn and Rackley, 2017a: 2; Powell and Henry, 2017a: 7; 2016a: 2–3 and 2016b: 10; Powell et al, 2018a: 310).

While there is no existing data to confirm how common it is for sexual offenders to create and/or distribute sexual assault images, a number of high-profile cases and recent decisions of the appellate courts in various jurisdictions suggest it is a growing trend (Powell and Henry, 2017a: 130–31; Powell et al, 2018b: 93). Although they accept that there is currently a lack of empirical data on the prevalence of online forms of sexual violence and harassment, Henry and Powell (2016a) conceptualise technology-facilitated sexual violence as a form of gender-based violence for three interconnected reasons.

Firstly, research to date supports the theory that, although not the exclusive victims, women and girls are the main targets of online digital sexualised violence and of the non-consensual distribution of intimate images online. Secondly, the impacts of these behaviours are gendered because women and girls may experience adverse impacts due to the persistence of outdated myths and expectations surrounding sexual norms. Thirdly, regardless of the gender of either the perpetrator or the victim, a key factor underlying the perpetration of sexual violence is what the authors describe as the social and structural context of gender hierarchisation, an 'historically constructed pattern of power relations between men and women and definitions of femininity and masculinity' (Henry and Powell, 2016a: 398–99, citing Connell, 1987: 98–99; see also Citron and Franks, 2014: 353–54; Henry and Powell, 2016b: 1–2 and 2014: 99, fn 2; McGlynn and Rackley, 2017a: 11 and 13–14; and Powell, 2009: 7). Drawing these three strands together, Powell concludes:

> 'It is difficult to imagine rapists taking and distributing images of their assault, boasting online to their peers and to a wider public audience, if there were not a culture of societal tolerance, even acceptance, of rape … [P]erpetrators of rape have long used various strategies to intimidate, harass and humiliate their victims and arguably to prolong the experience of power and entitlement; recording and distributing images of the rape may just be an extension of these practices' (Powell, 2015: 575; see also Henry and Powell, 2014: 92; Powell and Henry, 2017a: 90; and Powell et al, 2018b: 98).

Why do Offenders Film Rape and Sexual Assault?

As the filming of sexual assault and any subsequent distribution of the footage so often involves the internet and social media, it has been suggested that the public, law enforcement and the judiciary sometimes struggle to understand the mechanics of the conduct and the effect that it has on the victim (Citron and Franks, 2014: 347; see also Henry and Powell, 2015a: 760, 766–67 and 2014: 92; McGlynn and Rackley, 2017a: 21; and Powell, 2009: 6). Even where criminal justice stakeholders do have an understanding of the mechanics involved, it is often difficult for professionals to keep up to date with developments in technology as offenders use and adapt new services, software applications and websites to facilitate their offending (Powell and Henry, 2016b: 12).

In seeking to explore the circumstances in which videos and photographs of criminal activity are produced and the role that such filming plays in offending behaviour – 'the underlying motivations and socio-cultural structures that lead offenders in the middle of committing an offence to reach for their smartphones' – Sandberg and Ugelvik examined 51 decisions of the Norwegian higher courts in which the offender (or at least one in a group of offenders) had either taken a picture or recorded video footage of the offences as they were happening (Sandberg and Ugelvik, 2017: 1027). The authors identify three cultural trends to explain why images are recorded as part of the commission of crime: firstly, to produce what they term 'pornography'; secondly, to further hurt and humiliate the victim; and thirdly, as an impulse to document extraordinary events (Sandberg and Ugelvik, 2017: 1028). Sandberg and Ugelvik stress, however, that the cultural trends are not mutually exclusive; they often operate simultaneously in specific cases to form a bricolage of offender motives embedded in recent socio-cultural and technological developments (2017: 1034–35; see also Henry and Powell, 2016b: 10, fn 4).

The Production of 'Pornography'

Sandberg and Ugelvik explain that many of the offences in their study were clearly shaped, or even instigated, to create 'a certain visual product'. One of the most common reasons for recording an offence was to produce what the authors term 'pornography' (2017: 1028). It may be questioned whether, in the context of rape and sexual assault, 'pornography' is an appropriate term. In their discussion of 'revenge pornography' (a term routinely used in various media as a catch-all phrase to include a wide variety of non-consensual image-based harms) McGlynn and Rackley suggest that this term is problematic for two reasons. Firstly, it concentrates on the *motives* of the perpetrators, rather than on the *harm* to victims. Secondly, the term 'pornography' tends to instil what the authors describe as a sense of 'choice and legitimacy' that is inappropriate when discussing the creation and/or distribution of sexual images without consent, again particularly as it fails to focus on the harms of these practices (McGlynn and Rackley, 2017a: 3; see also McGlynn and Rackley, 2016 and 2015b: 3; Powell and Henry, 2017a: 118 and 2014a: 122, fn. 4; Powell et al, 2018a: 306; and Wright, 2019: 527–28). A further objection voiced by McGlynn et al is that the language of 'porn' risks eroticising the harms of image-based sexual abuse and may encourage the media's salacious interest and reporting of such cases (McGlynn et al, 2017: 38).

Arguably 'non-consensual pornography' – sexually graphic images of individuals taken without their consent, including recordings of sexual assaults (see Citron and Franks, 2014: 346 and Henry et al, 2017: 3) – would be a more appropriate term in the cases discussed by Sandberg and Ugelvik. Nevertheless, Sandberg and Ugelvik identify the creation of pornography as an underlying motive in 27 of the 51 Norwegian court cases examined in their study, mostly in cases of sexual offending (Sandberg and Ugelvik, 2017: 1028). Offenders recorded sexual assaults and rape as digital 'souvenirs' or 'visual mementos' which allowed them to 'relive or even re-enact episodes later'. In such cases, the victims 'are used against their will as props for the offenders' future enjoyment' (2017: 1028–29; see also Franklin, 2013: 59 and 2004: 29–30).

Sandberg and Ugelvik consider that the filming of sexual assaults reflects a highly gendered process of sexualisation and 'pornographication' of society (Sandberg and Ugelvik, 2017: 1028–29). For commentators such as Alexa Dodge (2016: 66), the filming of such offences raises disturbing questions about the way in which sexual violence can be normalised and condoned and the role that new media increasingly plays in the perpetration of such violence. Cases such as those examined in Sandberg and Ugelvik's study demonstrate the ways in which new media exacerbates issues surrounding sexual violence by creating 'digital spaces' in which its perpetuation and legitimisation takes on new qualities (Dodge 2016: 66).

Further Humiliation of the Victim

Henry and Powell suggest that, in the majority of cases of technology-facilitated sexual violence, the motivation for the offender's behaviour stems essentially from the objectification and debasement of the victim (Henry and Powell, 2016a: 399). In 17 of the 51 cases in Sandberg and Ugelvik's study, it appears that images were recorded to further humiliate the victim as part of sexual or physical abuse. The authors cite one example of severe violence and humiliation in which the act of filming was a central part of the events described in court documents. Following an altercation at a party, several youths ganged up on the victim, a young woman. The group proceeded to assault her; they forced her to pose in degrading positions and to perform sex acts in front of those assembled. The incident was filmed on a mobile phone; laughter and comments from those present could be heard in the background (Sandberg and Ugelvik, 2017: 1030).

Sandberg and Ugelvik (2017: 1031) consider that such sexual assaults are often about control: the use of a camera during the offence further strengthens the unequal power relationship while also making the abuse appear less impulsive and more calculated. The authors conclude:

> 'The very act of filming or taking pictures furthers the humiliation because it demonstrates the power of the offender to direct or objectify the victim and turn her or him into an image. It also adds to the pain of a violent or sexual assault by demonstrating to the victims that they are being watched not only by the offenders and bystanders, but also potentially by many others if the images are distributed' (2017: 1031–32).

The Compulsion to Document

Sandberg and Ugelvik found 'a compulsion for documentation' to be the third reason for offenders filming or recording their offences. The authors link this will or urge to document with modern 'snapshot culture'. Camera phones have become taken-for-granted parts of social life in general; individuals frequently use them to engage with social media, documenting dramatic or unusual events to reveal a sense of who they are or of how they wish to be perceived (Sandberg and Ugelvik, 2017: 1032, 1035; see also Pennington and Birthisel, 2016: 2436). When cameras are so ubiquitous, videos and images of an offence may be recorded 'just because it feels like the appropriate thing to do' (Sandberg and Ugelvik, 2017: 1036).

In a similar vein, Yar (2012) considers the ways in which the rise of new media challenge commonplace criminological assumptions about the crime/media interface. Yar suggests that the filming of, for example, sexual assault may not be coincidental or opportunistic but may rather be a key driver of the offence itself:

> 'Today we see the spectacle of (predominantly) young people *performing* acts of crime and deviance in order to record them, share them and upload them to the Internet. This kind of "will to communicate" or "will to representation" may be seen in itself as a new

> kind of causal inducement to law- and rule-breaking behaviour … [I]nstead of asking whether "media" instigates crime or fear of crime, we must ask how the very possibility of *mediating oneself* to an audience through self-representation might be bound up with the genesis of criminal behaviour' (Yar, 2012: 246, emphasis per original).

Yar explains that an offence may be engineered or instigated with the specific and express purpose of recording it, thereafter disseminating the footage via electronic networks of communication. In such cases, the desire to represent the (criminal) self becomes a criminogenic factor: people offend so that they may be seen by others (Yar, 2012: 252–53). Yar elaborates:

> '[T]he yearning to represent and mediate the self in the act of "transgression" comes to serve as a motivation for violence – the desire to been [*sic*] seen and to seek recognition from others for one's acts, underpins the instigation of criminal acts … [T]he flagrant eschewal of anonymity and the public sharing of images that amount to an admission of guilt make perfect sense if we grasp the role played by the desire for mediated self-representation in the genesis of transgression' (Yar, 2012: 253–54).

In recent years, several commentators have highlighted a phenomenon described as 'rape culture', namely the social, cultural and structural discourses and practices in which sexual violence is tolerated, accepted, eroticised, minimised and trivialised. A pernicious effect of such rape culture is that victims are routinely disbelieved or blamed for their own victimisation; perpetrators, meanwhile, are rarely held accountable or their behaviours are seen as excusable or understandable (see Powell and Henry, 2017a: 102–5 and 2014b: 2; and Sills et al, 2016: 936). Following Yar, Powell considers that there are arguably links between the 'will-to-representation' and the pervasiveness of 'rape culture' that can begin to explain why particular sexual offenders are driven to film and share recordings of their crimes, despite the images having the potential to be used as evidence against them in subsequent criminal proceedings (Powell, 2015: 576; see also McGlynn and Rackley, 2017a: 16–18 and Powell et al, 2018a: 311–312). Sandberg and Ugelvik's 'compulsion for documentation' (or Yar's 'will-to-representation') is identified in 24 cases in the authors' study. In some cases, the taking of pictures or the recording of video footage happened impulsively, while in others, the images were staged or enacted for the camera for maximum effect (Sandberg and Ugelvik, 2017: 1032).

The Convergence of the Three Trends and Motivations

To illustrate the way in which the three cultural trends and offender motivations (generation of (non-consensual) pornography, humiliation of the victim and the compulsion to document a dramatic or extraordinary event) can intertwine, Sandberg and Ugelvik discuss a further case of sexual assault drawn from their study. Court documents recorded that two young men ('A' and 'B') sexually abused a young girl, who was at the time drunk and unconscious, while a third ('C') filmed the offence. The offenders later posted an image on Instagram along with disparaging comments about the victim. Sandberg and Ugelvik note that the court regarded C's conduct as positively encouraging A and B's actions. A, B and C can be seen and heard on the video discussing ways in which to further assault and humiliate the victim. They suggest ways in which to subject the victim to further sexual degradations, including penetrating her with objects and these suggestions are acted upon (Sandberg and Ugelvik, 2017: 1034).

Sandberg and Ugelvik note that, initially, C documents the sexual assault – an 'extraordinary event' – in a detached manner. Yet, at a certain point in the episode, the role of the camera changes from the *passive recording* of a sexual assault to the *active staging* of abuse for the camera. The authors explain that the camera appears to coax the youths into doing more than they would have otherwise, to create a 'better', more extreme video (Sandberg and Ugelvik, 2017: 1034). It appears that as the abuse continues, the *filming* becomes increasingly important and the offenders' *sexual desire* plays a less important role (Sandberg and Ugelvik, 2017: 1034–35). In this regard, Judith Butler suggests that the camera can promote 'a festive cruelty' in which, for example, a rapist uses a camera phone to capture and commemorate his offence. In such circumstances, Butler explains, the photograph or video may already be at work in prompting, framing and orchestrating the rape or sexual assault, even as the photograph or video captures the offence at the moment of its commission (Butler, 2007: 959).

In the Scottish decision in *Gay v HMA*,[9] for example, the 16-year-old appellant was convicted of sexually assaulting a young child.[10] The offence took place in a dormitory at a Sea Cadets training camp. The appellant, a senior Sea Cadet, encouraged a younger boy to sexually assault the victim while he was asleep. The victim's clothes were removed and he was digitally penetrated. The appellant filmed the offence on his mobile phone and later showed the video to another cadet. The appellant could be heard laughing and giggling on the video as he filmed the assault. It is clear from the evidence led at trial that, while the initial assault was spontaneous and unplanned, as the incident progressed, the primary focus of the two offenders' actions shifted to the staging of further and increasingly serious acts of sexual abuse for the camera.[11]

Similarly, in *Attorney General's Reference (Nos 15, 16 and 17 of 2013)*[12] two of the three respondents pleaded guilty to assault by penetration, while the third pleaded guilty to assault by penetration and sexual assault.[13] A charge of rape was ordered to lie on the file, the respondents' pleas to the lesser offences being regarded by the prosecution as adequate to the indictment as a whole. The victim in this case was an 18-year-old student. Having left a nightclub in the early hours of the morning, she met the three respondents and agreed to return home with them. More alcohol

[9] [2015] HCJAC 125; 2016 SCCR 87.
[10] Contrary to ss 19 and 20 of the Sexual Offences (Scotland) Act 2009.
[11] *Gay* (n 9) at [2].
[12] [2013] EWCA Crim 1041.
[13] Contrary to ss 2 and 3 of the Sexual Offences Act 2003 respectively.

was consumed, drinking games were played and 'sexual banter' took place. The victim appeared happy to engage in the games and jokes. The victim eventually passed out and was assaulted by two of the respondents. The third respondent filmed the assaults on the victim's own mobile phone. Due to the amount of alcohol she had consumed, the victim was unsure of what had happened; however, as she woke the following afternoon to find herself in bed with two of the respondents and subsequently experienced discomfort in her anal region, she suspected that she may have been sexually assaulted. Some four days later, she discovered the video footage of the assault on her mobile phone. The Court of Appeal's description of the footage illustrates the way in which, as explained by Sandberg and Ugelvik (2017: 1034–35), the role of the camera in such offences changes from the *passive recording* of a sexual assault to the *active staging* of abuse.

The Court noted that the footage lasted some 20 minutes. It commenced with the three respondents discussing the victim's physical appearance and the possibility of uploading the recording to Facebook although, in the event, they refrained from doing so. There was much laughing and giggling by the respondents; they egged one another on in what the Court described as 'very coarse terms'.[14] Having been so encouraged by the other respondents, the first respondent placed his private parts on the victim's face while she lay comatose on a bed. The abuse then escalated to digital penetration of the victim's hinder parts by the second respondent. The sexual abuse culminated with either the first or the second respondent repeatedly inserting an object into the victim's hinder parts. The abuse was filmed by the third respondent; while he did not physically touch the victim, he offered enthusiastic encouragement to the first and second respondents.[15] The third respondent later claimed that he had filmed the events as 'a drunken bit of fun'.[16] The Court increased the sentences imposed on the respondents from three-and-a-half years' imprisonment to five-and-a-half years, reduced from seven-and-a-half years to reflect their guilty pleas.[17]

In the later case of *R v S*,[18] the appellant was convicted of raping and sexually assaulting his former wife. The offences only came to light when the victim discovered 11 DVDs in the course of clearing the former matrimonial home. The DVDs all contained video footage, filmed by the appellant, of his raping the victim and subjecting her to other sexual indignities, including penetrating her private and hinder parts with various objects and foodstuffs. The victim had no recollection of the offences, having been either asleep or unconscious at the time, possibly through intoxication.[19] It transpired that the appellant had set up his own pornographic website to which he uploaded the videos.[20]

[14] *Attorney General's Reference (Nos 15, 16 and 17 of 2013)* (n 12) at [6].
[15] Ibid at [7] and [8].
[16] Ibid at [9].
[17] Ibid at [30]. On the operation of plea-based sentencing reductions in England and Wales, see Chapter 4.
[18] [2015] EWCA Crim 2527.
[19] Ibid at [2].
[20] Ibid at [8] and [19].

The offences are described in graphic detail in the Court's judgment.[21] Unlike the case of sexual assault discussed by Sandberg and Ugelvik (2017: 1034–35) or *Gay*[22] and *Attorney General's Reference (Nos 15, 16 and 17 of 2013)*[23] considered above, the appellant in *R v S* committed the offences alone. The Court's description of the offences, however, in particular the assaults by penetration, demonstrates that the appellant moved from 'passively' recording the sexual assault of his wife to *actively staging* increasingly depraved acts of sexual violence. Indeed, during a debate on whether the jury was required to view the video footage, prosecuting counsel noted that in her 24 years in practice in the criminal courts, this was the most unpleasant material she had ever been required to view.[24] These later instances of assault by penetration, committed by the appellant using a disparate and increasingly bizarre range of objects, appear to have been specifically staged for the camera and with a view, ultimately, to the appellant 'commemorating' his offences by uploading the videos to his own pornographic website. On appeal, the appellant was sentenced to 12 years' imprisonment on the charges of rape (reduced from 15 years to reflect his guilty pleas), with concurrent sentences of 10 and seven years imposed in respect of the charges of sexual assault.[25]

The same escalation from 'passive' recording to 'active staging' is evident in *Ronald (Marc) v HMA*,[26] where the appellant was convicted of three charges of sexual assault and two charges of rape committed against his former partner. The facts of the case are similar to *R v S*.[27] The offences came to light when the victim discovered video footage on the appellant's laptop computer. It transpired that the appellant had abused the victim over a period of some two years. The offences were committed when the victim was unconscious through drug or alcohol intoxication. The appellant filmed the abuse using a video camera. The abuse began with the appellant sexually assaulting the victim. He then dressed her in nappies or plastic underwear, raped her and urinated and ejaculated on her. The appellant provided a running commentary when committing the offences; he repeatedly made sexual and derogatory remarks about the victim and announced his intention to rape her. As part of the 'active staging' of the offences, the appellant placed the victim in various positions on a sofa prior to assaulting her and repeatedly checked her eyes to ensure that she remained unconscious throughout. The appellant's appeal against the *cumulo* sentence of nine years' imprisonment was refused (see Brown, 2018a: 5–6).

In such cases, where an offender's need to document the abuse is part of the motivational structure, offenders appear to spend as much (or indeed more) effort

[21] Ibid at [2].
[22] *Gay* (n 9).
[23] *Attorney General's Reference (Nos 15, 16 and 17 of 2013)* (n 12).
[24] *S* (n 18) at [4].
[25] Ibid at [23].
[26] High Court of Justiciary on appeal, 31 May 2018, unreported (see the case note by Brown, 2018a).
[27] *S* (n 18).

on the staging of a desired image than on the offence itself. The elements of staging and committing the offence merge and the two become inseparable:

> 'The cinematic quality of the act is part and parcel of the act itself. Committing the crime and taking the picture is the same thing. In some of these cases, the victim is no longer a human being; he or she is reduced to a theatrical prop' (Sandberg and Ugelvik, 2017: 1036).

The victim is thus severely degraded throughout the process. The act of filming is a crucial part of the humiliation. This continues if images or video recordings of the assault are shown and distributed to others (Sandberg and Ugelvik, 2017: 1035).

The Filming of Multiple Perpetrator Rape

In recent years, filming has become an increasingly prominent feature of multiple perpetrator rapes[28] (see Chambers et al, 2013: 253 and Chambers et al, 2010: 1136). This development further illustrates the functional overlap between the three reasons for digitally recording offences – namely the production of (non-consensual) pornography, further humiliation of the victim and a compulsion to document – suggested by Sandberg and Ugelvik (2017). Karen Franklin (2013), for example, studied media coverage of multiple perpetrator rapes involving 25 high-profile cases. Most of these were reported in the United States, Australia and the UK between 2002 and 2011 (2013: 37). Franklin reports that in almost half of the cases of multiple perpetrator rape in which it was technically feasible to do so, offenders and/or observers went to great lengths to 'choreograph' the offence and to capture it on mobile phones. The images – 'electronic memorialisations' of the offences – were then circulated amongst a larger audience through word of mouth or by posting the footage on social networking sites (2013, 53; see also Densley et al, 2013: 267).

In nearly every case examined by Franklin, the victims were subjected to gratuitous physical abuse. In several cases, ever-more-extreme forms of non-consensual pornography were created by the filming of acts such as the insertion of cigarettes, pool cues and bottles into the orifices of the unconscious victims. As in *Attorney General's Reference (Nos 15, 16 and 17 of 2013)*[29] many of the offenders in Franklin's study verbally denigrated the victim and celebrated the commission of their offences in coarse terms while filming or photographing the acts of abuse (Franklin, 2013: 53).

The Effect on the Victim

Victims of sexual assault whose ordeals are filmed by their abusers can experience severe emotional distress and anxiety (Citron and Franks, 2014: 351;

[28] For a discussion of multiple perpetrator rape, see Chapter 2.
[29] *Attorney General's Reference (Nos 15, 16 and 17 of 2013)* (n 12).

Henry et al, 2017: 5). The offender's actions in filming the abuse is particularly traumatic for, as Sandberg and Ugelvik (2017: 1030) explain, '[t]he cold, penetrating gaze of the camera lens is, in effect, like a "double rape"'. Victims may also experience shame and humiliation; altered relationships with others; reputational damage; loss of employment prospects; victim blaming; withdrawal from social life; anxiety, paranoia, depression and low self-esteem (see Bates, 2017: 23; Bloom, 2014: 240–43; Henry and Powell, 2016a: 403; McGlynn and Rackley, 2015b: 2; Powell and Henry, 2017a: 137; and Powell et al, 2018a: 310). While many of these sequelae are also evident in more conventional forms of sexual violence and abuse,[30] it is important to recognise the unique harms that occur when technologies such as mobile phones and the internet are used in the commission of sexual offences (Powell and Henry, 2016b: 14).

Victims of rape and sexual assault whose ordeals are filmed or photographed by their attackers have no control over the future dissemination of the footage or images. As the internet readily enables re-posting, it may be impossible to retract an image once it has been distributed (Bates, 2017: 23; Bloom, 2014: 246; Cecil, 2014: 2515–16; Henry and Powell, 2016a: 405 and 2014: 88; O'Malley, 2016: 216; Powell, 2010: 85 and 2009: 9–10; and Powell and Henry, 2017a: 138, 2016b: 9 and 2015: 3). As two respondents in Powell and Henry's empirical study into the effects of technology-facilitated sexual violence (a police officer and social worker) explained:

> 'They feel that they've got no control then of when is it going to be posted next or who has seen it and that embarrassment too. A lot of them worry about when they go for jobs, is it going to be seen? It's posted on Facebook and ends up on the internet … It's quite debilitating for a victim, to be honest […] [police officer].
>
> It just makes it worse because it never goes away, does it? … It's there and you know even if you're not watching it, somebody can be watching it, it's just floating around all the time … [T]here is no end date, it's infinity [social worker]' (Powell and Henry, 2016b: 9–10).

Similarly, in later work, Powell and Henry recount the following comments from another respondent (a police officer and member of a sex crime investigation unit) in their study:

> 'The harm is substantial and severe … It's ongoing forever because if that's on the internet then it will just pop up all the time. You can't erase it. Once it's on the internet it's there forever. There's no way you can track down a sex tape on the internet and erase every copy' (Powell and Henry, 2017a: 138).

Much academic discussion has focused on certain notorious cases in the United States (including the 'Steubenville rape' case) and Australia (the 'Werribee DVD' case). In these cases, young women were raped or sexually assaulted by groups of young men, often at high school or college parties; in some, but not all, instances

[30] For a full discussion of the psychological impact on victims of rape and sexual assault, see Chapter 2.

the victims were unconscious through alcohol intoxication. The perpetrators filmed the offences on mobile phones and subsequently distributed the footage amongst peer networks through social media. In some cases, the footage was posted online.

In the 2013 Steubenville case, for example, the rape and sexual assault of the intoxicated and incapacitated 16-year-old victim by two high-school football players was filmed by other students. The footage was then posted on Instagram, Twitter and YouTube and was distributed by mobile phone. In the 2006 Werribee case, a group of teenage boys filmed themselves urinating on the teenaged victim, setting her hair on fire, throwing her clothes into a river and subjecting her to sexual assault. The boys later transferred the footage on to DVD for sale online and in local schools in Melbourne; excerpts were also made freely available on YouTube. Eight of the youths were later charged with assault, manufacturing child pornography and procuring sexual penetration by intimidation in the Melbourne Children's Court.[31] In such cases the victim must cope not only with the effects of the sexual assault, but also with the humiliation of the assault being shared online (Sandberg and Ugelvik, 2017: 1030, 1036). The further distribution of the original image or video is itself a direct and continued violation of the victim's sexual dignity and autonomy (Henry and Powell, 2015a: 766; McGlynn and Rackley, 2017: 8, 13; 2016; and 2015a; Powell, 2010: 81 and 2009: 6).

Dodge explains that the posting of sexual assault images online or on social media allows the assault to be temporally extended. The sexual abuse can be 'memorialised' by social media users, with degrading and misogynistic comments about the victim frequently posted to social networking sites: 'with each share, like, tweet or comment, the sexual assault [is] reiterated over and over again' (Dodge, 2016: 68 and 70; see also Bluett-Boyd et al, 2013: 35–36; Butler, 2007: 961; McGlynn and Rackley, 2017a: 15; Pennington and Birthisel, 2016: 2440; Powell, 2015: 578; and Powell and Henry, 2015: 3). As Armstrong et al (2015: 253) observe of the posting of sexual abuse images to social networking sites, 'a tragic event in the life of one person is no longer isolated but relived and shared in a public vernacular, allowing comments and responses from strangers and further traumatizing the victim'. In this sense, the posting of the images online allows the abuse to continue; arguably, because of the image or video, the abuse continues indefinitely through both visual and discursive means (see Butler, 2007: 961, 965). The internet provides 'a staggering means of amplification' as images can be e-mailed or otherwise exhibited to a victim's family, friends, peers, employers and co-workers (Citron and Franks, 2014: 350; see also Bates, 2017: 23, Cecil, 2014: 2521–22; Henry and Powell, 2014: 84;

[31] See Armstrong et al, 2015; Bluett-Boyd et al, 2013: 39–40; DeKeseredy and Schwartz, 2016: 2; DeKeseredy et al, 2014: 181–82; Dodge, 2016: 65–66; Dodge and Spencer, 2017: 18; Fairbairn and Spencer, 2017: 7–9; Franklin, 2004: 32; Henry and Powell, 2014: 88; 2015a: 758–59; 2016a: 400 and 405; and 2016b: 5; McGlynn and Rackley, 2017a: 6–7 and 2017b: 42; McGlynn et al, 2017: 35; Pennington and Birthisel, 2016: 2435–36, 243–38 and 2440; Powell, 2015: 571–75; 2010: 81; 2009: 7; Powell and Henry, 2017a: 1–2, 88–89; 2017b: 208; 2014b: 18; Powell et al, 2018b: 91–93; and Yar, 2012: 253.

McGlynn and Rackley, 2017a: 2; Powell and Henry, 2017a: 131; and Woodlock, 2017: 596–97, 599).

The images and any resulting online bullying, harassment or abuse by the victim's peers[32] continue to *recreate* and *extend* the trauma of the sexual assault (Butler, 2007: 959; Dodge, 2016: 69; Powell, 2015: 575; Powell and Henry, 2017a: 89–90; 2016b: 9; and 2015: 3). Indeed, many commentators stress that, in addition to extending the trauma of sexual assault, the dissemination of photographs or videos of the offence is also a form of sexual violence *in and of itself*, the impact of which can, in some cases, be even more traumatic for the victim than the original assault. In this way, technology-facilitated sexual violence and image-based sexual abuse form part of the continuum of sexual violence (see Bluett-Boyd et al, 2013: 37; Citron and Franks, 2014: 362–64; Dodge, 2016: 67 and 69; Fairbairn et al, 2013: 9, 49; Henry and Powell, 2015b: 105, 113–14; Henry et al, 2017: 3–4; McGlynn and Rackley, 2017a: 3–4 and 2016; McGlynn et al, 2017: 28–29 and 36–38; Pennington and Birthisel, 2016: 2440; Powell, 2009: 6; and Powell and Henry, 2017a: 32–33, 309). The original violation is exacerbated by 'the unbounded nature of potential and perpetual public shame and humiliation' (Henry and Powell, 2015a: 767). Dodge elaborates:

> 'It is the photograph that allows the event to be shared and, thereby, allows the degradation of the event to continue indefinitely and its impact to broaden as others comment on the photo in ways that condone the event or offer additional insults. This is the photograph's power of temporal extension in action' (Dodge, 2016: 70; see also Butler, 2007: 958).

As Powell and Henry (2016b: 11) argue, in assessing the effects of technology-facilitated sexual violence, conventional conceptions of criminality which focus on corporeal or bodily forms of harm require an overhaul in both theory and practice. It is important that the structural, social, emotional and psychological harms caused by technology-facilitated sexual violence are recognised by the courts, particularly at the stage of sentencing.

The Effect on the Victim as a Factor in Sentencing: Recent Appellate Decisions

The trauma that can be caused by the filming of sexual assault is vividly illustrated by a number of recent decisions of the Court of Appeal (Criminal Division), particularly *R v Dale*,[33] *Attorney General's Reference (No 46 of 2013)*,[34] *Attorney General's Reference (Nos 15, 16 and 17 of 2013)*,[35] *R v Shahjahan*[36] and *R v K*,

[32] See Franklin, 2013: 54; Lindsay et al, 2016: 3176; Powell and Henry, 2015; Powell et al, 2018a: 311 and 2018b: 98–100; and Wellman et al, 2017: 93–95, 99–100.

[33] [2014] EWCA Crim 2286.

[34] [2013] EWCA Crim 1642.

[35] *Attorney General's Reference (Nos 15, 16 and 17 of 2013)* (n 12).

[36] [2011] 2 Cr App R (S) 94.

D and M.[37] In *Dale*, the appellant and the victim were both university students. On the evening of the offence, the appellant, one of his friends from his hometown and a group of fellow students, including the victim, went out drinking. The group eventually returned to the student flat where the appellant and others in the group lived. The victim went to sleep in a bedroom, where she lay naked under a duvet. The appellant and his friend, who were both drunk, entered the bedroom and pulled the duvet from the bed. The appellant's friend filmed the incident on his mobile phone. He continued to film the victim from the front and back as she lay on her side, asleep. The appellant then removed all his clothes except for his underwear, climbed on to the bed, took out his penis and brought it into contact with the victim's forehead, as if striking her with it. His friend proceeded to touch the victim's private parts. The appellant's friend later showed the video to his work colleagues who, in due course, reported the matter to police.

The appellant pleaded guilty to a charge of sexual assault and was sentenced to nine months' imprisonment. In refusing his appeal, the Court quoted at some length from the victim's personal statement ('VPS'):[38]

> 'When I initially found out by the police that a video had been made of me it made me feel sick and violated. I thought I was safe in my friend's house and nothing like this could ever happen to me … It has made me feel completely violated that two men [whom] I do not know would come into the room I was asleep in and sexually assault me and then go on to record what they did to me … Although the video has not been retrieved by the police this does not mean that it does not exist. It makes me think that it could still be out there in someone's possession and that anybody could have it. Knowing that it could exist petrifies me.'[39]

As the Court observed, the VPS highlighted in stark form the obvious, significant and continuing distress caused to the victim.[40] The Court considered that the sentencing judge had struck an appropriate balance between the mitigating and aggravating factors in the case. The recording of the offence was seen by the Court as an important aggravating factor.[41]

In *Attorney General's Reference (No 46 of 2013)*,[42] the Crown appealed against the sentence of six-and-a-half years' imprisonment imposed on the 52-year-old respondent following his conviction after trial of two charges of assault by penetration and one charge of rape committed against two separate victims. In both cases the respondent contacted the victims (aged 22 and 28) through Facebook, arranged to meet them and took them to his hotel room where he plied them with drink. From the evidence led at trial, both the sentencing judge and the Court of Appeal drew the inference that the respondent drugged both victims. In the case of the first victim, the respondent proceeded to remove her clothing and fondle her

[37] [2014] 1 Cr App R (S) 5.
[38] On the use of victim statements in the sentencing process, see Chapter 2.
[39] *Dale* (n 33) at [12].
[40] Ibid at [13].
[41] Ibid at [14] and [18].
[42] *Attorney General's Reference (No 46 of 2013)* (n 34).

breasts before digitally penetrating her. He filmed the assault on his mobile phone. When the victim regained consciousness, she was unaware of what had happened. In the case of the second victim, the respondent waited until she too had passed out. He then removed her clothing, penetrated her mouth with his penis to ejaculation and digitally penetrated her private parts. Once again, the respondent recorded the offences, this time taking photographs with his mobile phone.

The offences came to light when the second victim contacted the police: she could not remember much of what had happened and, despite the respondent's assurances that nothing untoward had taken place, the victim began to have suspicions. The respondent was arrested some three weeks later. His mobile phone was seized, on which police discovered the film of the offences committed against the first victim, along with the photographs of the second victim. As a result, the identity of the first victim was discovered. Forensic analysis of the respondent's laptop revealed that he had been in contact with up to 100 women in various parts of the country via Facebook.

As in *Dale*,[43] the Court referred to the victim personal statements available to the sentencing judge. The first victim reiterated that she had no idea that any sexual activity had taken place until she was visited by police and informed of the existence of the video recording. The victim explained in her VPS that she felt 'dirty and ashamed'; she had been prescribed anti-depressant medication by her GP and her condition was such that she had lost her job.[44] The second victim, meanwhile, referred in her VPS to the devastating impact of the rape and to the fact that she had taken an overdose of tablets. She was shown the photographs taken by the respondent and described her reaction: 'When I saw them I felt absolutely disgusted. This was one more violation to heap on to the mess I felt I was in.'[45] In allowing the Crown's appeal, the Court noted that the planning, filming and photographing of the offences were aggravating factors.[46] The total sentence was increased to nine years' imprisonment.[47]

In *Attorney General's Reference (Nos 15, 16 and 17 of 2013)*[48] where, as we have seen, the victim was sexually abused by three men while unconscious through alcohol intoxication, the episode having been recorded by one of the respondents on the victim's own mobile phone, the victim's VPS was summarised by the Court as follows:

> '[The complainant] describes herself as a private person who felt totally broken when she arrived home on the day in question. After the event she blamed herself for what had happened and felt self-hatred. She spoke of the indignities of the examination she had to undergo and of the need to disclose very private and personal information to the

[43] *Dale* (n 33).
[44] *Attorney General's Reference (No 46 of 2013)* (n 34) at [13].
[45] Ibid at [14].
[46] Ibid at [26] and [27].
[47] Ibid at [30].
[48] *Attorney General's Reference (Nos 15, 16 and 17 of 2013)* (n 12).

police. She had to attend a clinic to be tested for sexually transmitted disease, including HIV. When she had seen the footage, some four days after the events, she had become hysterical and it had left her feeling devastated, humiliated and embarrassed. She lived in fear of people finding out about what had happened to her. She had been forced to disclose what had happened to her university because of time she had had to take off away from her studies. She had needed to take sleeping tablets in order to be able to sleep and had lost social confidence and been unable to go out for a time. The incident had left her having difficulty trusting men who were not family or close friends. She felt that her life had been significantly affected.'[49]

In allowing the reference and increasing the sentences imposed on both respondents from three-and-a-half years to five-and-a-half years' imprisonment, the Court specifically referred to the effect that the offence had had on the victim.[50] It also regarded the filming of the offences as a particularly serious aggravation.[51]

The victim in *Shahjahan*[52] had attended a party at the appellant's flat where she became so intoxicated that she passed out. While unconscious, she was sexually assaulted and raped by the appellant. The victim had been unaware of what happened until the appellant's co-accused showed her video footage and a photograph of the assaults which he had taken with his mobile phone. In the course of its judgment, the Court referred to the VPS:

> '[W]hen she first saw the images she felt quite sick and went into shock. She had many sleepless nights since and suffered with stress. She felt embarrassed about going to court and others seeing the images. The complainant was no longer an outgoing person and she was nervous that friends would find out what had happened. She had changed; she was no longer a bubbly person and felt that her life had changed forever.'[53]

In *R v K, D and M*,[54] where the 14-year-old appellant and his two co-accused used a mobile phone to record their sexual assault of the intoxicated 14-year-old victim in a public park, the Court of Appeal also referred to the VPS. The Court noted that the victim now found school difficult, being uncomfortable at the rumours and gossip that had circulated following the offence. She had lost interest in her studies and had lost the respect of her friends.[55] In imposing a 12-month detention and training order, subsequently upheld on appeal, the sentencing judge noted that the three accused had all got drunk together and had all encouraged each other in their abuse of the victim. The judge stated that the filming of the offence 'suggested a slippage into truly barbaric behaviour' with the result that, in his view, such 'loss of civilised behaviour' had to be dealt with in an exemplary way.[56]

[49] Ibid at [15].
[50] Ibid at [30].
[51] Ibid.
[52] *Shahjahan* (n 36).
[53] Ibid at [8].
[54] *K, D and M* (n 37).
[55] Ibid at [13].
[56] Ibid at [19].

That the impact of an offender photographing or filming acts of sexual abuse and subsequently distributing, or threatening to distribute, the images online can, in some cases at least, be even more traumatic for the victim than the initial sexual assault is demonstrated by the sentencing notes of Dunningham, J of the High Court of New Zealand in *R v Hammond*.[57] Here, the accused was convicted of 95 charges involving various sexual offences, including rape, committed against two children over a 10-year period. The accused photographed and video recorded much of the abuse, the images having been recovered from the accused's mobile phone. Analysis of the accused's computer equipment demonstrated that he had traded these images online with other paedophiles to receive similar images.[58] The seriousness of the accused's offending behaviour is reflected in the sentence of 22 years' imprisonment imposed by the trial judge.[59] In giving her reasons for sentence, Justice Dunningham observed that the impact of the offences had been clearly expressed in the VIS provided by one of the two victims. In a passage addressed directly to the accused, the victim said this:

> '[T]he part that makes me most sick of all … is that my images, my body is always going to be out there for perverts like you, or maybe just someone I know clicks on the wrong thing and wham, bam there I am. You will never understand the fear of this happening, the pain of having to explain why I am all over the internet, because I always will be.'[60]

Finally, in *R v Mortensen*,[61] the accused was convicted in the High Court of New Zealand of sexual offences committed against four young children over a period of eight years. The accused inveigled himself into positions of trust within the victims' families; he then groomed the victims before committing various indecent acts. The accused photographed his abuse of two of the victims. In respect of the second victim, B, an eight-year-old girl, the sentencing judge, Justice Kós, described the images as 'vile beyond description'.[62] The accused traded the images of B on a paedophilic website and chatroom for similar images of child sex abuse. In imposing a sentence of preventive detention with a minimum term of five-and a half-years' imprisonment, Justice Kós referred to the impact that this aspect of the accused's offending had had on B:

> 'Victim B … is suffering from Post-Traumatic Stress Disorder. Having managed to repress her memory of the things you did to her she then learned that you had posted your appalling photographs of her on the internet. Although the police have removed the images of Victim B from websites they have come across, there is no control as to further distribution of the images by and to other paedophiles on the internet. This is a

[57] [2015] NZHC 1030.
[58] Ibid at [11]–[13].
[59] Ibid at [56]–[58].
[60] Ibid at [35].
[61] [2012] NZHC 2478.
[62] Ibid at [9].

fact that Victim B will have to live with for the rest of her life. The suggestion that your counsel makes in his written submissions that there may be more pornographic internet images "than grains of sand on a beach" will be of no comfort to Victim B.'[63]

Empirical Studies of Technology-Facilitated Sexual Violence

Empirical research into the prevalence, perpetration and impact of technology-facilitated sexual violence is important, not only to establish sustainable and effective prevention strategies (Henry and Powell, 2014: 86, 92) but also to inform the appropriate legal responses including, for present purposes, the sentencing decisions of the courts. While filming a sexual assault and posting images of sexual abuse online will clearly have a serious impact upon a victim's wellbeing, the *extent* to which images of rape or sexual assault are distributed in this way is unclear. As Henry and Powell (2016b: 1–2, 9–10) acknowledge, there is a dearth of empirical research examining the varied nature and prevalence of sexually abusive behaviour involving technology (see also Henry and Powell, 2014: 97–98; Powell and Henry, 2017a: 3, 2016b: 3 and 2015: 1, 3; and Powell et al, 2018a: 307, 312).

In one of the few empirical studies exploring the prevalence, nature and impacts of technology-facilitated sexual violence victimisation amongst adults, Powell and Henry conducted an online survey of the experiences of 2,956 Australian adults aged 18 to 54 recruited via an online panel provider (Powell and Henry, 2016a: 9). Lifetime technology-facilitated sexual violence victimisation for men and women was not found to be significantly different, although men were more likely to report victimisation through the distribution of non-consensual images. In particular, almost 10 per cent of male respondents and almost 7 per cent of female respondents, reported that they had suffered unwanted sexual experiences that had been either photographed or filmed. Similar numbers of respondents (almost 10 per cent of male respondents and just over 7 per cent of female respondents), reported that images or videos of their unwanted sexual experiences had been posted online or sent to others (2016a: 12 and 18–19; see also Powell and Henry, 2017a: 134 and Powell et al, 2018a: 307).

While acknowledging that since respondents self-selected from a population of individuals who had agreed to be contacted for research purposes and that, accordingly, the sample was likely to incorporate some representative biases as compared with the general population (Powell and Henry, 2016a: 9, 21), the authors conclude that technology-facilitated sexual violence victimisation is common and while lifetime prevalence of such victimisation is similar for males and females, the experiences of such abuses are sexed and gendered in particular ways. Women, for example, were found to report significantly higher rates of digital

[63] Ibid at [27].

sexual harassment; women were also significantly more likely to report experiencing negative impacts as a result of victimisation (Powell and Henry, 2016a: 22–23; see also Powell and Henry, 2015: 1).

A larger programme of research into the extent, nature and impacts of image-based abuse amongst youths and adults in Australia, New Zealand and the UK and the legal responses to image-based abuse in a comparative context, was conducted by Henry et al (2017). In discussing their key findings from the first stage of the research (a further Australian online survey of 4,274 participants aged 16 to 49), the authors state that one in five respondents reported experiencing at least one form of image-based abuse victimisation (2017: 4). Eighty per cent of victims who had experienced threats to distribute a sexual image reported high levels of psychological distress consistent with a diagnosis of moderate to severe depression and/or anxiety disorder. Levels of psychological distress were also high for other victims of image-based abuse: 67 per cent of those whose images were taken without their consent and 75 per cent of those whose images were distributed, also reported symptoms of moderate to severe depression and/or anxiety. The authors conclude that these findings are important as they demonstrate the severity of the harm that is associated with image-based abuse victimisation (2017: 5; see also Powell et al, 2018a: 307–9).

Powell observes that, as increasingly seen from media and court reports, while some sex offenders appear to record assaults for their own personal use, other offenders share their recordings with their peers. Images and video recordings of rape and sexual assault are shared through social media such as Twitter, Facebook and Instagram, as well as on online forums and websites dedicated to sharing user-generated explicit content (Powell, 2015: 574; see also Armstrong et al, 2015: 252 and DeKeseredy and Schwartz, 2016: 2). Nevertheless, in contrast to the academic commentary on the notorious 'Steubenville rape' case in the United States and the 'Werribee DVD' case in Australia,[64] the Norwegian study by Sandberg and Ugelvik (2017) found that images of sexual assault were *not* widely distributed. The authors report that of the 51 court decisions in which offences were filmed or photographed by offenders, distribution occurred in only 12 cases: one image was uploaded to Instagram for a very short period; one image was posted to an internet site hosting child pornography; and a further 10 cases involved what the authors describe as very limited private sharing of images with friends (Sandberg and Ugelvik, 2017: 1030–31). In none of the cases examined by the authors were images posted on Snapchat, YouTube, Facebook or similar platforms (2017: 1038).

Bates conducted a study of the mental health issues faced by victims of so-called 'revenge pornography', conducting interviews with 18 individuals in Canada, the United States and England who had experienced the trauma of having intimate photographs or videos of themselves posted online or distributed amongst friends and acquaintances (Bates, 2017: 27–28). One of Bates' respondents, identified

[64] Discussed above.

by the pseudonym 'Regina', had been drugged by her ex-husband. She had no memory of what subsequently happened but later discovered that she had been raped by her ex-husband and another man. Some months after their divorce, Regina's ex-husband sent a video containing footage of the rape to the school board where she worked; she was immediately dismissed from her job as a school superintendent (2017: 29). Bates reports the following excerpt from her interview with Regina who explained the impact this had on her mental health:

> 'When the actual video was released, um, well, I can admit now that I was suicidal … I lost my reputation … financially I'm ruined, I lost my career, a 25-year stellar career … I had a doctorate degree. I lost everything. So, how did that make me feel? Um, devastated. I just don't even have words to describe it. Horrifying, humiliated, embarrassed, betrayed … How could he do something like this? So I just felt very, very worthless' (2017: 32; see also Bates, 2015: 64).

The Response of the Courts and the Legislatures

The additional trauma that victims of sexual assault endure by virtue of having the offence filmed is such that Sandberg and Ugelvik call for the filming of offences to be treated as an aggravating factor at the sentencing stage (Sandberg and Ugelvik, 2017: 1038). In 24 of the 51 cases examined in the Norwegian study, the act of recording images explicitly led the courts to increase the sentence, while in the remaining 27 cases, the images were simply presented as evidence without any further comment by the court (2017: 1027). The photographing or recording of sexual offences is also considered to be an aggravating factor by the courts in other jurisdictions.

England and Wales

Filming Rape and Sexual Assault – Attorney General's Reference (Nos 3, 73 and 75 of 2010) *and the Definitive Guideline*

It is in England and Wales that we see the most sophisticated approach to the sentencing of offenders who record acts of rape and sexual abuse. We have already seen how in *Attorney General's Reference (Nos 3, 73 and 75 of 2010)*[65] the Court of Appeal (Criminal Division) held that the taking of photographs should always be treated as a very serious aggravating factor in cases of sexual assault.[66] The recording of an offence now features as an integral part of the present Definitive Guideline on Sexual Offences issued by the Sentencing Council for England and

[65] *Attorney General's Reference (Nos 3, 73 and 75 of 2010)* (n 1).
[66] Ibid at [7](2).

Wales (Sentencing Council, 2013a). The structure and operation of the present English guidelines, in force since 1 April 2014, are fully considered in Chapter 4. For present purposes, however, it is sufficient to note that the guidelines set out a staged approach for judges to follow in imposing sentence, comprising a series of distinct 'steps'. The gravity with which the English courts now view an offender's creation of a permanent record of his sexual offence is such that, rather than simply *listing* the recording of a sexual offence as an aggravating factor, recording an offence is now to be *factored into* the first step of the process of imposing sentences for various sexual offences including rape (assault by penetration and sexual assault (Sentencing Council, 2013a: 10, 14, 18).

The first step of the process mandated by the Definitive Guideline involves the sentencing judge assessing the degree of *harm* caused by the particular offence and the level of the offender's *culpability*. These combinations of harm and culpability generate a matrix; the sentencing judge must then proceed to use the corresponding starting points to reach a sentence within the appropriate category range (see Wasik, 2014: 276–77). The first step in the process is regarded as being one of the most important as it involves a judicial assessment of the seriousness of the particular case (Hutton, 2013: 98–99). Recording of an offence is listed as a *culpability factor* rather than an *aggravating factor* in the current Definitive Guideline (Sentencing Council, 2013a: 10). The seriousness of recording a sexual offence is thus reflected in the fact the Definitive Guideline views the practice as affecting the offender's *culpability* for that offence (Rook and Ward, 2016: 25–26). In England and Wales, recording or taking photographs of a rape or sexual assault is no longer simply one factor in a list of aggravating factors which the sentencing judge must consider (*cf* Sentencing Council, 2013a: 11). The practice is now seen as being inextricably linked to the seriousness of the offence itself. This is an important factor both in punishing rape and sexual assault appropriately (McGlynn et al, 2017: 40) and in taking steps towards restoring and affirming a victim's dignity at the sentencing stage (see McGlynn and Rackley, 2017a: 19).

'Extreme Pornographic Images' – Section 63 of the Criminal Justice and Immigration Act 2008: Possession of Images of Rape and Sexual Assault

In England and Wales, there are legislative provisions directed against extreme pornography that specifically target the possession of images of rape and sexual abuse. Section 63 of the Criminal Justice and Immigration Act 2008 ('the 2008 Act') makes it an offence to possess an 'extreme pornographic image' (ie one that is both pornographic and which constitutes an extreme image).[67] The 2008 Act defines an image as *pornographic* if it is of such a nature that it must reasonably

[67] Criminal Justice and Immigration Act 2008, s 63(2).

be assumed to have been produced solely or principally for the purpose of sexual arousal.[68] The Act defines an *extreme image* as one which is grossly offensive, disgusting or otherwise of an obscene character[69] *and* which is *either* an explicit and realistic portrayal of an act of rape,[70] an act of assault by penetration[71] *or* any of a number of other acts including, *inter alia*, acts which result, or are likely to result, in serious injury to a person's anus, breasts or genitals.[72] Images depicting rape or sexual assault were added by section 37(2)(c) of the Criminal Justice and Courts Act 2015 to address criticism that the definition of 'extreme pornographic image' as originally enacted did not cover most images of rape and to bring the law into line with the position in Scotland (see Antoniou and Akrivos, 2017: 168–73; Chalmers and Leverick, 2017: 651, fn 31; Foster, 2010: 25–26; McGlynn, 2010b: 192, 197–98; and McGlynn and Rackley, 2009: 249–50).[73]

Possession of an extreme pornographic image depicting rape or assault by penetration is punishable by up to three years' imprisonment following conviction on indictment[74] and up to 12 months' imprisonment on summary conviction.[75] While McGlynn and Rackley (2009: 256) suggested some 10 years ago that sentencing guidelines for the offence of possessing extreme pornography should be issued, such guidelines have yet to emerge. Unlike offences related to indecent images of children, there are at present no sentencing guidelines for the offence of possessing extreme pornographic images, including possessing extreme pornographic images depicting rape or assault by penetration (Antoniou and Akrivos, 2017: 205). As Antoniou and Akrivos suggest, guidance to promote a more consistent approach to sentencing extreme pornography offences across England and Wales would be a useful way forward (2017: 220, see also McGlynn and Rackley, 2009: 256).

Scotland

Filming Rape and Sexual Assault – The Decisions in Robertson, JT *and* CH

The first cases considered by the Appeal Court which featured the photographing of acts of sexual abuse were the decisions in *Robertson v HMA*[76] (an appeal against sentence) and *HMA v JT*[77] (a Crown appeal against sentence), both heard

[68] Ibid, s 63(3).
[69] Ibid, s 63(5A)(b).
[70] Ibid, s 63(5A)(a) and s 63(7A)(a).
[71] Ibid, s 63(5A)(a) and s 63(7A)(b).
[72] Ibid, s 63(5A)(a) and s 63(7)(a)–(d).
[73] For the background and legislative history of the offences under s 63 of the 2008 Act, see Antoniou and Akrivos, 2017: Chapter 3; Easton, 2011: 391–96; McGlynn and Rackley, 2007: 679–80; and Rackley and McGlynn, 2013: 401.
[74] Criminal Justice and Immigration Act 2008, s 67(2)(b).
[75] Ibid, s 67(2)(a) and (4).
[76] 2004 JC 155.
[77] 2005 1 JC 86.

by the Court in 2004. Both cases involved the accused photographing themselves sexually abusing young girls. Although in disposing of the appeals, the Court in neither *Robertson* nor *JT* considered the acts of the accused in photographing their respective offences in any detail, it appears that the taking of photographs was nevertheless recognised as an aggravating factor in both cases. In *Robertson*, the appellant's photographing of the offences was libelled in one of the charges on the indictment; it appears to have been one of several aggravating features of the case that led the Court to refuse the appellant's appeal against the imposition of a discretionary life sentence.[78]

In *JT*, meanwhile, the Court allowed the Crown's appeal against the sentence of five years' imprisonment on the ground of undue leniency and imposed an extended sentence of 13 years with a custodial term of eight years. In the course of submissions, the Lord Advocate specifically referred to the respondent's photographing the acts of abuse as a 'significant feature' of the case, it being clear from the report prepared by a consultant forensic clinical psychologist that the respondent intended to use the photographs for his own sexual gratification.[79] Counsel for the respondent, meanwhile, accepted that 'photography represented an extension of the abuse of the [victims]'.[80] The Appeal Court made specific reference to the respondent having taken photographs of the victims in allowing the Crown's appeal.[81]

The development of technology, in particular the ubiquity of the smartphone and the associated rise in perpetrators of sexual offences recording or photographing their victims led the Appeal Court to consider the issue in some detail in the later decision in *HMA v CH*,[82] another Crown sentence appeal. In *CH*, the respondent pleaded guilty in the High Court to statutory charges of orally raping a three-year-old boy and to making indecent images of the victim by filming the offence on his mobile phone. The respondent committed the offences while babysitting the victim and his elder brother. The Crown appealed as unduly lenient the sentence of three years and nine months' imprisonment, discounted from a headline sentence of five years' imprisonment to reflect the respondent's guilty pleas[83] imposed by the sentencing judge.

In allowing the Crown's appeal, the Appeal Court considered in some depth the reasons why an offender's actions in filming or recording his commission of a sexual offence will amount to a serious aggravation. Importantly, the Court did so by reference both to English case law and to the research literature. The Court found there to be 'considerable force' in the Crown's submission that, as well as constituting a separate statutory offence of making an indecent image of a child,

[78] *Robertson* (n 76) at [32]–[36].
[79] *JT* (n 77) at [24].
[80] Ibid at [25].
[81] Ibid at [34] and [43].
[82] [2017] HCJAC 82; 2017 SCCR 587.
[83] On the operation of the guilty plea discount in Scotland, see Chapter 5.

the respondent's video recording of the rape on his mobile phone constituted an additional and significant aggravation of the charge of rape.[84] The Court continued:

> 'Such is the prevalence of use of mobile phones and such is the ease of making, retaining and transmitting (or 'sharing') still and moving images using their associated technology that it has become increasingly common for perpetrators of sexual offences or their associates to record the commission of an offence, or to take photographs of the victim, on a mobile phone ... While so doing may have the result that perpetrators thereby document their offending and generate evidence which may incriminate them, as in the present case, the practice has what the Court of Appeal (Criminal Division) described in *Attorney General's Reference (Nos 3, 73 and 75 of 2010)* ... as 'pernicious' effects ... [A] victim's suffering is intensified by the knowledge that such a recording or image exists and that little can be done to control the use to which it may later be put or the extent to which it may be circulated ...'[85]

The Court then adopted what was said by the Court of Appeal in the *Attorney General's Reference (Nos 3, 73 and 75 of 2010)* concerning the recording of images of sexual offending constituting a very serious aggravation of the offence in question.[86] In allowing the Crown's appeal and substituting a sentence of six years' imprisonment, discounted from a headline sentence of eight years, the Court stated that it had been 'particularly influenced' by the fact that the respondent had recorded his rape of the victim and continued:

> 'That this was to be regarded as a material aggravation (and therefore a factor pointing to a higher sentence than would otherwise have been imposed simply for the rape) was enunciated in *Attorney General's Reference (Nos. 3, 73 and 75 of 2010)* and reiterated in the subsequently published *Definitive Guideline*. That is a position that we would endorse.'[87]

This is not, in fact, an accurate statement of the development of English sentencing practice in this area and suggests a misunderstanding by the Appeal Court of the operation of the relevant English sentencing guidelines. As we have seen,[88] the recording of a sexual offence appears as a *culpability factor* rather than as a mere *aggravating factor* in the current Definitive Guideline (Sentencing Council, 2013a: 10). It follows that the Appeal Court erred in stating that the appellate guidance in the *Attorney General's Reference* was simply 'reiterated' in the current guideline. Although in the event nothing turned on this point in the disposal of the Crown's appeal, it does evidence a lack of understanding by the Court of the development of the relevant English sentencing jurisprudence. This is regrettable given the Court's otherwise detailed treatment of how judges are to approach the issue of sentence in cases that feature image-based, or technology-facilitated, sexual abuse.

[84] *CH* (n 82) at [35].

[85] Ibid, references omitted.

[86] Ibid. For a full discussion of the decision in *Attorney General's Reference (Nos 3, 73 and 75 of 2010)* (n 1), see above.

[87] *CH* (n 82) at [39].

[88] See the discussion above.

Nevertheless, the decision in *CH* is to be welcomed as an example of the Appeal Court developing an important point of principle through the issuing of sentencing guidance. In so doing, the Appeal Court brought Scottish sentencing practice into line with practice in England and Wales.

'Extreme Pornographic Images' – Section 51A of the Civic Government (Scotland) Act 1982: Possession of Images of Rape and Sexual Assault

The statutory offence of possession of an extreme pornographic image, contrary to section 51A of the Civic Government (Scotland) Act 1982 ('the 1982 Act'), was created in 2010 following a government consultation. The legislation came into force in March 2011: section 42(2) of the Criminal Justice and Licensing (Scotland) Act 2010 inserted the relevant provisions into the 1982 Act.[89] The offence is committed if a person possesses an 'extreme pornographic image', (ie an image which is obscene, pornographic and extreme).[90] An image is deemed extreme if it depicts, in an explicit and realistic way, any of five acts including 'rape or other non-consensual penetrative sexual activity'.[91] In determining whether an image is extreme, the legislation provides that reference may be had to the context, in particular how the image is (or was) described, or any sounds accompanying the image.[92] The maximum penalty on summary conviction is 12 months' imprisonment and a fine of the statutory maximum.[93] Following conviction on indictment, the maximum penalty is three years' imprisonment and a fine.[94]

It appears that the Crown has not routinely made use of these statutory provisions. In particular, it has not been the Crown's practice to libel charges of possession of extreme pornographic images depicting rape or other non-consensual penetrative sexual activity in cases where an accused charged with such offences has photographed or filmed the abuse. Although such cases have featured in the law reports[95] and in certain press reports, none of the accused were charged with offences involving the possession of extreme pornographic images. It appears that the Crown's practice is simply to libel the fact that the sexual abuse was photographed or filmed in the indictment, rather than making the photographing or filming the subject of a specific charge.[96]

[89] For a full discussion of the statutory provisions, see Chalmers and Leverick, 2017: 651–52 and Jones and Taggart, 2015: 354–55.

[90] Civic Government (Scotland) Act 1982, s 51A(1) and (2).

[91] Ibid, s 51A(6)(c).

[92] Ibid, s 51A(7)(a) and (b) respectively.

[93] Ibid, s 51A(8)(a).

[94] Ibid, s 51A(8)(b).

[95] See, for example, *Gubinas and Radavicius v HMA* [2017] HCJAC 59; 2018 JC 45 and *Ronald v HMA* (n 26).

[96] See, for example, *Fenton v HMA* [2014] HCJAC 70; 2014 SCCR 489 at [1], specifically the conduct libelled in charge (005).

In *HMA v CH*,[97] the Appeal Court made certain observations regarding the risk of 'double counting' when an offender has filmed acts of sexual abuse. The Court noted that where child pornography offences are libelled alongside offences involving contact sexual abuse of the child, the sentencer must ensure that there is no 'double counting'.[98] In other words, while the filming of acts of child rape and other child sexual abuse amounts to serious aggravations of such offences, the offender must not be punished twice for the same offence if he is also convicted of specific charges relating to, for example, the making and possession of indecent images of the child in question. In *CH*, the Court addressed the problem of double counting by ordering the sentence imposed on the child pornography charge to run concurrently with the sentence imposed on the lead offence of rape.[99] It is reasonable to conclude that the Court's warning against 'double counting' in respect of child pornography offences would apply *mutatis mutandis* to offences involving the possession of extreme pornographic images in circumstances, firstly, where the offender films or photographs the rape of an adult victim and, secondly, where the indictment libels an offence under section 51A(1) of the 1982 Act involving the possession of extreme pornographic images in respect of the filming or photography of the sexual abuse in question.

Other Jurisdictions

New Zealand

In New Zealand, the Court of Appeal's judgment in *R v AM*,[100] in which certain guidelines were set out for the offences of rape and unlawful sexual connection, lists the videotaping or photographing of an offence as an example of conduct that further degrades the victim. Such degradation was held to increase the offender's culpability.[101] Thus, photographing or filming an offence is one of several 'culpability assessment' factors[102] which judges must consider in imposing sentence, the decision as to the appropriate sentence in a particular case being a matter that involves 'an evaluative exercise of judgment' on the part of the sentence.[103] The New Zealand courts have routinely applied the guidance in *R v AM* in treating the filming of sexual abuse as a relevant factor in fixing the appropriate banding and starting point sentence.[104]

[97] *CH* (n 82).
[98] Ibid at [36].
[99] Ibid at [40]. For criticism of this part of the Court's decision, in which it misdirected itself as to its sentencing powers, see Brown 2018b: 6.
[100] *R v AM* [2010] NZCA 114; [2010] 2 NZLR 750. The decision is fully considered in Chapter 7.
[101] Ibid at [47].
[102] Ibid at [34] et seq.
[103] Ibid at [79].
[104] See, for example, the decisions in *R v Senior* [2015] NZHC 236 at [20]; *R v Walker* [2015] NZHC 1525 at [22](e); and *R v Page* [2014] NZHC 2092 at [53].

The Republic of Ireland

Although at present there are no formal sentencing guidelines for rape in the Republic of Ireland (O'Malley, 2016: 369),[105] the making of a video recording of the assault or the photographing of the victim are both regarded as aggravating factors by the Irish courts (O'Malley, 2016: 216 and 395). In *People (DPP) v Finn*,[106] for example, the appellant pleaded guilty to two charges of rape. The offences were committed in the grounds of a church over a period of some two-and-a-half hours. During the assault, the appellant used his mobile phone to photograph the victim's naked breasts and genitals. In sentencing him to 12 years' imprisonment, the sentencing judge listed the appellant's actions in photographing the victim as aggravating features of the offence. In refusing the subsequent appeal against sentence, the Court of Criminal Appeal found no fault with the sentencing judge's approach.

Canada

In many Canadian territories and provinces, the courts apply a comparatively low starting point sentence of three years' imprisonment for rape.[107] In *R v Katsnelson*,[108] however, the offender's use of his mobile phone to film his co-accused sexually assaulting the victim was regarded by MacDonnell J of the Ontario Superior Court of Justice as an aggravating factor in imposing a sentence of eight years' imprisonment.[109]

[105] Sentencing practice for rape in the Republic of Ireland is fully considered in Chapter 6.
[106] [2009] IECCA 96.
[107] See the discussion in Chapter 5.
[108] 2010 ONSC 2246.
[109] Ibid at [52] and [60].

4

From Guidance to Guidelines

Rape Sentencing in England and Wales

Introduction

In England and Wales, the law relating to sexual offences is governed by the Sexual Offences Act 2003 ('the 2003 Act') which came into force on 1 May 2004. The 2003 Act represented the most important overhaul of the law on sexual offences in modern times. It was designed to respond to criticisms that the common law on rape, particularly regarding the issue of consent, was vague, confusing and was a factor that contributed to low conviction rates (McGlynn, 2010a: 143).

Some offences were abolished, a range of new offences were created and certain existing offences were redefined under the 2003 Act (Ormerod et al, 2018: 315; Richardson, 2018: 2310). The definition of rape was expanded by section 1(1)(a) of the 2003 Act to include oral as well as vaginal and anal penetration by a penis (Ashworth, 2015: 144; Ashworth and Temkin, 2004: 329; Rook and Ward, 2016: 9). Under section 1(4) of the 2003 Act, the maximum sentence for the offence is life imprisonment.

From *Billam* to the Definitive Guideline: The Development of Rape Sentencing Guidelines in England and Wales

The English judiciary has traditionally insisted that a degree of judicial discretion is essential for the just application of legal rules and principles, since rigid rules are incompatible with the judge's duty to take account of the complex combination of facts that arise in individual cases (Player, 2012: 248). The result has been a judicial focus on conformity (or uniformity) of *approach* to sentencing, rather than seeking a conformity (or uniformity) of *outcome* (Player, ibid). As Lord Lane CJ observed in delivering the judgment of the Court of Appeal (Criminal Division)[1] in *R v Bibi*:[2] 'We are not aiming at uniformity of sentence; that would be impossible. We are aiming at uniformity of approach.'[3]

[1] Hereinafter 'the Court of Appeal'.
[2] (1980) 2 Cr App R (S) 177.
[3] Ibid at 179.

While uniformity of approach is a difficult thing to measure, it is (as Wasik observes) 'unbelievable' that a system which operates sentencing guidelines is no more consistent or principled than one which operates without them (Wasik, 2008: 259). Ashworth and Roberts explain that the sentencing guideline movement in England and Wales has evolved rapidly in recent years: the development of English guidelines can be seen, broadly, as comprising four 'phases' (Ashworth and Roberts, 2012: 881–82 and 891). The first phase comprised the handing down of guideline judgments by the Court of Appeal. The second phase involved the issuing of draft sentencing guidelines by the Sentencing Advisory Panel ('SAP'). In the third phase, Definitive Guidelines were issued by the Sentencing Guidelines Council ('SGC'). Finally, the fourth phase saw the establishment of the Sentencing Council, which replaced the SAP and SGC. Sentencing guidelines for rape have been issued at each of these four phases.

The First Phase – The *Roberts* and *Billam* Guidelines

Guideline Judgments by the Court of Appeal

In the first phase of the development of English sentencing guidelines, in the 1960s the Court of Appeal began to set out various statements of general principle in certain of its judgments in appeals against sentence. This was a slow and essentially reactive way by which to develop sentencing principles; however, the Court of Appeal began to develop a more active role in this regard from the 1980s through to the late 1990s (Ashworth, 2013: 16 and 2009: 243; see also Judge, 2014a: 679–80; Leveson, 2013a: 2; Maguire, 2016: 311; O'Malley, 2018: 9–10; and Roberts, 2019: 191). The Lord Chief Justice would select a particular appeal case, or several cases listed together, in which to deliver a guideline judgment. The Court's judgment would set out the parameters of sentencing for a range of variations of the crime in question (Ashworth, 2009: 243; Ashworth and Roberts, 2017: 855–56; Henham, 1995: 220–21; Wasik, 2008: 253). The Court's aim in issuing such guideline judgments was to foster consistency in sentencing (Ashworth and Roberts, 2013: 3). The judgments often set out one or more starting points along with various aggravating and mitigating factors (Ashworth, 2001: 73; Easton and Piper, 2016: 48; O'Malley, 2016: 13–14). As Thomas noted of the system as it then operated, such guideline judgments began to provide a framework for sentencing the offence in question around which judges could analyse the circumstances of the individual case (Thomas, 1987: 19; see also Ranyard et al, 1994: 203–4).

The Roberts Guidelines

The Court of Appeal first provided general sentencing guidelines for the crime of rape in early 1982 in its judgment in *R v Roberts and Roberts*.[4] It was held that

[4] (1982) 4 Cr App R (S) 8.

an immediate custodial sentence was called for in all but wholly exceptional circumstances, the length of the sentence depending on all the circumstances of the particular case.[5] Several general aggravating factors were set out including, *inter alia*, the use of a weapon; serious injury; and abuse of a position of trust.[6] While the guidance in *Roberts* was an important first step in the development of sentencing guidelines for rape, nothing explicit was said about the level of sentencing in either normal or aggravated cases (Temkin, 2002: 31).

At the time of the decision in *Roberts*, it was well settled in the English common law of sentencing that a plea of guilty would normally attract a reduction in sentence, with the scale of the reduction being greater the earlier the plea was intimated (see Ashworth, 2015: 179, Thomas, 1979: 50 and the decision in *R v De Haan*[7]). The issue of plea-based sentence reductions was not, however, considered by the Court in *Roberts*. Thus, as Temkin (2002: 31) concludes, the *Roberts* guidelines were too vague to be of much assistance.

The Billam *Guidelines*

Amidst mounting public concern about sentencing in rape cases (Rumney, 2003: 870; Temkin, 2002: 30–33), more extensive guidance for sentencing rape was subsequently provided by the Court of Appeal in its guideline judgment in *R v Billam and others*.[8] Ten cases of rape or attempted rape involving 12 different appellants were listed together to give the Court the opportunity to 'restate principles', as the Lord Chief Justice put it, which were to guide sentencing in what was acknowledged to be a 'difficult and sensitive' area of the criminal law.[9] Thus, on one view, as Thomas notes in his commentary to the decision, the sentencing guidelines were intended to restate the practice of the Court rather than establish a new approach (Thomas, 1986: 348). Temkin, however, considers that the guidelines were necessary to deal with the relatively lenient approach to rape sentencing adopted by some judges. Her view is persuasive given that, in the course of delivering the new guidelines, the Court in *Billam* specifically stated that sentences imposed for rape were too low.[10]

The comments with which the Lord Chief Justice prefaced the new sentencing guidelines demonstrated that the Court was aware of changing societal attitudes towards the seriousness of rape and, in particular, to the psychological harm sustained by victims. His Lordship observed that it was the experience of the Court that, in recent years, the 'nastiness' of offences of rape had increased, with what had hitherto been regarded as 'incredible perversions' now being commonplace.[11]

[5] Ibid at 10.
[6] Ibid at 10 and 11.
[7] (1968) 52 Cr App R 21. See also the discussion below.
[8] (1986) 8 Cr App R (S) 48.
[9] Ibid at 49.
[10] Ibid at 50.
[11] Ibid at 49.

Having reviewed the statistics on the length of custodial sentences imposed for the crime of rape in 1984, the Court considered that the sentences imposed were too low.[12] Thus, despite the Court's apparent declaration to the contrary,[13] one of the major rationales for the guidelines in *Billam* was to increase levels of sentence for rape: the decision was clearly one manifestation of the increasing seriousness with which the offence had come to be viewed by society since the 1970s (Ranyard et al, 1994: 205; see also Warner, 2002: 506). While the Court acknowledged that the variable factors in cases of rape were so numerous that it was difficult to lay down guidelines as to the proper length of sentence in terms of years,[14] it proceeded to set out guidelines based on four separate starting points reflecting different levels of seriousness.

Firstly, for a rape committed by an adult without any aggravating or mitigating features, five years' imprisonment was set as the starting point in a contested case. Secondly, a starting point of eight years' imprisonment was set for cases in which a rape was committed by two or more men acting together; by an offender who had broken into or otherwise gained access to a place where the victim lived; by an offender who was in a position of responsibility towards the victim; or by an offender who abducted and held the victim captive. Thirdly, for an offender who had carried out a campaign of rape against a number of different women and who was thus to be regarded as representing more than an ordinary danger to the public, the starting point was set at 15 years or more. Finally, the Court considered that where the offender's behaviour displayed what was described as 'perverted or psychopathic tendencies or gross personality disorder' and where he was likely to remain a danger to women for an indefinite time, a life sentence would not be inappropriate.[15]

The Court also set out certain aggravating factors.[16] These broadly mirrored the guidance provided in *Roberts*[17] and included the effect on the victim. The Court stated that the effect on the victim, whether physical *or* mental, was 'of special seriousness'.[18] As Temkin notes, however, the effects of rape are almost invariably serious or very serious for its victims and it was not entirely clear what extra evidence was necessary for the effect to constitute an aggravating feature (Temkin, 2002: 40). Temkin suggests that serious injury (whether physical or psychological) would seem to qualify, as presumably would pregnancy or disease. Nevertheless, the Court in *Billam* went further than in *Roberts* by directing judges to have particular regard to the physical and mental effect of the offence on the victim.

The Court went on to say that where any one or more of the aggravating factors was present, the sentence should be substantially higher than the figure suggested

[12] Ibid at 50.
[13] Ibid at 49.
[14] Ibid at 50.
[15] Ibid at 50 and 51.
[16] Ibid at 51.
[17] *Roberts and Roberts* (n 4).
[18] *Billam* (n 8) at 51.

as the starting point.[19] However, it attached no specific weight to the various aggravating factors, either singly or in combination (Ashworth, 2000: 113–14; Thomas, 1986: 348). Ashworth considered this to be a major shortcoming of the guideline: its vagueness on this point made it difficult to state how closely *Billam* governed sentencing for rape (2000: 114).

Guidance was also provided in *Billam* on the effect of a guilty plea on sentence. The Court considered that the extra distress which giving evidence can cause to a victim meant that a guilty plea, perhaps more so than in other cases, should normally result in some reduction from what would otherwise be the appropriate sentence, although the amount of such a reduction would depend on all the circumstances.[20]

With regard to the behaviour of the victim prior to the offence, the Court stated that it was not a mitigating factor that the victim may have exposed herself to danger by acting imprudently; similarly, her previous sexual experience was irrelevant.[21] This finally laid to rest the notion that a victim could be found to have been 'contributory negligent' in her own rape (Thomas, 1986: 349; *cf* Warner, 2002: 518). Although an offender's previous good character was said to be only of minor relevance in sentencing, the Court allowed some scope for mitigation in circumstances where the victim had behaved in a manner such as to suggest to the offender that she would consent to sexual intercourse.[22] Finally, with regard to the sentencing of offenders under the age of 21, it was noted that most offences of rape are so serious that a non-custodial sentence cannot be justified. In the ordinary sense, the appropriate sentence would be one of youth custody, following the term suggested as terms of imprisonment for adults but making some reduction to reflect the offender's youth.[23]

Towards Consistency of Approach – An Assessment of the Billam *Guidelines*

While the *Billam*[24] guidelines were far more specific than those set out in *Roberts*[25] (Temkin, 2002: 33), the post-*Billam* sentencing practice of the courts was criticised by some commentators who suggested that judges had failed to adhere to the new guidelines (Ranyard et al, 1994: 209–15; Rumney, 1999: 259–65; Warner, 2002: 504; *cf* Moxon, 1988: 11–13; and Robertshaw, 1994: 344–45). In spite of this, the *Billam* guidelines were widely used by the courts and were consistently applied in subsequent appellate cases (Banks, 2003: 484; Henham, 1994: 506–7; Lacey and Wells, 1998: 401; O'Malley, 2013a: 659; Wells and Quick, 2010: 536). The Court of Appeal

[19] Ibid.
[20] Ibid.
[21] Ibid.
[22] Ibid.
[23] Ibid.
[24] *Billam* (n 8).
[25] *Roberts and Roberts* (n 4).

often referred to the guidelines in hearing appeals against sentence in cases of rape and they had a clear impact in driving up sentences for the offence (Temkin, ibid 36– 7; see also Lacey and Wells, 1998: 401 and Moody, 1995: 235, fn 72).

Temkin reports that, on the whole, the Court of Appeal applied the starting points set out in *Billam*:[26] while both the five- and eight-year starting points were observed, sentences were frequently imposed well above the level of eight years where aggravating features were present (Temkin, 2002: 37–38). Indeed, having undertaken a review of case law from the late 1980s and early 1990s, Temkin concludes that some decisions of the Court of Appeal suggested a rule of thumb by which a year was added to the eight-year starting point for each aggravating factor present in a given case; paradoxically, however, rape committed in abuse of a position of trust tended to attract sentences at a lower level (2002: 38–39). Temkin also demonstrates that previous convictions for rape substantially increased the offender's sentence (2002: 39) and that the list of aggravating factors set out in *Billam* were not treated by the courts as exhaustive (2002: 40).

The *Billam* guidelines were thus an important step both in guiding judges towards consistency in sentencing rape and, crucially, in developing judicial understanding of the emotional and psychological effects of the offence on victims. As with other guideline judgments issued by the Court of Appeal – an innovation which, as Ashworth notes, the senior judiciary could rightly be proud (Ashworth, 2001: 74) – the decision in *Billam* provided direction to sentencers in a judge-friendly way and based on judicial experience, to shape judicial sentencing discretion without constraining it too tightly.

One important area which the Court in *Billam* did not consider – and, indeed, given the state of English criminal law in 1986, *could not* consider – was the approach to sentencing in cases of marital rape (Warner, 2000: 595). As the law stood at the time that the *Billam* guidelines were issued, a husband could not be found guilty of raping his wife. The 'marital immunity' rule was later abolished in 1991 in *R v R*,[27] a decision upheld by the House of Lords the following year in *R v R*[28] (see Munro, 2014: 751). Thus, following *R*, from a definitional perspective at least, the law of rape made no distinction between marital and extra-marital rape (Rumney, 1999: 243): women had the right to full protection from sexual violation whatever the status of their attacker (Fenwick, 1992: 871). In delivering the judgment of the Court of Appeal in *R*, for example, Lord Lane CJ remarked that 'a rapist remains a rapist subject to the criminal law, irrespective of his relationship with his victim'.[29] Shiels observes that, while this observation was made in the context of removing a husband's immunity from rape, it could also be taken to mean that the *Billam* sentencing guidelines should apply equally in cases of marital rape (Shiels, 1992: 366).

[26] *Billam* (n 8).
[27] (1991) 93 Cr App R 1.
[28] (1992) 94 Cr App R 216.
[29] *R* (n 27) at 8.

As sentencing for marital rape was not an issue for the Court in *Billam*, the relevance of a past or present sexual relationship with the victim was not mentioned (Warner, 2000: 595); nor did the Court consider sentencing for relationship or acquaintance rape other than to state, as we have seen, that the victim's previous sexual experience was 'irrelevant'.[30] As Rumney (1999: 247) observes, however, the broad wording of this part of the *Billam* guidelines did not prevent the courts from using the existence of a previous sexual relationship between the victim and the offender as a *mitigating* factor in sentencing.

Development of the Billam *Guidelines: Relationship/Marital Rape and the Decisions in* Berry, Thornton *and* W

The first post-*Billam* case to consider the relevance to sentence of a pre-existing relationship between an offender and his victim was *R v Berry*[31] in which the appellant pleaded guilty to the rape of a former partner. In allowing the appeal against a sentence of six years' imprisonment and substituting a sentence of four years, the Court of Appeal remarked that the rape of a former sexual partner *may* be less serious than rape committed by a stranger. The Court considered that while the woman who is raped by a stranger will inevitably be 'violated' and 'defiled', these features are not always present to the same degree when the offender and the victim had previously had 'a long-standing sexual relationship'.[32] The implication seemed to be that although a previous settled relationship may have some mitigating effect in a case of rape, that effect is relatively limited (Thomas, 1988: 325).

Rumney criticises the decision as fundamentally flawed in a number of respects: the Court provided little explanation for the basis of its decision and failed to consider the realities of stranger and marital rape (Rumney, 1999: 247–48; see also Rumney, 2003: 871–72 and Warner, 2002: 512–13 and 2000: 600–1). Underlying the Court's reasoning was the assumption that the fact that a woman had previously had *consensual* intercourse with her partner would then diminish the gravity of any subsequent *non-consensual* intercourse (Rumney, 1999: 248). For Rumney, this approach was based on a false premise: that rape and consensual intercourse are, in many respects, the same thing, while many victims of marital rape in fact perceive the act as one of violence and humiliation.[33]

The decision in *Berry* thus de-emphasised the violence and trauma which are inherent within the act of non-stranger rape (Rumney, 1999: 248). The Court of Appeal failed to provide a detailed rationale for its view of non-stranger rape and the decision distorted the application of the *Billam* guidelines (Rumney, 2003: 871–72; 2002: 1282). The reasoning in *Berry* was nevertheless subsequently approved by

[30] *Billam* (n 8) at 51.
[31] (1988) 10 Cr App R (S) 13.
[32] Ibid at 15.
[33] See the discussion in Chapter 2.

the Court of Appeal in *Attorney General's Reference (No 7 of 1989) (sub nom R v Thornton)*.[34] It was held that the fact that the parties had cohabited for some two years prior to the offence was 'a factor to which some weight can be given by the sentencing court' in mitigation.[35]

Thornton was subject to trenchant academic criticism. The *ratio* of the decision was that the length of cohabitation was a factor in sentencing cases of relationship rape (Rumney, 1999: 249; see also Warner, 2000: 597). For Fenwick (1992: 871), this raised the unwelcome possibility of sentencing in cases of marital and relationship rape involving 'a crude categorisation of domestic rapists': at one end of the sentencing scale would be husbands of long standing who lived with their wives at the time of the rape and, at the other, would be former lovers who had cohabited with the victim for only a few months.

As in *Berry*, the court in *Thornton* did not explain how or why a long-term sexual relationship between a rapist and his victim should reduce the seriousness of the rape (Rumney, 1999: 249). Indeed, it could be argued that the consequences for the victim of being raped by a long-term partner would be *greater* than for victims who had been in such relationships for a shorter period of time: to be raped by a man with whom the victim had shared intimacy and trust over a long period might be viewed as particularly shocking and psychologically devastating (Rumney, 1999: 249; see also Temkin, 2002: 41; Warner, 2002: 512–13 and 2000: 602; and Wells and Quick, 2010: 537).

The appropriate sentence for rape committed by a husband upon his wife was subsequently considered in *R v W*.[36] This was the first case in which the Court of Appeal gave consideration to a case of marital rape where the victim and the offender were still co-habiting at the time of the offence (Rumney, 1999: 250; see also Temkin, 2002: 4; Warner, 2000: 597; and Wasik, 2001: 316–17). In refusing the appeal against a sentence of five years' imprisonment, the Court distinguished between marital rapes involving neither violence nor threats, where more lenient sentences could be given and those where the conduct was 'gross' and did involve threats or violence, where the *Billam* standard should apply.[37]

The decision in *W* was criticised as being inconsistent with the guidance in *Billam* since, on an application of that guidance, the sentence should have been considerably higher than five years on account of the presence of various aggravating factors (see Rumney, 1999: 250–51; Lacey and Wells, 1998: 401; Temkin, 2002: 43; Warner, 2000: 598–99; and Wells and Quick, 2010: 536–37). For commentators such as Rumney, Temkin and Warner the decision in *W* appeared to indicate that the courts were unwilling to view even grave cases of marital rape in the same manner as stranger rapes. Throughout the 1980s and 1990s, sentences imposed for marital rape almost invariably continued to fall short of the *Billam* standard, with

[34] (1990) 12 Cr App R (S) 1.
[35] Ibid at 6.
[36] (1993) 14 Cr App R (S) 256.
[37] Ibid at 260.

the courts continually distinguishing these cases from other cases of rape (Temkin, 2002: 42–43; see also Warner, 2000: 600).

While women's actual experiences are central to understanding what rape is, its impact and its wider societal significance, the various judicial pronouncements on the trauma of non-stranger rape in *Berry*, *Thornton* and *W* took no account of women's experiences (Rumney, 1999: 253). In particular, Rumney considers that the judiciary was, at this stage in the development of sentencing guidelines for the offence, working from the perspective that some forms of rape were more akin to sexual intercourse and should not, therefore, be subject to the same level of criminal sanction as 'real' (ie 'stranger') rape. This, Rumney maintains, was the product of an approach to understanding rape which took no account of the available research evidence on rape trauma (see also Temkin, 2002: 44; Warner, 2002: 511–13, 523 and 1998: 174, 188; and Wells and Quick, 2010: 536). This unsatisfactory position persisted until the Court of Appeal, acting on the advice of the then recently created Sentencing Advisory Panel, issued its judgment in *R v Millberry and others*[38] in December 2002.

The Second Phase – The *Millberry* Guidelines

The Establishment of the Sentencing Advisory Panel

The second phase of the development of English sentencing guidelines had commenced in 1998 with the creation of the Sentencing Advisory Panel ('SAP'). The government at the time had been persuaded that a new machinery for generating sentencing guidelines should be tried (Ashworth, 2013b: 16). The main arguments in favour of this development were threefold: firstly, that although discretion in sentencing was recognised as essential, it was thought that greater attention should be paid to the rule of law and to the articulation of common principles and standards of sentencing; secondly, that this would be best achieved through a coordinated set of sentencing guidelines which would bring greater consistency of approach to sentencing (the Court of Appeal having insufficient time and resources to develop such coordinated guidelines); and thirdly, that since the task was one of policy creation, the guidelines should be created not only by judges but also by those with experience of other aspects of the criminal justice system (Ashworth, 2009: 244).

The new system aimed to draw into the process a wider range of experience of sentencing, while preserving the authority of the Court of Appeal to issue guideline judgments (Ashworth, 2013b: 16). To this end the SAP, a statutory body established under sections 80 and 81 of the Crime and Disorder Act 1998, came into being on 1 July 1999. It started England and Wales 'upon the journey towards more structured sentencing' (Roberts, 2012a: 333).

[38] [2003] 2 Cr App R (S) 31.

The SAP's function was to make proposals for new guidelines which the Court of Appeal could issue when a suitable case or cases came before the Court (Easton and Piper, 2016: 49). The SAP prepared guidelines for sentencing particular offences, conducted professional and public consultations on the proposed guidelines and remitted its advisory guidelines to the Court of Appeal (Roberts, 2012a: 333 and 2019: 191–92; see also Ashworth, 2013b: 16; 2008: 113; and 2006: 3; and Roberts and Ashworth, 2016: 334). The Court was free to adopt, amend or reject the SAP's proposals so the power, authority and, above all, the discretion of the Court of Appeal was preserved (Ashworth, 2013b: 16–17). In practice, however, the SAP's proposed guidelines were usually accepted and were incorporated, sometimes with modifications, into guideline judgments when a convenient case arose (Roberts, 2012a: 333; Ashworth, 2010: 389). The authority of these judgments stood on the same foundations as those of earlier guideline judgments devised by the Court of Appeal itself (Ashworth, 2009: 244).

The Millberry *Guidelines*

A series of developments since the *Billam* guidelines were issued in 1986 indicated a need for revised and updated sentencing guidelines for rape. In addition to the legal recognition of marital rape and an increase in the number of cases of non-stranger rape reported to the police (Rumney, 2003: 871), major changes to the substantive law of rape were made by the Sexual Offences Act 2003. The 2003 Act expanded the definition of rape to include oral as well as vaginal and anal penetration by a penis. Shortly before the 2003 Act was passed, the Court of Appeal, responding to advice from the SAP, handed down revised guidelines for the sentencing of rape in *R v Millberry*,[39] the first major revision to the English sentencing guidelines in 16 years (Ashworth, 2015: 144; Wells and Quick, 2010: 537).

In its advice to the Court of Appeal, the SAP identified three 'dimensions' to be used in assessing the gravity of an individual offence of rape: firstly, the degree of harm to the victim; secondly, the level of culpability of the offender; and thirdly, the level of risk posed by the offender to society (SAP, 2002: para 9). The SAP's advice regarding the sentencing of non-stranger rape was informed by commissioned research in which public attitudes to so-called 'date rape' and 'relationship rape', including the attitudes of some rape victims, were examined (Clarke et al, 2002). The SAP's advice was largely accepted by the Court of Appeal in *Millberry*.[40]

As a result of the SAP's advice, three applications for leave to appeal were listed so that the Court could consider what revised guidelines should be given.[41] The judgment in *Millberry* was issued by the Lord Chief Justice, Lord Woolf. The guidelines retained the general structure and levels of the previous *Billam*[42] guidelines

[39] *Millberry* (n 38).
[40] Ibid.
[41] Ibid at [1].
[42] *Billam* (n 8).

with some minor but significant changes to take account of both the new legislation and changes in the nature of the offence since the *Billam* guidelines were issued (Ashworth, 2005: 128; Bottoms, 2010: 42, fn 14; SAP, ibid para 6; Shapland and Hall, 2010: 182). In particular, the Court accepted the SAP's proposals that judges should consider each of the three dimensions of harm, culpability and risk whenever a sentence for rape was imposed.[43]

Following the structure of the *Billam* guidelines, the general starting point for a conviction for rape after a contested trial in cases featuring no aggravating circumstances was set at five years' imprisonment.[44] A general starting point of eight years was set where one or more of seven stated factors were present:

- the rape being committed by two or more offenders acting together;
- the offender being in a position of responsibility towards the victim, or the rape being committed in breach of trust;
- abduction of the victim;
- rape of a child, or an especially vulnerable victim;
- racially aggravated rape and other cases where the victim is targeted because of his or her membership of a vulnerable minority;
- repeated rape in the course of one attack; and
- rape by a man who is knowingly suffering from a life-threatening sexually transmissible disease.[45]

The eight-year starting point in such cases was recommended by the SAP either because of the impact of the offence upon the victim, or the level of the offender's culpability, or both.[46] A starting point of 15 years was set where the offender had either repeatedly raped the same victim over a course of time or where multiple victims were involved.[47] Finally, again as in *Billam*, a life sentence was not considered to be inappropriate where the offender 'manifested perverted or psychopathic tendencies or gross personality disorder' or where the offender was likely to remain a danger to women for an indefinite time.[48]

From the appropriate starting point the court would move downwards to take account of any mitigating factors and an offender's plea of guilty and upwards to take account of any aggravating factors not otherwise built into the sentence. The nine aggravating factors identified by the SAP and with which the Court agreed, were as follows:

- the use of violence over and above the force necessary to commit the rape;
- use of a weapon to frighten or injure the victim;

[43] *Millberry* (n 38) at [7].
[44] Ibid at [19].
[45] Ibid at [20].
[46] Ibid at [21].
[47] Ibid at [22].
[48] Ibid at [23].

- planning of the offence;
- an especially serious physical or mental effect on the victim;
- further degradation of the victim;
- rape in which the offender broke into or otherwise gained access to the victim's home;
- the presence of children when the offence is committed;
- the covert use of a drug to overcome the victim's resistance and/or obliterate their memory of the offence; and
- a history of sexual assaults or violence by the offender against the victim.[49]

With regard to mitigating factors, the Court referred to the statutory requirement to have regard to an offender's plea of guilty.[50] It also endorsed the view of the SAP that while an offender's previous good character should not be ignored, it did not justify a substantial reduction of what would otherwise be the appropriate sentence[51] (see generally Ashworth, 2005: 128).

As the Court accepted the comments of the SAP as to starting points, there was no substantial departure from the general approach laid down in *Billam*[52] (Thomas, 2003: 109). As Ashworth notes, however, what was new about the SAP's advice and the Court's guidelines in *Millberry*[53] was a change in the approach to relationship rape, where the parties had recently been, or were still, involved in a sexual relationship (Ashworth, 2005: 129). One of the clear findings of the research commissioned by the SAP (Clarke et al, 2002) was the view that relationship rape was no less traumatic and therefore no less serious, than stranger rape. In particular, the breach of intimate trust involved in relationship rape could have equally severe effects on the victim and relationship rape was experienced as harder to deal with and to recover from by victims. Thus, in its advice to the Court, the SAP said this:

> '… the Panel proposes that the Court of Appeal should make a clear statement to the effect that the starting point for sentence is that cases of "relationship rape" and "acquaintance rape" are to be treated as being of equal seriousness to cases of "stranger rape", with the sentence increased or reduced, in each case, by the presence of specific aggravating or mitigating factors.'[54]

This recommendation amounted to the effective reversal of the *Berry*[55] formulation that non-stranger rape was to be viewed as a less serious offence than stranger rape (Rumney, 2003: 872). The Court stated that it was in general agreement with

[49] Ibid at [32].
[50] Ibid at [27]–[28]. See below.
[51] Ibid at [29].
[52] *Billam* (n 8).
[53] *Millberry* (n 38).
[54] Ibid at [9].
[55] *Berry* (n 31).

these propositions[56] but qualified its acceptance of this part of the SAP's advice. The Court considered there to be some cases of relationship rape (eg where a woman is raped by her partner after he consumed so much alcohol that he 'failed to show the restraint he should have') which it would be 'contrary to common sense' to treat as being equivalent to stranger rape.[57]

The Court also considered that, in cases of stranger rape, judges should not overlook the fact that 'the victim's fear can be increased because her assailant is an unknown quantity', in the sense that the victim will not know whether her attacker is also a murderer as well as a rapist.[58] The Court did, however, agree with the SAP that the same guidelines and starting points should apply, in principle, to male rape, to female rape[59] and to historic cases of rape;[60] and that no inherent distinction should be made in sentencing between anal and vaginal rape.[61] With regard to the effect on sentence of the victim's behaviour, the Court agreed with the SAP that the offender's culpability would, as in all offences, inevitably vary from case to case and that the degree of the offender's culpability should be reflected in the sentence.[62]

A Question of Balance – An Assessment of the Millberry *Guidelines*

By largely accepting the SAP's advice on the seriousness of relationship and acquaintance rape, the *Millberry*[63] guidelines went a considerable way towards breaking from past sentencing practice in which stranger rape was perceived as the paradigm of 'real' rape (Rumney, 2003: 872, 883; Warner, 2002: 511). The change in the Court's approach to the sentencing of relationship rape was significant. Judicial views that relationship and acquaintance rape were less serious than stranger rape had been so entrenched that when the SAP first put the findings of the empirical study by Clarke et al (2002) (that relationship rape was no less traumatic than stranger rape due to the deeply unsettling aspect of breach of trust) to the judges of the Court of Appeal, the judges found the findings so counter-intuitive that some of their Lordships questioned whether the research had been properly conducted (see Ashworth, 2013b: 18). It was only when the judges had received assurances that the research was reliable that the guideline judgment in *Millberry* was issued.

As Rook and Ward (2004: 12) observe, however, the Court in *Millberry* was reluctant to place the culpability of the 'stranger' rapist and the 'relationship' or 'acquaintance' rapist on precisely the same footing. This aspect of the Court's

[56] *Millberry* (n 38) at [9].
[57] Ibid at [26].
[58] Ibid at [13].
[59] Ibid at [10].
[60] Ibid at [17].
[61] Ibid at [11].
[62] Ibid at [14].
[63] *Millberry* (n 38).

judgment is criticised by Rumney (2003: 883) who considers that the judicial view of non-stranger rape continued to be obscured and distorted by conceptions of harm and seriousness that failed to consider the full range of impacts experienced by rape victims. Rumney considers that the Court tended to minimise the offender's culpability in cases of non-stranger rape (2003: 878–81). For Rumney, the breach of trust inherent in cases of relationship and acquaintance rape ought to have been regarded by the Court in *Millberry* as a distinct aggravating factor in sentencing as it constitutes a distinct, additional and ultimately unique harm not present in cases of stranger rape (2003: 881–83).[64]

One aspect of the decision in *Millberry* that is arguably insufficiently recognised by Rumney, however, is the fact that the Court stressed the importance of flexibility in the application of the guidelines. The various starting points did not mean that the sentence would be the same in the case of all offences to which the respective starting point applied for, as the Court stated, '[a]ll the circumstances of the particular offence, including the circumstances relating to the *particular victim* and the *particular offender* are relevant' (emphasis added).[65] In explaining how the guidelines were to operate and in emphasising the importance of judicial discretion in sentencing rape, the Court said this:

> '[W]e would emphasise that guidelines such as we have set out above can produce sentences which are inappropriately high or inappropriately low if sentencers merely adopt a mechanistic approach to the guidelines. It is essential that having taken the guidelines into account, sentencers stand back and look at the circumstances as a whole and impose the sentence which is appropriate having regard to all the circumstances … Guideline judgments are intended to assist the judge [to] arrive at the current sentence. They do not purport to identify the correct sentence. Doing so is the task of the trial judge.'[66]

This view on the use of guideline judgments was subsequently adopted in Scotland by the High Court of Justiciary on Appeal in issuing one of its first guideline judgments in *HMA v Graham*.[67] According to the Court in *Millberry*, the task facing the judge was said to be one that involved a balancing exercise – balancing any circumstances of mitigation against the aggravating circumstances.[68] The Court in *Millberry* did not specifically regard the breach of trust in relationship or acquaintance rape as an aggravating factor. Nevertheless, its emphasis on flexibility in the application of the guidelines, its reference to the importance of judicial discretion and its observations on the limited extent to which an offender's previous good character could operate to mitigate a sentence meant that judges were well placed to *increase* sentences arrived at through an application of the *Millberry* guidelines where this was warranted due to breach of trust by the offender.

[64] See the discussion in Chapter 2.
[65] *Millberry* (n 38) at [13].
[66] Ibid at [34].
[67] [2010] HCJAC 50; 2011 JC 1 at [22].
[68] *Millberry* (n 38) at [13].

This appears to be accepted by Rumney towards the end of his critique where, having set out at length his criticisms of the decision in *Millberry*, he concedes both that 'cases of non-stranger rape, as with cases of stranger rape, will have to be sentenced on a case-by-case basis' and that '[t]he nature and perhaps quality of the relationship may have a bearing on sentencing decisions in the context of breach of trust' (2003: 882). Rumney acknowledges that the Court in *Millberry* had issued general guidance and could not be expected to explore every possible eventuality (2003: 883); however, he concludes his argument by making only brief mention of the fact that the Court warned against the mechanistic application of the guidelines (2003: 883–84). Nevertheless, in focusing mainly on the perceived shortcomings of the judgment in *Millberry* and by omitting consideration of the discretion that judges retained, Rumney's account arguably fails to recognise a key point in sentencing: the discretionary and individualised nature of the sentencing task (see Aas, 2005: 86–87; Brown, 2017a; Krasnostein and Freiberg, 2013: 267 and Tombs, 2008: 84–85). Allowing sentencing judges sufficient discretion and manoeuvrability to tailor their sentences to the circumstances of the particular offence and the particular offender, was still an important feature of sentencing practice at this stage in the development of sentencing guidelines in England and Wales.

The decisions which sentencers are called upon to make are fact specific and individual offences and offenders are infinitely complicated (Padfield, 2011: 99). Individualised justice remained possible under the *Millberry* guidelines because the principles laid down in the judgment operated at a higher level of generality than rules. These principles were sufficiently flexible to permit departure and variation when the particular circumstances of a case so demanded (see O'Malley, 2013a: 533). Although most sentences subsequently imposed in the Crown Court reflected the guidance in *Millberry*,[69] the discretion afforded to judges enabled them, once they had taken the *Millberry* guidelines into account, to 'stand back', to consider the circumstances of the particular case as a whole and to impose the sentence which was appropriate 'having regard to all the circumstances'.[70] This could result in the imposition of custodial sentences either below the levels set by the Court of Appeal in *Millberry*[71] or above (sometimes substantially above) the levels set by the Court,[72] provided that there were good reasons for applying the necessary flexibility.[73]

[69] See *Attorney General's References (Nos 37, 38, 44, 54, 51, 53, 35, 40, 43, 45, 41 and 42 of 2003)* [2004] 1 Cr App R (S) 84 at [7], *cf Attorney General's References (No 153 of 2004 and Nos 14 and 2 of 2005)* [2005] EWCA Crim 954 at [3].

[70] *Millberry* (n 38) at [34].

[71] See, for example, *Attorney General's Reference (No 80 of 2006)* [2006] EWCA Crim 2305 (two-and-a-half years' imprisonment upheld); *Attorney General's Reference (No 96 of 2006)* [2007] 2 Cr App R (S) 30 (community order upheld) and the observations at [14] and [15] of *Attorney General's Reference (No 62 of 2004)*, [2004] EWCA Crim 2036.

[72] See, for example, *R v S* [2005] EWCA Crim 3520 (life imprisonment upheld) and *R v B* [2006] 2 Cr App R (S) 60 (detention for life upheld).

[73] See *Attorney General's Reference (No 36 of 2006)* [2007] 1 Cr App R (S) 38 at [13].

The principles in *Millberry* thus helped judges to navigate their way through the facts to arrive at an acceptable sentence. The guidelines led to a more structured, principled and informed approach to sentencing and were arguably flexible enough to allow judges to impose sentences commensurate with the offender's culpability and both the physical and psychological harm caused to the victim.

The Third Phase – The Sentencing Guideline Council's Definitive Guideline on the Sexual Offences Act 2003

In 2004, the development of English sentencing guidelines entered its third phase with the creation of the Sentencing Guidelines Council ('SGC') under section 167 of the Criminal Justice Act 2003. This marked a significant change in the production of sentencing guidance. Under section 170(9) of the 2003 Act, the SGC had the power to issue 'Definitive Guidelines'. In terms of section 172(1)(a) of the Act, judges were obliged to 'have regard' to any guidelines which were relevant to an offender's case. Section 174(2) of the Act imposed a duty on judges to give reasons for departing from a Definitive Guideline and section 170(5) of the Act imposed on the SGC the aim of having regard to the need to promote consistency in sentencing (see Ashworth, 2013b: 23; O'Malley, 2006: 59–60; Roberts, 2011: 1001; and Roberts and Baker, 2008: 568–569). Thus, although the SGC was comprised of judicial and lay members and was chaired by the Lord Chief Justice, it effectively assumed the Court of Appeal's responsibility for issuing guidelines (Easton and Piper, 2016: 49). This change accelerated the development of definitive sentencing guidelines in England and Wales, which became the only country outside the United States to implement a detailed, national system of guidelines containing specific sentence ranges (Ashworth and Roberts, 2013: 1–2; Oleson, 2017: 369; Roberts and Ashworth, 2016: 310, fn 3; Wiles, 2015: xi).

In this third phase of development, the SAP performed much the same function as before; however, it advised the SGC rather than the Court of Appeal (Wasik, 2008: 253). The SGC was then required to formulate draft guidelines and to consult government ministers and a Parliamentary Committee; it was then authorised to lay down definitive sentencing guidelines (Ashworth, 2010: 389). The work of the SAP and the SGC resulted in the creation of a substantial corpus of sentencing guidelines, including guidelines on sexual offences (Ashworth, 2010: 389; Ashworth and Roberts, 2012: 882; Pina-Sánchez, 2015: 77; and Roberts and Ashworth, 2016: 334).

The guidelines issued by the SGC tended to consist of two parts. The first was essentially narrative; it discussed the features of the particular offence and factors that might increase or decrease its seriousness. The second consisted chiefly of a sentencing table for the offence; it set out three or four levels of seriousness and assigned a sentencing range to each of them. The guidelines included a narrative description of the table and its levels of seriousness in the preceding pages. A list of aggravating and mitigating factors appeared beneath the table (Ashworth, 2009: 245;

Roberts, 2019: 192–93). The aim of these guidelines was not to eliminate proper decision-making by judges, but to structure it (Wasik, 2008: 255).

The Sexual Offences Act 2003 contained a significant number of new or amended offences for which there was no sentencing case law (Cooper, 2008: 281) so, on 30 April 2007, the SGC published its Definitive Guideline on the sentencing of offenders convicted of offences under the 2003 Act (SGC, 2007a). The guidelines applied to all offenders sentenced on or after 14 May 2007, irrespective of the date of the offence. The guidelines used the starting point of five years' imprisonment for the rape of an adult with no aggravating or mitigating factors derived from the decision in *R v Millberry*[74] as the baseline from which all other sentences for sexual offences in the guideline were calculated.

The guidelines for the offences of rape and assault by penetration were set out at pages 23 to 30 of the Definitive Guideline.[75] In relation to rape, the guideline adopted the starting points established in *Millberry*; namely five years where no aggravating factors were present and eight years where any of the particular aggravating factors identified were involved (SGC, 2007a: 23). The starting points and sentencing ranges for rape, set out in tabular form, ranged from a starting point of five years' imprisonment (with a sentencing range of between four and eight years) for a single offence by a single offender committed against a victim aged 16 or over; through a starting point of eight years' imprisonment (with a sentencing range of between six and 11 years) for rape accompanied by any one of six specified aggravating factors; to a starting point of 15 years' imprisonment (with a sentencing range of between 13 and 19 years) for the repeated rape of the same victim over a course of time or for rape involving multiple victims (SGC, 2007a: 25). The aggravating factors specified in the guideline comprised:

- abduction or detention;
- knowingly suffering from a sexually transmitted infection;
- more than one offender acting together;
- abuse of trust;
- an offence motivated by prejudice; and
- a sustained attack.

The guidelines stressed, however, that the figures of five, eight and 15 years were simply starting points: the existence of such aggravating factors could significantly increase the sentence (SGC, 2007a: 23).

The guidelines also discussed the harm caused by non-consensual sexual offences, noting that such offences involved the violation of the victim's sexual autonomy and that the seriousness of the violation may depend on several factors. The nature of the sexual behaviour would, however, be the primary

[74] *Millberry* (n 38).

[75] For a concise overview of the relevant SGC guidelines applicable to the crime of rape, see Rook and Ward, 2008: 1–10 and 2010: 10–23.

indicator of the degree of harm caused in the first instance (SGC, 2007a: 19). The principle established in *Millberry*[76] that judges should adopt the same starting point for 'relationship' rape or 'acquaintance' rape as for 'stranger' rape was applied to all non-consensual offences in the guideline. The SGC explained: 'Any rape is a traumatic and humiliating experience and, although the particular circumstances in which the rape takes place may affect the sentence imposed, the starting point for sentencing should be the same.' This section of the Definitive Guideline finally laid to rest the debate as to whether 'relationship rape' or 'acquaintance rape' should attract the same sentence as 'stranger rape' (Rook and Ward, 2010: 14).

The extreme youth or old age of a victim was stated to be an aggravating factor. In addition, the SGC considered that, in principle, the younger the child and the greater the age gap between the offender and the victim, the higher the sentence should be, account being taken in all cases of the youth and immaturity of the offender. It considered that all offences of rape involved a high level of culpability on the part of the offender since the person will have acted either deliberately without the victim's consent or without giving due consideration to whether the victim was able to or did, in fact, consent (2007a: 19, 21).

With regard to offences involving children under 13, including the rape of a child under 13,[77] the SGC noted that there would be cases involving victims under 13 where there was, *in fact*, consent where, *in law*, such consent could not be given. In such circumstances, the SGC considered that the presence of consent could be material in relation to sentence. This was said to be particularly so in relation to a young offender where there was close proximity in age between the victim and the offender or where the mental capacity or maturity of the offender was impaired. The fact that an offender had a reasonable belief that the victim was aged 16 was said to be capable of being taken into consideration as a mitigating factor (SGC, 2007a: 21).

This section of the Definitive Guideline developed the principles previously set out by the Court of Appeal in *R v Corran*.[78] The guidance in *Corran* was provided by the Court in the expectation that the SGC would pronounce on the subject (Rook and Ward, 2010: 183). Judges were required to undertake a significant weighing of interests in such cases (Selfe, 2011: 6). The Definitive Guideline did not amplify the point about consent so it was left to the judge to decide how significant the presence of actual consent should be in any given case (Thomas, 2008: 159).

The SGC also referred to the Court of Appeal in *Millberry*[79] having established that an offender's culpability would be 'somewhat less' where the victim had consented to sexual familiarity with the offender on the occasion in question, than in cases where the offender had set out with the intention of committing rape

[76] *Millberry* (n 38).
[77] Contrary to s 5 of the 2003 Act.
[78] [2005] 2 Cr App R (S) 73 at [6]–[10]. For criticism of the decision, see McGlynn, 2010a: 145–46.
[79] *Millberry* (n 38).

(SGC, 2007a: 21). In broadly accepting this statement but also in elaborating upon it, the SGC noted that:

> 'Save in cases of breach of trust or grooming, an offender's culpability may be reduced if the offender and victim engaged in consensual sexual activity on the same occasion and immediately before the offence took place. Factors relevant to culpability in such circumstances include the type of consensual activity that occurred, similarity to what then occurs and timing. However, the seriousness of the non-consensual act may overwhelm any other consideration.'

The guideline stated that planning an offence indicated a higher level of culpability than an opportunistic or impulsive offence (SGC, 2007a: 21). The guideline also contained cross-references to associated criminal activity (most importantly the Definitive Guideline on Domestic Violence (SGC, 2006a)) which ensured that the wider aim of the criminal justice system to extend protection to victims of crime in all areas of life was achieved. While in the past there had been a worrying tendency within the criminal justice system to treat domestic violence as less serious than other crimes, the guidelines played a significant role in drawing domestic violence into the mainstream of criminal behaviour by stating that it was to be treated as seriously as other cases of violence (Cooper, 2008: 282).

Despite the imposition of the statutory duty under section 172 of the 2003 Act to 'have regard' to the relevant sentencing guidelines in cases of rape, judges still retained a significant degree of sentencing discretion. As the Court of Appeal observed in *R v Oosthuizen*,[80] the first decision of the Court concerning the treatment of Definitive Guidelines issued by the SGC, 'having regard' to a relevant guideline did not mean that it had to be followed.[81] Some three months later, in *R v Matthews*,[82] the Court noted that section 172 fell well short of 'a demand for robotic adherence'.[83]

The Court of Appeal would frequently stress that the final responsibility for determining a just and appropriate sentence lay with the judge and that sentencing guidelines were simply an aid which allowed the judge to effectively exercise his or her discretion in the individual case (see Thomas 2008: 160 and Ashworth, 2013b: 23). In the years following the implementation of this third phase of guidelines, the Court of Appeal observed that sentencing was not a mathematical exercise since it was infinitely more complex and refined than mathematical problems;[84] the Court noted that, as each case is different, the judge had to ensure that each case was assessed on an individual basis[85] and it stressed the importance of doing 'justice in the circumstances of an individual case'.[86] Judges were, the Court stated,

[80] [2006] 1 Cr App R (S) 73.
[81] Ibid at [15].
[82] [2005] EWCA Crim 2768.
[83] Ibid at [9].
[84] *R v Martin* [2007] 1 Cr App R (S) 3 at [18] and [21].
[85] *Attorney General's References (Nos 32 to 34 of 2007)* [2008] 1 Cr App R (S) 35 at [16].
[86] *Attorney General's References (Nos 7 to 9 of 2009)* [2010] 1 Cr App R (S) 67 at [39].

entitled to disregard a Definitive Guideline if an injustice would result from following it: sometimes justice would require a more merciful sentence than indicated in a guideline, sometimes a more severe one.[87]

In *R v Larcombe*,[88] the Court discussed the way in which judges should use the Definitive Guideline on Sexual Offences. In delivering the judgment of the Court, Pitchford J explained that the sentencing tables did not stand alone and noted that judges would be misled if they neglected the principles and the explanatory guidance which applied to them.[89] His Lordship noted that flexibility is required in the sentencing of sexual offences; that the starting points and ranges are not rigid; and that movement both within and between ranges would depend on the circumstances of individual cases, particularly the aggravating and mitigating features.[90]

An Assessment of the Sentencing Guideline Council's Definitive Guideline

In a valuable critique of the system of sentencing guidelines under the SGC, the barrister John Cooper QC commends its work in amalgamating various key decisions of the Court of Appeal since the implementation of the Sexual Offences Act 2003 into a fully developed sentencing guideline (Cooper, 2008: 281–82). This, Cooper notes, was of particular assistance to the legal profession: as a general proposition, providing sentencing guidelines to judges and practitioners on a range of offences and sentencing options provided an 'invaluable tool' to enable the Crown and the defence to focus on the important issues that would affect the mind of the sentencer (2008: 278). Such guidelines lead to predictability and consistency in the field of sentencing; they allow relevant and defined argument to take place in court; they permit counsel to manage the lay client's expectations of the sentencing outcome; and assist the Crown in managing the expectations of victims of crime. With regard to the guideline on sexual offences in particular, Cooper notes that the SGC provided 'a welcome consolidation of the pre-existing and new sexual offences sentencing regimes into one document'; he considers that 'any initiative which seeks to make available a complex series of sentencing developments in one document will be favourably received by those who practise' (2008: 282).

Cooper does not, however, consider the third phase of sentencing guidelines under the SGC to be an unqualified success. He expresses some important reservations with regard to what members of the criminal Bar perceived to be an apparent erosion of judicial discretion in sentencing (2008: 279). In particular, he reports that the majority of both the judiciary and the legal profession perceived that the guidelines were heavily prescriptive, if not, in fact, mandatory, with the Crown all

[87] Ibid.
[88] [2008] EWCA Crim 2310.
[89] Ibid at [10].
[90] Ibid at [11] and [13].

too often presenting the guidelines to the judge 'as if written in stone'. A common complaint from the Bar was that the SGC's guidelines had resulted in the sentencing process becoming a 'box ticking' exercise at the expense of a flexible sentencing regime (2008: 279–80). Indeed, the layout of the guidelines lent itself to what Cooper describes as a 'multiple choice' approach (2008: 280). Practitioners saw the guidelines being used by judges not as helpful signposts to a proper disposal, but rather as 'fireproofing' against any subsequent appeal against sentence.

For Cooper (2008: 284), the sentencing regime requires sophistication rather than prescription. It appeared that, despite the observations of Pitchford J in *R v Larcombe*[91] on the proper approach to the application of the guideline,[92] practitioners were of the view that judges applied it rigidly, inflexibly and in a mechanistic fashion. Sentencing, however, is not – and never should be – a rigid and formulaic process (Selfe, 2012: 4).

In Cooper's view, the approach of the SGC prioritised sentencing the *offence*, rather than the *offender*, thus making a constructive disposal highly unlikely. Although the seriousness of rape meant that cases where the court was able to impose a non-custodial disposal were few in number, from the practitioner's perspective, there nevertheless existed a fundamental conflict between the need for conformity and certainty in sentencing and the reality that each case would inevitably depend upon its own facts (Cooper, 2008: 285). Inherent within this problem was the erosion of judicial discretion to deal with each case individually and, ultimately, fairly (2008: 286). This is a concern which Cooper would come to raise again in his critique of the present format of English guidelines issued by the Sentencing Council.[93]

The Fourth Phase – The Sentencing Council's Definitive Guideline

The Establishment of the Sentencing Council and the New Format of Sentencing Guidelines

The task of issuing amended guidelines fell to the Sentencing Council for England and Wales ('the Council'). The Council was established in April 2010 under the Coroners and Justice Act 2009.[94] The 2009 Act changed the previous arrangements for the issuing of guidelines in two important ways. Firstly, the courts' duty to comply with sentencing guidelines was amended. While the previous statutory

[91] *Larcombe* (n 88).

[92] Ibid at [10], [11] and [13], discussed above.

[93] See below.

[94] For the background to the 2009 Act and the changes to the sentencing environment it introduced, see Ashworth, 2013b: 24–25 and 2010: 389–90; Ashworth and Roberts, 2013: 5 and 2012: 882; Easton and Piper, 2016: 50–52; Roberts, 2019: 193–94; 2013: 3, 2012a: 334–35, 2012b: 270–71 and 2011: 998–99, 1006–9; and Roberts and Ashworth, 2016: 334–35.

requirement was for judges to 'have regard' to any relevant guidelines, section 125(1) of the 2009 Act introduced the requirement that judges *must follow* the relevant guidelines, unless satisfied that it would be contrary to the interests of justice to do so (see Ashworth, 2012: 93–94; Ashworth and Roberts, 2017: 857 and 2012: 882; Leveson, 2013a: 5; O'Malley, 2016: 14; Roberts and Ashworth, 2016: 336–37; and Satish, 2017: 120). Secondly, the Council, established under section 118(1) of the 2009 Act, replaced both the SAP and the SGC.

The Council began to issue its own guidelines in 2011. These follow a different structure from those issued by the SGC. They set out a multi-stage process for determining sentence and, in so doing, seek to promote what Roberts describes as 'uniformity' [*sic*] and consistency in sentencing (Roberts, 2013: 5 and 22). Section 120 of the 2009 Act requires the Council to prepare sentencing guidelines. These may be general in nature or limited to a particular offence, category of offence or particular category of offender. Under section 121, the guidelines should specify the 'offence range' appropriate for a court to impose on an offender convicted of that offence and, if the guidelines describe different categories of case, they should specify for each category a 'category range' within the offence range (Wasik, 2014: 48–49). The guidelines should also specify the 'starting point' within the offence range or within each category range (Wasik, 2014: 49; see also Maslen, 2015: 173).

Under this fourth phase in the development of English sentencing guidelines, judges are directed to undertake a nine-step process in arriving at sentence (Allen, 2016: 9–10; Ashworth and Roberts, 2017: 857 and 2013: 6; Roberts, 2012b: 275–78 and 2011: 1011; Roberts and Rafferty, 2011: 682). To date, most Council guidelines have followed the style of the Definitive Guideline on Assault which came into effect on 13 June 2011 (Sentencing Council, 2011). While the assault guideline was intended to serve as a model for all future guidelines issued by the Council (Roberts, 2013: 4), it need not necessarily serve as the model or template for all future guidelines since the 2009 Act gives the Sentencing Council discretion as to the form that a guideline takes (see Harris and Gerry, 2013: 240).

The first step in the nine-step process involves the judge determining which of three levels of seriousness is appropriate in a particular case. Once the judge has determined the appropriate category range, she will use the starting point within the range as a point of departure. Secondly, the judge will then 'fine tune' the sentence within the chosen range by considering other factors relating to the seriousness of the crime as well as any personal mitigation (Wasik, 2014: 51–52). These first two steps are regarded as the most important in the process as they involve a judicial assessment of the seriousness of the case (Allen, 2016: 10; Hutton, 2013: 98–99).

The judge must then follow seven further steps, which are required mainly for technical or legal reasons (Hutton, 2013: 96), to determine the final sentence, namely:

- consideration of whether the sentence should be reduced to reflect assistance provided to the prosecution or police;
- consideration of whether to reduce the sentence for a guilty plea;

- consideration of whether to impose an extended sentence;
- consideration of the totality principle and whether the sentence is proportionate;
- consideration of whether to make a compensation or other ancillary order;
- explanation of the effect of the sentence; and
- consideration of any time served on remand.

(For a full discussion, see Ashworth and Roberts, 2013: 8–9; Brown, 2017a: 148–49; Roberts, 2019: 205–07 and 2013: 10–11; and Wasik, 2014: 52–53.)

Julian Roberts, a former member of the Sentencing Council, explains that the present format of sentencing guidelines structures the decision-making process by effectively creating what he describes as an 'algorithm' for judges to follow (Roberts, 2011: 1011; see also Hutton, 2013: 95). The result, as Roberts observes, is a detailed and relatively prescriptive sentencing scheme (Roberts, 2012b: 283).

The Development of the Sentencing Council's Definitive Guideline on Sexual Offences

By 2012 the Sexual Offences Act 2003 had been in force for eight years. A clearer picture had emerged of the way in which the courts were approaching the use of certain new offences introduced under the Act. Also, the nature of certain established offences had changed. For example, as we have seen in Chapter 3, technology was increasingly used in the commission of sexual offences, with offenders photographing or filming the abuse of their victims. It was evident that the SGC's Definitive Guideline on Sexual Offences had to be amended to reflect such developments (Sentencing Council, 2012: 6).

The process of issuing the new Definitive Guideline began in December 2012 when the Council issued its draft guideline for consultation (Sentencing Council, 2012). The Council's review of the existing guideline took place against a background of a greater awareness of sexual offending that extended to an increased understanding of the impact of sexual abuse upon victims and their families (Rook and Ward, 2014: x; 2016: 1800; and 2019: 410). In its consultation document, the Council stressed that the perspective of victims was central to its considerations (Sentencing Council, 2012: 5). The gravity of sexual offending and the very particular emotional and physical harm experienced by victims meant that engagement with victims and with those who work with them was a vital part of the Council's development of the guidelines (2012: 12). In particular, the Council commissioned research into victim and public attitudes to the sentencing of sexual offences (Nicholls et al, 2012). A key issue to emerge from the research was a strong desire from victims for the criminal justice system to demonstrate an accurate understanding of the overarching and long-term harmful effects of sexual violence and abuse, of how it impacts on the life of the victim and their family and to consider this to a greater extent within the sentencing process (2012: 58–59). The Council considered these matters in identifying harm factors for each of the offences in the guideline (Sentencing Council, 2012: 12).

The Operation of the Definitive Guideline

The new sentencing guidelines for rape are particularly important. As the Council noted in its consultation, they set a benchmark for the sentence levels for many other sexual offences (Sentencing Council, 2012: 15). Following the consultation period, the new Sexual Offences Definitive Guideline was published by the Council on 12 December 2013 (Sentencing Council, 2013a). The guideline applies to the sentencing of all adult sex offenders from 1 April 2014, whenever the offences were committed. In particular, in accordance with the guidance given by the Court of Appeal in *R v H*[95] and *R v Forbes*,[96] an offender is to be sentenced in accordance with the regime applicable at the date of sentence and thus the new Definitive Guideline applies to cases of historic sexual abuse (see Rook and Ward, 2016: 16, 1800–2 and 2019: 9, 349–64). The Definitive Guideline is gender neutral and applies equally to male and female offenders (*Attorney General's Reference (No 85 of 2014)*[97]).

A press release issued by the Council when the new Definitive Guideline was published stated that the intention was to reflect more fully the psychological and longer-term effects on victims of sexual abuse (see Wasik, 2014: 276). The new guideline places an emphasis on the *harm* caused by sexual offences and on the *culpability* of the offender. The structure for determining these aspects varies according to the offence concerned so that, in theory, the guideline is tailored to the particular offending behaviour (Rook and Ward, 2014: xi and 2016: 1803). Rather than focusing on the nature of the particular sexual activity, the guideline focuses on the extent of the harm caused to the victim. A number of models for addressing harm and culpability are used for offences in the Definitive Guideline, each of which are different from the model used in the previous Sentencing Council guidelines (Rook and Ward, 2019: 410).

As the Council explained in its consultation, the first step that the court must take is to consider the main factual elements of the offence; the judge will do this by considering the harm to the victim and the culpability of the offender. In the Council's previous guidelines on assault and burglary the formulation of harm and culpability was achieved by recourse to a number of factors that indicated greater or lesser harm and higher or lower culpability (Sentencing Council, 2012: 15). The Council explained that it moved away from this formulation in recognition of the fact that all rape is extremely harmful to the victim (ibid). The approach recommended in the consultation (and carried through to the final guideline) was to assume that there is *always* a baseline of harm, for as the Council explained: 'The violation of the victim through the act of rape is harm in itself. It would be unhelpful to articulate this as 'lesser harm' as these offences are inherently harmful' (2012: 16).

[95] [2012] 2 Cr App R (S) 21 at [16], [46] and [47a]–[47g].
[96] [2016] 2 Cr App R (S) 44 at [4].
[97] [2015] 1 Cr App R (S) 14 at [27].

While the previous guideline on sexual offences considered the gravity of the offence in terms of the *physical nature* of the sexual activity, the Council was concerned that simply labelling sentence levels in terms of activity did not fully reflect the seriousness or complexity of the offence. The model used for the majority of offences in the new guideline, including rape, thus has a lowest level (a baseline) in which inherent harm and culpability are assumed (Rook and Ward, 2016: 18 and 1802–3). An offence can be moved to a higher category of harm or culpability (with a correspondingly higher starting point) where one or more factors from an exhaustive list are present (2016: 28; see also Rook and Ward, 2019: 411).

The maximum penalty for rape is life imprisonment and the offence range specified by the guideline is four to 19 years' imprisonment. A sentence passed outside this range would be a departure from the guideline and, under section 174(6)(b) of the Criminal Justice Act 2003, would require the judge to give reasons why it would be contrary to the interests of justice to sentence within the offence range (Wasik, 2014: 276). The guideline does provide, however, that offences may be of such severity (eg involving a campaign of rape) that sentences of 20 years or more may be appropriate (Sentencing Council, 2013a: 10).

Harris (2015a: 653) observes that sentencing levels for serious sexual offences have increased dramatically in recent years to levels that 'would have been unthinkable just a short time ago'. In *R v Watkins*,[98] for example, a total custodial term of 29 years' imprisonment as part of an extended sentence was upheld on appeal for various sexual offences committed against children and young persons, while in *R v DJ*,[99] an extended sentence with a custodial term of 30 years was imposed on appeal following the appellant's conviction for a large number of sexual offences, including rape, committed against young girls.

In common with all other Council guidelines, the judge must first determine the offence category by assessing both the degree of harm and the level of culpability ('step 1'). The harm may fall into one of three categories, 1, 2 or 3. Category 2 provides a closed list of relevant factors:

- severe psychological harm (which need not be permanent – see *R v JM*[100]);
- severe physical harm;
- pregnancy or sexually transmitted infections as a consequence of the offence;
- additional degradation or humiliation;
- abduction;
- prolonged detention or the sustained nature of the incident;

[98] [2015] 1 Cr App R (S) 6.

[99] [2015] 2 Cr App R (S) 16.

[100] [2016] 1 Cr App R (S) 21 at [8]. In *R v Chall* [2019] EWCA Crim 865, the Court of Appeal held that expert evidence is not an essential precondition of a finding that a victim has suffered severe psychological harm. The judge may assess that such harm has been suffered based on evidence from the victim, including evidence contained in a victim personal statement.

- the use of violence or the issuing of threats (beyond that which is inherent in the offence);
- forced or uninvited entry into the victim's home; and
- the particular vulnerability of the victim due to personal circumstances (which can include the victim's intoxication – see *Attorney General's Reference (No 51 of 2015)*;[101] Ormerod et al, 2018: 322; and Rook and Ward, 2016: 22 – see Sentencing Council, 2013a: 10).

The harm caused by a particular offence *may* fall within category 1 as a result of the 'extreme nature' of one or more category 2 factors, or the 'extreme impact' caused by a combination of category 2 factors (Sentencing Council, 2013a: 10).[102] This approach relies on the judge, in full possession of all the facts of the case, being best placed to determine whether a particular case should be so elevated (see Rook and Ward, 2014: 6–7). It is not essential for there to be a psychiatric or psychological report before the court for a judge to find severe psychological harm to be present (Rook and Ward, 2019: 4). In *R v Forbes*,[103] Lord Thomas CJ observed that a judge who has heard evidence from the victim will be well placed to make an assessment of the effect of the offending on them.[104] His Lordship continued:

> 'However, it must be borne in mind, so that double counting is avoided, that the starting points and sentencing ranges provide for the effect on the victim which is the inevitable effect of this type of serious criminal behaviour. There has to be significantly more before harm is taken into account as a distinct and further aggravating factor and or before a judge makes a finding of extremely severe psychological or physical harm so as to justify placing the offence in the top category of harm.'[105]

Category 3 applies where the factor(s) in categories 1 and 2 are not present. This is designed to indicate to judges that once an offender has been found guilty of rape, they do not need to identify additional factors for the offence to be deemed harmful or serious (see Rook and Ward, 2014: 5).

With regard to culpability, levels are described as A or B, rather than 'higher' or 'lower' as in certain other Council guidelines. A case will fall within culpability level A where:

- there has been a significant degree of planning;
- the offender acts together with others to commit the offence (the wording of the Definitive Guideline in this respect is to be read 'objectively and sensibly'; the lack of intent by any co-accused may have some bearing upon the ultimate overall assessment of the position for sentencing purposes, but that does not of

[101] [2015] EWCA Crim 1699.
[102] See, for example, *R v Mamaliga* [2018] EWCA Crim 515.
[103] *Forbes* (n 96).
[104] Ibid at [26].
[105] Ibid. See also *R v Chall* (n 100) at [36].

itself remove a case from the categorisation under Culpability A – see *Attorney General's Reference (No 133 of 2015)*[106]);

- alcohol or drugs are used on the victim to facilitate the offence;
- there is an abuse of trust;
- previous violence has been used against the victim;
- the offence is committed in the course of a burglary;
- the offence is recorded;[107]
- there is commercial exploitation and/or motivation in committing the offence;
- the offence is racially or religiously aggravated; or
- the offence is motivated by hostility to the victim based either on his or her sexual orientation, transgender identity, or disability (Sentencing Council, 2013a: 10).

With regard to offences that exhibit a significant degree of planning, the issue needs to be considered in the overall context and cases will be fact-specific (Rook and Ward, 2019: 5–6). The Court of Appeal held in *R v Teklu*[108] that a 'significant' degree of planning within the meaning of the Definitive Guideline is not an absolute concept.[109] Similarly, in *R v Dogra*[110] the Court of Appeal noted that the higher level of culpability denoted by a significant degree of planning must be 'a matter of judgment based on all the facts of the case'.[111]

A case will fall into culpability level B if the factors in category A are not present (Sentencing Council, 2013a: 10). No factors are listed in culpability level B to reflect the fact that the act of rape inherently involves a high level of culpability. Thus, level B is not a 'lower' culpability category, but simply reflects the absence of any of the additional factors found in culpability level A; it also indicates the baseline of culpability that exists whenever rape is committed (Rook and Ward, 2014: 11).

These combinations of harm and culpability generate a matrix (Wasik, 2014: 277). The judge must proceed to 'step 2' by using the corresponding starting points to reach a sentence within the appropriate category range (Sentencing Council, 2013a: 10):

- Category 1 harm has a starting point of 15 years' imprisonment (with a range of between 13 and 19 years) where the culpability falls within level A and a starting point of 12 years (with a range of between 10 to 15 years) where the culpability falls within level B;

[106] [2016] 1 Cr App R (S) 70 at [26].
[107] See Chapter 3.
[108] [2018] 1 Cr App R (S) 12.
[109] Ibid at [10].
[110] [2019] 2 Cr App R (S) 9.
[111] Ibid at [32].

- Category 2 harm has a starting point of 10 years' imprisonment (with a range of between nine and 13 years) where the culpability falls within level A and a starting point of eight years (with a range of between seven and nine years) where the culpability falls within level B; and
- Category 3 harm has a starting point of seven years' imprisonment (with a range of between six and nine years) where the culpability falls within level A and a starting point of five years (with a range of between four and seven years) where the culpability falls within level B (Sentencing Council, 2013a: 11; see also Wasik, 2014: 277 and Ashworth, 2015: 144).

As part of 'step 2' the judge is also directed to consider a list of aggravating and mitigating factors to either increase or reduce the seriousness of an offence (Sentencing Council, 2013a: 11). The aggravating factors are listed as follows:

- the statutory aggravating factors of previous convictions (having regard to the nature of the previous convictions, their age and their relevance to the current offence) and whether the current offence was committed while on bail;
- specific targeting of a particularly vulnerable victim;
- ejaculation;
- blackmail or the use of threats;
- location and timing of the offence;
- the use of a weapon to frighten or injure the victim;
- the victim being compelled to leave their home;
- failure to comply with current court orders;
- commission of the offence while on licence;
- exploitation of contact arrangements with a child to commit an offence;
- presence of others (especially children);
- any steps taken to prevent the victim reporting the offence and/or from assisting or supporting the prosecution;
- attempts to dispose of, or conceal, evidence; and
- commission of the offence while under the influence of alcohol or drugs (Sentencing Council, 2013a: 11).

The considerably shorter list of mitigating factors comprises the following:

- an absence of previous convictions or relevant/recent convictions;
- remorse;
- previous good character and/or exemplary conduct. This is different from having no previous convictions and the more serious the offence, the less weight will be attached to this factor. In the context of rape, previous good character or exemplary conduct should not normally be given any significant

weight and will not normally justify a reduction in what would otherwise be the appropriate sentence. In *R v Forbes*,[112] Lord Thomas CJ stated that what is of material significance is proper evidence of positive good character and the court must examine carefully all the circumstances of the particular case;[113]
- age and/or lack of maturity where it affects the offender's responsibility; and
- mental disorder or learning disability, particularly where linked to the commission of the offence (Sentencing Council, 2013a: 11).

The relevant factors are specifically stated to be non-exhaustive. The presence of aggravating or mitigating factors entitles the judge to move up or down within the category range or to move into a different category from that selected at step 1 (Sentencing Council, 2013a: 11). In particular, relevant recent convictions are specifically stated to be a factor likely to result in an upward adjustment. Thereafter, the judge is directed to follow the remaining seven steps[114] to reach the final sentence (2013a: 12); in particular, an appropriate reduction should normally be made to reflect an offender's plea of guilty at step 4.

Relationship Rape and Abuse of Trust under the Definitive Guideline

The issue of whether rape committed within an established relationship should automatically constitute an abuse of trust, such as to bring such a case within culpability level A of the Definitive Guideline, was considered by the Court of Appeal in *R v DO*.[115] The term 'abuse of trust' used in the Definitive Guideline is wider than the term 'abuse of a position of trust', which was a factor indicting higher culpability in the consultation draft. The Court in *DO* held that the Sentencing Council did not intend that every case of rape within an established relationship should be treated as an abuse of trust. In the Court's view, the Council's use of the term 'abuse of trust' was intended to include circumstances where the offender may not hold a formal position of trust in relation to the victim, but where they abused the trust engendered by their status and/or standing.[116] The Court held that the fact that, in this case, the rape took place within a relationship was not sufficient for the offence to represent an abuse of trust; however, it did constitute 'a gross betrayal' which was itself an aggravating feature (the victim had herself described the offence as a 'betrayal').[117]

Agreeing with the victim that the offence represented a 'gross betrayal' yet concluding that the offence did not involve a breach of trust is, as Harris (2015b: 380) observes, somewhat dichotomous: the Court regarded the offence as a

[112] *Forbes* (n 96).
[113] Ibid at [24].
[114] See above.
[115] [2015] 1 Cr App R (S) 41.
[116] Ibid at [31].
[117] Ibid.

betrayal, but a betrayal of what? Harris suggests that while not every rape committed within a relationship will amount to an abuse of trust, the majority of such cases will, in fact, either be considered culpability A cases or receive sentences in line with those imposed for cases involving abuse of trust on the basis of 'betrayal' constituting an aggravating feature.

In the later decision in *R v CC*,[118] the appellant was convicted of various offences, including four charges of rape, one of controlling or coercive behaviour in an intimate or family relationship and six charges of assault. The evidence at trial disclosed that the victim was in a relationship with the appellant for some three months. The relationship was violent almost from the outset. During the latter part of the relationship, the appellant raped the victim on an almost daily basis. Due to threats made by the appellant and his coercive and controlling behaviour, the victim felt powerless to prevent what was happening to her. The trial judge considered that the appellant's violent and coercive behaviour constituted an abuse of trust, indicating that '[the victim] trusted you to do right by her and you abused that trust'.[119] The Court of Appeal considered that the trial judge's conclusion in relation to abuse of trust represented 'an unwarranted extension of that term'.[120] In the circumstances of the case, however, other factors justified a finding that the appellant's offending fell within category 2A of the Definitive Guideline.[121]

Guidelines, Not Case Law

In delivering the judgment of the Court of Appeal in *R v Thelwall*,[122] Lord Thomas CJ stated that the English sentencing system 'now proceeds on the basis of guidelines, not case law'.[123] This, his Lordship continued, meant that the citation before either a sentencing judge or the Court of Appeal of appellate decisions which are simply illustrations of the operation of a sentencing guideline on particular facts are unlikely to be of assistance.[124]

Lyndon Harris (2017: 242) considers that the courts' move in the past 10 years or so towards reliance only on cases that establish or develop principles of sentencing is laudable; however, to suggest that cases interpreting or at least illustrating the application of a guideline are 'unlikely to be of assistance', as the Court of Appeal put it in *Thelwall*, is deeply regrettable. Harris demonstrates, by reference to certain authorities on a variety of offences, how such cases can, in fact, be useful. For Harris, the Court's position in *Thelwall* disregards the need for consistency in sentencing and risks, or indeed invites, a divergence in practice. Rook and Ward (2019: 409), meanwhile, note that while the Court's frustration at the unnecessary

[118] [2018] EWCA Crim 2704.
[119] Ibid at [48].
[120] Ibid.
[121] Ibid.
[122] [2016] EWCA Crim 1755.
[123] Ibid at [22].
[124] Ibid.

citation of previous decisions is understandable, it is unrealistic to treat all guidelines as being sufficiently clear that they can be applied simply as they stand. There are, for example, references throughout the Definitive Guideline to factors such as 'abuse of trust',[125] 'grooming' and 'significant disparity in age' that are not defined and that need elaboration if their ambit is to be properly understood (2019: 410). In cases where the applicability of such terms is a live issue, it is essential that counsel look to previous appellate decisions in which the issues have been considered. By so doing, counsel can assist the courts in developing a broadly consistent approach to the application of key terms used in the Definitive Guideline.

An Assessment of the Sentencing Council's Definitive Guideline

Rook and Ward welcome the introduction of the new Definitive Guideline, noting that it is important that sentencing guidelines adapt to long-term changes associated with the particular criminal behaviour to which they relate, particularly so in relation to the sensitive and complex area of sexual offending (Rook and Ward, 2014: x). The authors consider that the guideline addresses core aspects of harm and culpability in sexual offending, whilst retaining sufficient flexibility to accommodate future developments and increased understanding (ibid; see also Leveson, 2013b and Treacy, 2013).

The Council's Response to the Consultation itself discloses that 165 responses were received from the judiciary, legal practitioners, victims' groups, academics and the public, 92 of which addressed the draft sentencing guidelines for rape (Sentencing Council, 2013b: 5, 9). The Council prefaced its discussion of the responses with an excerpt from the response of the Police and Crime Commissioner for Northumbria who, in commending the 'comprehensive and welcome piece of guidance' said this:

> 'In my opinion this guidance has the potential to reach much further than its original intent of delivering tougher and more appropriate sentences … It isn't often that sentencing guidelines are capable of changing the public perception of an offence but these draft guidelines might just help to do that' (Baird, 2013, cited in Sentencing Council, 2013b: 4).

The following comments from Dr Fiona Mason, a consultant forensic psychiatrist and specialist in the psychiatric treatment of rape victims, are cited by the Council as reflecting the generally positive responses it received to its proposed sentencing guidelines for rape:

> 'The proposed guidelines are a welcome move in the right direction in the campaign for justice for victims of rape and serious sexual assault. They acknowledge the psychological harm suffered by victims and shift the exclusive focus on physical harm. Importantly, vulnerable victims are given particular emphasis, especially children and people with a mental disorder' (Mason, 2013, cited in Sentencing Council, 2013b: 9).

[125] See above.

In particular, the majority of respondents favoured the move away from the structure of previous Council guidelines in assessing harm and culpability and the introduction of a 'baseline' for these factors which reflected the harm and culpability inherent in the act of rape (Sentencing Council, 2013b: 10). With regard to the specific culpability factors at step 1 of the guideline, the Council reports a high level of agreement by respondents both with the proposed approach and with the individual factors included in culpability level A (2013b: 15). Similarly, there were high levels of agreement with those factors that the Council had identified as specific aggravating factors in cases of rape (2013b: 15–16).

There was disquiet amongst some respondents at the consideration of any *mitigating* circumstances in the guideline due to the nature of the harm caused by rape and the very high culpability of any offender convicted of the offence. The Council, however, considered that as a general principle and for reasons of transparency, it was important that common mitigating factors were listed in the guideline so that the judge's difficult task of weighing the various factors was understood (Sentencing Council, 2013b: 17). While a number of respondents queried the inclusion of remorse as a specific mitigating factor on the basis that it could be easily faked or 'switched on' by manipulative offenders, the Council noted that it is a factor that appears in all Council guidelines and is one that judges are adept at assessing.

The concern expressed by certain victims' groups over the inclusion of previous good character and/or exemplary conduct as mitigating factors met with a similar response from the Council. The Council noted that judges would carefully assess the relevance of previous good character in the particular case (Sentencing Council, 2013b: 18). In any event, the Court of Appeal had previously recognised that this factor should have only limited impact in sexual offences; in this regard the Council made reference to the decisions in *Attorney General's Reference (No. 38 of 2013), (sub nom R v Hall)*[126] and *R v Millberry.*[127]

Finally, with the regard to the sentence levels for rape, the Council noted that the levels proposed in the draft guideline retained the starting points in the previous SGC guideline of five and eight years' imprisonment; however, what it termed a 'clearer articulation of the culpability of the offender' meant that these starting points increased to seven and 10 years' imprisonment in the final guideline, for Category 3A and 2A cases respectively (Sentencing Council, 2013b: 19). The Council reports that the government, the Crown Prosecution Service, the Law Society, the Criminal Bar Association, the Council of HM Circuit Judges and the Police Federation all agreed with the proposed sentence levels. The increased sentence levels reflected current sentencing practice in England and Wales which, the Council noted, had seen average sentences for sexual offences rise since 2005.

In late 2018, the Sentencing Council published an assessment of how the courts have implemented the Definitive Guideline (Carline et al, 2018). In addition to statistical analysis of sentences imposed for sexual offences, the study also

[126] [2014] 1 Cr App R (S) 61.
[127] *Millberry* (n 38).

included semi-structured interviews with 26 Crown Court judges. The majority of respondents were recruited from the Sentencing Council's existing research 'pool', a list of judges who had previously indicated willingness to be contacted for research purposes. As the judges who participated in the study were self-selecting, however, the authors of the study acknowledge that the research findings should be regarded as indicative and not conclusive (Sentencing Council, 2013b: 9, fn 18).

Through conducting these interviews, the authors of the study aimed to explore with judges the extent to which the Definitive Guideline was used in practice, whether or not they faced any difficulties when applying the guideline and the perceived existence of any unanticipated consequences (Carline et al, 2018: 9). With regard to the offence of rape, the study found that judges were generally positive about the guideline. In particular, judges found the structure in relation to the categorisation of harm and culpability helpful when sentencing. Most of the harm and culpability factors were considered appropriate by respondents and were used accordingly (2018:13). Judges generally agreed that the guideline's recognition of psychological harm was to be commended; however, the lack of a definition of 'severe psychological harm' was seen by some judges as causing difficulties and further guidance on the issue would, the authors note, be useful. Several judges also emphasised the importance and, indeed, the *necessity* of flexibility when determining the appropriate offence category in any given case (2018:13).

Despite the generally favourable responses of self-selecting judges to the use of the Definitive Guideline as reported in the Sentencing Council's study, practitioners have nevertheless expressed certain important reservations. Criticism has tended to focus on the format of the new system of sentencing guidelines and on the potential for injustice that a rigid adherence to guidelines may cause. Although the barrister Lyndon Harris welcomes the greater focus on the psychological harm caused by offences, noting that sentences should reflect all the factors in a particular case and that the new guideline ought to facilitate this, he criticises the format of the guideline itself (Harris, 2013: 847). For Harris, the problem is that the culpability and harm assessment still gives no assistance as to how much weight judges should ascribe to a particular factor (Harris, 2015c: 828–29 and 2015d: 7). Harris posits the example of a case where violence is used: if such violence is worth, say, a 12-month uplift (this itself being unclear as the guideline provides no details), then how much is extreme violence worth? While these factors will result in different uplifts, with the sentence being adjusted differently in different cases, no guidance is provided as to how to sentence in such cases (Harris, 2013: 847). Harris explains:

> 'The conclusion to be drawn is that the guidelines, regrettably, offer little assistance. In terms of the most common examples of each offence, they probably work quite well. Ironically, these are the offences where sentencers and practitioners need little assistance. The cases in which most help is needed are the unusual cases, those on the borders, the extreme examples of the offence (be they high or low) and yet these cases are the ones in which the new sexual offences guideline fails miserably (Harris, 2013: 847).'

In an earlier paper written in response to the Sentencing Council's consultation on the new guideline, Harris and Gerry criticise the guideline's format as unduly mechanistic and restrictive (Harris and Gerry, 2013: 239). The authors consider that the guidelines fail to appreciate the often-complex nature of offending and that such a 'broad brush' methodology has the potential to result in serious injustice. In particular, Harris and Gerry consider the Council's system of ranges and starting points to be an artificial method of calculating sentence (2013: 241). The system places what Harris and Gerry consider to be undue emphasis on a mathematical approach to sentencing: as we have seen, once the category is selected, movement up or down within the range is based on reference to a list of factors; however, judges are given no assistance as to the weight to attribute to each factor. As the authors explain:

> 'The focus is placed on the presence or absence of the factors, as opposed to identifying the real feature of the offending. The danger in this approach in relation to sexual offending is that the default option is a custodial penalty and the only issue is for how long, regardless of the fact-specific nature of the case before the Judge … [T]he reliance on the mechanistic and arbitrary factors to determine category, list and aggravation or mitigation results in unfairness, confusion and perverse results … What is required at sentence is a true examination of the offending behaviour in order to ensure the correct sentence is imposed' (Harris and Gerry, 2013: 241–42; see also Harris, 2015d: 7 and Weitzdörfer et al, 2018: 198).

Experience in the criminal courts has shown that the problem with the mechanistic approach of the Council's guidelines is that, in many cases, sentencing hearings are reduced to 'unseemly exercises in trading figures' that the public finds impossible to follow (Harris and Gerry, 2013: 240). Victims, for example, may not understand why a particular sentence has been chosen on the *facts*, merely that it has been chosen on the Council's *figures*. In many situations, recourse to the Council's guideline hinders the judge's ability to do justice (Harris and Gerry, 2013: 242; see also Harris, 2016: 73). Harris and Gerry conclude that the present format of sentencing guidelines has 'led to an over-dependence on mathematics and undue criticism of judges who take a fact-based approach' (Harris and Gerry, 2013: 242).

They are not alone in their criticism of the new system of sentencing guidelines. The award-winning legal commentator the 'Secret Barrister' similarly criticises the format of the guidelines, noting that the guidelines operate 'by way of convoluted flow charts and grids'; that many of the guidelines 'tie the judge's hands in irrational binds'; that their application often leads to 'perverse' results; and that none of the guidelines are easily explicable to the public (Secret Barrister, 2019: 291–94). Public understanding of the guidelines appears to be a particular problem. Empirical research undertaken by Professor Sir Anthony Bottoms on behalf of the Sentencing Council found that victims do not always understand the complexity of the multi-step approach adopted in the present system of sentencing guidelines (Bottoms, 2018: 15).

Professor Nicola Padfield, an academic and barrister who sat as a part-time judge in the Crown Court for 12 years between 2002 and 2014, considers the Council's guidelines 'quite complicated' (Weitzdörfer et al, 2018: 192), 'less easy to apply' and 'more difficult to use' than the guidelines issued by the SGC (Padfield, 2013: 35).

Padfield and Ashworth acknowledge that the current system of sentencing guidelines is 'more rigid' than the system under the SGC and they express concern that the 'user-friendliness' of the current guidelines is not monitored (Ashworth and Padfield, 2015: 658). That the algorithmic guidelines issued by the Sentencing Council are becoming 'increasingly complex' is acknowledged by Julian Roberts, himself a former member of the Council (see Roberts and Hough, 2015: 13). This amounts to a rare example of self-reflection since, as Roberts himself acknowledges, the Sentencing Council has not been particularly self-critical over the years (Roberts, 2019: 231).

In his case commentary to the decision in *R v Karam*,[128] a case involving the rape of an intoxicated 17-year-old girl, the late Dr David Thomas QC criticises the nine-step process involved in the Council's guidelines as 'increasingly mechanistic', as a 'time-consuming and not often productive process of analysing … statements of the obvious' and as having the potential to turn judges into 'mere technicians oiling the wheels' (Thomas, 2013: 1000). For Thomas, the advent of the new system of guidelines under Sentencing Council means that the judgement of experienced sentencers counts for less and less: what matters is simply the detailed application of a quasi-statutory scheme (Thomas, 2013: 999–1000; *cf* Treacy, 2014). Dr Thomas was one of the leading authorities on English sentencing law and practice whose commentaries on decisions of the Court of Appeal in the *Criminal Law Review* were regarded as a cornerstone of English sentencing jurisprudence (see Ashworth and Ormerod, 2013: 946; Judge, 2014b and 2009; Padfield, 2016a: 231; and Walston et al, 2009: 51). Given Dr Thomas's status as one of England's foremost sentencing scholars, such trenchant criticism of the current system of guidelines in England and Wales cannot lightly be dismissed.

In a critique of the current system of sentencing guidelines, John Cooper QC persuasively argues that the new guidelines format focuses on offence severity and offender culpability at the expense of personal mitigation (Cooper, 2013: 158), a view shared by Harris and Gerry (2013: 240; see also Weitzdörfer et al, 2018: 198). Cooper regards the Council's approach as, on the whole, victim centric. He suggests that the Council has gone so far as to interpret public opinion (with what the Council perceives to be public distaste for personal mitigation) as being 'the arbiter of how the guidelines should be calibrated' (Cooper, 2013: 163).

While the approach of the SGC was to provide guidance by means of specific fact-based scenarios, judges are now directed to weigh harm (in its new, expanded, form incorporating psychological harm) and culpability equally to reach a specific category of offence within the guidelines (Cooper, 2013: 159). Cooper maintains that as seriousness is the overwhelming determinant of sentencing severity, the influence of personal mitigation has been marginalised and reduced to the extent that it is hardly mentioned in any of the Sentencing Council's guidelines. For Cooper, the Council's tendency to present long lists of aggravating factors but correspondingly short lists of mitigating factors in its guidelines puts personal

[128] [2013] 2 Cr App R (S) 65.

mitigation into a subordinate position and makes it, to a significant extent, reliant upon judicial inclination: the more serious the offence, the less likely it is in practice that the judge will take personal mitigation into account (Cooper, 2013: 163).

The juxtaposition of a detailed matrix of criteria linked to aggravating factors and seriousness with the paucity of guidance in relation to personal mitigation also drew adverse comment from the Howard League in its response to the Sentencing Council's consultation on the draft guidelines for sentencing rape. The Howard League considered that this tendency, 'connotes a reluctance to include mitigating factors in the sentencing guideline and suggests that the consideration of mitigating factors is not an important element in [the] sentencing of sexual offences' (Howard League, 2013, cited in Sentencing Council, 2013b: 17). These comments drew the ire of the Sentencing Council. The Council replied that they strongly refuted such a suggestion and stated that they had spent much time considering mitigation, ensuring that common factors were included to achieve transparency for victims, offenders and sentencers (Sentencing Council, 2013b: 17).

Nevertheless, Cooper (2013: 160) considers that the Sentencing Council interprets personal mitigation very narrowly. In practice, the only real mitigating factors available for the judge to consider will be issues relating to remorse and assisting the police. Personal mitigation is, however, a more complex consideration than the Council seems to acknowledge. In Cooper's view, the concept remains underdeveloped as the Council has concentrated upon seriousness and on aggravating circumstances (2013: 160).

Cooper argues that the focus on aggravating factors at the expense of mitigation clearly affects the ability of judges to respond to the characteristics of the individual offender. In order to address these problems, he suggests listing mitigating factors in a separate step of the guideline methodology; expanding the list of guideline factors relating to personal mitigation (to include, for example, pressing personal or family need, the offender's mental health[129] and exceptional personal responsibilities undertaken by the offender); and the issuing of a generic guideline on personal mitigation to list the 'enormously wide' range of factors advanced in mitigation. This, Cooper suggests, would ensure a more consistent and principled approach to the consideration of mitigating factors (2013: 161–62; see also Allen, 2016: 18 and Bottoms, 2018: 18).

Cooper considers that there is no principled reason why personal mitigation should play a lesser role in sentencing for serious crimes such as rape; he stresses that the pursuit of fairness and justice must include a central role for personal mitigation (Cooper, 2013: 164). In a scathing criticism of the Sentencing Council's approach, Cooper concludes:

> 'The sentencing of offenders is a complex and individual exercise; there is no blueprint or a "one size fits all" solution. In the Council's quest for consistency the complex and idiosyncratic nature of offenders has been shelved in place of a process which,

[129] The Sentencing Council launched a three-month consultation on its proposed guideline on Sentencing Offenders with Mental Health Conditions or Disorders (Sentencing Council, 2019) on 9 April 2019. For discussion, see Padfield, 2019.

> it is argued, can be easily understood by the public. This approach is superficial and perhaps worse, it is patronizing. Sometimes, sentencing cannot be reduced to this two-dimensional approach … [I]t is time to acknowledge that the sentencing exercise is often difficult, sometimes complex and always individualized' (Cooper, 2013: 164; see also Gerry, 2011a; Gerry and Sjölin, 2012; Lovegrove, 2010: 921–23; and Ormerod, 2013: 183).

Thus, for academic commentators such as Padfield, Thomas and Lovegrove and practitioners such as Cooper, Gerry and Harris, the ability of the judge to do justice in sentencing a particular case of rape may be hampered by the format of the Sentencing Council's Definitive Guideline. The nature of rape is such that, in many cases, any personal mitigation will either be completely outweighed by the seriousness of the offence or may only be afforded a certain weight depending on the facts of the individual case. Cases of rape do arise, however, in which the factors advanced in mitigation are so compelling as to warrant the imposition of non-custodial sentences. This may arise in cases involving rape or other sexual offences committed by young defendants (see Harris, 2016: 73).

Perhaps the paradigm example in this regard is the decision in *R v Charles and others*,[130] decided in July 2011, where the previous guidelines issued by the SGC were in force. Here, the six appellants, all of whom were young men of previous good character, pleaded guilty to charges of rape of a child under 13.[131] The two complainants were both aged 12, with one of them being four weeks short of her thirteenth birthday; however, they both had the appearance of being over 16. All six appellants believed the complainants to be over 16. One of their number had specifically enquired about their ages; the complainants both told him that they were 16. The appellants were sentenced on the basis that they had committed the rapes in the belief that they had not been acting unlawfully. The complainants had both been willing participants; one of them consented to sexual activity with five of the six appellants.

The appellants were sentenced to two years' detention in the Crown Court. In the subsequent appeals against sentence the Court of Appeal acknowledged the difficult nature of the case. The Court concluded its narration of the facts of the case by noting that 'these young men fell to be punished for taking the chance that the girls were younger than the age they said they were and they appeared to be, by committing casual sex with them, a not uncommon feature of youth'.[132] In quashing the custodial sentences and imposing suspended sentences of 12 months with 12 months' supervision, the Court made the following observations on the use of the sentencing guidelines:

> 'The difficulty with the guidelines is that they are designed to ensure consistency in sentencing and to reflect the public perception and Parliament's perception of the gravity of the offences. But that objective is inept where the facts are wholly different from those envisaged in the guideline … [W]e endorse the views previously expressed by this

[130] [2012] 1 Cr App R (S) 74.
[131] Contrary to the Sexual Offences Act 2003, s 5 (so-called 'statutory rape' (see Gerry, 2011a: 314)).
[132] *Charles* (n 130) at [23].

Court that there will be cases where the guidelines are not suitable for offences where young men have sexual activity with girls whom they believe to be over 16.'[133]

Felicity Gerry QC reports that the families of the convicted young men, who were present in court, 'erupted with delight' when the judgment was handed down, while in the press, 'rape victims reacted with horror'. In commenting on the decision, Gerry continues:

> 'It is such cases which demonstrate what a difficult exercise sentencing can be. No one wants their 12-year-old daughter to be sexually active. No one wants their sons to have sex with underage girls … In an age where "sick" means "good", trying to teach chivalry through the criminal law leads to cases, such as this, where the courts have to pick up the pieces of other peoples' lives and try to do justice to both sides' (Gerry, 2011b: 454).

Similarly, in *R v B*,[134] the appellant and the complainant had corresponded via Facebook when he was 18 and she was 12. The complainant claimed to be 16. She consented to and indeed initiated, sexual intercourse with the appellant. On appeal, the suspended sentence of six months' imprisonment with a 12-month supervision requirement was quashed and a conditional discharge substituted.

The facts of the decisions in *Charles*[135] and *B*[136] illustrate the position advanced by Joanne Conaghan (2019: 178) that, rather than being static, universal and insensitive to social and cultural specificities, rape is, in fact, 'a remarkably fluid concept' (see also Martin Alcoff, 2018: 4–5; 15–16). As such, there is a need for flexibility in rape sentencing guidelines and for judges to be able to exercise their discretion. Nevertheless, with the Sentencing Council having imposed an 'algorithmic' approach which prioritises consistency or perhaps even 'uniformity', in sentencing (Roberts, 2013: 5 and 22 and 2011: 1011); the fact that the Definitive Guideline is presumptively binding on judges; that judges have to justify any departure from the guideline; and, perhaps most importantly, the fact that the judge's assessment of sentence will take place against a background of numerous aggravating factors with correspondingly few mitigating factors, the imposition of constructive disposals *in appropriate cases* (such as *Charles*[137] and *B*[138]) will, arguably, now be far less likely. Harris (2013: 848), for example, suggests that since the implementation of the new Definitive Guideline, defence counsel find it 'harder to mitigate for a defendant convicted of a sexual offence'. As Gerry and Sjölin (2012) observe:

> '[I]n the drive for consistency it is sometimes forgotten that sentencing is a human process … It is important to ensure that any individual is sentenced for what they have done in the light of who they are … Despite tighter and tighter sentencing guidelines, cases will stubbornly continue to involve real people in really different circumstances … The tighter the guidelines the more difficult it is, in our view, for judges to dispense justice.'

133 Ibid at [26].
134 [2011] EWCA Crim 165.
135 *Charles* (n 130).
136 *B* (n 134).
137 *Charles* (n 130).
138 *B* (n 134).

Rape Sentencing and Plea-based Sentence Reductions

At step 4 of the Sentencing Council's Definitive Guideline, judges are directed to make an appropriate reduction in the sentence to reflect an offender's plea of guilty (Sentencing Council, 2013a: 12). Cole and Roberts (2018: 44) consider the term 'reduction' more appropriate than 'discount'.[139] The authors consider that 'discount' implies 'an unprincipled departure from an appropriate tariff' whereas plea-based reductions follow a principle, albeit one which is not retributive in nature (ibid, fn 1).

The allowance of a plea-based sentence reduction, or discount, is a long-standing but not uncontroversial aspect of English criminal procedure (Ashworth, 2015: 179–85, 186–88; Ashworth and Roberts, 2017: 861; Campbell et al, 2019: 327). It is also one of the most important principles in sentencing as it arises in the majority of cases falling to be sentenced by the courts (Wasik, 2014: 71), albeit that a lower proportion of those charged with sexual offences – and with rape in particular – plead guilty compared to those charged with other offences. In 2011, for example, 7,061 defendants were tried at the Crown Court for sexual offences, of whom 2,713 (38.4%) pleaded guilty. The pleas varied by sexual offence group, however, with defendants charged with rape of a female having the lowest proportion of guilty pleas at 20.8 per cent (see Ministry of Justice et al, 2013: 34).

In terms of section 144(1) of the Criminal Justice Act 2003, in sentencing an offender who has pleaded guilty to an offence, the court must take into account (a) the stage in the proceedings at which the offender indicated his intention to plead guilty; and (b) the circumstances in which this indication was given. Sentencing practice is governed by the Sentencing Council's Definitive Guideline on Reduction in Sentence for a Guilty Plea (Sentencing Council, 2017), an updated version of the guideline issued by the Sentencing Guidelines Council 10 years previously (SGC, 2007b). The purpose of the guideline is to encourage those who are going to plead guilty to do so as early in the court process as possible (Sentencing Council, 2017: 4). The guideline lists the standard rationales for allowing a reduction in sentence for a guilty plea: the plea normally reduces the impact of the crime upon victims; saves victims and witnesses from having to testify; and saves public time and money on investigations and trials (Sentencing Council, 2017: 4).

Judges are directed to consider the guilty plea independently of the offender's personal mitigation (Sentencing Council, 2017: 4). Thus, the guilty plea discount principle derives from the need for the effective administration of justice and not as an aspect of mitigation. The maximum level of reduction in sentence for a guilty plea is a third, this being appropriate where the plea is indicated at the first hearing of the case. If the plea is indicated after the first stage of proceedings, then the discount reduces to a quarter. There is a sliding scale of reduction thereafter, decreasing to a maximum of one-tenth on the first day of trial. The reduction should normally be decreased further, even to zero, if the guilty plea is entered during the trial (2017: 5).

[139] *Cf* the terminology used by the courts in Scotland ('guilty plea discounts'), considered in Chapter 5.

The Sentencing Council issued a consultation paper in February 2016 on reductions in sentence for a guilty plea prior to issuing the Definitive Guideline (Sentencing Council, 2016). The Council's proposals were criticised by practitioners as prioritising consistency at the expense of defendants (Cohen-Lask, 2016: 9); as writing out the role and value of defence counsel in assessing the evidence in any given case (Harris, 2016: 15); as placing pressure on certain defendants to plead guilty (Padfield, 2016b: 302); and as circumscribing judicial discretion, depriving judges of the ability to do justice in the individual case (Stanbury, 2016: 6–7; *cf* Treacy, 2016).

Particular tensions surround the practice in cases such as rape where the offence is especially serious and morally repugnant (Leverick, 2014: 348 and 2013: 263).[140] While condign punishment is usually required for offences of rape, the benefits of a guilty plea – principally, in cases of rape, saving the victim from what may be the ordeal of giving evidence and cost savings to the criminal justice system – accrue equally in cases where the offender's conduct is morally reprehensible as from less serious offences.

A related question is whether an offender who has no realistic option other than to plead guilty should still receive credit for his plea? Although pre-guideline practice suggested that the discount or reduction could be withheld in such circumstances (Ashworth, 2015: 184; Easton and Piper, 2016: 97; Thomas, 2012: 562; Wasik, 2014: 74; and the decision in *R v Costen*[141]), the Definitive Guideline now states that the benefits of a guilty plea apply regardless of the strength of the evidence against an offender. Judges are specifically directed that they should not take the strength of the evidence into account when determining the level of reduction (Sentencing Council, 2017: 4). This can be compared with the previous SGC guideline, in force until 31 May 2017, which stated that where the prosecution case was 'overwhelming' it may not be appropriate to give the *full* reduction of one third; while there was previously a presumption in favour of the full reduction, a lesser reduction of 20 per cent could be given for a plea at the first reasonable opportunity where the Crown case was indeed overwhelming (SGC, 2007b: 6).

The tensions that arise in such cases and the subsequent balance that the court must attempt to strike, are well illustrated by the decision in *R v Wilson*.[142] Here, the appellant pleaded guilty within a few days of his arrest to two counts of rape of a child under 13 and to various other sexual offences committed against teenaged girls over the internet. The victims in the charges of rape were two three-year-old girls; the appellant filmed himself on his mobile phone orally penetrating both girls. The appellant committed the rapes in the course of his employment at a nursery which the victims attended. Following his pleas of guilty, the judge sentenced him to life imprisonment on the two counts of rape with a minimum term of 15 years on each count. While the judge reduced the sentences imposed in respect

140 See the discussion in Chapter 5.
141 (1989) 11 Cr App R (S) 182.
142 [2012] 2 Cr App R (S) 77.

of the internet offences to reflect the appellant's guilty pleas, she declined to allow a discount in sentence for the rapes, noting that the appellant had 'no option but to plead guilty'.[143] On appeal, it was argued, *inter alia*, that the judge had misdirected herself by withholding any credit for the guilty pleas on the charges of rape.

In allowing this aspect of the appeal, the Court referred to the SGC Definitive Guideline then in force and noted that a guilty plea has a distinct benefit even in an overwhelming case.[144] While the Court understood the sentencing judge's reluctance to make any allowance for the guilty pleas in relation to the charges of rape, it considered that uncertainty and inconsistency in sentencing would result if the guideline were to be disregarded.[145] In the circumstances, it was held that the sentencing judge should have made some allowance for the appellant's guilty pleas. The Court took what it described as 'a broad view' of the appropriate allowance and did not permit itself to be 'beguiled by mathematics': the notional determinate sentence was reduced from 30 years to 27 years.[146] This approach was later endorsed by the Court of Appeal in *R v Caley*[147] where it was noted that the various public benefits which underlie the practice of guilty plea reductions apply just as much to overwhelming cases as to less strong ones.[148] The Court also noted that while it cannot be assumed that defendants will make rational decisions or ones which are born of any inclination to cooperate with the system, those who do so merit recognition.[149]

The message from the Court of Appeal is clear. One can sympathise with the judge who, when faced with a defendant who has pleaded guilty to rape, either allows a lesser reduction in sentence than is mandated in the Sentencing Council's Definitive Guideline, or declines to allow a reduction at all due to the serious nature of the offence. The judge who follows this course will, however, have misdirected herself and will, in all likelihood, have her sentence overturned on appeal.[150] A plea of guilty to a charge of rape will result in the same administrative benefits as a plea of guilty to a lesser offence and the rapist is entitled to credit for his guilty plea in the same way as any other offender.

[143] Ibid at [25].
[144] Ibid at [29].
[145] Ibid at [30]–[32].
[146] Ibid at [33].
[147] [2013] 2 Cr App R (S) 47.
[148] Ibid at [24].
[149] Ibid.
[150] Compare the approach in Scotland and the decision in *Murray v HMA* [2013] HCJAC 3; 2013 SCCR 88, discussed in Chapter 5.

5

A 'Radically Different' Approach

Rape Sentencing in Scotland

Introduction

The law relating to sexual offences in Scotland was completely recast by the Sexual Offences (Scotland) Act 2009.[1] The 2009 Act comprised a comprehensive rewriting and codification of the substantive law of sexual offences. It broadly followed the recommendations of the Scottish Law Commission's *Report on Rape and Other Sexual Offences* (SLC, 2007) and adopted the terms of the Commission's draft Bill. The Act abolished certain common law offences and previous statutory sexual offences; created new offences; and redefined certain existing offences. Some of the redefined offences were modelled on the provisions in the Sexual Offences Act 2003, which recast the law of sexual offences in England and Wales[2] (AN Brown, 2015: 1).

The definition of rape was extended by section 1 of the 2009 Act to include vaginal, oral and anal penetration. Section 1 came into force on 1 December 2010. In terms of section 1(1) of the Act:

> 'If a person ('A') with A's penis –
>
> (a) without another person ('B') consenting and
> (b) without any reasonable belief that B consents,
>
> penetrates to any extent, either intending to do so or reckless as to whether there is penetration, the vagina, anus or mouth of B, then A commits an offence, to be known as the offence of rape.'

The scope of the crime was thus widened beyond that of the previous common law offence of rape, which required penile penetration of the vagina and which could only be committed against a woman (Christie, 2001: 508). The 2009 Act abolished the offence of rape at common law.[3] The inclusion of references to the anus and mouth in section 1 of the 2009 Act recognised for the first time in Scots law that men could be victims of rape (Cowan, 2019: 24); male-on-male rape had previously been prosecuted in Scotland as indecent assault.

[1] Hereinafter 'the 2009 Act'.
[2] See Chapter 4.
[3] The 2009 Act, s 52(a)(i).

The relevant penalties are set out in Schedule 2 of the Act, the maximum sentence for rape being life imprisonment. As Freiberg observes, the statutory maximum penalty serves important symbolic and practical functions by providing both the public and sentencers with a guide to the seriousness with which the community views the offence. The maximum sentence of life imprisonment thus reflects the level of communal abhorrence while also providing a directive to judges on how to weigh the gravity of the offence (Freiberg, 2002: 242).

Another common law offence which the 2009 Act abolished[4] was that of 'clandestine injury to women'. This offence was traditionally libelled as an alternative to common law rape in circumstances where the accused had intercourse with a woman who was either sleeping or who had been rendered unconscious by alcohol or drugs (Christie, 2001: 517). Until 2002, the *actus reus* of rape required that the woman's will had been overcome by force, or the threat of force on the part of the accused (Christie, 2001: 508–12). Since the act of rape required force, intercourse with a sleeping or unconscious woman was not regarded as rape. In these circumstances, the crime of 'clandestine injury' would be libelled, this offence being a species of indecent assault rather than rape (see Chalmers, 2010: 30; Chalmers and Leverick, 2017: 459; Cowan, 2010: 155; Gane, 1992: 46–7; and the decision in *Rodgers v Hamilton*[5]).

Concern about the narrow *actus reus* of rape at common law led the Lord Advocate, the head of public prosecutions in Scotland, to make a reference to the High Court in 2001. In *Lord Advocate's Reference (No 1 of 2001)*[6] the Court, on a majority of five to two, fundamentally altered the common law of rape by overruling previous authority and recasting the *actus reus*: rather than requiring force or the threat of force, the new *actus reus* was constituted by a man having sexual intercourse with a woman 'without her consent'.[7] Thus, clandestine injury as a crime distinct from rape arguably ceased to exist following the changes to the definition of common law rape effected by the *Lord Advocate's Reference*[8] (Christie, 2005: 146; Cubie, 2016: 185; Jones and Taggart, 2015: 244).[9] Between 22 March 2002 when the decision in the *Lord Advocate's Reference*[10] was issued and the coming into force of section 1 of the 2009 Act, cases where the victim was asleep, intoxicated or unconscious, which would previously have been regarded as clandestine injury rather than rape, were properly regarded as rape (Chalmers and Leverick, 2017: 515). As we shall see, however, the sentences imposed by the Scottish courts for offences of rape involving unconscious victims (ie rapes that would *formerly* have been libelled as clandestine injury) have heavily influenced the setting of 'benchmark' or 'starting point' sentences in all cases of rape.[11]

[4] Ibid, s 52(a)(ii).
[5] 1994 SLT 822.
[6] 2002 SCCR 435.
[7] Ibid at [44] (per the Lord Justice General (Cullen)).
[8] *Lord Advocate's Reference (No 1 of 2001)* (n 6).
[9] Ibid at [32] and *Spendiff v HMA* 2005 1 JC 338 at [5].
[10] *Lord Advocate's Reference (No 1 of 2001)* (n 6).
[11] See below.

A final point relating to the substantive law of rape that appears to have influenced sentencing practice is the distinction between so-called 'forcible' and 'non-forcible' rape. Following the decision in the *Lord Advocate's Reference*[12] and the new *actus reus* which focused on the issue of consent rather than force, a distinction came to be drawn between 'forcible' and 'non-forcible' rape by academic commentators (eg see Ferguson and Raitt, 2006: 188, 190; and Chalmers, 2004: 145), by practitioners (see Scott, 2005: 68) and by the Appeal Court itself in a line of cases commencing with *Gilmour v HMA*[13] and concluding, most recently, with *Lennie v HMA.*[14] In *Keaney v HMA*,[15] however, a Bench comprising Ladies Paton, Smith and Cosgrove disapproved this distinction:

> 'The crime of rape is not subdivided into two subsets – forcible and non-forcible rape. There is a single crime and it occurs when a man has non-consensual sexual intercourse with a woman in circumstances where he has the relevant *mens rea*. That *mens rea* is unitary in character; it concerns a single concept, namely, the intention to have non-consensual intercourse with a woman knowing that she does not consent or being reckless (i.e. not caring) about that. The fact that the presence of that intention can be established in two different ways – knowledge of lack of consent and recklessness regarding consent – does not mean that different criminal conduct is involved.'[16]

In the recent decision in *Jamal v HMA*,[17] the Appeal Court observed that rape is regarded as a serious offence because it involves a violation of an individual's physical and sexual autonomy.[18] As we shall see, while the Appeal Court has disapproved the distinction between so-called 'forcible' and 'non-forcible' rape, there is nevertheless a marked difference in the sentences imposed for offences of rape committed using force and rapes where no force is used, often due to the victim's voluntary intoxication.[19]

Pragmatism, Flexibility and Individualisation: How Scottish Judges Sentence

The Traditional Approach to Sentencing

Scottish judges have traditionally enjoyed a very wide sentencing discretion (Hutton, 1999: 173; Moody, 1995: 219–20). There was no concept of a 'tariff' or

[12] *Lord Advocate's Reference (No 1 of 2001)* (n 6).
[13] 1993 JC 15 at 16.
[14] [2014] HCJAC 103; 2014 SCL 848 at [14].
[15] [2015] HCJAC 3; 2015 JC 259.
[16] At [15], *cf* Cowan, 2019: 31–32.
[17] [2019] HCJAC 22; 2019 SCCR 135.
[18] Ibid at [19].
[19] See below.

'going rate' for specific offences in Scotland (Hutton and Tata, 2010: 272). The High Court of Justiciary sitting as a court of appeal[20] was slow to issue any form of sentencing guidelines (Brown, 2017a: 163; AN Brown, 2010: 162; Hutton, 2008: 144; Sentencing Commission for Scotland, 2006: 15; Tata, 2013: 238). Nicholson reports that it was customary for judges hearing sentence appeals to say no more than was strictly necessary for the disposal of the particular case. The Appeal Court, Nicholson observes, had always adopted 'a pragmatic and individualised approach to questions of sentence' with cases being decided on their own facts and circumstances, rather than based on any declared principles (1992: 177; see also Stewart, 1997: 221).

The traditional antipathy of the Scottish judiciary towards sentencing guidelines may have been due to a fear that such formal guidelines would inhibit some of the flexibility of Scottish sentencing practice (Nicholson, 1992: 178; see also *HMA v May*[21]). Senior judges in Scotland were traditionally suspicious of developing any policy on sentencing. They saw the existence of any such policy as potentially undermining the principles of judicial independence and individualised justice in which every case is considered unique and is dealt with as such (Brown, 2017a: 64 and 166; Hutton and Tata, 2010: 272; Tata, 2010: 197). The traditional approach of Scottish judges to sentencing is explained by Tombs:

> 'In producing coherent sentencing narratives, sentencers consider the "facts" of the cases presented to them, the information provided about the circumstances surrounding the crime and offender in question and create interpretive frameworks within which those facts and circumstances considered relevant are evaluated … [I]n order to sentence individuals (as opposed to legal categories of offenders), [the Scottish judiciary] continue to draw on traditional sentencing values (for example, showing mercy) and their creative abilities in constructing meaningful stories about the crimes committed by contextualised individuals' (Tombs, 2008: 84–5).

This individualised approach to sentencing, in which judicial experience is a key factor, accords with practice in other common law jurisdictions in which judges enjoy a wide sentencing discretion. Indeed, in *Gemmell v HMA*,[22] a full Bench of the Appeal Court approved the view of the Canadian Supreme Court of sentencing as 'a delicate art' based on 'competence and expertise'[23] and the view of the High Court of Australia that sentencing is an 'instinctive synthesis' of the particular circumstances of the case and all relevant aggravating and mitigating factors.[24] In delivering the leading opinion[25] in *Gemmell*, the Lord Justice

[20] Hereinafter 'the Appeal Court'.

[21] 1995 SCCR 375 at 378.

[22] [2011] HCJAC 129; 2012 JC 223.

[23] See the decisions in *R v M (CA)* [1996] 1 SCR 500 and *R v LM* [2008] 2 SCR 163 approved in *Gemmell* (n 22) at [59].

[24] See the decision in *Markarian v The Queen* [2005] HCA 25 approved in *Gemmell* (n 22) at [59].

[25] In Scotland, judgments of the Appeal Court are referred to as 'opinions' (see Duncan, 1992: 79).

Clerk (Gill) stressed that the assessment of sentence is 'not a matter of precise arithmetical calculation' and noted that the exercise 'involves the making of an overall judgment from a consideration of numerous factors based on judicial experience'.[26]

Lord Gill's comments were later cited with approval by his successor as Lord Justice Clerk, Lord Carloway, in the decisions in *McGill v HMA*,[27] *Ferguson v HMA*[28] and *Wilson v Shanks*.[29] In *Ferguson*, for example, his Lordship explained, by reference to Lord Gill's observations in *Gemmell*, that:

> 'Sentencing is "a delicate art based on competence and expertise" rather than an exact science. A judge should not have to go through a formal checklist of procedures before arriving at the appropriate and proportionate sentence … [The sentencing decision], although often involving a complex matrix of factual and legal material, will be instantaneous, if not quite instinctive, once the material is ingathered and understood.'[30]

The debate over whether sentencing should involve structured decision-making or the judge's instinctive, or intuitive, synthesis of the particular facts and circumstances has been played out in the Australian courts over a number of years, with the High Court ultimately confirming instinctive synthesis as the correct sentencing methodology (see the decisions in *Markarian v The Queen*,[31] *Hili v The Queen*,[32] *Barbaro v The Queen*[33] and the discussion by Bagaric et al, 2018: 34–40; Brown, 2017a: 29–47; Freiberg, 2014: 228–33; and Krasnostein, 2015: 36–40). In *Gemmell*,[34] *McGill*,[35] *Wilson*[36] and *Ferguson*,[37] Scotland's two most senior judges similarly came down in favour of the instinctive synthesis approach. Thus, Scottish judges should aggregate and assess the factors bearing on a sentencing decision in a single, global process of reasoning. The judge must identify all relevant factors but, rather than ascribing a weight to each of them, she will simply arrive at an end sentence that represents her own intuitive synthesis of them. The decisions in *Gemmell, McGill, Wilson* and *Ferguson* all stress the importance of judicial knowledge, experience and discretion in sentencing. This does not mean, however, that judicial sentencing discretion in Scotland is entirely unconstrained, or that it is exercised without any regard to issues of principle.

[26] *Gemmell* (n 22) at [59].
[27] [2013] HCJAC 150; 2014 SCCR 46 at [13].
[28] [2014] HCJAC 19; 2014 SCCR 244.
[29] [2018] HCJAC 50; 2019 JC 1 at [18], the opinion of the Court being delivered by Lord Carloway as Lord Justice General.
[30] *Ferguson* (n 28) at [103] and [104], references omitted. See also Carloway, 2014: 18 and 22.
[31] *Markarian* (n 24).
[32] [2010] HCA 45.
[33] [2014] HCA 2.
[34] *Gemmell* (n 22).
[35] *McGill* (n 27).
[36] *Wilson* (n 29).
[37] *Ferguson* (n 28).

The Move Towards Sentencing Guidelines in Scotland

While discretion continues to be the hallmark of Scottish sentencing, the Appeal Court has a statutory power to issue sentencing guidelines (Ashworth and Roberts, 2017: 856). On one view, it would be *ultra vires* for the Appeal Court to give an exposition of sentencing policy in generality for similar cases (Shiels et al, 2015: 504). Section 118(7) of the Criminal Procedure Scotland Act 1995, however, allows the Appeal Court, when disposing of any solemn appeal, to 'pronounce an opinion on the sentence or other disposal or order which is appropriate in any similar case' – in other words, to issue sentencing guidelines. The recently established Sheriff Appeal Court is given the same power to issue guideline judgments in respect of summary appeals under section 189(7) of the 1995 Act. Under section 197 of the 1995 Act, a court passing sentence 'shall have regard' to any such guideline judgment. Thus, while the appellate courts are empowered to issue guidelines, they are very different in nature from the system of presumptively binding guidelines in England and Wales. As we have seen, English judges *must follow* any sentencing guidelines which are relevant to the offender's case unless satisfied that it would be contrary to the interests of justice to do so;[38] Scottish judges, however, are directed merely to *have regard* to any appellate guidelines. Sentencing guidelines in Scotland are merely directory: there is no statutory presumption that they will be followed by the judge in the individual case.

Formal sentencing guidelines took some time to emerge from the Appeal Court. The first case to make explicit use of the statutory provisions on sentencing guidelines was *Du Plooy and others v HMA*[39] on the operation of guilty plea discounts (see Leverick, 2008a: 44; 2008b: 308). The change in the attitude of the senior judiciary towards the desirability of sentencing guidelines is well illustrated by the remarks of the present Lord Justice General, Lord Carloway, in delivering the 2013 Sacro lecture. Having referred to the traditional approach of the Appeal Court in which, in an effort to preserve judicial discretion and flexibility in sentencing, no more was said in disposing of sentence appeals than was necessary to deal with the particular case, his Lordship continued:

> '[A]lthough a legal system ought to be careful and guard what is good in its traditions, built as they are upon the wisdom of generations, if the essentials are out of kilter with the fundamentals applied in all other similar civilised legal systems, it will often be time to look again at the domestic regime with a heavier degree of scrutiny' (Carloway, 2013: 10).

More recently, the former Lord Justice General, Lord Gill, notes how Scottish criminal law, procedure and sentencing have developed through an increased willingness to learn from other common law jurisdictions. In particular, his Lordship has remarked upon the trend in recent years for the Appeal Court to consider sentencing guidance from the courts of England, Canada, Australia and

[38] Coroners and Justice Act 2009, s 125(1), discussed in Chapter 4.
[39] 2005 1 JC 1.

New Zealand, along with academic and research literature, in issuing its own sentencing guidelines. This, his Lordship contends, is evidence of 'the new internationalism of Scottish jurisprudence … in which an open-minded High Court is prepared to derive every possible benefit from good law and good theory that is available in other jurisdictions in the English-speaking world' (Lord Gill, 2016: 17–18; see also Lord Reed, 2015: 13).[40]

The number of formal guideline judgments issued by the Appeal Court under section 118(7) of the 1995 Act has increased substantially in recent years. Such guidelines tend to be issued in relation to offences about which there is public or political concern, such as so-called 'cannabis farming',[41] downloading and distributing child pornography[42] and sexual offences committed in breach of a position of trust.[43] Guidelines may also be issued in relation to offences in respect of which the Appeal Court perceives there to be a degree of disparity in the sentences imposed by the lower courts. For example, the *Du Plooy*[44] guidelines on the practice of guilty plea discounting were later refined in *Spence v HMA*[45] and were subsequently tightened in *Gemmell v HMA*[46] and *Murray v HMA*.[47] As the Court explained in *Spence*,[48] the refined and clarified guidelines were required because of the inconsistent manner in which the courts had implemented the original *Du Plooy* guidelines (see Orr, 2007). Sentencing guidelines have thus been promulgated by the Appeal Court in respect of a variety of offences either to direct judges on to the path of consistency in approach, or to ensure that disposals are proportionate to the nature and seriousness of the offence in question (Brown, 2017a: 164).

The traditional concern of the Scottish judiciary that sentencing guidelines fetter the judge's discretion and inhibit the flexibility of the system has been addressed by repeated statements from the Appeal Court emphasising the discretionary nature of such guidelines. The Court has, for example, stressed that sentencing guidelines 'provide a structure for, but do not remove, judicial discretion';[49] that sentencing should 'always involve the sentencer's judgment and discretion';[50] that guidelines are intended to help sentencers, rather than being 'straitjacket[s] from which they cannot escape';[51] and that they are not to be 'interpreted and applied in a mechanistic way'.[52] The Appeal Court has also made it clear that, while guidelines 'assist

[40] *Cf* Cowan (2019: 46) who laments 'the worrying tendency of the Scottish courts to take a narrow view of the extent to which other jurisdictions have much to teach us' [*sic*].

[41] *Lin v HMA* [2007] HCJAC 62; 2008 JC 142.

[42] *HMA v Graham* [2010] HCJAC 50; 2011 JC 1 and *Wood v HMA* [2017] HCJAC 2; 2017 JC 185.

[43] *HMA v Collins* [2016] HCJAC 102; 2017 JC 99, discussed later in this chapter.

[44] *Du Plooy* (n 39).

[45] [2007] HCJAC 64; 2008 JC 174.

[46] *Gemmell* (n 22).

[47] [2013] HCJAC 3; 2013 SCCR 88, discussed later in this chapter.

[48] *Spence* (n 45) at [14].

[49] *Graham* (n 42) at [21].

[50] Ibid at [22].

[51] Ibid.

[52] *Neill v HMA* [2014] HCJAC 67 at [11].

in the exercise of [the sentencer's] discretion', the decision as to the appropriate sentence lies with the sentencing judge alone.[53] As the Lord Justice Clerk (Gill) stated in his dissenting opinion in *Mitchell v HMA*,[54] sentencing guidelines are subject always to the discretion of the sentencer and, on appeal, to the discretion of the Appeal Court.[55]

The Use of English Sentencing Guidelines as a 'Cross-Check'

While neither guideline judgments from the English Court of Appeal (Criminal Division), nor Definitive Guidelines issued by the Sentencing Guidelines Council and latterly by the Sentencing Council in England and Wales[56] apply in Scotland, the Appeal Court has acknowledged that Scottish judges may, in certain circumstances, find reference to English sentencing guidelines useful. The Appeal Court has, on several occasions, encouraged judges to have regard to English sentencing guidelines in appropriate cases.

The first decision of the Appeal Court that specifically approved recourse to English sentencing guidelines, albeit with certain caveats, was the Crown appeal against sentence in *HMA v Roulston*.[57] *Roulston* involved a conviction for causing death by dangerous driving under section 1 of the Road Traffic Act 1988 (a UK statute), an offence in respect of which sentencing guidelines had been issued by the Court of Appeal some two years earlier in *R v Cooksley*.[58] In the course of its appeal against the sentence of three years' imprisonment imposed on the respondent on the grounds of undue leniency, the Crown relied on various factors based on the English guidelines. In delivering the opinion of the Court allowing the Crown's appeal, the Lord Justice Clerk (Gill) noted that:

> 'It is helpful, particularly in offences under UK legislation, to look at the guidelines applied by the English courts and to consider, to the extent that they are relevant, the specific factors on which those guidelines are based. But in doing so the court should not lose sight of its overall duty to assess the sentence that in all the circumstances of the case most justly reflects the culpability of the accused and the mitigating factors, if any, that are found to exist.'[59]

In a series of more recent decisions, the Appeal Court has approved judicial recourse to English sentencing guidelines, including the Sentencing Council's Definitive Guideline on Sexual Offences (Sentencing Council, 2013a), as a form

[53] *Jakovlev v HMA* [2011] HCJAC 90; 2012 JC 120 at [11]. See also *Rippon v HMA* 2012 SCCR 699 at [3], *Deeney v HMA* [2015] HCJAC 5; 2015 SCL 329 at [2], and *Wood* (n 42) at [28].

[54] [2011] HCJAC 10; 2012 JC 13.

[55] Ibid at [15].

[56] See the discussion in Chapter 4.

[57] [2005] HCJAC 12; 2006 JC 1.

[58] [2004] 1 Cr App R (S) 1.

[59] *Roulston* (n 57) at [17]. See also *HMA v Macpherson* 2004 SCCR 579 at [10] and *Gill v Thomson* [2010] HCJAC 99; 2012 JC 137 at [20].

of comparator or 'cross-check'. This effectively amounts to Scottish judges proofing their proposed sentences against the guidelines operating in England and Wales. In delivering the opinion of the Court in *HMA v AB*,[60] a Crown appeal against sentence in a case of rape, the Lord Justice Clerk (Carloway) provided the following guidance for Scottish judges on how the English Definitive Guideline on Sexual Offences could be used:

> 'The Sexual Offences Definitive Guideline is a useful comparator from a neighbouring jurisdiction, but one which should not be applied too rigidly … It must be borne in mind that in England and Wales there are statutorily defined sentencing purposes (Criminal Justice Act 2003, s.142) which are not directly applicable in Scotland. Nevertheless, *the relevant sentencing range is a matter with which a sentence selected in Scotland might be cross checked to see if any major disparity appears*.'[61]

In *Sutherland v HMA*,[62] an appeal against sentence following the appellant's conviction for having been concerned in the large-scale supply of heroin contrary to section 4(3)(b) of the Misuse of Drugs Act 1971 (again, a UK statute), the Lord Justice Clerk (Carloway) echoed the dicta of Lord Justice Clerk Gill in *Roulston*[63] when he stated that:

> 'Definitive Guidelines from the Sentencing Council of England and Wales often provide a useful cross-check for sentences in Scotland especially where the offences are regulated, as here, by a UK statute and there are identical sentencing *maxima*. They should not, however, be applied in Scotland in a rigid or mechanistic fashion, given the differences in sentencing purposes, practices and regimes between the two jurisdictions.'[64]

The Appeal Court has thus cautioned against uncritical acceptance and application of English sentencing guidelines. In so doing, it has stressed the importance of Scottish judges relying on domestic precedent. In *Geddes v HMA*,[65] for example, the Lord Justice Clerk (Carloway) opined that:

> 'It is important to observe that, while the court has encouraged sentencing judges to 'have regard' to the English guideline[s] … it has not said that [they] should 'be interpreted and applied in a mechanistic way' … In order to ensure a degree of consistency in this jurisdiction, albeit paying due regard to local circumstances, it may be equally important to have regard to existing precedent.'[66]

Lord Carloway later reiterated this proposition in delivering the opinion of the Court in *Scottish Power Generation Ltd v HMA*.[67] By reference to the decision in *Geddes*,[68] his Lordship confirmed the importance of Scottish judges looking to

[60] [2015] HCJAC 106; 2016 SCCR 47.
[61] Ibid at [13], emphasis added and references omitted.
[62] [2015] HCJAC 115; 2016 SCCR 41.
[63] *Roulston* (n 57).
[64] *Sutherland* (n 62) at [20].
[65] [2015] HCJAC 43; 2015 SCCR 230.
[66] Ibid at [18].
[67] [2016] HCJAC 99; 2017 JC 85.
[68] *Geddes* (n 65).

existing Scottish precedent in order to discover what levels of penalty are appropriate for the offence in question, albeit acknowledging that this task may involve a cross-check with any relevant English guidelines.[69] Most recently, in *HMA v Collins*,[70] a differently constituted Bench made the following observations on judicial recourse to sentencing guidelines from other jurisdictions and on the use of domestic precedent:

> 'Among the purposes of issuing sentencing guidelines is the identification of a general consensus as to what is appropriate in respect of particular types of offending in particular circumstances so that then, by an application of the guideline, the court can achieve a degree of consistency which commends itself as rational and just. Regard can of course be had to the practice in other jurisdictions but where there is no domestic guideline … the first resort in attempting to identify what level of penalty is generally considered appropriate to a particular sort of case should be Scottish precedent.'[71]

It is clear that while it is appropriate in sentencing cases of rape for Scottish judges to have regard to the current English guidelines (Sentencing Council, 2013a),[72] a rigid or mechanistic adherence to those guidelines is to be avoided. What the Appeal Court described in *HMA v McKeever*[73] as 'slavish adherence' to English guidelines is certainly not appropriate for, as the Court observed in *Milligan v HMA*,[74] in what was arguably something of an understatement, the Scottish approach to sentencing is 'rather less formulaic than the English sentencing guidelines'.[75] Furthermore, Scottish judges must have regard, in the first instance at least, to existing Scottish precedent in reaching their decisions as to sentence. Thus, in sentencing rape, the English Definitive Guideline is to be used as a cross-check on the sentence arrived at once the judge has considered relevant domestic authority to see if any major disparity appears.

Although it seems that, in the event of such a major disparity arising, Scottish judges are expected to increase or decrease their proposed sentences for rape to bring them broadly into line with the ranges set out in the English Definitive Guideline, the extent to which this is routinely done by judges is questionable. Certainly, the Appeal Court has not led by example in this regard.

The decision in *HMA v CH*,[76] for instance, has already been considered in Chapter 3; it established the principle that filming or photographing a sexual offence is to be regarded by the Scottish courts as a serious aggravating factor in sentencing.[77] To recap, in this case the Crown successfully appealed as unduly lenient the *cumulo* sentence of three years and nine months' imprisonment, discounted

[69] *Scottish Power Generation Ltd* (n 67) at [35] and [38].
[70] *Collins* (n 43), considered later in this chapter.
[71] Ibid at [30] per Lord Brodie delivering the opinion of the Court (references omitted).
[72] See Chapter 4.
[73] [2016] HCJAC 43; 2016 SCL 564 at [16].
[74] [2015] HCJAC 84; 2015 SCL 984.
[75] Ibid at [5].
[76] [2017] HCJAC 82; 2017 SCCR 587.
[77] See Chapter 3.

from a headline sentence of five years, imposed following the respondent's pleas of guilty to charges of orally raping a three-year-old boy and to making indecent images of the child by filming the offence on his mobile phone. In allowing the Crown's appeal and imposing concurrent sentences of six years (discounted from eight years) on the charge of rape and 24 months (discounted from 32 months) on the indecent images charge, the Appeal Court considered the English Definitive Guideline. The Court accepted the Crown's submission that the preponderance of aggravating factors present in the case would shift the sentence indicated by the guideline upwards from the starting point of 13 years towards 15 years, prior to any discount for the respondent's guilty plea.[78] In making reference to certain domestic authorities cited by counsel for the respondent, however, the Court continued:

> 'Against that, while we did not find [counsel] for the respondent's review of previous cases of direct assistance, given their different factual circumstances, overall these cases do suggest that, for whatever reason, the English regime as expressed in the Definitive Guideline produces a level of sentence which is higher than that which would be considered appropriate in Scotland in cases of this sort. Useful as the English guidelines have been found to be as a cross check or comparator, such instances of divergence in result will occur.'[79]

The Court, therefore, declined to apply the English Definitive Guideline, although it was held that the various aggravating factors within the Guideline identified by the Crown were all considerations that were required to be taken into account when assessing the relative seriousness of an offence committed in Scotland.[80] Nevertheless, the disposal in this case is troubling and raises important issues of proportionality in the Scottish courts' sentencing of rape, particularly from a comparative perspective. It is surely a matter of concern that even following the Crown's successful appeal in *CH*, the respondent's headline sentence of eight years' imprisonment selected by the Appeal Court for the offence of rape of a young child was still, as the Court itself acknowledged, some seven years less than the respondent would have received for the corresponding offence in England and Wales, had the offence been committed in similar circumstances (see Brown, 2018b: 6). Rather than simply noting that 'such instances of divergence in result will occur',[81] it would arguably have been preferable for the Appeal Court to have issued its own sentencing guidelines for rape by fully discussing relevant aggravating and mitigating factors (Brown, 2018b: 7).

This aspect of the decision in *CH* also raises questions as to what a judge should do when, in sentencing in a case of rape, an application of the English Definitive Guideline highlights a major disparity between her proposed sentence and the range of sentence applicable in England and Wales. Given that the Appeal Court

[78] *CH* (n 76) at [33].
[79] Ibid at [37].
[80] Ibid at [38].
[81] Ibid at [37].

in *CH* acknowledged that more severe sentences are imposed by the English courts for the crime of rape, the judge's proposed sentence is likely to be lower than is indicated by the Definitive Guideline. In these circumstances, should the judge follow the Appeal Court's guidance in *AB*[82] and *Sutherland*,[83] use the Definitive Guideline as a cross-check, apply it in a flexible manner and perhaps increase her sentence accordingly? Alternatively, is it acceptable for the judge to follow the same course as the Appeal Court in *CH*,[84] note that divergences in result will occur and impose the sentence that she had originally considered appropriate, even though there may be many years' difference between her sentence and that indicated by the Definitive Guideline?

Recent appellate decisions suggest that neither sentencing judges nor the Appeal Court itself routinely apply the Definitive Guideline as a cross-check in sentencing rape. The decision in *Gubinas and Radavicius v HMA*,[85] for example, has already been considered in Chapter 1. This was a case of multiple perpetrator rape. The two appellants and a co-accused abducted the intoxicated victim and forced her to consume more alcohol before sexually assaulting and raping her over several hours. The assaults were filmed using mobile phones. Given that the appellants were convicted after trial, there was no question of their receiving a discount in sentence to reflect any guilty plea. Nevertheless, the appellants and their co-accused were each sentenced to four-and-a-half years' imprisonment at Glasgow High Court.

Perhaps unsurprisingly, the appellants sought only to appeal their convictions (the appeals ultimately being unsuccessful) and did not seek leave to appeal what appear to be, in the circumstances, remarkably lenient sentences (see Brown, 2017b: 8). The case featured six of the eight 'harm' factors set out in the English Definitive Guideline (namely the abduction of the victim; her prolonged detention; the sustained nature of the incident; the additional degradation of the victim; her vulnerability; and the additional violence used against her) and four 'culpability' factors (the significant degree of planning; the fact that there were multiple perpetrators; the use of alcohol on the victim to facilitate the offences; and the recording of the offences). Thus, it fell to be considered as a 'Category 1A' case on an application of the English guidelines (Sentencing Council, 2013a: 10). In terms of the Definitive Guideline, this results in a starting point of 15 years' imprisonment (more than three times the sentence imposed on the appellants at Glasgow High Court), with a range of 13 to 19 years' imprisonment (Sentencing Council, 2013a: 11).

Thus, in terms of the decision in *AB*,[86] a 'major disparity' clearly exists. It appears that the sentencing judge in *Gubinas and Radavicius* did not use the Definitive Guideline as a cross-check. Had his Lordship done so, it would have

[82] *AB* (n 60).
[83] *Sutherland* (n 62).
[84] *CH* (n 76).
[85] [2017] HCJAC 59; 2018 JC 45.
[86] *AB* (n 60).

been evident that the sentences of four-and-a-half years' imprisonment were arguably unduly lenient in terms of the test set by the Appeal Court in *HMA v Bell*,[87] in that they fell outside the range of sentences which the judge, applying his mind to all the relevant factors, could reasonably have considered appropriate.

Amongst other recent examples, reference can be made to the decisions in *JGC v HMA*[88] and *Ahmadi v HMA*.[89] The appellant in *JGC* was convicted after trial of certain historic sexual offences, including rape at common law, committed against his fiancée's younger sister when she was aged between seven and 12. The victim was raped on over 10 occasions over a period of some four-and-a-half years, the appellant having groomed her from the age of seven. The trial judge imposed a *cumulo* sentence of 10 years' imprisonment. Although the sentence was upheld on appeal, if the provisions of the Definitive Guideline for the corresponding offence in England and Wales (rape of a child under 13) were to be applied, a sentence in the range of 13 to 19 years' imprisonment is indicated, with a starting point of 16 years (Sentencing Council, 2013a: 29–30). The existence of certain additional aggravating factors, including the appellant's previous convictions for child pornography offences, ejaculation and the location of the offences in the family home (Sentencing Council, 2013a: 31), would arguably result in an upward adjustment towards 17 or perhaps 18 years' imprisonment had the appellant been convicted of similar offences in England and Wales (see Brown, 2018c).

In *Ahmadi*,[90] in which the appellant raped the intoxicated victim having entered her bedroom uninvited, a sentence of seven years' imprisonment was reduced on appeal to five years with a two-year extension period. The circumstances were such that an application of the Definitive Guideline suggests that a starting point of eight years' imprisonment was appropriate, with a range of between seven and nine years. Thus, the original sentence, whilst arguably somewhat lenient, should have remained undisturbed (see Brown, 2016a).

Taken together, the decisions in *CH*,[91] *Gubinas and Radavicius*,[92] *JGC*[93] and *Ahmadi*[94] suggest that judges, both at first instance and also in the Appeal Court, do not, in fact, apply the guidance in *AB*.[95] The English Definitive Guideline on Sexual Offences (Sentencing Council, 2013a) does not appear to be routinely used as a cross-check by Scottish judges to gauge their disposals in sentencing cases of rape. Were the Definitive Guideline to be used as a cross-check, it would, in all likelihood, result in the consistent imposition of more severe sentences for rape in the Scottish courts.

[87] 1995 SCCR 244 at 250.
[88] [2017] HCJAC 83; 2017 SCL 1042.
[89] [2016] HCJAC 7; 2016 SCL 329.
[90] *Ahmadi* (n 89).
[91] *CH* (n 76).
[92] *Gubinas and Radavicius* (n 85).
[93] *JGC* (n 88).
[94] *Ahmadi* (n 89).
[95] *AB* (n 60).

The Scottish Sentencing Council

The Scottish Sentencing Council ('the SSC'), an advisory body chaired by Scotland's second most senior judge, the Lord Justice Clerk, was established in October 2015 by sections 1 to 13 of the Criminal Justice and Licensing (Scotland) Act 2010.[96] Although the 2010 Act received Royal Assent on 6 August 2010, the provisions establishing the SSC were not brought into force for almost five years (see Brown, 2017a: 160 and Chalmers, 2019: 487).

The SSC has six judicial members, including the Lord Justice Clerk as chair, three legal members and three lay members.[97] It is tasked with promoting consistency in sentencing, assisting the development of sentencing policy and promoting greater awareness and understanding of sentencing policy and practice.[98] The SSC has a statutory duty to prepare sentencing guidelines for submission to the High Court of Justiciary for its consideration.[99] Its proposed guidelines are submitted to the High Court following a period of consultation.[100] The High Court may either approve or reject the proposed guidelines in whole or in part, with or without modifications[101] (see Ashworth and Roberts, 2017: 858; Brown, 2017a: 160–62; and Dorrian, 2017). The primacy of the High Court as a source of sentencing guidance is thus preserved. In the course of its opinion in *HMA v Collins*,[102] for example, the Appeal Court provided a reminder that the SSC does not itself determine what sentences are appropriate, that its role is simply to advise the Court and that it is an advisory body.[103]

If the High Court does approve guidelines submitted by the SSC, then all courts are then required to 'have regard' to them[104] and to state their reasons if the guidelines are not followed.[105] Thus, unlike in England and Wales, the guidelines do not have a binding status (Carloway, 2016: 14). This ensures that the principle of judicial autonomy in relation to sentencing is retained (Welsh, 2010: 810).

The Council's First Guideline and the Principle of Proportionality

On 30 October 2018, the High Court of Justiciary approved the SSC's first (and so far, only) guideline on the *Principles and Purposes of Sentencing* (SSC, 2018a). The guideline, which followed a three-month public consultation period in 2017, came into effect on 26 November 2018 and applies to all offenders sentenced in Scotland.

[96] Hereinafter 'the 2010 Act'.
[97] Criminal Justice and Licensing (Scotland) Act 2010, Sch 1, para 1.
[98] Ibid, s 2.
[99] Ibid, s 3.
[100] Ibid, s 4.
[101] Ibid, s 5(3).
[102] *Collins* (n 43).
[103] Ibid at [29].
[104] Criminal Justice and Licensing (Scotland) Act 2010, s 6(1).
[105] Ibid, s 6(2).

The core principle expressed in the guideline is that 'sentences in Scotland must be fair and proportionate' (SSC, 2018a: 3). It then sets out a series of requirements following from this principle. They comprise the requirement that 'all relevant factors' be considered by the sentencer (including the seriousness of the offence, the impact on the victim and the offender's circumstances) and acceptance of the principle of parsimony in sentencing. Certain duties required of sentencers follow, namely a duty to give reasons; a duty to act lawfully and to 'have regard to any sentencing guidelines which are applicable'; to treat people equally and without discrimination; and to 'treat similar cases in a similar way, assisting consistency and predictability' (SSC, 2018a: 3).

Moving to the purposes of sentencing, the guideline states that '[t]he sentence selected should best achieve the purposes of sentencing that are appropriate to the particular case but should always reflect the core principle of fairness and proportionality' (SSC, 2018a: 4). The guideline then lists the following purposes of sentencing: protection of the public; punishment; rehabilitation of offenders; reparation; and denunciation. Interestingly, these purposes are listed 'in no particular order' (ibid) so it is left to the individual sentencer to balance the purposes according to the facts and circumstances of the particular case.

In an accompanying press release, the Lord Justice Clerk (Dorrian), as chair of the SSC, lauded the High Court's approval of the guideline as 'an historic moment … [marking] a new approach to supporting sentencing consistency and decision making'. Her Ladyship suggested that, as the fundamental principles and purposes of sentencing had never before been expressly defined in Scotland, the guideline 'will have significant benefits both to the public and the courts'. Her Ladyship noted that the SSC had 'drawn on expertise and research from across Scotland and other jurisdictions … We were clear from the outset that our approach to developing guidelines will always be evidence-based' (SSC, 2018b).

A somewhat different, and arguably more realistic, view of the SSC's guideline is offered by John Scott QC. A solicitor advocate, Scott was appointed as the SSC's first solicitor member in 2015 and held the post until October 2018. In an interview in the *Journal of the Law Society of Scotland* at the time of demitting office, Scott acknowledged that the guideline is essentially 'a statement to the public primarily of what our system is about'. Scott very candidly accepted that '[s]ome of it, to some people, is going to seem like a statement of the obvious', but proceeded to suggest that the guideline could serve an educational purpose for those unfamiliar with the Scottish criminal justice system and with Scottish sentencing law, procedure and practice (Scott, 2018: 14).

The guideline uses non-technical language throughout and has clearly been drafted for the benefit of the public, rather than the judiciary or the legal profession. It does no more than re-state principles and purposes that are well understood by judges and practitioners, albeit in terms readily understood by the layperson. For example, the duty that the guideline imposes on judges to 'have regard to any sentencing guidelines which are applicable' (SSC, 2018a: 3) is no more than a restatement of the statutory duty imposed on judges to have regard to guidelines.[106] The guideline's list of penal purposes, meanwhile, are familiar to all judges and have always influenced sentencing decisions (see Brown, 2017a: 113–20; Lothian, 2004: 44; Nicholson, 1992: 178–82 and 1981: 201–6). Even its identification of proportionality as the key principle governing sentencing amounts to nothing new since proportionality has always had a role both in sentencing policy (O'Malley, 2011: 10; von Hirsch, 2017: 20; 2009: 118; von Hirsch and Ashworth, 2005: 131) and in the sentencing practice of the Scottish courts.[107]

The guideline also bears a striking similarity to section 142 of the Criminal Justice Act 2003.[108] This section, which sets out the purposes of sentencing in England and Wales in near identical terms to the SSC's guideline, has been widely criticised both by academics and the senior judiciary. The main criticism of section 142 is that while it provides a list of sentencing purposes, like the SSC's guideline, it does not provide any hierarchy between them (see Brown, 2017a: 113–14; Dingwall, 2008: 402; Koffman, 2006: 296; Tarling, 2006: 39; von Hirsch and Roberts, 2004: 642; and Weitzdörfer et al, 2018: 208).

It is self-evident that the purposes of sentencing listed in both section 142 of the 2003 Act and the SSC's guideline are not always consistent: reform, rehabilitation and punishment are often not easily reconciled (see Judge, 2015: 263; Mosonyi, 2017: 284, 288; and Padfield, 2016a: 250; 2013: 33–34). As Ashworth and Player (2005: 825) observe, it is 'plain as a pikestaff' that these purposes may (and, in fact, often will) conflict in their application to particular cases. In criticising section 142 of the 2003 Act as 'fatuous', Ashworth (2004: 528) explains that 'it is simply a list that provides no means of resolving the inevitable conflict between purposes and establishes no order of priority'. Indeed, Ashworth (2015: 100) suggests that declarations such as section 142 'serve no useful purpose and should be abolished'. In particular, Ashworth argues that such declarations are 'confusing and unhelpful, inasmuch as they proceed without apparent awareness of the deficiencies of principle and of evidence affecting some of the declared purposes' (ibid).

Precisely the same criticism can be levelled at the SSC's guideline. The guideline is of very little practical value since it merely reflects pre-existing sentencing law and fails to offer any guidance as to when one purpose should take precedence over the others (see generally O'Malley, 2011: 239). Given the Lord Justice Clerk's emphasis on the guideline being 'evidence-based' and having drawn from research in other jurisdictions (SSC, 2018b, above), the SSC's decision to frame its first guideline in terms so similar to the much criticised English statutory provisions appears ill-considered and is both ill-advised and perplexing.

Sentencing statutes in other common law jurisdictions frequently include a list of penal purposes in similar terms to both section 142 of the 2003 Act and the SSC's guideline (O'Malley, 2016: 44–45, 2011: 238). The explicit recognition of the

[106] Under the Criminal Procedure (Scotland) Act 1995, s 197 and the Criminal Justice and Licensing (Scotland) Act 2010, s 6(1). See above.

[107] See, for example, the decisions in *Gorrie v MacLeod* [2014] HCJAC 10; 2014 SCCR 187 and *Ferguson v HMA* (n 28) at [103].

[108] Hereinafter 'the 2003 Act'.

importance of proportionality in the SSC's guideline does, at least, bring Scotland into line with jurisdictions such as the Republic of Ireland,[109] New Zealand[110] and South Africa.[111] Read as a whole, however, informed professional opinion must inevitably conclude that far from being the 'historic development' claimed by the Lord Justice Clerk (SSC, 2018b), the SSC's first guideline is, in fact, simply a statement of the (blindingly) obvious (see Brown, 2018d).

Future Guidelines from the Scottish Sentencing Council

In its second business plan, the SSC announced its intention to prepare a guideline or guidelines on sexual offences and noted that consideration was ongoing as to the precise scope of work in this area (SSC, 2018c: 29–30). In a letter to the Cabinet Secretary for Justice dated 13 May 2019 (and subsequently published on the SSC's website), the Lord Justice Clerk announced that the SSC would develop multiple guidelines on sexual offences, beginning with guidelines for rape, sexual assault and offences involving indecent images of children (Dorrian, 2019). The decision to issue offence-specific guidelines, rather than a single sentencing guideline covering all sexual offences, was taken due to the wide-ranging nature of sexual offending and to ensure that guidelines are produced more quickly.

The Lord Justice Clerk explained that the SSC's work programme would be re-prioritised to place more emphasis on the development of sentencing guidelines for sexual offences. Her Ladyship also noted that it was difficult to say with any certainty how long the first guidelines on sexual offences would take to develop, with much depending on the complexities encountered as the SSC begins work on each topic and on feedback received during the consultation process (Dorrian, 2019).

At least one of the catalysts for the SSC's re-prioritisation of its work appears to have been a motion for a parliamentary debate on sentencing heard in the Scottish Parliament on 27 February 2019. In particular, a motion was raised by Daniel Johnson MSP in the following terms:

> 'That the Parliament believes that transparency and consistency are fundamental to ensuring that victims' and wider society's interests are served by the justice system … [The Parliament] is concerned that it has taken three-and-a-half years for the Scottish Sentencing Council to produce one set of sentencing guidelines; notes that guidelines on sexual assaults will not be available until after 2021 and considers this unacceptable.'[112]

At the time of writing, the SSC had yet to issue sentencing guidelines for any sexual offence. In June 2019, however, a draft guideline was issued entitled *The Sentencing*

[109] See Chapter 6.
[110] See Chapter 7.
[111] Ibid.
[112] Motion S5M-16013, lodged on 25 February 2019. The motion was tabled, debated, and passed with certain amendments.

Process (SSC, 2019a); a three-month public consultation followed (SSC, 2019b). The draft guideline seeks to provide 'a framework for the sentencing process' (SSC, 2019a: 3) by setting out a sequence of actions or 'steps' which courts should follow to reach a sentencing decision. The draft guideline sets out a series of eight 'steps' in tabular form: (1) assessment of the seriousness of the offence in terms of culpability and harm; (2) selection of a sentencing range; (3) consideration of aggravating and mitigating factors; (4) determination of the 'headline sentence'; (5) consideration of any guilty plea; (6) consideration of any time spent in custody; (7) consideration of any ancillary orders; and (8) imposition of sentence and the provision of reasons (SSC, 2019a: 4–5). A further explanation of the process then follows (SSC, 2019a: 6–13).

The draft guideline initially appears to be a radical departure from the sentencing methodology of instinctive, or intuitive, synthesis traditionally employed by Scottish judges.[113] Upon closer inspection, however, it becomes clear that even if the draft guideline is submitted to the High Court for approval in its current form and if the High Court does, in fact, decide to approve it without any modifications, then judges are still not precluded from sentencing by way of the instinctive synthesis, as approved by the Appeal Court in decisions such as *Gemmell v HMA*[114] and *Ferguson v HMA*.[115] The draft guideline states:

> 'The sentencing decision may be made swiftly … In those cases the court may appear to consider all relevant factors at the same time. *Where a court does not expressly take any step or steps, that does not in itself amount to a decision not to follow the guideline*. A court may choose to explain aspects of a sentence it has passed by reference to a specific part of this guideline. But *[a court] does not have to give full reasons as to how each part of the process has affected the sentence*' (SSC, 2019a: 3, emphasis added).

Thus, as with the SSC's first guideline on the *Principles and Purposes of Sentencing* (SSC, 2018a), the draft guideline appears to be aimed primarily at improving the public's understanding of the sentencing process. While this is a laudable goal in and of itself, a recent study that combined empirical research with Scottish sentencers with one of the most thorough reviews of sentencing scholarship in recent years demonstrates both a judicial preference for sentencing by way of instinctive synthesis and the superiority of this methodology in terms of achieving *individualised* justice (see Brown, 2017a). It is to be hoped that, rather than introducing a paradigm shift in the methodology by which Scottish judges impose sentences, the eventual guideline on *The Sentencing Process* will, as with the SSC's first guideline on the *Principles and Purposes of Sentencing* (SSC, 2018a), simply serve an educational purpose for those unfamiliar with Scottish sentencing law, procedure and practice.

This review of Scottish sentencing methodology demonstrates that sentencing in this jurisdiction remains an individualised process. Discretion has long been

[113] See above.
[114] *Gemmell* (n 22) at [59], discussed above.
[115] *Ferguson* (n 28) at [103] and [104], discussed above.

the hallmark of sentencing in Scotland. This continues to be the case, although sentencers' discretion is increasingly structured by guideline judgments from the Appeal Court in respect of certain offences. Although at present there is no guideline judgment on the sentencing of rape, appellate guidance encourages judges to have regard to the relevant sentencing guidelines operating in England and Wales as a form of 'cross-check' or comparator. Whether judges do, in fact, proof their proposed sentences against the English guidelines, at least in respect of sentencing for rape, is, however, open to question. In the absence of rape sentencing guidelines (either in the form of a guideline judgment from the Appeal Court, or guidelines from the SSC), the discussion now turns to an examination of how the Scottish courts sentence the offence and the limited guidance on issues of principle issued by the Appeal Court.

Early Appellate Guidance on Rape Sentencing

Limited Appellate Guidance and the Crown's Request for Sentencing Guidelines: The Decision in *Shearer*

A review of certain decisions of the Appeal Court from the late 1980s to the early 1990s suggests that sentences imposed by Scottish judges for rape were broadly in line with the sentencing guidelines then operating in England and Wales, as set out by the Court of Appeal (Criminal Division) in *R v Billam and others*.[116] In particular, Moody suggests that a starting point of five years tended to be seen as the appropriate figure by Scottish judges, although she acknowledges that judgments in Scottish sentencing appeals were at that time much terser and less developed than in England and Wales (Moody, 1995: 221). Similarly, Robertshaw's analysis of UK sentencing statistics suggests that there were marked similarities in outcome between the two jurisdictions at this time (Robertshaw, 1994; see also Kelly, 1993: 157–58 and Nicholson, 1992: 246–47).

The Appeal Court never formally approved the *Billam* guidelines, nor did it approve the revised sentencing guidelines issued by the Court of Appeal in *R v Millberry and others*,[117] let alone either of the Definitive Guidelines issued successively by the Sentencing Guidelines Council (2007a) and the Sentencing Council (2013a).[118] For many years, the only real guidance that the Appeal Court provided in relation to the sentencing of rape committed against adult victims comprised certain observations in *HMA v Shearer*.[119]

[116] (1986) 8 Cr App R (S) 48, discussed in Chapter 4.
[117] [2003] 2 Cr App R (S) 31, discussed in Chapter 4.
[118] See Chapter 4.
[119] 2003 SCCR 657.

Shearer was a Crown appeal against sentence in which the respondent was convicted after trial of raping the victim in an hotel room. The indictment recorded that the rape was committed while the victim was 'unconscious or asleep and under the influence of alcohol'. The Crown appealed against the sentence of 18 months' imprisonment imposed by the sentencing judge on the ground of undue leniency. The respondent was convicted approximately a year after the law of rape in Scotland had been fundamentally altered by the decision in *Lord Advocate's Reference (No 1 of 2001)*.[120] Thus, while the respondent in *Shearer* was convicted of rape, the facts were such that, prior to the *Lord Advocate's Reference*, the offence would have been treated as 'clandestine injury' at common law.[121]

In his report to the Appeal Court,[122] the sentencing judge in *Shearer* remarked that in assessing the appropriate sentence and the culpability of the respondent, he took account of all the circumstances of the case. These included the fact that the crime was committed because the victim was incapable of giving her consent, rather than by the fact that her will and resistance were overcome by the use or the threat of force. The sentencing judge continued:

> 'It appears to me to be absurd to suggest, as appears to be suggested [by the Crown in the note of appeal against sentence], that (other considerations being equal) the culpability of an accused is the same in either case.'[123]

The Crown's appeal was heard by a Bench chaired by Scotland's most senior judge, the Lord Justice General. The Court allowed the Crown's appeal, quashed the sentence of 18 months' imprisonment and imposed a sentence of three-and-a-half years. In so doing, the Appeal Court expressed concern that the sentencing judge appeared to take the view that the respondent's culpability and hence the appropriate sentence, should be affected materially by the fact that the victim was incapable of giving consent, rather than it being a case of her will and resistance having been overcome by the use of force or the threat of force.[124] In delivering the opinion of the Court, the Lord Justice General (Cullen) explained:

> 'It is important, in our view, for the sentencer to avoid treating the fact that the [victim] was asleep or unconscious as if it lessened the gravity of the accused having sexual intercourse with the [victim] without her consent. While there are no doubt cases of rape in which the use of force or the threat of force call for very substantial sentences, we demur from the view that the present type of case should be regarded as substantially less serious, for example, than one in which the [victim] was conscious but in which the least amount of force was used or threatened and the [victim] experienced relatively

[120] *Lord Advocate's Reference (No 1 of 2001)* (n 6), discussed above in the introduction to this chapter.

[121] Discussed above in the introduction to this chapter.

[122] A particular feature of Scottish criminal procedure is that in appeals against conviction or sentence, the presiding judge must provide a written report giving her opinion on the case generally and on the grounds contained in the note of appeal (see the Criminal Procedure (Scotland) Act 1995, section 113).

[123] *Shearer* (n 119) at [6].

[124] Ibid at [12].

> little fear, distress or anger at the time. The culpability of the accused in each of these cases would, in our view, be broadly similar.'[125]

The Court in *Shearer* did not consider that the sentences which had, in the past, been imposed for cases of clandestine injury provided 'a reliable guide for the future' in sentencing cases of rape.[126] This represented a marked departure from previous sentencing practice since clandestine injury was an offence which the courts generally treated as far less serious than rape (Cowan, 2010: 166) and in respect of which non-custodial disposals appear to have been commonplace, if not the norm. Non-custodial sentences were, for example, imposed on appeal in the two cases of clandestine injury that appear in the law reports: *Paton v HMA*[127] and *Fox v HMA*.[128]

In *Paton*, the appellant (a 41-year-old first offender) pleaded guilty in the High Court to a charge of clandestine injury by having intercourse with the victim while she was unconscious, asleep and under the influence of alcohol. The victim, who was very drunk, met the appellant outside a nightclub. They returned to the appellant's flat and went to bed together, where consensual sexual intimacy took place. The victim then went to sleep and later woke to find the appellant having intercourse with her. The appellant's explanation for the offence was that it was a momentary act carried out under the influence of drink taken on top of certain prescribed medication. The judge imposed what she regarded as a sentence at the lower end of the scale for an offence of this sort, namely two years' imprisonment. In the subsequent appeal against sentence, the Appeal Court stated that cases of clandestine injury tended to 'turn upon their own particular circumstances' and concluded that: 'clandestine injury is an offence which may be of an unusual character and may merit an unusual form of disposal, that is, a non-custodial form'.[129] The appeal was allowed, the custodial sentence quashed and a sentence of 300 hours of community service was substituted.

The appeal by Richard Fox also illustrates the attitude of the Scottish courts towards sentencing clandestine injury. The decision in *Fox v HMA*,[130] an appeal against conviction, is well-known to Scottish lawyers as the leading decision on the use of circumstantial evidence as corroboration in criminal trials (see Ross and Chalmers, 2015: 75–81). The appeal against conviction having been refused, the outcome of Mr Fox's subsequent sentence appeal is perhaps less well known. The appellant, Fox, had been sentenced to two-and-a-half years' imprisonment following his conviction in the High Court for clandestine injury. The appellant

[125] Ibid.
[126] Ibid at [13].
[127] 2002 SCCR 57.
[128] 1998 GWD 24–1215.
[129] *Paton* (n 127) at [6].
[130] 1998 JC 94.

and the 16-year-old victim had attended a party. Both were drunk. The victim went to bed and awoke to find the appellant having intercourse with her. In allowing Fox's appeal against sentence, the Appeal Court held that the sentence was excessive given, firstly, that the offence was 'less serious than rape' [*sic*] and, secondly, that the victim had 'not suffered physical injury'. The custodial sentence was quashed and a community service order of 200 hours was substituted.[131]

In the course of its submissions in *HMA v Shearer*, the Crown had invited the Court to provide sentencing guidelines as to the range of sentences appropriate for cases involving the rape of 'vulnerable females'.[132] Given the context of the offence in question, it appeared that the Crown were specifically requesting sentencing guidelines for cases of so-called 'non-forcible' rape in which the victim is raped while in a state of unconsciousness due either to voluntary intoxication or through the voluntary ingestion of drugs. The Appeal Court, however, expressly declined to issue sentencing guidelines, the Lord Justice General observing that:

> 'Cases of the type with which we are concerned in this appeal are relatively unusual in their circumstances. We have already indicated how such cases might be compared with cases in which the [victim] is conscious. Beyond that it does not appear to us to be useful or practicable for us to indicate what sentences would be appropriate, since so much will depend upon the circumstances of the individual case.'[133]

These comments were, with respect, unfortunate. It is disappointing that the Appeal Court did not accept the Crown's invitation to provide sentencing guidelines for rape, or at least for so-called 'non-forcible' rape. As the Lord Justice Clerk (Carloway) was later to observe in *HMA v Cooperwhite*,[134] experience has shown that cases of the type under consideration in *Shearer* are not at all unusual.[135]

In his commentary to the decision in *Shearer*, Sir Gerald Gordon QC notes that although the Court's opinion made it clear that 'rape is rape is rape, whether or not the [victim] is asleep', it also indicated that if the victim was asleep or unconscious then the crime would perhaps be 'at the lower end' of the scale of seriousness. The decision in *Shearer*, Sir Gerald observes, shifts the emphasis for sentencing purposes from the consciousness or otherwise of the victim to the degree of force (or, perhaps, degrading behaviour) employed by the offender (Gordon, 2003: 663). Perhaps the most important, and regrettable, aspect of the decision in *Shearer*, however, is the fact that it has come to be used by judges as a form of anchoring point in sentencing rape.

[131] *Fox* (n 128).
[132] *Shearer* (n 119) at [8].
[133] Ibid at [13].
[134] [2013] HCJAC 88; 2013 SCCR 461, discussed later in this chapter.
[135] Ibid at [19].

The Three-and-a-half-year 'Benchmark': The Courts' Use of *Shearer* as an Anchoring Point

The Shearer *Benchmark and the Incapable Victim*

In *HMA v Cooperwhite*,[136] Lord Justice Clerk Carloway observed that although the Appeal Court in *HMA v Shearer*[137] ultimately declined to issue sentencing guidance for so-called 'non-forcible' rape, the sentence of three-and-a-half years' imprisonment imposed by the Court had 'undoubtedly been used by sentencers as the benchmark'[138] for sentencing rape.

Following the decision in *Shearer*, the Scottish courts have routinely imposed sentences around the *Shearer* benchmark of three-and-a-half years' imprisonment in cases where offenders have raped victims who were so intoxicated that they were incapable of giving or withholding consent. For example, in *Allan v HMA*,[139] an appeal against sentence decided some six months after the Court delivered its opinion in *Shearer*, the appellant pleaded guilty to rape. The victim and her boyfriend attended a Christmas party at the hotel where the appellant worked as a waiter. A substantial amount of alcohol was consumed. At the end of the night, the victim and a number of her friends continued drinking in her hotel room. The victim then fell asleep. The appellant later entered the victim's room, digitally penetrated her, licked her private parts and raped her. The appellant was a complete stranger to the victim; she awoke during the commission of the offence and erroneously thought that the appellant was her boyfriend. On appeal, the sentence of four-and-a-half years' imprisonment, with an extension period of 18 months, was quashed and a conventional custodial sentence of four years' imprisonment was imposed.

In *Crombie (Gerald) v HMA*,[140] the 60-year-old appellant was convicted after trial of rape at common law. The appellant lived in a sheltered housing complex with his wife. The elderly victim lived in a neighbouring flat; she was severely disabled and relied heavily on the appellant and his wife for her day-to-day needs. The appellant held a New Year party at his flat. The victim became very drunk and had to be helped to bed by the appellant's wife. In the early hours of the morning the appellant, who was also very drunk, entered the victim's flat where he raped her vaginally and orally in her bed. On appeal, the custodial sentence of six years' imprisonment was quashed and a sentence of four years' imprisonment was imposed, with an extension period of 12 months.

The 21-year-old appellant in *JD v HMA*,[141] a first offender, was convicted after trial of raping the victim at a party at which significant amounts of alcohol had

[136] *Cooperwhite* (n 134), discussed later in this chapter.
[137] *Shearer* (n 119).
[138] *Cooperwhite* (n 134) at [19].
[139] 2004 SCCR 278.
[140] High Court of Justiciary on appeal, 24 September 2008, unreported.
[141] High Court of Justiciary on appeal, 9 December 2014, unreported (see the case note by Brown, 2015a).

been consumed by all those present. On appeal, the sentence of six years' imprisonment imposed by the trial judge was quashed and a sentence of three years' imprisonment was substituted. The Appeal Court considered the victim's actions in willingly consuming alcohol to excess to be 'the most salient feature of the case'[142] and that the case fell 'very much towards the lower end of the spectrum of seriousness' when considering cases of rape.[143]

In *Lee v HMA*,[144] meanwhile, the appellant was convicted after trial of raping a university student. The victim had been spent the night drinking heavily with friends in a nightclub; she became separated from her group and had no memory of meeting the appellant, let alone of having intercourse with him. The first time she became aware of the possibility that she had been raped was when she awoke the next morning in the back of the appellant's van, parked in a supermarket car park, whereupon the appellant told her that she had 'better take the morning after pill'. Subsequent analysis of CCTV footage showed the appellant following the victim out of the nightclub, of his guiding her into his van and of the van driving off a short time later. The appellant was sentenced to four-and-a-half years' imprisonment. He did not seek leave to appeal the sentence and his appeal against conviction was refused.

In *McDermott (John) v HMA*,[145] the 19-year-old appellant (aged 17 at the date of the offence) was convicted after trial of having raped the 14-year-old victim at a party while she was severely intoxicated and unable to give or withhold her consent. The appellant was a first offender with a troubled upbringing. He was sentenced to five years' detention. On appeal, the Court accepted that the trial judge had given no real consideration either to the impact of the appellant's age at the time of the offence or to the appropriate sentencing aims of rehabilitation and reintegration into society, these being particularly important in sentencing youths. The appeal was allowed, the sentence of five years' detention quashed and a sentence of three-and-a-half years' detention was substituted.

The Shearer *Benchmark and the Intoxicated Victim*

The Scottish courts have also used the benchmark of three-and-a-half years' imprisonment set in *Shearer*[146] in cases where, although the victims have not drunk themselves into a condition of incapability or unconsciousness, they have nonetheless been heavily under the influence of alcohol or drugs at the time of the offence. In *Tough v HMA*,[147] for example, the 23-year-old appellant pleaded

[142] Ibid at [8].
[143] Ibid at [9].
[144] [2016] HCJAC 39; 2016 JC 133.
[145] High Court of Justiciary on appeal, 20 September 2017, unreported (see the case note by Brown, 2017b).
[146] *Shearer* (n 119).
[147] [2012] HCJAC 119.

guilty to the sexual assault and rape of the 12-year-old victim, the offences involving oral and digital penetration and masturbation. On the night of the offence the victim had been drinking alcohol in a park with other youths. They were joined by the appellant and, at his invitation, the group went on to his aunt's house which was empty at the time. More alcohol was consumed and the victim became very drunk. The appellant took her to a bedroom where the offences took place. The appellant was assessed as having a low IQ and a mild learning disability although he was able to live unassisted. On appeal, the custodial sentence of three years and nine months, discounted from five years to reflect the appellant's guilty plea, was quashed and a sentence of 27 months' imprisonment was imposed, along with an extension period of two years.

Sentences of five years' imprisonment were imposed on the appellant and his co-accused in *Lennie v HMA*[148] in circumstances where they both raped the intoxicated victim at a party. The appellant did not seek leave to appeal his sentence. Given the victim's vulnerability by reason of her intoxication and the fact that the appellant and his co-accused acted together in raping the victim, an offence committed in similar circumstances in England and Wales would be likely to attract a sentence in the region of nine to 13 years' imprisonment, with a starting point of 10 years (a 'Category 2A' case under the relevant sentencing guidelines (Sentencing Council, 2013a: 10–11)).[149]

Although the case report in *Parker v HMA*[150] omits certain important details regarding the circumstances of the offence and the sentence imposed, the appellant was convicted after trial of vaginally and anally raping the 21-year-old victim before ejaculating over her. The victim had spent the night drinking at various bars and a nightclub with a female friend until 3 am. They both went on to a party attended by the appellant. After consuming more alcohol, the victim went to sleep in a bedroom. The appellant later entered the room and committed the offences, during which the victim awoke but pretended to be asleep and offered no resistance. The appellant, a 42-year-old with a previous conviction for assault to severe injury, was sentenced to five years' imprisonment. The appellant did not seek leave to appeal his sentence and his appeal against conviction was refused.[151] Again, using the English Definitive Guideline as a cross-check, it is likely that an offence committed in similar circumstances in England and Wales would result in a sentence in the region of seven to nine years' imprisonment, with a starting point of eight years (a 'Category 2B' case, Sentencing Council, 2013a: 10–11).[152]

Most recently, in *Ferguson v HMA*,[153] the 29-year-old appellant was convicted of rape after trial at Glasgow High Court. The victim was aged 22. After a night

[148] [2014] HCJAC 103; 2014 SCL 848.
[149] See Chapter 4.
[150] [2016] HCJAC 40; 2016 SCL 520.
[151] Ibid at [6].
[152] See Chapter 4.
[153] [2019] HCJAC 1; 2019 JC 53.

spent drinking in various pubs, the victim and a female friend were invited by a stranger to a party hosted by the appellant. Once at the party, the victim continued drinking and took cannabis, which made her sick. The appellant invited her to rest in his bed. The victim awoke at 3 am to find the appellant getting into bed with her. He proceeded to rape her. In the course of the assault, the appellant removed the victim's clothes, bit her neck and digitally penetrated her anus and vagina before raping her. The appellant was sentenced to four years' imprisonment. While he did not appeal his sentence, his appeal against conviction was refused. An application of the English Definitive Guideline as a cross-check suggests that, given the additional degradation of repeated digital vaginal and anal penetration, the victim's vulnerability and the appellant having abused the victim's trust, an offence committed in similar circumstances south of the border would result in a sentence in the region of nine to 13 years' imprisonment, with a starting point of 10 years (a 'Category 2A' case, Sentencing Council, 2013a: 10–11). Had the appellant been convicted of this offence in England and Wales, he would almost certainly have received a custodial sentence at least two-and-a-half to three times that imposed by the trial judge at Glasgow High Court.

Perhaps the most controversial example of a sentencing judge apparently using the three-and-a-half-year benchmark set by the Appeal Court in *Shearer*[154] is the recent decision in *Gubinas and Radavicius v HMA*,[155] a case involving the multiple perpetrator rape of the intoxicated victim in which the appellants were both sentenced to four-and-a-half years' imprisonment. As we have seen, offences of this nature attract sentences in the region of 13 to 19 years' imprisonment in England and Wales.[156]

The Shortcomings of the Shearer *Benchmark*

It is a matter of grave concern that the sentence of three-and-a-half years' imprisonment imposed on appeal in *Shearer*[157] operates as a form of benchmark, or anchoring point, in sentencing rape. It is highly debatable whether it should continue to do so, either in the sentencing of cases involving an incapable or intoxicated victim or, indeed, in sentencing rape generally. While there is no longer any need for the victim's will to be overcome by force or the threat of force for the crime of rape to be committed,[158] a *de facto* hierarchy of seriousness remains, with so-called 'forcible rape' at the apex (see Campbell, 2017: 480). There is a clear tendency for the courts to treat instances of rape in which the victim was either drunk, or incapable of giving or withholding consent due to intoxication, as lying

[154] *Shearer* (n 119).
[155] *Gubinas and Radavicius* (n 85), discussed above.
[156] Ibid.
[157] *Shearer* (n 119).
[158] See the discussion in the Introduction to this chapter.

at the lower end of the spectrum of seriousness when considering contraventions of section 1 of the Sexual Offences (Scotland) Act 2009. In so doing, the courts arguably perpetuate the outdated view that violent rape by a stranger is the paradigm of 'real rape' (see Rumney, 2003: 872 and 883; and Warner, 2002: 511).

Another key problem with the Scottish courts' use of the *Shearer* benchmark in cases where the victim was either drunk or was incapable of giving or withholding consent due to intoxication is that the imposition of sentences at or around the benchmark of three-and-a-half years arguably amounts to acceptance, by certain judges, of certain rape myths,[159] while also perhaps perpetuating stereotypical views of acceptable female socio-sexual behaviour. In regarding such cases, as the Appeal Court did in *JD v HMA*,[160] as lying at the lower end of the spectrum of seriousness, it could be argued that the courts view the victim's intoxication as 'sufficient grounds for her partial condemnation' (Stormo et al, 1997: 303) since, in drinking to excess:

> '[S]uch a complainant appears to have violated feminine gender norms by becoming intoxicated. Moreover ... she has exhibited a reckless disregard for her own safety by sending out a message of sexual interest through her intoxication and by placing herself in a position in which she is vulnerable [...]' (Finch and Munro, 2007: 594–95; see also Lovett and Horvath, 2009: 128–29 and Richardson and Hammock, 1991: 91).

Such views are supportive of what Finch and Munro (2007: 595), in their study of mock jurors' deliberations in rape cases involving intoxication, describe as 'contributory negligence' on the part of the rape victim (see also Ellison and Munro, 2009b: 295–97; Finch and Munro, 2005: 35–36; Horvath and Brown, 2007: 425–26; McGlynn, 2010a: 147–50; and Munro and Kelly, 2009: 289–92). The sentences imposed by the Appeal Court in cases such as *JD v HMA*[161] and by the High Court in cases such as *Gubinas and Radavicius v HMA*,[162] could be said to evidence a judicial perception that 'real rape' 'is inspired by violence, pathology and deviance rather than by excesses of male sexuality and wilful obliviousness to tokens of resistance or lack of affirmative consent' (Ellison and Munro 2009b: 301; see also Brown and Horvath, 2009: 326–27).

These 'common sense' understandings of what constitutes 'real' rape are concerning (Cowan, 2019: 47). Yet, as Thomas O'Malley, a barrister and the leading commentator on Irish sexual offences law and practice, observes, '[t]he study of sexual offences is in many ways a study of social values' (O'Malley, 1995: 1). Stewart et al (1996: 159–61) acknowledge that rape myths and stereotypes are so embedded in society that people, including certain judges, routinely draw upon them. Sentencing has long been recognised as a human process (see Brown, 2017a; Cooke, 1987: 58; Gerry and Sjölin, 2012; Hall, 2007a: 254; Hogarth, 1971; Judge, 2007: 1; and O'Malley, 2011: 29) and judges are themselves social actors.

[159] See Chapter 2.
[160] *JD* (n 141).
[161] Ibid.
[162] *Gubinas and Radavicius* (n 85).

These myths and stereotypes surrounding rape shape our daily social reality and those of certain judges, to the extent that they come to be accepted as 'normal' (Brown and Horvath, 2009: 326–27; Horvath and Brown, 2009: 7–8; Leahy, 2019: 4; Spies, 2016: 403).

As Hunter (2016: 327) explains, subconscious acceptance of 'real-rape' stereotypes trigger complex social and psychological reactions in criminal law's actors that 'flow into all aspects of the criminal justice system'. The same view of certain rape victims being 'contributorily negligent' as a result of engaging in risky behaviour or by drinking alcohol to excess is, for example, shared by other professionals within the criminal justice system, including certain prosecutors and defence counsel (Cowan, 2019: 34–5; Smith and Skinner, 2017: 449–58; and Temkin et al, 2018: 212–13), as well as physicians tasked with performing forensic medical examinations of rape complainants (McMillan and White, 2015 and White and McMillan, 2018: 103–5).

While in terms of the judicial oath, judges are bound to 'do right to all manner of people after the laws and usages of this realm, without fear or favour, affection or ill will' (Hodge, 2016: 2), they remain susceptible to the same human frailties and cognitive biases as the rest of us (Secret Barrister, 2019: 282). Du Bois-Pedain (2017: 396), for example, notes that judicial decision-making, like all human behaviour, is subject to heuristic shortcuts and is affected by subconscious attitudes and biases. Thus, in the context of rape and sexual assault, judges, as social actors, are no different from anyone else in relying 'on the same taken-for-granted explanations and assumptions about reality' (Stewart et al, 1996: 160). As Craig explains in her study of Canadian sexual assault trials, all judges can be expected, at times, unknowingly to resort to what she describes as 'schematic or stereotype-based thinking' (Craig, 2018: 206).

As Du Mont et al (2003: 469–70) explain, within the criminal justice system more generally traditional notions of chastity and respectability have been seen as effectively disqualifying those women who frequent pubs and nightclubs and who drink to excess from claiming or achieving 'real victim status' (see also Stormo et al, 1997: 299–303). Larcombe (2011: 37) suggests that while the 'ideal victim' may no longer be sexually chaste she is, however, 'consistent, rational and self-disciplined'; the 'ideal victim' neither drinks alcohol to excess nor otherwise engages in 'risky' behaviour. In Scotland, offenders convicted of raping victims who do not conform to this image of the 'ideal victim' routinely receive sentences around, and sometimes below, the *Shearer*[163] 'benchmark' of three-and-a-half years' imprisonment.[164] Arguably, this evidences what Gotell (2010: 219) describes as decontextualised judicial understandings of rape that reinforce individual responsibility and new forms of victim blaming.

It must also be questioned whether the benchmark set by the Appeal Court in *Shearer*[165] adequately reflects current societal attitudes towards the crime of rape,

[163] *Shearer* (n 119).
[164] See the discussion of recent case law above.
[165] *Shearer* (n 119).

since most common law jurisdictions adopt higher starting points for sentencing the offence. In England and Wales, for example, the general starting point for a conviction for rape after a contested trial in cases featuring no aggravating circumstances has long been set at five years' imprisonment (*R v Billam*;[166] *R v Millberry*[167]). The starting point under the current guidelines remains five years, with a sentencing range of between four and seven years' imprisonment (Sentencing Council, 2013a: 10–11).[168] In the Republic of Ireland, case law indicates that where an offender pleads guilty to rape in circumstances which involve no additional gratuitous humiliation or violence beyond that ordinarily involved in the offence, a sentence in the region of five years' imprisonment is usually imposed (see O'Cathaoir, 2012; O'Malley, 2013a: 648–58; and the decision in *People (DPP) v Drought*[169]). In New Zealand, meanwhile, the starting point range for offences at the lower end of the spectrum, where aggravating features are either not present or are present only to a limited extent, is six to eight years' imprisonment.[170] In comparison with many other common law jurisdictions, the *Shearer* benchmark of three-and-a-half years' imprisonment fails entirely to reflect what in England and Wales is referred to as 'the "baseline" of culpability and harm inherent in rape' (see Rook and Ward, 2016: 18 and 1802–3 and Sentencing Council, 2012: 16).

The *Shearer* Benchmark – A Comparison with Canadian Sentencing Practice

Scottish sentencing practice for rape involving incapable or intoxicated victims is most closely aligned with practice in certain Canadian provinces and territories. Canada is another jurisdiction in which judges have traditionally enjoyed, and indeed continue to enjoy, a very wide sentencing discretion (see Brown, 2017a: 25–28; Foy, 2018: 78–79; Manson, 2001: 56, 61; and Manson et al, 2016: 38). Before examining the sentences imposed for such offences in the Canadian courts, it is necessary to outline the main features of the law relating to rape and sexual assault in this jurisdiction.

Sexual Assault under the Canadian Criminal Code

In a major redrafting of the Canadian Criminal Code in 1982, the old offences of rape, attempted rape and indecent assault were repealed and replaced with the

[166] *Billam* (n 116).
[167] *Millberry* (n 117).
[168] Namely, a 'Category 3B' case. See the discussion in Chapter 4.
[169] [2008] 1 IR 308 at [36], discussed in Chapter 6.
[170] *R v AM* [2010] NZCA 114; [2010] 2 NZLR 750, discussed in Chapter 7.

offence of sexual assault (see Benedet and Grant, 2010: 324). There are three levels of sexual assault under sections 271 to 273 of the Canadian Criminal Code.[171] The essential nature of these offences is seen to be a violent assault against the person and, as an acknowledgement of this, they are found in Part VIII of the Code ('Offences Against the Person and Reputation'). As Ruby et al (2017: 1017) explain, the substance of section 271 to 273 of the Code accommodates the fact that the seriousness of a sexual assault does not necessarily turn on whether or not actual penetration within the old definition of rape has occurred.

Under section 271 of the Code, the first level of sexual assault is a hybrid offence punishable either on summary conviction or by a maximum of 10 years' imprisonment. Under section 272, sexual assault involving the use of a weapon, threats to a third party, the causing of bodily harm to the victim or participation in an offence committed with other offenders is punishable by up to 14 years' imprisonment. Under section 272(2)(a), a minimum sentence of four years' imprisonment is required where a firearm is used in the commission of the offence. Finally, the most serious category, aggravated sexual assault under section 273, is punishable by life imprisonment; it includes a sexual assault which 'wounds, maims, disfigures, or endangers the life of the complainant' (see Ruby et al, 2017: 1017–18). Certain mandatory minimum sentences apply in respect of sexual assault committed against children (see Benedet, 2019).

The Three-Year Starting Point in *Sandercock*

A traditional feature of sentencing practice in various Canadian provinces has been the use of 'starting points'. Starting point sentences were pioneered by the Alberta Court of Appeal in the 1970s in an attempt to provide judges in the lower courts with a place to start the consideration of what sentence to impose (Manson, 2001: 67; for a full discussion, see Brown, 2017a: 37–39 and Ruby et al, 2017: 866–75).

Over 30 years ago, in *R v Sandercock*,[172] the Alberta Court of Appeal set a starting point of three years' imprisonment for what it described as 'major sexual assault'.[173] The three-year starting point was said to apply to mature offenders of previous good character and with no criminal record.[174] The Court defined a 'major sexual assault' as one where the offender, 'by violence or threat of violence, forces an adult victim to submit to sexual activity of a sort or intensity such that a reasonable person would know beforehand that the victim likely would suffer

[171] RSC.1985, c. C-46, hereinafter 'the Code'.

[172] 1985 ABCA 218; (1985) 22 CCC (3d) 79. In more recent times, the decision was approved by the Alberta Court of Appeal in *R v Arcand* 2010 ABCA 363.

[173] *Sandercock* (n 172) at [17].

[174] Ibid.

lasting emotional or psychological injury, whether or not physical injury occurs'.[175] The Court considered the category of major sexual assaults to include rape and forced oral and anal penetration.[176] In terms of a sentencing methodology, judges sentencing major sexual assaults were directed to acknowledge the starting point of three years' imprisonment, before expressing and reflecting all mitigating and aggravating factors in arriving at the final sentence.[177]

Sandercock remains one of the leading cases on sentencing for sexual offending in Canada and has influenced sentencing practice for sexual assault across the country (see Manson et al, 2016: 75; Mosonyi, 2017: 294; and Nightingale, 1991: 82, fn 42). The Saskatchewan Court of Appeal, for example, adopted a starting point of three years' imprisonment for major sexual assault in *R v WJV*.[178] The Saskatchewan courts have consistently followed the principles articulated in *Sandercock*. In the recent decision in *R v Lemaigre*[179] the Saskatchewan Court of Appeal noted that a three-year sentence was 'the standard reference point'[180] for major sexual assault. In *R v AJPJ*,[181] meanwhile, the Northwest Territories Court of Appeal followed *Sandercock* in holding that the starting point sentence for sexual assaults involving non-consensual intercourse is three years' imprisonment; the three-year starting point was later affirmed by the Supreme Court of the Northwest Territories in *R v Jacobson*.[182]

As Ruby et al (2017: 1019) note, however, the starting point approach is not followed in every Canadian province and territory; in *R v Glassford*,[183] for example, the Ontario Court of Appeal rejected the starting point concept. In particular, the Court in *Glassford* considered, firstly, that each case must be decided on its own facts and, secondly, that the *Sandercock* starting point of three years did not necessarily reflect the seriousness of major sexual assaults.[184] More recently, O'Malley has similarly noted that a starting point of three years' imprisonment arguably does not reflect current societal attitudes towards the crime of rape: most common law jurisdictions adopt higher starting points for sentencing the offence (O'Malley, 2013a: 661; see also Brown, 2015a: 8).

The *Sandercock* Starting Point and the Intoxicated Victim

Having undertaken an extensive review of the authorities from across Canada, Ruby et al (2017: 1022–23) conclude that sentences at or below the starting point

[175] Ibid at [13].
[176] Ibid.
[177] Ibid at [21].
[178] [1991] SJ No 41, 90 Sask R 110; see also *R v MS* 2003 SKCA 33 at [29].
[179] 2018 SKCA 47.
[180] Ibid at [20].
[181] 2011 NWTCA 2.
[182] 2014 NWTSC 33.
[183] [1988] OJ No 359, 42 CCC (3d) 259.
[184] Ibid at 265.

of three years' imprisonment set in *Sandercock*[185] tend to be imposed in cases involving the rape of a victim who is either intoxicated or unconscious following voluntary consumption of alcohol or drugs. The cases considered by Ruby et al which feature disposals below the *Sandercock* starting point of three years include *R v GM*[186] (90 days' imprisonment increased on a Crown appeal to 18 months); *R v Kozy*[187] (18 months' imprisonment); *R v Cubillan*[188] (two years' imprisonment); and *R v Laz-Martinez*[189] (two years' imprisonment).

With regard to cases in which the starting point sentence was imposed, in both *R v Owusu*[190] and *R v Lyons*[191] the Alberta Court of Appeal imposed sentences of three years' imprisonment on the respondents following successful Crown appeals against the conditional sentences imposed at first instance. In *Owusu*, the 18-year-old respondent was convicted of vaginally and orally raping a 17-year-old girl who had been lured to a motel room and plied with alcohol; the victim was also raped by the respondent's friend and the Court noted that the offence had 'overtones of a gang rape'.[192] In *Lyons*, meanwhile, the 54-year-old respondent orally and vaginally raped a 14-year-old girl who was unconscious through alcohol and drug intoxication.

While in both *Owusu* and *Lyons* the Court saw fit to impose the starting point sentence that it had earlier established in *Sandercock*,[193] these cases would attract substantially higher sentences in other common law jurisdictions. An application of the *Millberry*[194] sentencing guidelines then in force in England and Wales, for example, demonstrates that an offence with similar facts and circumstances to *Owusu* committed in that jurisdiction would have attracted a starting point of eight years' imprisonment due to the respondent having acted along with a co-accused.[195] The eight-year starting point would then have been increased, due to the aggravating factor of the offence having been planned,[196] to perhaps nine years' imprisonment – three times the sentence imposed by the Alberta Court of Appeal. An offence committed in similar circumstances today would, following the English Sentencing Council's Definitive Guideline on Sexual Offences (Sentencing Council, 2013a: 10–11), attract a starting point of 10 years' imprisonment, with a range of between nine and 13 years.[197]

By reference to the decision in *R v Rose*[198] – a case in which the alcoholic accused was sentenced to 12 months' imprisonment for raping a drinking

[185] *Sandercock* (n 172).
[186] 2015 BCCA 165.
[187] [1990] OJ No 954, 58 CCC (3d) 500.
[188] 2015 ONSC 2747.
[189] 2011 ONCJ 115.
[190] 2006 ABCA 239.
[191] 2005 ABCA 258.
[192] *Owusu* (n 190) at [6].
[193] *Sandercock* (n 172).
[194] *Millberry* (n 117). See Chapter 4.
[195] Ibid at [20].
[196] Ibid at [32].
[197] See the discussion in Chapter 4.
[198] [1979] MJ No 482, 5 Man R (2d) 211.

companion – Ruby et al (2017: 1023) report that, historically, it was suggested by the courts that the victim 'should surely [recognise] the increasing danger of her situation' when she remained in the company of 'unsavoury characters'.[199] The Supreme Court of Canada has since made it clear that the fact that a complainant placed herself in danger by, for example, agreeing to accompany the offender is not a relevant sentencing consideration.[200] Nevertheless, in what is arguably a tacit acknowledgement of the operation of rape myths in Canadian sentencing, Ruby et al (2017: 1023–24) consider that certain comments made by the Canadian courts concerning rape complainants 'are less a criticism of the victims' incaution than an attack on their perceived immorality'. The authors also note the 'archaic tendency [of the Canadian courts] to punish victims who could be viewed as less than chaste' (2017: 1024; see also Craig, 2018: 206–7).

Appellate Views on Sentencing Relationship and Acquaintance Rape: The Decisions in *Ramage* and *Petrie*

In addition to the three-and-a-half-year 'benchmark' for sentencing rape set by the decision in *Shearer*,[201] the Appeal Court in Scotland has also provided certain sentencing guidance on an issue which is not uncontroversial: namely, the extent to which the nature of a pre-existing relationship between a rapist and his victim palliates the sentence imposed. The Appeal Court's traditional view was that an existing or a pre-existing sexual relationship between the parties was a mitigating factor in sentencing. In *Ramage v HMA*,[202] the appellant pleaded guilty to pinning the victim down, digitally penetrating her and raping her. The offence took place in the victim's home. The appellant and the victim had had a sexual relationship some six years before the commission of the offence. They had become friendly again about four months before the offence; the appellant would often call at the victim's home late at night while drunk and, while the victim would occasionally let him in, she made it clear that she did not wish to resume a sexual relationship. On the night of the offence, the appellant had spent around three hours drinking with the victim and one of her friends. When her friend left about 3 am, the victim asked the appellant to leave. The appellant refused and, when the victim rejected his advances, he proceeded to rape her.

The appellant was sentenced to five years' imprisonment and appealed on the basis that the period of imprisonment was excessive; in particular, it was submitted that the sentencing judge had not taken account of the fact that the appellant had resumed a relatively close relationship with the victim. While the Appeal

[199] Ibid at 213.
[200] See *R v Seaboyer* [1991] 2 SCR 577.
[201] *Shearer* (n 119).
[202] 1999 SCCR 592.

Court considered this to be 'a serious crime',[203] it considered that the previous sexual relationship between the parties and the fact that they had resumed their friendship 'could perhaps justify treating the case as being less serious than would normally be the case with a rape offence'.[204] Although the Court acknowledged that the victim had in no way given the appellant cause to think that she wished to resume their sexual relationship, it considered that 'there was perhaps room for the appellant to delude himself as to what the position was on that point'.[205] In the circumstances, the Court quashed the sentence of five years' imprisonment and imposed a sentence of three years and six months[206] – the same sentence that, four years later, the Court was to set as the 'benchmark' sentence in *Shearer*.[207]

As the Lord Justice Clerk (Carloway) was later to observe in *HMA v Cooperwhite*,[208] the Court's repetitive use of the word 'perhaps' in its opinion in *Ramage* shows that it may have felt 'somewhat uncomfortable with what it was saying' and, indeed, with the import of its decision.[209] Nevertheless, as his Lordship also noted, the decision in *Ramage* appeared to be clear authority for the proposition that a prior sexual relationship between a rapist and his victim was to be regarded as a mitigating factor by the Scottish courts.[210] The Lord Justice Clerk concluded his review of the decision in *Ramage* by noting that, following the logic of the dictum, mere acquaintanceship between the parties may be a mitigating factor in sentencing, at least compared with the rare 'stranger rape'.[211]

It may be thought that *Ramage*, decided as it was in 1999, simply reflected judicial views about the nature and effect of rape (albeit erroneous and outdated) at the time. This is not to condone the Court's decision to allow the appeal against what was, arguably, already a lenient sentence for relationship rape. Rumney, for example, demonstrates that there was a considerable research literature on rape trauma available at the time of the decision which discussed the very serious emotional and psychological effects of marital and relationship rape (Rumney, 1999: 254–57).[212] This literature would have been available to the Court had it requested submissions from counsel or, alternatively, had the Court conducted its own researches. This was never likely to happen, however, as the sentence appeal in *Ramage* was heard at a time when, as we have seen, the Appeal Court decided cases on their own facts and circumstances, rather than on the basis of any declared principles (Nicholson, 1992: 177).[213]

[203] Ibid at 594.
[204] Ibid.
[205] Ibid.
[206] Ibid.
[207] *Shearer* (n 119).
[208] *Cooperwhite* (n 134), discussed later in this chapter.
[209] Ibid at [18].
[210] Ibid.
[211] Ibid.
[212] See Chapter 4.
[213] See above.

In Scotland, as in England and Wales, complete marital immunity from prosecution for rape had traditionally been recognised (Hume, 1797: 306). Hume's statement that a husband 'cannot himself commit a rape on his own wife, who has surrendered her person to him in that sort' was plainly outdated in modern society (see MacDonald, 1989: 208 and Ferguson, 1993: 197) and was, indeed, an indefensible anachronism (Jones, 1989: 279). The statement was declared unsound in *Stallard v HMA*[214] and the rule that marriage implied irrevocable consent to sexual intercourse was abolished. The decision in *Ramage*,[215] however, suggested that even if *legally* spousal immunity from prosecution for rape had long since been abolished, the idea that stranger rape was more serious than relationship rape persisted amongst Scottish judges.

The Appeal Court's view that relationship rape was less serious than stranger rape was confirmed some 12 years later in *Petrie v HMA (sub nom JP v HMA)*.[216] In *Petrie*, the appellant was convicted after trial of assaulting and repeatedly raping his partner. The offence took place following the couple's return from a party at which they had both drunk to excess. The victim awoke in the early hours of the morning to find the appellant touching her private parts. Despite her protestations that she did not want to engage in sexual activity, the appellant assaulted the victim by digitally penetrating her, restraining and biting her and by raping her twice. The trial judge considered this to be a frightening and distressing attack. Contrary to the position in *Ramage*,[217] the judge regarded the fact that the appellant co-habited with the victim at the time of the offence as being an *aggravating* factor since, in his view, it involved a breach of trust. The judge imposed an extended sentence of 10 years, comprising a custodial term of seven years and an extension period of three years.

On appeal, it was argued for the appellant, by reference to *Ramage*,[218] that the custodial term was excessive as the judge had given insufficient weight to the mitigating circumstances, in particular the relationship between the parties. In allowing the appeal, quashing the custodial term of seven years and substituting a custodial term of five years, the Court said this:

> 'While the element of breach of trust involved in any domestic assault is an important factor in determining the appropriate penalty, the significance of an ongoing sexual relationship in determining the penalty in a case such as this, where the gravest feature is that there was penile penetration and the conviction is for rape, is a much more complex issue. The fact of the relationship is one of a complex host of facts and circumstances that have to be taken into account in determining the appropriate sentence. In this case we consider that the trial judge gave insufficient weight to the fact that the couple had regularly engaged in sexual intercourse over a period of two years up to the night of the offence … [H]aving regard to the whole circumstances, particularly

[214] 1989 SCCR 248.
[215] *Ramage* (n 202).
[216] [2011] HCJAC 1; 2012 JC 1.
[217] *Ramage* (n 202).
[218] Ibid.

the ongoing sexual relationship between the [parties], the custodial term imposed can properly be described as excessive.'[219]

Petrie affirmed the Appeal Court's view that the existence of a prior sexual relationship between a rapist and his victim was a factor – perhaps, as the Lord Justice Clerk later noted in *Cooperwhite*,[220] a significant factor – that would serve to mitigate a sentence imposed for rape. Yet, the decision arguably goes further in positively *rejecting* the position of the sentencing judge that the existence of such a relationship should be regarded as an *aggravating* factor due to the breach of trust involved in the offence. This was a troubling development since, in re-affirming the position taken in the earlier decision in *Ramage*, the Court in *Petrie* adopted what the Lord Justice Clerk later described as 'a radically different approach' towards the sentencing of 'relationship rape' and 'acquaintance rape' from the approach taken by the English courts.[221] As we saw in Chapter 4, the Court of Appeal (Criminal Division) had long since taken the opposite view to the Scottish Appeal Court, in holding that cases of relationship rape and acquaintance rape were to be treated as being of equal seriousness to cases of stranger rape.[222]

Unlike in *Ramage*,[223] decided in 1999, the English sentencing guidelines on the relevance of a relationship between a rapist and his victim issued by the Sentencing Guidelines Council (SGC, 2007a) were available to the court in *Petrie*.[224] It appears, however, that neither the prosecutor nor counsel for the appellant drew the English guidelines to the attention of the Appeal Court; indeed, the submissions by counsel for the appellant went no further than referring to the earlier decision in *Ramage*.

This is disappointing given that, as O'Malley (2001: 136) observes, sentencing systems which operate with wide judicial discretion and which rely mainly or exclusively on appellate review (such as the system operating in Scotland[225]) place the onus on counsel as much as on judges to develop principled sentencing through a dynamic reliance upon existing precedents and the fashioning of new ones. When one also considers the observations of the Lord Justice Clerk (Gill) in *HMA v Roulston*,[226] that it is helpful to look at the sentencing guidelines applied by the English courts and to consider, to the extent that they are relevant, the specific factors on which those guidelines are based, it can be seen that the Court in *Petrie* was not favoured with comprehensive submissions on comparative sentencing jurisprudence. This was most regrettable for, as the Appeal Court

[219] *Petrie* (n 216) at [7] and [8].
[220] *Cooperwhite* (n 134) at [20].
[221] Ibid at [22].
[222] See Chapter 4.
[223] *Ramage* (n 202).
[224] *Petrie* (n 216).
[225] Subject to the issuing of guidelines by the Scottish Sentencing Council and their approval by the High Court (see above).
[226] *Roulston* (n 57) at [17], considered above.

was later to observe in *Rodger v HMA*,[227] when sitting in its appellate capacity the High Court of Justiciary is, generally, a court of final instance and hence a supreme court; as such, it should be afforded the assistance of a commensurately high quality of advocacy from those who undertake the important professional responsibility of presenting appeals before it.[228]

The result in *Petrie*[229] was a decision that appears to have been reached in ignorance both of English sentencing practice and the research literature on rape trauma upon which English sentencing jurisprudence in this area had long been based.[230] In adhering to a radically different view of the seriousness of relationship and acquaintance rape from that taken by the English courts, the Appeal Court in *Petrie* perpetuated a view of rape that was outdated and at odds with modern societal views on the nature of the offence. In disapproving the sentencing judge's view that the existence of the sexual relationship between the parties in *Petrie* fell to be regarded as an aggravating factor, the Court can arguably be seen as regarding sexual violence by an intimate partner as less serious than stranger rape (see generally Martin et al, 2007: 332; McGregor, 2005: 6, 65 and 91–92; and Kift, 1995: 60, 76 and 80). This is perhaps a position with subtle undertones of 'victim blaming': one in which some victims of rape (specifically, those who have never engaged in sexual intimacy with their attackers) are seen as more 'deserving' in the eyes of the courts than others, with concomitant implications for the length of sentence. As Kift (1995: 91) observes, however, no amount of consensual sex is likely to lessen the humiliation and degradation associated with rape, let alone the fear generated and the resultant harm suffered, regardless of the relationship between the victim and the offender.

The decisions in *Ramage*[231] and *Petrie*[232] are demonstrative of a flawed approach to the sentencing of rape by the Appeal Court. The decisions demonstrate the Court's tendency to categorise the victim in terms of being an ex-partner or an acquaintance of the offender and to *then* determine the gravity of the offence and the culpability of the offender for sentencing purposes according to the victim's designated status. The Court thus makes assumptions as to the likely effect of the crime on the victim that bear no relationship to the *particular* victim's reaction (see Kift, 1995: 74). For Kift, such an approach consequently fails to assess the offender's true culpability.

The Appeal Court was not alone in its flawed approach to the sentencing of relationship and acquaintance rape. A similar approach has traditionally been taken by the Canadian courts. Having undertaken a comprehensive review of the authorities, Ruby et al (2017: 1022–23) conclude that sentences of four years'

[227] [2014] HCJAC 133; 2015 JC 215.
[228] Ibid at [13].
[229] *Petrie* (n 216).
[230] See the discussion in Chapter 4.
[231] *Ramage* (n 202).
[232] *Petrie* (n 216).

imprisonment or less still tend to be imposed on offenders who rape their partners or women with whom they have had a prior relationship. In the cases considered by Ruby et al, the sentences imposed by the Canadian courts for relationship rape range from four months' imprisonment,[233] to four years for a rape committed at knifepoint.[234]

Some of the more recent cases noted by Ruby et al include *R v PB*[235] and *R v Stewart*.[236] In *PB*, the offender, aged 60 at the time of the offence, raped his wife of seven years. The victim was hospitalised following the rape and continued to suffer from anxiety and depression. The couple immediately separated after the offence and later divorced. The offender was sentenced to seven months' imprisonment, with a further two years' probation. In *Stewart*, meanwhile, a sentence of three years and eight-and-a-half months' imprisonment was imposed following the appellant's conviction for raping a woman with whom he had an abusive on/off relationship.

In his commentary to the decision of the Appeal Court in *Petrie*,[237] Sheriff Tom Welsh QC (2011: 429) acknowledges that sentencing judges have 'a most unenviable task' in sentencing cases of relationship rape. Sheriff Welsh raises the question, however, of whether there is any validity in the notion that a rape will be any less traumatic or less psychologically damaging for the victim just because, in the past, the parties had consensual sexual intercourse in the course of a stable relationship (2011: 428–29)? These issues and others, were subsequently considered by the Appeal Court in in *HMA v Cooperwhite*.[238]

Towards Improved Reasoning in Rape Sentencing: The Decision in *Cooperwhite*

The Need for Consistency and Predictability in Sentencing Rape: The Majority View in *Cooperwhite*

In *HMA v Cooperwhite*,[239] the Crown unsuccessfully appealed the *cumulo* sentence of six years' imprisonment imposed on the respondent following his conviction after trial of two charges of rape committed against two former partners. The respondent raped his wife on a single occasion in 2002 when she was pregnant and suffering from medical complications that made it unsafe to have

[233] See *R v Gulliver* [1991] NJ No 145.
[234] See *R v Draper* [1978] OJ No 886, 4 CR (3d) S-20.
[235] 2009 ONCJ 303.
[236] 2013 ONCA 579.
[237] *Petrie* (n 216).
[238] *Cooperwhite* (n 134).
[239] Ibid.

intercourse. Having later divorced his wife, the respondent also raped his subsequent partner on at least four occasions in 2009 and 2010 after she rejected his advances; throughout the period during which these rapes took place, consensual intercourse also occurred. The Crown appealed the *cumulo* sentence on the grounds of undue leniency, submitting that the sentence did not reflect the gravity of the offences, the need for retribution and deterrence and the need to protect the public.[240] Counsel for the respondent submitted that the decisions in *Ramage v HMA*[241] and *Petrie v HMA*[242] demonstrated that 'familiarity' between a rapist and his victim was regarded by the courts as a factor justifying a more lenient sentence than might normally have been thought appropriate. It was submitted that the sentence of six years' imprisonment had been within the range open to the trial judge.[243]

The appeal was heard by a Bench chaired by the Lord Justice Clerk (Carloway). The Court reached the view that the sentence imposed on the respondent was not unduly lenient 'without any difficulty'.[244] It considered that the trial judge had taken all of the various factors into account when selecting the period of custody 'which would inevitably follow from a conviction for rape'.[245] In particular, the trial judge had balanced the repeated nature of the offending in relation to the second victim against the respondent's absence of previous convictions and his assessment as presenting a low risk of re-offending. The Court concluded that although the sentence of six years was lenient, it still fell within the range of sentences reasonably open to the trial judge.[246]

In delivering the leading opinion, the Lord Justice Clerk proceeded to make a number of further observations regarding sentencing for the crime of rape.[247] His Lordship observed that the significance to sentence of a pre-existing, or existing, sexual relationship between a rapist and his victim was 'one of continuing debate'; he considered it to be an issue which the Appeal Court should address, firstly, in the interests of certainty in sentencing policy and, secondly, to promote consistency in sentencing.[248] While it had intended to use the Crown's appeal in *Cooperwhite* as a vehicle through which to issue sentencing guidelines, it became clear at the hearing that, due to administrative error, the possibility of the Court issuing such guidelines had not, in fact, been canvassed with the parties. The result was that the Court did not hear submissions on the general points of principle involved.[249]

[240] Ibid at [12].
[241] *Ramage* (n 202).
[242] *Petrie* (n 216).
[243] *Cooperwhite* (n 134) at [14].
[244] Ibid at [15].
[245] Ibid at [16].
[246] Ibid.
[247] Ibid at [17]–[23].
[248] Ibid at [17].
[249] Ibid.

The Lord Justice Clerk accepted, by reference to *Ramage*[250] and *Petrie*,[251] that it was 'undoubtedly correct' that the existence of both a pre-existing and an existing sexual relationship between a rapist and his victim had been regarded by the Appeal Court, in the past, as a mitigating circumstance.[252] Although neither the Crown nor counsel for the respondent referred in their submissions to any comparative authority, the Lord Justice Clerk stated that the Court was conscious of the work which had been undertaken in other jurisdictions in an attempt to provide judges with useful guidance on how to approach sentencing in rape cases generally and in cases of relationship rape in particular.[253] In this regard, the Lord Justice Clerk referred to the English guidelines then in force (SGC, 2007a) and to the earlier decision of the Court of Appeal (Criminal Division) in *R v Millberry*.[254] With regard specifically to relationship rape, the Lord Justice Clerk observed that the principle in England and Wales was that judges should adopt the same starting point for relationship rape or acquaintance rape as for stranger rape.[255] This, the Lord Justice Clerk noted, was 'radically different' to the approach in Scotland. This difference would, his Lordship stated, 'require to be expressly addressed in any future consideration'.[256] The Lord Justice Clerk concluded with the following comments:

> 'It is of course possible to say that, in relation to any sentence for criminal conduct, each case will depend upon its facts and circumstances; as indeed it will. However, it is important that general principles are established in order to ensure both consistency and predictability insofar as that is possible and desirable. First-instance courts normally benefit from clear statements of principle from the appellate courts, as was the case in England following *Millberry* [...].'[257]

In an address delivered some five months later, the Lord Justice Clerk stressed the importance of the Appeal Court issuing statements of principle in sentencing and, in particular, of the Court issuing sentencing guidelines, rather than continuing with what he described as the traditional 'haphazard and inconsistent approach with no defined principles' (Carloway, 2013: 25). In *Cooperwhite*, the Lord Justice Clerk was clear that any future guideline judgment from the Appeal Court dealing with sentencing for relationship or acquaintance rape should be informed by a comparative consideration of sentencing practice, both in England and Wales and in other common law jurisdictions:

> 'In a matter of such importance as that under consideration, the court would hope also to have the benefit of guidance from the jurisdictions in the Commonwealth and

[250] *Ramage* (n 202).
[251] *Petrie* (n 216).
[252] *Cooperwhite* (n 134) at [18] and [20].
[253] Ibid at [21].
[254] *Millberry* (n 117).
[255] *Cooperwhite* (n 134) at [21] and [22].
[256] Ibid at [22].
[257] Ibid at [23].

beyond when it comes to address the significance of the relationship between a rapist and his victim in the future.'[258]

Judicial Sentencing Discretion 'Soundly Exercised'? Lord Eassie's Partial Dissent in *Cooperwhite*

Although Lord Bracadale concurred both with the decision to refuse the Crown's appeal and with the Lord Justice Clerk's comments regarding the need for sentencing guidance,[259] the third member of the Bench, Lord Eassie, expressed certain reservations with regard to the latter point. Although his Lordship agreed that the Crown's appeal should be refused, Lord Eassie was not persuaded that there was any evident need for the Appeal Court to issue sentencing guidelines for rape.[260] His Lordship stated that he was not aware of 'any wide discrepancy or difference of approach in the sentencing of those convicted of rape and similar sexual offences' in Scotland and considered that the discretion of sentencing judges was 'generally soundly exercised' in this regard. Rape cases, his Lordship stated, tended to be 'particularly "fact-specific"'; relationships between victims and perpetrators 'may vary considerably in their nature and quality'; and, for these reasons, Lord Eassie declared that he had reservations as to whether, in practice, the issuing of guidelines in this area would prove to be of any real assistance to sentencing judges.[261] His Lordship concluded by stating that, in his view, it is necessary 'to exercise caution when considering sentencing guidance issued in other jurisdictions' as the general sentencing framework may be very different and may include provisions not available in Scotland.[262]

Lord Eassie's comments were regrettable since, as we have already seen,[263] sentencing lends itself particularly well to comparative treatment. What is more, his Lordship's comments were at odds with decisions of the Appeal Court which stressed the importance of considering comparative jurisprudence in sentence appeals. Although in the recent past the Appeal Court may not have entirely approved of attempts by counsel to cite English case law in sentence appeals (see Lord Rodger of Earlsferry, 2010: xviii), even in 2013 when the opinions in *Cooperwhite* were delivered (some two years before the Court began to encourage judges to have regard to English sentencing guidelines as a 'cross-check' on their sentences[264]) it was recognised that where principles of sentencing law and practice were in issue, it was legitimate (and perhaps even expected) for the Court to look

258 Ibid.
259 *Cooperwhite* (n 134) at [30].
260 Ibid at [28].
261 Ibid.
262 Ibid at [29].
263 See the discussion in Chapter 1.
264 See above.

to jurisprudence beyond its own case law for assistance (see *HMA v Roulston*[265] and *McCourt v HMA*[266]).

Reflecting 'Modern Thinking' on Relationship Rape: The Decision in *SSK*

Following its decision in *HMA v Cooperwhite*,[267] an opportunity arose for the Appeal Court to issue sentencing guidance for relationship rape some two-and-a-half years later in a subsequent Crown sentence appeal, *HMA v SSK*.[268] In *SSK*, the respondent was convicted after trial of seven charges of sexual offences committed against two former partners and their two children over a period of some six years. Some of the offences preceded the commencement of the Sexual Offences (Scotland) Act 2009 while others were committed after the 2009 Act had come into force. The two adult victims were the respondent's mistress, CD, and his wife, AM. In respect of the offences committed against CD, the respondent was convicted of indecently assaulting her at common law by continuing to anally penetrate her after she had withdrawn her consent; of indecently assaulting her on several occasions at common law by again anally penetrating her; and of anally raping her on several occasions contrary to section 1 of the 2009 Act. In respect of his wife, AM, the respondent was convicted of the same statutory charge of anal rape.

The Crown appealed the extended sentence of seven years, comprising a custodial term of five years and an extension period of two years, imposed by the trial judge on the grounds of undue leniency. Given that some of the offences of anal rape against CD were libelled as indecent assault at common law while others were libelled as the statutory offence of rape, with the statutory offence of rape also libelled in respect of AM, the trial judge imposed separate sentences for each offence. The custodial sentences imposed by the judge ultimately amounted to two years' imprisonment for the three charges of anal rape of CD; a concurrent sentence of one year's imprisonment for the anal rape of AM; and three years' imprisonment in respect of the sexual offences committed against CD and AM's children. Thus the respondent received an effective custodial sentence of two years' imprisonment for the various anal rapes committed against his former wife and his mistress.

The evidence at trial disclosed that the respondent and the victims CD and AM were all involved in the 'swinging', or 'partner swapping', scene in Glasgow. Evidence was led regarding the sexual promiscuity in which the parties indulged

[265] *Roulston* (n 57) at [17].
[266] [2012] HCJAC 32; 2012 JC 336 at [16].
[267] *Cooperwhite* (n 134).
[268] [2015] HCJAC 114; 2016 SCCR 74.

at 'swinging' parties. In his report to the Appeal Court the trial judge made various controversial remarks about the two victims which partly explained why the sentences he saw fit to impose were so low. The judge referred to AM as a person who 'acknowledged few if any sexual boundaries'. He quoted from her testimony about her sexual exploits which, his Lordship remarked, provoked periodic 'incredulous mirth' amongst the jurors. The judge proceeded to describe the degree of force involved in the anal rape of AM as 'not great'. He described the level of the respondent's criminality in respect of the rape and the level of harm suffered by the victim as 'minor', involving only 'a transient sense of violation'. The judge considered that this incident equated with an assault which might have been prosecuted at summary level.[269]

The trial judge's comments in respect of the victim CD were no less extraordinary. He described her as 'sexually confident' in relation to her involvement in the swinging scene; he referred to her decision not to report the rapes at the time; and described her as 'condoning' or 'acquiescing in' [*sic*] the rapes. The judge also referred to CD freely choosing to continue to live with the respondent after the rapes had occurred. The judge regarded this as such 'powerful mitigation' [*sic*] that he might have considered admonishing the respondent, had the convictions involving CD stood alone.[270]

The main thrust of counsel's plea in mitigation before the trial judge was the impact of the offences on the adult victims, against the background of what was described as general sexual promiscuity. The trial judge described the offences in his report to the Appeal Court as 'essentially non-violent relationship rapes'. The judge expressed the view that juries do not convict of such rapes because, according to 'received wisdom', High Court sentences for such offences are disproportionate. The judge also questioned whether all rapes needed to be tried by a jury. This appears to amount to a suggestion that certain rapes ought to be tried summarily by a sheriff or summary sheriff sitting alone, in which case the sentencing powers of the court would be limited to 12 months' imprisonment. While he considered that the rapes were 'at the lower end of the seriousness scale', the trial judge reported that he did not regard the respondent's relationships with the adult victims as a mitigating factor *per se*.[271]

On appeal, the Crown submitted that the overall sentence failed to give adequate weight to the gravity of the respondent's crimes, the extended period over which they took place and the effect on the victims. In particular, it was submitted that had the Definitive Guideline on Sexual Offences (Sentencing Council, 2013a) applicable in England and Wales been applied, a much higher sentence would have been imposed. The Crown also referred to the guideline judgment

[269] Ibid at [5].
[270] Ibid at [7].
[271] Ibid at [11].

of the New Zealand Court of Appeal in *R v AM*[272] where, in setting out ranges of sentence for the offence of rape, it was held that 'culpability is not reduced by any sense of entitlement associated with a current or previous relationship' and that '[t]here is no separate regime for sexual violation of a spouse or partner or those who have previously been in a relationship'.[273] While the Crown in the present case considered the sentences 'derisory', it did not consider this to be a suitable case for the Appeal Court to issue sentencing guidelines, given the existence of offences involving both adult and child victims.[274]

In allowing the Crown's appeal, the Court (a Bench chaired, as in *Cooperwhite,*[275] by Lord Justice Clerk Carloway) began its discussion of how the Scottish courts should sentence relationship rape by noting the trial judge's 'pithy remarks' about prosecution policy for rape and related matters, before continuing:

> 'The short point is that, whatever a judge's own views may be, he must sentence on the basis of the crimes of which the respondent has been convicted, albeit in the contexts in which these crimes have been committed, in light of current Scottish sentencing principles and practice.'[276]

With regard to the issue of relationship rape it was held, by reference to the decision in *R v AM*[277] that: '[t]he court finds the general reasoning of the New Zealand Court of Appeal in this area as generally persuasive and reflective of modern thinking'.[278] The Appeal Court, however, added the following caveat:

> 'That is not to say that the existence of a continuing relationship is irrelevant. It may bear upon sentence insofar as it may (or may not) indicate the impact on the victim. However, given the status of crime as a public wrong, the victim's view, even if regarded as genuine, "normally cannot overwhelm the outcome."'[279]

The Court considered that in the present case, the trial judge had afforded too much weight to the victims' past sexual experience and to the existence of both prior and continuing sexual relationships between the parties.[280] The Crown's appeal was allowed, the sentences imposed by the trial judge quashed and, having regard to the principle of totality, an overall custodial sentence of eight years' imprisonment was imposed, with an extension period of four years.[281]

The decision in *SSK* is to be welcomed as going a considerable way towards settling the debate in Scottish sentencing jurisprudence as to whether 'relationship'

[272] *AM* (n 170), considered in Chapter 7.
[273] Ibid at [61].
[274] *SSK* (n 268) at [14].
[275] *Cooperwhite* (n 134).
[276] *SSK* (n 268) at [23].
[277] *AM* (n 170).
[278] *SSK* (n 268) at [27].
[279] Ibid at [26] citing *R v AM* (n 170) at [64].
[280] *SSK* (n 268) at [27].
[281] Ibid at [27]–[28].

rape should attract the same sentence as 'stranger' rape.[282] Although a prior relationship does not reduce an offender's culpability and the same sentencing regime now applies to both relationship and stranger rape, this is subject to the Appeal Court's own observation that the existence of a continuing relationship is not irrelevant as it may (or may not) indicate the impact on the victim. This aspect of the decision in *SSK* breaks from past sentencing practice in which stranger rape was arguably perceived as the paradigm of 'real' rape (see Brown, 2016b: 6). In this regard, the decision in *SSK* is a good example of how a reflective judgment from an appellate court can identify the need for a change of direction, in terms of the factors to be taken into account in sentencing (see O'Malley, 2016: 18–19).

Certain of the comments made by the trial judge in *SSK* rightly attracted trenchant criticism. For Sharon Cowan the judge's comments amount to victim blaming: he downplayed both the impact of sexual assault upon the victims and the culpability of the respondent. For Cowan, the trial judge's reasoning was troubling in that it evidenced a reluctance to take sexual offending seriously (2019: 48–49). Andrew Tickell, who aptly describes the trial judge's disparaging comments about the victims as 'appalling', notes that:

> 'It is remarkable – quite remarkable – that any trial judge would treat a note of appeal against sentence as an opportunity for a general meditation on such diverse topics as prosecution policy and jury reactions to [victims] … But it is the attitudes disclosed in the judge's note which are most disturbing … [T]he sections related stand starkly at odds with the hard-won modern understanding that rape is a distinctive and serious wrong … The idea that a victim "condoned" their own rape, or that they "acquiesced" in it – the idea that the "guilt" of victims … weighs against a more severe penalty being imposed on their abuser – I'm stunned that any judge of the High Court would even contemplate these views, never mind setting them down in writing for senior colleagues, reviewing their sentencing decision. Just stunned. Wrongheaded, outdated and wrong, wrong, wrong' (Tickell, 2015).

Although undoubtedly warranted, such criticism arguably deflected attention from an important shortcoming of the Appeal Court's decision. Despite the welcome comments regarding the sentencing of relationship rape, the decision in *SSK* does nothing to alter the *levels* or *ranges* of sentence for rape. In the absence of any guidelines from the Appeal Court, the starting point sentence for rape, or the 'benchmark' as it was described by the Lord Justice Clerk in *Cooperwhite*,[283] remains three-and-a-half years' imprisonment following the decision in *Shearer*.[284] Most common law jurisdictions, however, adopt higher – sometimes significantly higher – starting points for sentencing rape. As we have seen in Chapter 4, the

[282] See the discussion of the decisions in *Ramage* (n 202), *Petrie* (n 216), and *Cooperwhite* (n 134), above.
[283] *Cooperwhite* (n 134) at [19].
[284] *Shearer* (n 119).

starting point in England and Wales has long been set at five years and there is now a sentencing range of between four and seven years (Sentencing Council, 2013a: 10–11). In New Zealand, as we shall see in Chapter 7, the starting range set by the Court of Appeal in *R v AM*[285] is six to eight years' imprisonment.

While the Appeal Court in *SSK* stressed the importance of judges sentencing rape 'in light of current Scottish sentencing principles and practice'[286] this observation is problematic for two reasons. Firstly, there are, in fact, very few principles for sentencing rape in the Scottish courts, at least when compared with other common law jurisdictions. Secondly, Scottish sentencing practice for the offence remains significantly out of line with practice in other such jurisdictions.[287] Despite the Crown's submission to the contrary, the appeal in *SSK* presented an opportunity for the Appeal Court to address these problems by issuing formal sentencing guidelines. Given the Court's evident willingness in *SSK* to engage with sentencing jurisprudence from England and Wales and New Zealand, it would have been preferable had the Court issued its own sentencing guidelines for rape. By using the decision of the New Zealand Court of Appeal in *R v AM*[288] as a template, or at least a point of departure, the Appeal Court could have issued such guidelines by fully discussing relevant aggravating and mitigating factors and by setting out appropriate ranges of sentence which reflect those factors.

One of the difficulties with the present system of appellate sentencing guidance that operates in Scotland, whether in the form of formal guideline judgments or through appellate statements of principle, is that the Appeal Court has to wait for a suitable case to arise on appeal before a guideline judgment can be issued.[289] The system is essentially reactive, with the Appeal Court being confined to making statements of principle in response to the issues raised by the particular case under consideration (Brown, 2017a: 158). Crown appeals against sentence on the grounds of undue leniency have often afforded the Court a valuable opportunity to issue sentencing guidelines on a variety of offences and in relation to various aspects of sentencing procedure.[290] Insofar as it broadly aligns the approach of the Scottish courts towards the sentencing of relationship rape with practice elsewhere, the decision in *SSK* is to be welcomed. In declining to issue its own guidelines to assist judges in sentencing rape, however, the decision represents something of a missed opportunity for the Appeal Court.

[285] *AM* (n 170).

[286] *SSK* (n 268) at [23]. See also the discussion of the decisions in *Geddes v HMA* (n 65), *Scottish Power Generation Ltd v HMA* (n 67), and *HMA v Collins* (n 43) above in which the Appeal Court emphasised the need for judges to consider Scottish precedent as a first resort.

[287] See Chapters 4, 6, and 7.

[288] *AM* (n 170) at [34] to [64].

[289] See, however, the discussion of the role of the Scottish Sentencing Council, above.

[290] See, for example, *HMA v Graham* (n 42) on child pornography offences; *HMA v Boyle* [2009] HCJAC 89; 2010 JC 66 on the imposition of punishment parts in life sentences; and *Spence v HMA* (n 45) on guilty plea discounts.

Further Developments in Rape Sentencing: The Decisions in *AB* and *Collins*

Considerations in Sentencing Oral Rape – The Crown Appeal in *AB*

A further Crown sentence appeal, *HMA v AB*,[291] was heard by the Appeal Court along with the appeal in *SSK*.[292] In *AB*, the Crown successfully appealed as unduly lenient the sentence of three years' imprisonment imposed on the respondent following his conviction after trial of orally raping his 14-year-old stepdaughter. The appeal was allowed, the sentence of three years' imprisonment quashed and a sentence of five years' imprisonment was substituted. In her report to the Appeal Court, the trial judge acknowledged that the respondent had been in a position of trust. She took into account the respondent's lack of analogous offending and explained that she had also had regard to the absence of 'penile penetration or other activity that physically damaged the [victim's] physical integrity' [*sic*].[293]

AB was the first occasion on which the Appeal Court was required to consider the appropriate sentence in a case of oral rape, the definition of rape having been expanded on 1 December 2010 to include oral penetration.[294] Following the trial judge's comments, in which her Ladyship appeared to suggest that oral rape was less serious than vaginal rape, the Court made the following observations on sentencing cases of oral rape:

> '[The Court] recognises, as it may always have done, that an act of oral rape may be as abhorrent, demeaning and traumatising as vaginal rape … It must always be a question of facts and circumstances whether an act of oral rape will attract a higher sentence than a vaginal rape or vice versa. The factors to be considered will include, in each case: the level of violence used; the relationship between the offender and the victim; the age or other vulnerability of the victim; the degree of psychological as well as physical harm caused; the age, previous convictions and character of the offender and any degree of remorse. There are, of course, many other variables.'[295]

Following *AB* the position in Scotland now mirrors that in England and Wales, in that it cannot be said that any one form of non-consensual penetration is inherently a more serious violation of the victim's sexual autonomy than another. While this is not expressly stated in the English Definitive Guideline (Sentencing Council, 2013a), the position in England is well settled and no distinction is made as between types of penetration (see Rook and Ward, 2016: 39).

[291] *AB* (n 60).
[292] *SSK* (n 268). Both Crown appeals were heard on 9 October 2015.
[293] *AB* (n 60) at [5].
[294] Under section 1 of the Sexual Offences (Scotland) Act 2009, discussed in the introduction to this chapter.
[295] *AB* (n 60) at [11] and [12].

In *AB*, the Court's inclusion of the relationship between the offender and the victim in the list of aggravating factors in cases of rape is significant. While, as we have seen, in *HMA v SSK*[296] the same Bench broadly approved the observation of the New Zealand Court of Appeal in *R v AM*[297] that an offender's culpability is not *reduced* 'by any sense of entitlement associated with a current or previous relationship',[298] this part of the decision in *AB* goes further in suggesting that, in appropriate circumstances, a relationship between the parties – be it a sexual relationship or, as in *AB*, a familial relationship – can be an *aggravating* factor (*cf*, in England and Wales, the decision in *R v DO*[299]). The Court in *AB* was, however, careful to stress the importance of sentencing judges having regard to all the facts and circumstances of the individual case.[300] Perhaps the most that can be said is that the fact that the parties were in an established relationship may well be an aggravating factor in sentencing, although not every case will be treated as such.[301]

A particularly troubling aspect of the decision in *AB* concerns the trial judge's view of oral rape as being somehow less serious than vaginal rape. The section of the judge's report to the Appeal Court in which she discussed the issue was, at best, inelegantly worded, with her Ladyship making reference to the absence of any activity that 'physically damaged the [victim's] physical integrity'.[302] It may be that the trial judge intended to refer to the victim having sustained no physical injury. Even if this were so, it would not amount to a mitigating factor since, as we have seen, in the majority of cases of rape, victims in fact sustain no physical injuries.[303]

As the remarks of the trial judge in *AB* are reported, however, it appears that in her Ladyship's view, instances of oral rape have no effect on the victim's physical integrity. This is a matter of concern. It may be that these remarks were overshadowed by the reported comments of the trial judge in *SSK*.[304] The Appeal Court issued its opinion in *SSK* eight days after it issued its opinion in *AB* and, as we have seen, certain remarks made by the trial judge in the latter case were the subject of critical opprobrium. In any event, the remarks by the trial judges in these cases suggest that there is an inability or failure amongst certain Scottish judges to comprehend the nature of rape and the true dynamics of the offence. This may have been due to both the trial judges in *AB* and *SSK* having practiced predominantly at the civil Bar prior to their appointment to the Bench. One effect of the specialisation increasingly demanded of counsel is that an individual who may well be appropriate for judicial appointment may have little, if any, experience in criminal law and of the sentencing process (see Brown, 2017a: 94–96

[296] *SSK* (n 268).
[297] *AM* (n 170).
[298] Ibid at [61] approved in *SSK* (n 268) at [27].
[299] [2015] 1 Cr App R (S) 41 considered in Chapter 4.
[300] *AB* (n 60) at [12].
[301] See *R v DO* (n 299) at [31].
[302] *AB* (n 60) at [5].
[303] See Chapter 2.
[304] *SSK* (n 268), discussed above.

and, for similar observations in respect of the Canadian and Australian judiciaries see, respectively Craig, 2018: 208–210 and Krasnostein, 2015: 116 and McClellan, 2012: 26). This clearly has important implications for judicial training and professional development.

The failure to understand the nature and effect of rape is not, however, limited to the Bench. Despite the Court in *AB* being clear that oral rape is not necessarily less serious than vaginal rape, the import of the decision was overlooked by counsel (an experienced member of the criminal Bar) in *Ronald (Marc) v HMA*.[305] In the appeal against sentence following the appellant's conviction of, *inter alia*, one charge of vaginal rape and one charge of oral rape, counsel submitted that the charge of oral rape was less serious because it involved non-vaginal penetration. The Appeal Court refused counsel's submission and the appeal against sentence was refused.

Sentencing Sexual Offences Committed in Abuse of a Position of Trust – The Crown Appeal in *Collins*

The most recent opinion of the Appeal Court to examine questions of principle in the sentencing of sexual offences is *HMA v Collins*.[306] In this case, the respondent was convicted after trial of five charges of indecent behaviour towards vulnerable girls aged between 12 and 16 and of repeatedly raping one of the victims. The offences were committed between 1995 and 2006 at secure residential units where the victims resided and where the respondent was employed as a care worker. The Crown appealed as unduly lenient the *cumulo* sentence of six years' imprisonment imposed by the trial judge.

In allowing the appeal and substituting a *cumulo* sentence of 10 years' imprisonment, the Appeal Court reviewed the relevant Scottish case law on sentencing sexual offences committed in abuse of a position of trust and/or authority; extracted the relevant principles; and set out broad ranges of appropriate sentences, along with relevant aggravating and mitigating factors, in order to guide judges in the sentencing process.[307] The sentences ranged from four to nine years' imprisonment for historic charges of the common law crime of lewd and libidinous practices and behaviour (essentially child sexual abuse) or indecent assault;[308] and from eight to 10 years (or possibly longer in certain circumstances) in cases involving the rape of a victim in respect of whom the offender was 'in a position of trust or authority'.[309] The Court stressed the importance of the sentencer having regard in all cases

[305] High Court of Justiciary on appeal, 31 May 2018, unreported (see the case note by Brown, 2018a). For a full discussion of the facts of the case, see Chapter 3.

[306] *Collins* (n 43).

[307] Ibid at [40]–[42].

[308] Ibid at [40].

[309] Ibid at [41].

to the degree of harm, both physical and psychological, caused by the sexual abuse in question and to the violation of the victim's physical and psychological integrity.[310]

The Court stated that the sentencing guidance in this case applies, but is not limited, to cases in which an offender commits sexual offences in the course of his employment as a teacher, social worker, care worker, or his having held any other position of authority within an institutional and/or educational setting.[311] The guidance in *Collins* thus applies mainly, although not exclusively,[312] to sentencing sexual offences committed against children and young persons. In framing the guidance, the Court followed the more formal Definitive Guideline on Sexual Offences in England and Wales (Sentencing Council, 2013a) by focusing on the *harm* caused to the victim and the *culpability* of the offender.

The Sentencing Range for Rape in Scotland

We have seen in England and Wales that although there is always a baseline of harm in sentencing rape, the starting points range from five years' imprisonment (with a range of between four and seven years) for offences featuring the lowest level of harm and culpability, through to 15 years' imprisonment (with a range of between 13 and 19 years) for offences featuring the highest levels of harm and culpability.[313] To the extent that a 'tariff' or 'going rate' for sentencing rape has been developed by the Appeal Court in Scotland in recent years, how does it compare to practice south of the border?

Certain judges of the Appeal Court have not proved amenable to the concept of a tariff, starting point, or sentencing range for the crime of rape. In delivering the opinion of the Court in *Ahmadi v HMA*,[314] for example, Lord Menzies stated that:

> 'We make it clear that we are not setting down, nor are we to be taken to be setting down, any sort of minimum or indeed any sort of maximum [for sentencing rape]. We deal with this case and the circumstances of this case alone.'[315]

Notwithstanding the Court's reluctance to set a minimum sentence in *Ahmadi*, we have already seen how the Scottish courts have used the sentence of three-and-a-half years' imprisonment imposed in *HMA v Shearer*[316] as a starting point, or 'benchmark' as Lord Justice Clerk Carloway put it in *HMA v Cooperwhite*,[317]

[310] Ibid at [40] and [41].
[311] Ibid at [41].
[312] See, for example, *HMA v Murray* (n 47), discussed later in this chapter.
[313] See Chapter 4.
[314] *Ahmadi* (n 89).
[315] Ibid at [3].
[316] *Shearer* (n 119).
[317] *Cooperwhite* (n 134) at [19].

in sentencing rape.[318] This is not to suggest that the *Shearer* benchmark operates as a minimum sentence in cases of rape: cases will arise, albeit infrequently, where justice dictates that a lesser sentence is imposed or even, exceptionally, that no punishment be imposed at all. In *HMA v Cieslak*,[319] for example, Lady Scott, sitting at Glasgow High Court, discharged the accused absolutely following his plea of guilty to a statutory charge of raping a 12-year-old girl. The accused was a 19-year-old college student who met the victim in a taxi queue in Edinburgh city centre at 4 am. The victim, who had been drinking vodka with a group of older youths and who had the appearance and demeanour of being in her late teens or early twenties, took the accused to an impromptu party at the house of one of her friends. She told the accused that she was 16. Once at the party the accused and the victim paired off and had intercourse. Given the nature of the accused's culpability, Lady Scott considered that there was no need for, nor any public interest in, punishment. Her Ladyship concluded that justice was best served by taking what she described as 'the wholly exceptional decision' not to sentence the accused.[320] The decision in *Cieslak* is thus a paradigm example of an apparently aberrational sentence which, on closer scrutiny, is entirely justified by exceptional factors relating both to the offence and the offender (O'Malley, 2013b: 230).

We have seen that recent reported decisions from the Appeal Court suggest that the ordinary range of sentence imposed by the Scottish courts for the rape of an adult victim tends to range from three to six years' imprisonment:

- In *JD v HMA*,[321] a sentence of three years' imprisonment was imposed on appeal for the rape of the intoxicated victim at a party, the Appeal Court noting that the case fell 'very much towards the lower end of the spectrum of seriousness' when considering cases of rape.[322]
- In *Allan v HMA*,[323] a sentence of four years' imprisonment was imposed on appeal for the rape of the intoxicated, and initially unconscious, victim in her hotel room.
- In *Ferguson v HMA*,[324] a sentence of four years' imprisonment was imposed after trial for the rape of the intoxicated victim at a party.
- In *Crombie (Gerald) v HMA*,[325] a sentence of four years' imprisonment with a 12-month extension period was imposed on appeal for the rape of the intoxicated and disabled victim, the offence being committed in her own home.

[318] See above.

[319] Glasgow High Court, 17 March 2017, unreported (see the discussion by Brown, 2019a: 70–72 and 2017c).

[320] *Cf* the decisions of the Court of Appeal (Criminal Division) in *R v Charles* [2012] 1 Cr App R (S) 74 and *R v B* [2011] EWCA Crim 165, discussed in Chapter 4.

[321] *JD* (n 141).

[322] Ibid at [9].

[323] *Allan* (n 139).

[324] *Ferguson* (n 153).

[325] *Crombie* (n 140).

- In *Lee v HMA*,[326] a sentence of four-and-a-half years' imprisonment was imposed after trial for the rape of a vulnerable and intoxicated university student.
- In *Gubinas and Radavicius v HMA*,[327] sentences of four-and-a-half years' imprisonment were imposed after trial on both appellants for the abduction, detention and multiple perpetrator rape of the intoxicated victim over several hours, the offences being filmed on mobile phones.
- In *Lennie v HMA*,[328] sentences of five years' imprisonment were imposed after trial on both the appellant and his co-accused, both offenders having raped the intoxicated victim at a party.
- In *Parker v HMA*,[329] a sentence of five years' imprisonment was imposed after trial for the vaginal and anal rape of the intoxicated victim at a party.
- In *HMA v AB*,[330] a sentence of five years' imprisonment was imposed on a successful Crown appeal (increased from three years), the respondent having orally raped his 14-year-old stepdaughter.
- In *Ahmadi v HMA*,[331] a sentence of five years' imprisonment, with a two-year extension period, was imposed on appeal for the rape of the intoxicated victim, the appellant having entered her bedroom uninvited.
- In *HMA v Cooperwhite*,[332] a *cumulo* sentence of six years' imprisonment for two charges of rape committed against two former partners was upheld on an unsuccessful Crown appeal.

Further examples include the following recent appellate decisions:

- In *Walker v HMA*,[333] a sentence of four years' imprisonment was imposed on the appellant after trial. The appellant drove the victim to remote locations and raped her twice.
- In *Diba v HMA*,[334] a sentence of five years' imprisonment was imposed on the appellant after trial for raping a woman whom his friend had met in a nightclub.
- In *Watson v HMA*,[335] a sentence of five years' imprisonment was imposed on the appellant after trial for digitally penetrating and raping the intoxicated victim (a distant relative) at a party.

326 *Lee* (n 144).
327 *Gubinas and Radavicius* (n 85).
328 *Lennie* (n 148).
329 *Parker* (n 150).
330 *AB* (n 60).
331 *Ahmadi* (n 89).
332 *Cooperwhite* (n 134).
333 [2015] HCJAC 122; 2016 SCL 190.
334 [2015] HCJAC 123; 2016 SCL 186.
335 [2019] HCJAC 51.

- In *Gupta v HMA*,[336] a sentence of five-and-a-half years' imprisonment was imposed on appeal where the appellant had met the intoxicated victim in the street, took her back to his flat and raped her.
- In *Dalton v HMA*,[337] a sentence of six years' imprisonment was imposed on appeal following the appellant's conviction for raping his partner.
- In *Drummond v HMA*,[338] a sentence of six years' imprisonment, with an extension period of two years, was imposed on the appellant after trial for raping his partner and assaulting her to her severe injury and permanent disfigurement.

We have also seen, however, that many of these cases would have attracted considerably higher sentences had the offences been committed in England and Wales, following application of the Definitive Guideline on Sexual Offences (Sentencing Council, 2013a).[339]

Conscious of the baseline of harm inherent in all cases of rape (see Sentencing Council, 2012: 15–16) sentences imposed in what the Scottish courts have nevertheless regarded as particularly serious cases, often featuring numerous aggravating factors, multiple rapes, or rape accompanied by other sexual offences, tend to range between eight and 10 years' imprisonment:

- In *McMeekin v HMA*,[340] a *cumulo* sentence of eight years' imprisonment was imposed on the appellant following his conviction for raping two former partners. The appellant raped the first victim while she was asleep; he anally raped the second victim in the course of what had, up until that point, been consensual sexual activity.
- In *HMA v SSK*,[341] a sentence of eight years' imprisonment, with a four-year extension period, was imposed on a successful Crown appeal (increased from five years' imprisonment), the respondent having been convicted of seven charges comprising various sexual offences, including rape, committed against two former partners and their two children over a period of some six years.
- In *Livingstone v HMA*,[342] a sentence of eight years' imprisonment, with an extension period of three years, was imposed on the appellant after trial for assaulting and raping a former partner and for assaulting and raping a woman whom he had met via a social networking site.
- In *Falconer v HMA*,[343] a *cumulo* sentence of eight years' imprisonment, with an extension period of three years, was imposed on the appellant following his

[336] High Court of Justiciary on appeal, 10 January 2013, unreported.
[337] [2015] HCJAC 24; 2015 SCCR 125.
[338] [2015] HCJAC 30; 2015 SCCR 180.
[339] See above.
[340] [2019] HCJAC 53.
[341] *SSK* (n 268), discussed above
[342] High Court of Justiciary on appeal, 20 November 2014, unreported (the circumstances are briefly considered in the appellant's conviction appeal, reported at [2014] HCJAC 102; 2014 SCL 868).
[343] [2019] HCJAC 42.

conviction of three charges of assaulting and raping two former partners. In refusing the appeal against sentence, the Appeal Court stated that it regarded the sentence as 'a standard sentence for the sort of sexual offending that is in issue here'.[344]

- In *Ronald (Marc) v HMA*,[345] a *cumulo* sentence of nine years' imprisonment imposed on the appellant for three charges of sexual assault and two charges of rape committed against his former partner was upheld on appeal, the appellant having video recorded the offences.
- In *Anoliefo v HMA*,[346] a sentence of nine years' imprisonment was imposed on appeal for what the Appeal Court descried as 'a very serious' and 'predatory' offence.[347] The appellant had met the intoxicated victim outside a nightclub; he enticed her into his car, drove her to his flat where he detained her against her will and made her watch pornography on his computer, before assaulting and raping her.
- In *Graham v HMA*,[348] the appellant was convicted of assault, assault by penetration and rape; all three offences were committed against a former partner. The sentence of 10 years' imprisonment (comprising concurrent sentences of 18 months for the assault and three years for the assault by penetration, with a consecutive sentence of seven years' imprisonment for the rape) was upheld on appeal.

With regard to the upper range of sentence appropriate for rape, the Appeal Court made certain observations in *Greens v HMA*.[349] In *Greens*, the appellant pleaded guilty to assaulting the victim to her severe injury and to the danger of her life and to raping her. The victim was a Dutch tourist whom the appellant attacked, and subsequently abandoned, in a rural location. The appellant encountered the victim when he was driving on a remote road. He stopped his car, parked in a layby and approached the victim. He grabbed the victim, pushed her down an embankment, pushed her to the ground, pinned her down and threatened her with a knife before raping her. During the course of the rape the appellant repeatedly struck the victim in the face. Upon examination at hospital she was found to have sustained extensive injuries. Her right eye was swollen shut and she sustained a laceration over her nose, in addition to certain genital injuries. The victim was referred to a maxillofacial surgeon and was eventually left with scarring. Although she made a good physical recovery, the psychological effects of the offence were profound: her personality changed; she lost confidence and was afraid to leave her home; she felt anxious around men; and, in her daily life, she lost perspective so that even minor

[344] Ibid at [15].
[345] *Ronald* (n 305).
[346] High Court of Justiciary on appeal, 2 October 2012, unreported.
[347] Ibid at [10].
[348] [2018] HCJAC 69; 2019 JC 26.
[349] [2007] HCJAC 55; 2008 SCL 124.

setbacks caused her disproportionate distress, leaving her inconsolable for hours or even days. She was eventually referred to a psychiatrist.

The appellant was sentenced to 10 years' imprisonment, discounted from 12 years to reflect his guilty plea, with an extension period of seven years. In refusing the appeal against sentence, the Appeal Court made what it described as 'general observations'[350] on the sentencing of rape:

> '[T]he circumstances [in which rape is committed] vary enormously from what could be described as an amorous sexual encounter that has got out of control at one end of the scale to at the other an appalling attack on a woman by a complete stranger, unprovoked and without justification … There may be reasons why in relation to the former set of cases convictions are difficult to obtain. *When it comes to the latter type of case … it has to be recognised in the public domain that the courts will not tolerate this type of aggressive sexual conduct, to put it at its least, when imposing sentences.* If it is appropriate, and we have some hesitation whether it is, to scale the gravity of the crime of rape, this particular offence has to be placed at the highest level of it.'[351]

Turning to the circumstances of the case, the Court noted that the victim had been attacked by a complete stranger 'in a most brutal and aggressive way, quite apart from the sexual content'.[352] The Court described the victim's injuries as 'frankly horrific', noting that the violence used by the appellant went 'far beyond what might on one view be described as necessary for a rapist to achieve his sexual gratification'.[353] More important, however, was the psychological effect on the victim.[354] The Court concluded:

> '[T]his in our opinion is one of the worst cases of rape this court has had the misfortune to encounter for some time, when not connected also with murder … [W]e are entirely satisfied that the sentencing judge in setting the starting point for the custodial term at 12 years reflects no more than an acceptable sentence. A higher one could easily have been contemplated.'[355]

Two observations may be made regarding the decision in *Greens*. Firstly, the Court referred to a 'scale' of gravity in cases of rape comprising, at one end, 'an amorous sexual encounter that has got out of control' and, at the other, 'an appalling attack on a woman by a complete stranger, unprovoked and without justification'.[356] Crucially, the Court stated that it is apparently only the *latter* type of rape involving 'aggressive sexual conduct' that will not be tolerated.[357] Thus, the Court made a clear distinction between so-called 'forcible' and 'non-forcible' rape for the

[350] Ibid at [29].
[351] Ibid at [30] and [31], emphasis added.
[352] Ibid at [33].
[353] Ibid at [34].
[354] Ibid at [34] and [36].
[355] Ibid at [36] and [38].
[356] Ibid at [30].
[357] Ibid at [31].

purposes of sentencing. This may have been a well-intentioned attempt to simply highlight the truly appalling nature of the rape in *Greens*; however, in so doing the Court perpetuated the outdated and discredited view of violent rape by a stranger as being the paradigm of 'real rape' – a view which the Appeal Court disapproved some eight years later in *SSK*.[358]

Secondly, in placing the rape in *Greens* at 'the highest level'[359] of gravity, upholding the custodial sentence of 10 years (discounted from a headline sentence of 12 years) and noting that a higher sentence 'could easily have been contemplated',[360] the decision suggests that the upper range of sentence for rape of an adult lies in the region of perhaps 12 to 17 years' imprisonment. This proposition is borne out by the decision in *Murray v HMA*,[361] in which the appellant's sentence was increased on appeal to nine-and-a-half years' imprisonment, discounted from a headline sentence of 12 years, following his conviction for sexually assaulting two elderly residents in a care home and raping a third.

There are, as yet, no guidelines available for sentencing rape in Scotland[362] other than the Appeal Court's direction to judges to have recourse to the English Definitive Guideline as a 'cross-check' on their proposed sentences to see 'if any major disparity appears'.[363] If we apply the Definitive Guideline (Sentencing Council, 2013a: 10–11) as a cross-check to the sentence imposed in *Greens*, we see that, although the case falls into 'Category 1' in respect of the *harm* caused (having regard to the extreme violence used and the severe psychological impact on the victim), with regard to the appellant's *culpability* the case falls to be classified at level B since the offence appeared to be unplanned and none of the other culpability factors (such as recording of the offence, the presence of multiple perpetrators, or use of alcohol on the victim to facilitate the offence) were present. This results in a starting point of 12 years' imprisonment, with a sentencing range of between 10 and 15 years. Applying certain aggravating factors set out in the Definitive Guideline (the appellant's targeting of a lone female in a remote location, the fact that the appellant ejaculated and his use of a weapon) would increase the sentence from the starting point of 12 years towards perhaps 14 or 15 years. Thus, whilst the offence in *Greens* was described by the Appeal Court as one of the worst cases of rape it had encountered for some time,[364] cases featuring any of the culpability factors set out in the Definitive Guideline (all absent in *Greens*) would be more serious still. Such cases could result in a sentence in the region of perhaps 15 to 17 years' imprisonment.

[358] *SSK* (n 268), considered above.
[359] *Greens* (n 349) at [31].
[360] Ibid at [38].
[361] *Murray* (n 47), considered below.
[362] *Cooperwhite* (n 134) at [19] per the Lord Justice Clerk (Carloway).
[363] *AB* (n 60) at [13], considered above.
[364] *Greens* (n 349) at [36].

'Too Generous and Too Readily Given'? Guilty Plea Discounts in Sentencing Rape

The leading decisions in *HMA v Cooperwhite,*[365] *HMA v SSK,*[366] *HMA v AB,*[367] *HMA v CH*[368] and *HMA v Collins*[369] all concerned accused who were convicted after trial. A point which did not concern the Appeal Court in these Crown sentence appeals but which has generated considerable discussion in other cases, both in the Appeal Court and the Court of Appeal (Criminal Division),[370] in recent years, is the issue of granting a reduction, or discount, in sentence to an accused who pleads guilty.

The Development of Guilty Plea Discounting in Scotland

Unlike in England and Wales, guilty plea discounting is a relatively recent aspect of criminal procedure in Scotland. The statutory provisions relating to guilty plea discounting are contained in section 196 of the Criminal Procedure (Scotland) Act 1995 which are in broadly similar terms to the corresponding English provisions.[371] Yet a very different approach is taken by the Scottish courts to the practice of guilty plea discounting (see generally Brown, 2017a: Chapter 7; see also Brown, 2019b and 2017d).

Until late 2011, judges were directed to follow the approach to guilty plea discounting set out in *Spence v HMA*[372] in which the Appeal Court issued sentencing guidelines as to the expected levels of discount. These levels took the form of a sliding scale and were set at one-third for a guilty plea tendered at the first opportunity at an accelerated pleading diet, one-quarter for a plea tendered at a preliminary hearing and a maximum of one-tenth for a plea tendered on the day of the trial. This sliding scale was effectively identical to the guidelines then in force in England and Wales issued by the Sentencing Guidelines Council (SGC, 2007b; see Leverick 2008a: 44 and 2008b: 311).

Use of the sliding scale was, however, disapproved by the Lord Justice Clerk (Gill) in delivering the leading majority opinion in *Gemmell v HMA,*[373] decided on 20 December 2011, when a full Bench of five judges considered various questions of principle relating to the practice of guilty plea discounting. For present

[365] *Cooperwhite* (n 134).
[366] *SSK* (n 268).
[367] *AB* (n 60).
[368] *CH* (n 76).
[369] *Collins* (n 43).
[370] See Chapter 4.
[371] Ibid.
[372] *Spence* (n 45).
[373] *Gemmell* (n 22).

purposes, the important aspects of Lord Justice Clerk Gill's opinion comprised certain observations regarding the discretionary nature of guilty plea discounting. Lord Gill considered that 'the court's discretion to allow a discount should be exercised sparingly and only for convincing reasons';[374] that the size of any discount should be left to the sentencer's discretion, subject only to 'the broad principle that, in general, the discount will be the greater the earlier the plea';[375] and that as sentencing guidelines provide a structure for, but do not remove, judicial discretion, then where a sentencer has given cogent reasons for allowing a particular discount, or for declining to apply a discount at all, it would only be in exceptional circumstances that the Appeal Court should interfere.[376]

The only other member of the Court in *Gemmell* to address this issue was Lord Eassie. Although his Lordship agreed that the allowance of a discount was, 'in its essential nature, an exercise of discretion', his Lordship advocated recourse to the *Spence* sliding scale in all but exceptional circumstances.[377] Thus, judges were left to choose between Lord Gill's discretionary approach to guilty plea discounting and the more certain, although arguably more formulaic, approach advocated by Lord Eassie (see Leverick, 2012: 235). Although Lord Gill's discretionary approach was the subject of academic criticism, with one commentator arguing that it was expressed in vague terms and had the potential to result in inequalities in the application of guilty plea discounts (see Leverick, 2012 and 2013: 261–62), the discretionary approach to discounting was later affirmed by the Appeal Court in *Murray v HMA*.[378] *Murray* was an important decision that illustrates the difficulties which guilty plea discounting can cause in cases of rape.

Limiting the Discount in Rape Sentencing – The Decision in *Murray*

The decision in *Murray*[379] throws into sharp relief the problems that face the judge in discounting a sentence where the offender has pleaded guilty to rape or other serious sexual offences, for it is in cases where the offence is particularly morally repugnant that the tensions surrounding guilty plea discounting are most acute (Leverick, 2014: 348 and 2013: 263). In *Murray*, the appellant pleaded guilty at an accelerated pleading diet to various sexual assaults, including rape, committed against three elderly female residents of the care home in which he worked. The offences were described by the sentencing judge as truly shocking, depraved

[374] Ibid at [77].
[375] Ibid at [78].
[376] Ibid at [81].
[377] Ibid at [145].
[378] *Murray* (n 47).
[379] Ibid.

and as comprising an immense breach of trust.[380] All the victims suffered from severe dementia; the appellant admitted that he had targeted them because they were incapable of communication and were thus unable to report the offences. The offences only came to light when a colleague of the appellant discovered him sexually assaulting one of the victims late at night.

On appeal against the *cumulo* sentence of seven years' imprisonment, discounted from a headline sentence of nine years, imposed by the sentencing judge on the ground that a supposedly insufficient discount had been allowed, the Appeal Court exercised its rarely used statutory power[381] to *increase* the appellant's sentence (see Shaw, 2014 and Shead, 2008). In delivering the leading opinion, Lord Gill (now Lord Justice General), referred to the opinion he had delivered some 12 months previously in *Gemmell*[382] and reiterated that an accused is not *entitled* to any particular discount in return for a guilty plea; that the issue is one for the sentencer's discretion; and that to maintain public confidence in the criminal justice system and the credibility of sentences, this discretion should be exercised sparingly and only for convincing reasons.[383] The sentence of seven years' imprisonment was held to be unduly lenient. The appellant's sentence was increased to nine years and six months', discounted from a headline sentence of 12 years.[384]

The Appeal Court thus applied a discount of approximately a fifth to the appellant's sentence, as opposed to the discount of one third which would have been indicated under the earlier guidelines in *Spence*.[385] The factors in *Murray* that pointed to a substantial discount weighed heavily as there were significant benefits to avoiding a trial: there was no need for the witnesses and relatives of the victims to endure a distressing wait for what would have been a harrowing trial (see Leverick, 2013: 263 and 2014: 348). The factors that pointed to a longer sentence, however, such as the need to protect the public against a potentially dangerous offender and, particularly, the need for a disposal that reflected the moral gravity of the offence, weighed equally heavily (Leverick, 2013: 263).

The Appeal Court did not face an easy task in reconciling these concerns. On one view the Court in *Murray* may have been uncomfortable with awarding a larger discount because of the abhorrent nature of the appellant's crimes (Leverick, 2013: 263). As Lord Gill observed in *Gemmell*[386] the allowance of substantial discounts may cause the sentencing decisions of the criminal courts to lose credibility and in this way may erode the authority of the courts generally.[387] His Lordship also expressed concern about the possible perception of injustice that

[380] Ibid at [13].
[381] Under the Criminal Procedure (Scotland) Act 1995, s 118(4)(b).
[382] *Gemmell* (n 22).
[383] *Murray* (n 47) at [16] and [17].
[384] Ibid at [27]–[29], the Lord Justice Clerk (Carloway) and Lady Paton concurring.
[385] *Spence* (n 45).
[386] *Gemmell* (n 22).
[387] Ibid at [74].

guilty plea discounts can engender, particularly in cases (such as *Murray*) where severe sentences are warranted.[388]

The judicial move away from allowing substantial discounts in particularly serious cases is also evident in the later decision in *Geddes v HMA*.[389] In *Geddes*, the appellant tendered an early plea of guilty to a charge of causing death by dangerous driving whilst drunk, having been almost twice the then legal limit. In delivering the opinion of the Court, the Lord Justice Clerk (Carloway) again stressed that the selection of the appropriate discount is primarily a matter for the sentencing judge;[390] however, his Lordship also stated that 'the high level of headline sentence' (eight years' imprisonment in this case) was a factor that the sentencer can take into account in fixing the *level* of discount.[391] This is an important observation: it suggests that a lesser discount may be warranted when sentencing offences with inherently high levels of harm and culpability (Brown, 2015c: 6).

Since the decision in *Murray*[392] there have, as yet, been no further reported sentence appeals in cases of rape in which the discount has been restricted on the basis of the seriousness of the offence. This may be due to Lord Gill's dicta in *Gemmell*,[393] reiterated in *Murray*,[394] that strongly discouraged appeals against sentence based solely on the level of discount allowed by the sentencing judge.

The application of a guilty plea discount to serious cases such as rape can result in the sentencing process coming to be seen simply as an administratively convenient bargain unrelated to the offender or the moral gravity of his conduct (see Brown, 2017a: Chapter 7; see also Ashworth and Roberts, 2017: 861; and Mack and Roach Anleu, 1997: 132–33). The difficulty with treating offence seriousness as a relevant factor in discounting, however, is that guilty plea discounting is not a practice that lends itself to justification on intrinsic moral grounds. As Lord Gill himself acknowledged in *Gemmell*,[395] guilty plea discounting is most convincingly justified on the basis of cost savings to the criminal justice system. These benefits stem from cases where the offence is morally reprehensible just as they do from others and, again, as Lord Gill recognised in *Gemmell*,[396] the seriousness of the offence is appropriately reflected in the headline sentence, *not* the discount (Leverick, 2014: 348). Even so, Sheriff Christopher Shead observes that the decision in *Murray*[397] is evidence that a strand of judicial thinking has emerged which holds that 'discounts have become too generous and too readily given' (Shead, 2013: 95; see also Brown, 2017a: Chapter 7).

[388] Ibid at [76].
[389] *Geddes* (n 65).
[390] Ibid at [21].
[391] Ibid.
[392] *Murray* (n 47).
[393] *Gemmell* (n 22) at [81].
[394] *Murray* (n 47) at [26].
[395] *Gemmell* (n 22) at [34].
[396] Ibid at [27]–[32] and [37]–[39].
[397] *Murray* (n 47).

6

Proportionality and Individualised Justice

Rape Sentencing in the Republic of Ireland

Introduction

Two distinct forms of rape are currently recognised in the Republic of Ireland: so-called 'common law' rape and 'section 4' rape (Leahy and Fitzgerald O'Reilly, 2018: 13; O'Malley, 2013a: 35).[1] 'Common law' rape is something of a misnomer as the offence has, in fact, been defined by statute since 1981. Under section 2 of the Criminal Law (Rape) Act 1981 ('the 1981 Act'), as amended by section 21 of the Criminal Law (Rape) (Amendment) Act 1990 ('the 1990 Act'), common law rape consists of sexual intercourse by a man with a non-consenting woman. The offence is thus gender specific: it can be committed only by a male against a female. For the purposes of section 2 of the 1981 Act, 'sexual intercourse' means penetration of the vagina by the penis; other kinds of sexual penetration fall within the ambit of 'section 4' rape. A charge of rape libelled under section 4 of the 1990 Act consists of sexual assault involving forms of bodily penetration other than penile-vaginal intercourse, including penile penetration of the mouth or anus, or vaginal penetration by an object (O'Malley 2013a: 35 and 68; see also Bacik, 2002a: 149; and Leahy and Fitzgerald O'Reilly, 2018: 13, 59–60).

Under section 48 of the Offences Against the Person Act 1861 and section 4(2) of the 1990 Act respectively, both common law rape and section 4 rape are punishable with a maximum sentence of life imprisonment (Leahy and Fitzgerald O'Reilly, 2018: 60; O'Malley, 2016: 367 and 2013a: 68). The common law exception whereby a man could not be held guilty of raping his wife was abolished in the Republic of Ireland in 1991, when section 5 of the 1990 Act came into force (Leahy and Fitzgerald O'Reilly, 2018: 43–46).

[1] For a full discussion of 'common law' rape, see Leahy and Fitzgerald O'Reilly, 2018: Chapter 1 and O'Malley, 2013a: 35–68. For a full discussion of 'section 4' rape, see Leahy and Fitzgerald O'Reilly, 2018 Chapter 2 and O'Malley, 2013a: 68–69.

Sentencing in the Republic of Ireland

In common with jurisdictions such as Scotland[2] and New Zealand,[3] Ireland retains a largely discretionary sentencing system. There are few formal constrains on judicial sentencing discretion in Ireland, reflecting a commitment to individualised justice for offenders (Bacik, 2002b: 351; Campbell, 2008: 291–92; Edwards, 2019: 40–42; Maguire, 2012: 14 and 2008: 11; O'Flaherty, 2002: 375–76; O'Malley, 2018: 8; 2016: 1, 6; 2013b: 220; 2001: 135; 1994: 3). Indeed, individualised sentencing has long been seen as the foundation of the Irish sentencing system (Leahy and Fitzgerald O'Reilly, 2018: 212). Sentencing law in Ireland remains uncodified. While there is no single statute that governs sentencing law, or the procedural elements of it, the traditional purposes of punishment – retribution, deterrence, rehabilitation, incapacitation and denunciation – apply by virtue of the common law, with each rationale having been recognised by the appellate courts (O'Malley, 2016: 44–45). Judges, therefore, have a wide discretion in sentencing individual offenders and may impose any sentence up to the permitted statutory maximum (Conway et al, 2010: 179; O'Malley, 2013b: 220).

Kilcommins et al (2004: 145) criticise the judiciary for making sentencing decisions based on what they term a 'disjointed "instinctive synthesis" approach'. Although not referred to by the authors, the term 'instinctive synthesis' was first employed as a description of judicial sentencing methodology by the Victoria Court of Criminal Appeal in *R v Williscroft*.[4] We have already seen that this process involves the judge deciding the appropriate sentence by considering all factors of the case together, coming to a decision as to sentence without assigning a precise weight to individual factors.[5] This description and methodology was subsequently approved by the High Court of Australia in *Markarian v The Queen*[6] (see Bagaric et al, 2018: 34–40; Brown, 2019a: 55–59; Freiberg, 2014: 228–33; Krasnostein, 2015: 36–40; and Mackenzie, 2005: 17–19) and adopted by the Scottish High Court of Justiciary on Appeal in a series of recent decisions (see Brown, 2017a: 29–46).

It is debatable whether Irish judges do, in fact, sentence by way of *pure* 'instinctive synthesis' as Kilcommins et al suggest, at least insofar as the term is understood in Australian (and, more recently, in Scottish) sentencing jurisprudence. As we shall see, following the decision of the Supreme Court in *People (DPP) v M*,[7] Irish judges must, in fact, follow a staged or two-tiered approach to sentencing in which the judge firstly identifies a presumptively appropriate sentence before moving on to apply any mitigation to reach the final sentence.[8] The reasoning which a judge

[2] See Chapter 5.
[3] See Chapter 7.
[4] [1975] VR 292.
[5] See Chapter 5.
[6] [2005] HCA 25.
[7] [1994] 3 IR 306.
[8] See below.

undertakes at both of these stages may be that of 'instinctive synthesis', as it is a process that requires her to consider the relevant factors before making a decision without indicating the precise weight being attributed to individual factors or groups of factors. In the recent decision in *People (DPP) v O'Brien*,[9] the Court of Appeal elaborated on this aspect of Irish sentencing methodology:

> '[T]he Irish courts have never regarded the process of sentencing as amenable to a rigid algorithmic or mathematical approach, but rather have always recognised that each sentence must be individual and that in determining the overall weight to be afforded to factors weighing in the balance at either stage of the sentencing process, i.e. the assessment of gravity or the affording of discount for mitigation … the sentencing judge will bring to bear his or her professional experience, intuition and subjective judgment and arrive at a figure on the basis of what is sometimes called in the academic literature on sentencing 'instinctive synthesis'. The sentencing judge must be afforded a significant margin of discretion in doing so.'[10]

Notwithstanding judicial recourse to 'instinctive synthesis' at both stages of the sentence calculation, the very fact that Irish judges arrive at the final sentence by way of a two-tiered, or staged, approach militates against Irish sentencing methodology being seen in terms of a 'pure' instinctive synthesis of the type developed in Australian sentencing jurisprudence. In Australia, the sentence is determined in a single, global process of reasoning, all relevant considerations being simultaneously unified, balanced and weighed by the sentencing judge (see Bagaric et al, 2018: 31–40; Brown, 2017a: 29–46 and Krasnostein and Freiberg, 2013: 268). In any event, in Ireland, as in other common law jurisdictions in which judges do in fact employ the 'pure' instinctive synthesis approach to sentencing, judicial sentencing discretion is not entirely unconstrained. In selecting the appropriate sentence, judges must apply certain general principles established by the former Court of Criminal Appeal (now known as the Court of Appeal) and the Supreme Court (Cahillane, 2013: 12; Maguire, 2016: 303 and 2012: 27; O'Malley, 2016: 1 and 2013b: 220; and *People (DPP) v O'Brien*[11]). These principles typically indicate aggravating and mitigating factors that are either generally applicable or which are considered appropriate in certain circumstances (O'Malley, 2013a: 642). As Mr Justice Edwards of the Court of Appeal explains, the principles of sentencing law as expounded by the superior appellate courts operate to corral and guide the exercise of judicial discretion (Edwards, 2019: 41).

The provision of such appellate guidance results in judges exercising what O'Malley terms as 'principled discretion' (O'Malley, 2011: 5; 2001: 135). Under this system, judges retain the discretion they already enjoy, but exercise it in accordance with settled principles. Departure from these principles is, however, permissible when a novel or exceptional aspect of a particular case so requires (O'Malley, 2001: 135). Principled discretion thus results in *informed* judgment (O'Malley, 2011: 5).

[9] [2018] IECA 2.
[10] Ibid at [35].
[11] *O'Brien* (n 9) at [37].

The principles laid down by the appellate courts 'guide courts in navigating their way through the facts to arrive at an acceptable sentence' (O'Malley, 2013a: 533). This, in turn, leads to the development of a 'sentencing canon' of leading appellate decisions – decisions which are authoritative yet not inflexible (see O'Malley, 2001: 136; 1994: 9–10; see also Brown, 2017a: 168–69, 230–31 and Charleton and Scott, 2013: 21–22).

The Irish sentencing system thus produces a discretion underpinned by principles, rather than hemmed in by rules (O'Donnell, 2012: 256). It allows judges to retain sufficient flexibility to keep justice to the fore while injecting enough consistency to make sentencing outcomes more predictable (O'Donnell, 2012; 257). O'Malley explains that the Irish courts traditionally resisted the introduction of sentencing guidelines in any shape or form, preferring to rely on judicial discretion informed by such appellate guidance (2013a: 642; see also 2013b: 221 and 223; Bacik, 2002b: 348; Campbell, 2008: 292; and O'Flaherty, 2002: 375–76). In *People (DPP) v Tiernan*,[12] for example, the Supreme Court declined a specific invitation from the Attorney General to issue sentencing guidelines for rape in a similar manner to the guideline judgments then issued by the English Court of Appeal.[13] The Irish appellate courts also resisted specifying ranges of sentence in the sense of indicating appropriate bands or starting points for variants of particular offences (O'Malley, 2013a: 644). Indeed, in *People (DPP) v Kelly*,[14] the Court of Criminal Appeal implicitly disapproved this approach.

A 'Quiet Revolution' – The Court of Criminal Appeal's Guideline Judgments in *Ryan* and *Fitzgibbon*

While there was no change of judicial sentencing policy in the intervening years (Maguire, 2012: 24 and 2008: 28–29; O'Malley, 2016: 9–10; 2013a: 642; and 2013b), two decisions of the Court of Criminal Appeal and a recent decision of its successor, the Court of Appeal, indicate a move away from the traditional approach that eschewed either the use of sentencing guidelines or the setting of ranges of sentence, towards a new system of guideline judgments (Ashworth, 2015: 453; Davey, 2014: 31; O'Malley, 2016: 15–18). On 18 March 2014, the Court of Criminal Appeal handed down its judgments in *People (DPP) v Ryan*[15] and *People (DPP) v Fitzgibbon*.[16] In disposing of Mr Ryan's appeal against a sentence of four-and-a-half years' imprisonment following his pleas of guilty to certain

[12] *People (DPP) v Tiernan* [1988] IR 250, considered below.

[13] On the format of the guideline judgments issued by the Court of Appeal in England and Wales at this time, see Chapter 4.

[14] [2005] 2 IR 321 at 325.

[15] [2014] IECCA 11.

[16] [2014] IECCA 12.

firearms offences, the Court of Criminal Appeal considered the extent to which it had jurisdiction to provide general sentencing guidance.[17]

Although it recognised that sentencing is a complex matter, the Court in *Ryan* nevertheless considered it important that sentencers strive to maintain a level of consistency so that, at least in a general way, like cases are treated in a similar fashion.[18] The Court considered it appropriate to establish the broad legal principles by reference to which any sentencing exercise should be conducted, as well as providing, where possible, 'some guidance as to the broad range of sentences which should be imposed, all else being equal, across the spectrum of severity applicable to an offence under consideration'.[19] While acknowledging that it was bound by the decision in *People (DPP) v Tiernan*[20] in which the Supreme Court considered it inappropriate to constrain judicial sentencing discretion by specifying benchmark or tariff sentences, the Court of Criminal Appeal in *Ryan* did not read the judgment in *Tiernan* as precluding it from issuing 'some broad level of guidance … as to the range of sentences which may be appropriate for an offence under consideration on an appeal, having regard to the severity of the offence and the culpability of the accused.'[21]

In terms redolent of the approach of the Scottish Appeal Court towards the provision of appellate sentencing guidance,[22] however, the Court was careful to stress the importance of judicial discretion in applying such guidance:

> 'It clearly remains a matter for the sentencing judge to form a judgment, on all of the relevant facts, as to where on that range the offence for which the accused is to be sentenced lies. It is also clearly a matter for the sentencing judge to decide on the extent to which any aggravating or mitigating factors identified ought to increase or decrease the sentence to be imposed. Thus, *any such range provides broad guidance but does not seek to impose any form of standardisation of penalty*.'[23]

The Court proceeded to set out presumptive ranges of sentence for offences involving the possession of firearms[24] and identified the factors that were likely to influence the placing of a particular offence along the relevant scale.[25] This approach was endorsed in *Fitzgibbon*[26] in which the Court set out broad guidelines, again in the form of presumptive sentence ranges, for offences of assault causing serious harm.[27] As in *Ryan*, however, the Court stressed the importance of judicial discretion in the application of the guidelines.[28]

[17] *Ryan* (n 15) at para 1.3.
[18] Ibid, para 1.1.
[19] Ibid, para 1.2.
[20] *Tiernan* (n 12).
[21] *Ryan* (n 15) at para 2.3; see also para 3.4.
[22] See Chapter 5.
[23] *Ryan* (n 15) at para 2.3, emphasis added; see also O'Malley, 2016: 19.
[24] Ibid at para 7.16.
[25] Ibid at para 7.15.
[26] *Fitzgibbon* (n 16) at para 7.1.
[27] Ibid at paras 8.10–8.14.
[28] Ibid at para 8.11.

The decisions in *Ryan* and *Fitzgibbon* amount to a conscious departure by the Court of Criminal Appeal from established sentencing principles (Davey, 2014: 33). Indeed, O'Malley (2014) considers them to represent 'a quiet revolution' in the Irish criminal justice system. In examining the application of the *Ryan* and *Fitzgibbon* guidelines, he commends the initiative taken by the Court as an 'ice-breaking exercise'. O'Malley (2016: 17) suggests that judicially developed sentencing guidance is the most promising way forward in ensuring that sentencers' discretion is exercised in a principled manner. While such indicative guidelines are intended to strike a balance between doing justice to the individual offender and achieving a measure of consistency in sentencing, O'Malley cautions that sentencers must not apply the guidelines rigidly or automatically and without regard to any particular factors that might justify either an upward or downward departure from the recommended ranges (2017: 20).

Some 12 months later, in *People (DPP) v Counihan (sub nom People (DPP) v C)*,[29] a successful appeal by the Director of Public Prosecutions in which a suspended sentence imposed for rape and sexual assault was replaced with three years' imprisonment, the Court of Appeal reaffirmed its commitment to providing non-binding and flexible sentencing guidance. The Court acknowledged the difficulty of the task facing the sentencing judge and continued:

> 'This Court will endeavour over time to establish some consistent rules for the guidance of trial and sentencing judges. There is no question of this Court trying to lay down rigid propositions that sentencing courts must follow, but guidance is necessary and appropriate to let judges know how this Court approaches the issues of sentences in different classes of cases. It is in everybody's interest who is involved in the justice system or observing it to know how this Court approaches its task … It is … desirable that the courts should aim for consistency of approach in this important task. It is not satisfactory to have a wide range of sentencing practice depending on the inclination of the individual judge. Having said that, there will, of course, be variations in sentences, even in fairly similar cases because judges will inevitably differ to some degree in their assessment of the different elements that go into the sentencing process.'[30]

The Guideline Judgments in *Casey and Casey* and *Mahon*

On 26 April 2018, the Court of Appeal continued the work of the former Court of Criminal Appeal in crafting guideline judgments when it issued its own guideline judgment in *People (DPP) v Casey and Casey*.[31] The gap of some four years between the issuing of the guideline judgments by the Court of Criminal Appeal

[29] [2015] IECA 76, discussed later in this chapter.
[30] Ibid at [1] and [2].
[31] [2018] IECA 121.

in *Ryan*[32] and *Fitzgibbon*[33] and the Court of Appeal's judgment in *Casey and Casey* was due primarily to the Court of Appeal's workload since its establishment in October 2014. The Court inherited over 1,300 cases of all types from the Supreme Court, as well as 220 sentence appeals and 75 conviction appeals from the former Court of Criminal Appeal. It thus began work with a substantial acquired backlog; it also had to contend with resourcing issues, particularly with regard to the availability of judges. As the preparation of guideline judgments involves substantially more research than is required in the preparation of sentencing judgments that are confined to the circumstances of the individual case, the workload of the Court of Appeal precluded the issue of guideline judgments until early 2018 (see Edwards, 2019: 44).

In *Casey and Casey*, the Court identified a range of aggravating factors that may arise in cases of burglary, and divided the spectrum of penalties available into three parts: a low range, a medium range and a high range.[34] As in *Ryan*,[35] however, the Court stressed the continued importance of judicial discretion in placing a case within a particular range:

> 'The Court recognises that the circumstances surrounding individual offences can vary greatly and that is so even before one comes to consider the circumstances of the individual offender. While a consistency of approach to sentencing is highly desirable, it is not to be expected that there will be a uniformity in terms of the actual sentences that are imposed. There are just too many variables in terms of the circumstances of individual offences, but even more so in terms of the circumstances of individual offenders, for that to happen. Again, the Court recognises that there is no clear blue water between the ranges. Often the most that can be said is that an offence falls in the upper mid-range/lower higher range. In many cases whether an offence is to be labelled as being at the high end of the mid-range or at the low end of the high range for an offence is often a fine call. The judge's legitimate margin of appreciation may well straddle both.'[36]

O'Malley commends the decision in *Casey and Casey* as 'a significant development in sentencing law' and notes that the decision could lead to 'more coherent and structured sentencing in the future' (see Gallagher, 2018). The decision in *Casey and Casey* could herald the introduction of more guideline judgments from the Court of Appeal, including a guideline judgment for sentencing rape.

Twelve months after the Court of Appeal issued its decision in *Casey and Casey*,[37] the Supreme Court issued sentencing guidelines for manslaughter in *People (DPP) v Mahon*.[38] The Court continued the approach taken in previous

[32] *Ryan* (n 15).
[33] *Fitzgibbon* (n 16).
[34] *Casey and Casey* (n 31) at [46]–[49].
[35] *Ryan* (n 15) at para 2.3.
[36] *Casey and Casey* (n 31) at [49].
[37] *Casey and Casey* (n 31).
[38] [2019] IESC 24.

appellate judgments of setting out sentencing ranges, or bands.[39] Four such bands were identified: 'worst cases', namely those which are close to indistinguishable in culpability from murder; cases of 'high culpability', which tend to feature various aggravating factors; cases of 'medium culpability', where aggravating factors are either absent or are considerably lesser than in the higher range; and finally cases of 'lower culpability', which may include cases featuring diminished responsibility or extreme provocation.[40] The Court specifically listed attacks by men on women, and the use of lethal weapons such as knives, as aggravating factors in manslaughter.[41]

The Judicial Council Bill and the Sentencing Guidelines and Information Committee

Sentencing guidelines may, in the fullness of time, become a standard feature of Irish sentencing practice following the passing of the Judicial Council Bill 2017.[42] The Bill was passed on 9 July 2019 by the Oireachtas, the Irish legislature. The Bill provides, amongst other things, for the establishment of a Judicial Council.[43] Amongst its other duties, the Judicial Council is tasked with judicial training and investigating complaints against judges.[44]

The Bill also provides for the establishment of a Sentencing Guidelines and Information Committee ('SGIC') by the Judicial Council.[45] In a speech to the Dáil Éireann, the lower house of the Oireachtas, on 4 July 2019 during the second stage of the Bill, the Minister for Justice and Equality acknowledged that sentencing guidelines developed by the appellate courts were increasingly being used by judges as a technique for structuring their sentencing discretion. Nevertheless, the Minister considered that 'confidence in the criminal justice system would be enhanced by the production of formal guidelines' (Flanagan, 2019). It was in this context that amendments were made to the Bill during its passage which provided for the establishment of the SGIC, rather than a Sentencing Information Committee as originally proposed.[46]

The SGIC is to comprise judicial and lay members, with a judicial majority and a member of the judiciary as chairperson.[47] Its function is to prepare draft

[39] See the decisions in *Ryan* (n 15), *Fitzgibbon*, (n 16) and *Casey and Casey* (n 31), considered above.

[40] *Mahon* (n 38) at [51]–[73].

[41] Ibid at [74].

[42] Bill 33 of 2019, hereinafter 'the Bill'.

[43] Ibid, s 6.

[44] Ibid, s 7.

[45] Ibid, s 23.

[46] For a discussion of a recent unsuccessful legislative attempt to introduce a sentencing council in Ireland, see Edwards, 2019: 43, fn 21.

[47] Bill 33 of 2019, s 24. The SGIC will comprise 13 members, with eight judicial members nominated by the Chief Justice and five lay members appointed by the government (s 24(1) and (3)).

sentencing guidelines and submit them to the Judicial Council for review and adoption.[48] The SGIC will also prepare draft amendments to sentencing guidelines adopted by the Council and submit them to the Council for review;[49] monitor the operation of sentencing guidelines;[50] collate information on sentences imposed by the courts;[51] and disseminate that information.[52] In preparing draft sentencing guidelines, the SGIC is given various powers including the power to consult with such persons as it considers appropriate; to collate information on sentencing decisions; and to conduct sentencing research.[53]

In terms of section 92 of the Bill ('Courts to have regard to sentencing guidelines'):

> 'A court shall, in imposing a sentence, have regard to sentencing guidelines relevant to the proceedings before it, unless the court is satisfied that to do so would be contrary to the interests of justice and the reasons it is so satisfied shall be stated by the court in its decision.'

The status of any future sentencing guidelines issued by the SGIC are thus akin to guidelines issued by the Scottish Sentencing Council or by the appellate courts in Scotland.[54] Section 92 of the Bill is drafted in similar terms to the Scottish legislative provisions on sentencing guidelines.[55] As is the case with guidelines issued by the Scottish Sentencing Council and approved by the High Court of Justiciary, if draft guidelines are issued by the SGIC and are subsequently adopted by the Judicial Council, then Irish judges are required to *have regard* to them and to state their reasons if they decide not to follow a particular guideline.

Unlike the position in England and Wales,[56] there is no requirement that judges *must follow* any sentencing guideline unless satisfied that it would be contrary to the interests of justice to do so.[57] Thus, unlike guidelines issued by the English Sentencing Council, any future Irish sentencing guidelines emanating from the SGIC will not have a presumptively binding status. Indeed, Mr Justice Edwards of the Court of Appeal notes that a body established on a statutory basis to set presumptive determinate sentences would impinge significantly on judicial discretion (Edwards, 2019: 43). Mr Justice Edwards suggests that it could prove 'constitutionally problematic' if any such body were to be unduly preoccupied with generating consistency at the expense of more individualised sentencing (see also O'Malley, 2016: 20–21 and 769–71).

[48] Ibid, s 23(2)(a).
[49] Ibid, s 23(2)(b).
[50] Ibid, s 3(2)(c).
[51] Ibid, s 3(2)(d).
[52] Ibid, s 3(2)(e).
[53] Ibid, s 3(4).
[54] See Chapter 5.
[55] The Criminal Procedure (Scotland) Act 1995, s 197 and the Criminal Justice and Licensing (Scotland) Act 2010, s 6(1) and (2) considered in Chapter 5.
[56] See Chapter 4.
[57] See the Coroners and Justice Act 2009, s 125(1) considered in Chapter 4.

At the time of writing, the Judicial Council has yet to be established. Indications appear to be that the SGIC will be established, as part of the Judicial Council's remit, in 2020. Guilfoyle (2019) suggests, however, that it is premature to consider issuing sentencing guidelines until comprehensive statistics on sentencing practices and trends are available and maintains that such statistics are required to understand fully how judges currently sentence particular offences. He explains:

> '[I]ntroducing sentencing guidelines without an understanding of how offences are currently being sentenced would massively jeopardise the quality and integrity of the guidelines … Sentencing guidelines can improve Ireland's sentencing system but they can also damage it. One sure way of making the situation worse is to create a system where sentencing guidelines are drafted and monitored by a Committee that is underfunded, has unrealistic targets and is constrained in its abilities due to limited and substandard sentencing information.'

The Principle of Proportionality

Ireland has adopted proportionality as the primary distributive principle of sentencing. As von Hirsch explains, the principle of proportionality requires the *severity* of penalties to be determined by reference to the *seriousness* of crimes (von Hirsch, 2017: 63; see also von Hirsch et al, 2005: 201). The seriousness of a particular crime has two main elements: the *harmfulness* of the conduct and the extent of the offender's *culpability* (von Hirsch, 2017: 23; see also von Hirsch, 1993: 29 and Fox, 1994: 498). Thus, the sentences imposed by the Irish courts must be proportionate both to the gravity of the offence and to the personal circumstances of the offender (Conway et al, 2010: 162, 164; Edwards, 2019: 40–41; Kennefick and Fennell, 2017: 486; Leahy and Fitzgerald O'Reilly, 2018: 213, 219; Maguire, 2012: 18–19 and 2008: 17–20; O'Malley, 2017: 372; 2016: 63, 71; 2013a: 533–35; 2011: 81; and 2008: 10). One of the first decisions of the Court of Criminal Appeal to articulate the importance of proportionality in sentencing was *People (Attorney General) v O'Driscoll*[58] where it was stated:

> 'The objects of passing sentence are not merely to deter the particular criminal from committing a crime again but to induce him in so far as possible to turn from a criminal to an honest way of life and indeed the public interest would best be served if the criminal could be induced to take the latter course. It is therefore the duty of the Courts to pass what are the appropriate sentences in each case having regard to the particular circumstances of that case – not only in regard to the particular crime but in regard to the particular criminal.'

As O'Malley (2016: 69) explains, this statement is significant as it became the fountainhead of an elaborate body of proportionality jurisprudence later developed by the superior courts in Ireland. These decisions included *Lynch and*

[58] (1972) 1 Frewen 351.

Whelan v Minister for Justice[59] where, in a constitutional challenge to the mandatory life sentence for murder, the Supreme Court held that proportionality applies where the court has discretion as to sentence.[60] The statement of the Court of Criminal Appeal in *O'Driscoll* also demonstrates that the concept of proportionality is by no means inextricably linked with retributive theories of punishment (O'Malley 2016: 69; *cf* Maguire, 2016: 304–5). Thus, the circumstances of the individual offender may influence, if not determine, the policy objectives underpinning the sentence.

In the course of her judgment in *People (DPP) v M*,[61] Denham J noted that the 'nature of the crime and the personal circumstances of the appellant, are the kernel issues to be considered and applied in accordance with the principles of sentencing'.[62] Denham J explained the importance of the principle of proportionality in sentencing as follows:

> 'Sentences should be proportionate. Firstly, they should be proportionate to the crime. Thus, a grave offence is reflected by a severe sentence … However, sentences must also be proportionate to the personal circumstances of the appellant. *The essence of the discretionary nature of sentencing is that the personal situation of the appellant must be taken into consideration by the court* … Sentencing is a complex matter in which principles, sometimes being in conflict, must be considered as part of the total situation. Thus, while on the one hand a grave crime should be reflected by a long sentence, attention must also be paid to individual factors, which include remorse and rehabilitation, often expressed, *inter alia*, in a plea of guilty, which in principle reduce the sentence.'[63]

Similarly, the Court of Criminal Appeal stated in *People (DPP) v McCormack*:[64]

> 'Each case must depend upon its own special circumstances. The appropriate sentence depends not only upon its own facts but also the personal circumstances of the accused. The sentence to be imposed is not the appropriate sentence for the crime, but the appropriate sentence for the crime because it has been committed by that accused. The range of possible penalties is dependent upon those two factors.'[65]

Most recently, in *Gilligan v Ireland*,[66] the Supreme Court reiterated the importance of proportionality in sentencing:

> 'One of the hallmarks of the exercise of judicial discretion in sentencing is the application of the overriding principle of proportionality … By now, it is well established that the distributive principle of punishment under our law requires that, in general, every sentence must be proportionate to the gravity of the offence and take into account the

[59] [2010] IESC 34.
[60] Ibid at [55].
[61] *M* (n 7).
[62] Ibid at 317.
[63] Ibid at 316 to 318, emphasis added.
[64] [2000] 4 IR 356.
[65] At 359. See also *People (DPP) v Counihan* (n 29) at [4]; *People (DPP) v WC* [1994] ILRM 321 at 325; and *People (DPP) v O'Brien* (n 9) at [45].
[66] [2013] IESC 45.

> personal circumstances of the offender … Here, the term "proportionality" is used in the sense of the judicial task of striking a balance between the particular circumstances of the commission of the offence and the particular circumstances of the offender to be sentenced.'[67]

In this way, the principle of proportionality incorporates judicial discretion into the sentencing framework, allowing sentencing to be individualised based on the specific aggravating and mitigating factors in the particular case (Edwards, 2019: 41–42; Leahy and Fitzgerald O'Reilly, 2018: 219). In tailoring sentences to the individual circumstances of the case, judges are free to choose from multiple sentencing objectives such as retribution, deterrence, public protection and rehabilitation. The judge has a discretion as to which objective ought to be prioritised in the circumstances of the individual case and how best to structure the sentence to give effect to that objective (Edwards, 2019: 42; Maguire, 2012: 19–20 and 2008: 15–17). As with Scottish sentencing practice,[68] there is no stated hierarchical relationship between these aims. Nevertheless, Maguire argues that the fact that proportionality is the guiding principle suggests that retribution is the primary aim of Irish sentencing and it presumably trumps other philosophies (Maguire, 2016: 305; *cf* O'Malley, 2016: 69).

Conversely, in *People (DPP) v GK*,[69] the Court of Criminal Appeal stated that a sentencing court, or an appellate court in reviewing a sentence, should examine the matter 'from three aspects *in the following order of priority*, rehabilitation of the offender, punishment and incapacitation from offending and individual and general deterrence' (emphasis added). This statement that the penal objective of rehabilitation is *always* to be afforded the highest priority was disapproved by a differently constituted Bench of the Court of Appeal in *People (DPP) v O'Brien*.[70] In delivering the judgment of the Court, Edwards J said this:

> 'While we do not now think that this is necessarily a correct statement of principle and prefer an approach in which the correct prioritisation of penal objectives is to be determined by the circumstances of the particular case based on the evidence, we readily accept that in many cases it may indeed be appropriate to prioritise the penal objective of rehabilitation. There will, however, be other cases where it may be appropriate to prioritise deterrence, or retribution and incapacitation.'[71]

Sentencing Methodology – The Two-Tiered Approach

Following the decision of the Supreme Court in *People (DPP) v M*,[72] Irish judges must follow a two-tiered, or two-step, approach to sentencing. In the course of

[67] At [34] and [35] (references omitted).
[68] See Chapter 5.
[69] [2008] IECCA 110 per Finnegan J delivering the judgment of the Court.
[70] *O'Brien* (n 9).
[71] Ibid at [46].
[72] *M* (n 7).

his judgment in *M*, in which he considered the impact of mitigating factors in sentencing, Egan J explained:

> '[A] reduction in mitigation is not always to be calculated in direct regard to the maximum sentence applicable. One should look first at the range of penalties applicable to the offence and then decide whereabouts on the range the particular case should lie. The mitigating circumstances should then be looked at and an appropriate reduction made.'[73]

In her concurring judgment, Denham J said this:

> '[H]aving assessed what is the appropriate sentence for a particular crime it is the duty of the court to consider then the particular circumstances of the convicted person. It is within this ambit that mitigating factors fall to be considered.'[74]

Thus, in constructing a proportionate sentence, judges are required firstly to locate the particular offence on the overall scale of gravity to identify a presumptively appropriate, or 'headline', sentence. In so doing, the judge will have regard primarily to the gravity of the offence, as measured by reference both to the harm caused to the victim and to the offender's culpability as assessed at the time of the offence (O'Malley, 2016: 72–73; see also Maguire, 2016: 304; 2012: 25; and 2008: 22–23). As the Court of Appeal explained in *People (DPP) v Walsh*:[75]

> 'The assessment of the gravity of an offence involves a consideration of the offender's culpability and the harm done. In assessing culpability the court looks at the generic nature of the offence in terms of: its fundamental ingredients; the range of penalties available to address the various circumstances in which the offence may be committed, the particular circumstances in which the actual offence was committed; whether the offence was committed negligently, recklessly or intentionally; and any case specific circumstances tending to aggravate or mitigate the moral culpability of the offender. In assessing the harm done the court must consider the position of the victim, as well as the requirements of society in terms of the need to deprecate and deter future instances of the offending conduct.'

Aggravating circumstances of the offence are factored into the first stage of the sentencing process (Leahy and Fitzgerald O'Reilly, 2018: 222; O'Malley, 2016: 72–73; see also O'Malley, 2013b: 224–25, *People (DPP) v McC*,[76] *People (DPP) v Ryan*[77] and *People (DPP) v Mahon*[78]). The second stage of the process involves consideration of the offender's personal circumstances; in particular, the judge applies any mitigation to the headline sentence to reach the final sentence (Maguire, 2008: 15; O'Malley, 2016: 72–73; 2013b: 224; and 2008: 10).

In Australia, as we have seen,[79] the various appellate courts and the High Court have devoted much time and energy to considering the comparative merits of a

[73] Ibid at 315.
[74] Ibid. See also the decision of the Court of Criminal Appeal in *People (DPP) v Kelly* (n 14).
[75] [2017] IECA 187 at [13].
[76] [2008] 2 IR 92 at 104.
[77] *Ryan* (n 15) at para 3.2.
[78] *Mahon* (n 38) at [45].
[79] See above.

structured approach to sentencing versus the 'instinctive synthesis' approach. As O'Malley observes, the Irish courts have never agonised to the same extent over this issue (O'Malley, 2013b: 224). Nevertheless, the Court of Appeal has consistently stressed the need for judges to follow the staged approach to sentencing (Edwards, 2019: 48; O'Malley, 2016: 74). For example, in *People (DPP) v O'B*,[80] the Court described the staged approach as 'best practice', noting that in this case the sentencing judge's failure to do so made its own task in reviewing the sentence more difficult.[81] The Court repeated these observations in *People (DPP) v Flynn*[82] and *People (DPP) v Molloy (Richard)*.[83]

In commending the staged approach, the Court of Appeal has sought to promote greater consistency in sentencing. Perhaps more importantly, the Court views the staged approach as being conducive to better reasoning in sentencing, while also encouraging a greater rigour of analysis on the part of sentencing judges (Edwards, 2019: 48–49). As the Court of Appeal explained in *People (DPP) v Molloy (Raymond)*:[84]

> 'Sentencing should … be about substance over form, rather than the reverse, although it is increasingly recognised … [that] an accused is entitled to have the reasoning process, by means of which a sentencing court has arrived at the sentence which it has imposed upon him or her, rationally and adequately explained … We have … favoured the staged approach because it seems to us that it is likely to best focus judges at first instance on the overriding criterion of ensuring that sentences are proportionate both to the gravity of the offence and the circumstances of the offender … In addition, it has the advantage of producing better reasoned sentencing judgments, that better explain to the interested parties why a particular sentence was imposed and which are also more readily amenable to review at appellate level.'[85]

Discretion remains at the heart of the Irish sentencing system and, in that regard, the sentencing judge has a significant 'margin of appreciation' in terms of the sentence that she may impose in any particular case (Edwards, 2019: 52). While some structure in sentencing is favoured by the Court of Appeal, it is only as an aide to the correct exercise of the judge's discretion, rather than as a fetter on that discretion (Edwards, 2019: 52–53). Sentencing guideline judgments (such as *People (DPP) v Ryan*[86] and *People (DPP) v Fitzgibbon*[87]) serve to provide the judge with some assistance in undertaking the first stage of the process by identifying the presumptively appropriate penalty or range of penalties. Thereafter, the judge is still required, in terms of the second stage, to give credit for any mitigating factors.

[80] [2015] IECA 255.
[81] Ibid at [36].
[82] [2015] IECA 290 at [13]–[19].
[83] [2016] IECA 239 at [30]– [34]. See also *Mahon* (n 38) at [47].
[84] [2018] IECA 37.
[85] Ibid at [17] and [20], references omitted.
[86] *Ryan* (n 15).
[87] *Fitzgibbon* (n 16).

In this regard, the two-tiered approach for determining a proportionate sentence set out in *M*[88] remains intact (O'Malley, 2016: 74), albeit that the judge will make his or her decision at both stages by recourse to a form of 'instinctive synthesis' in which professional experience, intuition and subjective judgement are employed to make the decision as to sentence (see *People (DPP) v O'Brien*[89]).

The two-tiered approach to sentencing means that it is not unusual to find courts stating that a particular offence is 'high on the scale of gravity', 'in the upper reaches of the mid-range' or 'low on the overall scale' and so forth (O'Malley, 2013a: 644). Other than for cases involving possession of firearms, assault causing serious harm, burglary and manslaughter in which, as we have seen, appellate sentencing guidance has recently been issued,[90] judicial categorisation of types of offence and their gravity, to the extent that it exists, occurs purely on a case-by-case basis (O'Malley, ibid).

Sentencing Rape

The Decision in *Tiernan*

Until such time as the Court of Appeal extends the approach taken by its predecessor, the Court of Criminal Appeal, in *People (DPP) v Ryan*[91] and *People (DPP) v Fitzgibbon*[92] to the sentencing of rape and issues a guideline judgment for the offence, the decision of the Supreme Court in *People (DPP) v Tiernan*[93] remains the leading Irish authority on sentencing for rape (O'Malley, 2016: 369; 2011: 159; Scott, 2017: 1–2). The appellant was sentenced to 21 years' imprisonment following his plea of guilty to an abduction and vicious gang rape. Following the refusal of his appeal against sentence, the Attorney General certified that the case involved a point of law of exceptional public importance, namely the guidelines which the courts should apply in relation to sentences for rape. The case was appealed to the Supreme Court.

The Court allowed the appeal and reduced the sentence to 17 years' imprisonment, a majority of four to one holding that inadequate credit had been given for the appellant's guilty plea.[94] In so doing, however, the Supreme Court expressly declined to issue sentencing guidelines. Although parties made reference in their submissions to a number of decisions of appellate courts in various common law jurisdictions, including the sentencing guidance for the offence of rape provided by the superior courts in New Zealand and England and Wales, the Supreme Court

[88] *M* (n 7).
[89] *O'Brien* (n 9) at [35].
[90] See respectively *Ryan* (n 15), *Fitzgibbon* (n 16), *Casey and Casey* (n 31) and *Mahon* (n 38).
[91] *Ryan* (n 15).
[92] *Fitzgibbon* (n 16).
[93] *Tiernan* (n 12).
[94] Ibid at 256.

considered it inappropriate to lay down any 'standardisation or tariff of penalty' for sentencing cases of rape.[95] In so doing, the majority stressed the 'fundamental necessity' for judges to impose sentences which, in their discretion, appropriately met all the particular circumstances of the case and the particular circumstances of the accused.[96] This was a view shared by the dissenting judge, McCarthy J, who observed that: 'The trial judge … should have a true judicial discretion as to the sentence appropriate in any case.'[97] His Honour's view of the *Billam* guidelines which were then in force in England and Wales[98] as setting a 'minimum standard' for sentencing rape,[99] however, arguably rested upon a misunderstanding of the nature of the English Court of Appeal's guideline judgments.[100]

Thus, the Supreme Court refrained from issuing sentencing guidelines for rape as it was clearly opposed in principle to curtailing judicial sentencing discretion (Campbell, 2017: 481 and 2008: 292; Leahy and Fitzgerald O'Reilly, 2018: 213; Maguire, 2016: 311–12 and 2012: 50; O'Malley, 2011: 123–24 and 1994: 4–5). The Court did, however, set out certain fundamental principles applicable to the sentencing of rape and listed certain factors which are *not* to be treated as relevant to sentencing. Although the decision in *Tiernan* fell short of indicating appropriate ranges of sentence, it nevertheless provides many strands of useful guidance (Edwards, 2019: 45; Scott, 2017: 2). This guidance, the Court stated, was issued specifically with the intention of assisting sentencing judges:

> 'The crime of rape must always be viewed as one of the most serious offences contained in our criminal law even when committed without violence beyond that constituting the act of rape itself … The act of forcible rape not only causes bodily harm but is also inevitably followed by emotional, psychological and psychiatric damage to the victim which can often be of long term and sometimes of lifelong duration … Rape is a gross attack upon the human dignity and the bodily integrity of a woman and a violation of her human and constitutional rights. As such it must attract very severe legal sanctions.'[101]

In a critique of the decision in *Tiernan*, Campbell commends the Court's recognition of the multiplicity of harms inherent in rape; however, she argues that the Court's statement is questionable in two particular respects. Firstly, Campbell notes that the Court distinguishes between 'types' of rape. The Court classifies, and arguably ranks, them with what it describes as 'forcible rape' at the apex. This leads Campbell to suggest that although force or the threat of force is no longer necessary for a conviction for rape, it seems that 'a *de facto* hierarchy remains'

[95] Ibid at 254, per Finlay CJ delivering the leading majority judgment. See also the dissenting judgment by McCarthy J at 257.
[96] Ibid at 254.
[97] Ibid at 257. McCarthy J would have refused the appeal against sentence.
[98] *R v Billam and others* (1986) 8 Cr App R (S) 48, considered in Chapter 4.
[99] *Tiernan* (n 12) at 257.
[100] See the discussion in Chapter 4.
[101] *Tiernan* (n 12) at 253 per Finlay CJ.

(Campbell, 2017: 480). As we have seen, such a *de facto* hierarchy also appears to operate within the Scottish courts, where cases of so-called 'non-forcible rape' (including cases that would, in the past, have been prosecuted as the common law offence of clandestine injury) often attract far lower sentences than cases involving the use of force.[102] Secondly, Campbell suggests that the Court's perception of the inevitability of physical, emotional and psychiatric harm leaves little room for the agency of the victim; this, she argues, underlines the presumptions made about the victim and side-lines the victim's capacity and autonomy (2017: 480–81).

The Court in *Tiernan* considered that the seriousness of rape was such that the appropriate sentence would usually be 'a substantial immediate period of detention or imprisonment'.[103] Finlay CJ went on to explain:

> 'Whilst in every criminal case a judge must impose a sentence which in his [sic] opinion meets the particular circumstances of the case and of the accused person before him, it is not easy to imagine the circumstance which would justify departure from a substantial immediate custodial sentence for rape and I can only express the view that they would probably be wholly exceptional.'[104]

As the Court of Appeal later observed in *People (DPP) v ROD*,[105] the important element of this statement is that each case must be considered in light of its own facts and circumstances (see also Carney, 2002: 387 and O'Malley, 2006: 263 and 2013a: 656). The general principle that rape should be punished with a substantial term of imprisonment does not relieve the sentencing judge of the obligation to carefully consider the *particular* facts of each case, including the offender's personal circumstances, and to select an appropriate sentence (O'Malley, 2016: 368).

The aggravating features in Tiernan's case were listed as follows: the fact that the offence comprised a gang rape; that the victim was raped multiple times; that the rape was accompanied by acts of sexual perversion; the level of violence used; the abduction aspect of the offence; the psychological trauma caused to the victim; and the appellant's previous convictions.[106] Although the Supreme Court declined to approve the *Billam* guidelines then in force in England and Wales, these aggravating factors do, in fact, broadly correspond to the sentencing guidelines set out by the English Court of Appeal in *Billam*.[107] Similarly, the Court in *Tiernan* held that neither a victim's previous sexual experience nor the fact that she could be considered to have exposed herself 'by imprudence' to 'the danger' of being raped could conceivably be considered as mitigating circumstances in any rape.[108] These propositions were also set out by the Court of Appeal in *Billam*.

[102] See Chapter 5. See also the discussion there of the decision of the High Court of Justiciary on Appeal in *Greens v HMA* [2007] HCJAC 55; 2008 SCL 124.
[103] *Tiernan* (n 12) at 253 per Finlay CJ.
[104] Ibid.
[105] [2000] 4 IR 361 at 365.
[106] At [253]–[254].
[107] *Billam* (n 98), considered in Chapter 4.
[108] *Tiernan* (n 12) at 255.

Campbell, however, notes, firstly, that it is regrettable that such judicial pronouncements even need to be made and, secondly, that the Court's reference to 'the danger of rape' reframes the issue of sexual violence as one that seems to inexorably occur, rather than as the actions chosen and perpetrated by autonomous men (Campbell, 2017: 482). Campbell concludes that in seeking to ensure that sexual experience and behaviour do not mitigate, the Court's 'unfortunate choice of words' still serve to reproach the victim. The Court held that the only mitigating factor in Tiernan's case was his guilty plea.[109]

The Application of the *Tiernan* Principles

The two principles of rape sentencing set out in *Tiernan* (namely, the general requirement for an immediate and substantial prison sentence and the overarching need for individualised justice by imposing a sentence tailored to the facts and circumstances of the particular case) have been endorsed in subsequent decisions of the appellate courts (Leahy and Fitzgerald O'Reilly, 2018: 215). In *People (DPP) v Keane*,[110] for example, the respondent, a first offender aged 18 at the time of the offence, gained entry to the victim's house in the early hours of the morning. The victim awoke to find the respondent having intercourse with her. The respondent was sentenced to three years' imprisonment, suspended for five years. In the subsequent prosecution appeal against the sentence on the grounds of undue leniency, the Court of Criminal Appeal endorsed the *Tiernan* principles. In particular, with regard to the need for individualised justice in rape sentencing, the Court explained:

> '[The Court in *Tiernan*] was acknowledging that the ambit of a Judge's obligation under the law to impose a sentence which meets the particular circumstances of a case and of the accused person, even for an offence as grave as rape, does not in principle exclude the possibility of a non-custodial sentence in wholly exceptional circumstances. The wholly exceptional circumstances must be such as to justify a departure from the norm of a substantial custodial sentence.'[111]

The Court in *Keane* allowed the prosecution's appeal and substituted a sentence of 10 years' imprisonment with three years suspended and a one-year post-release supervision order, noting that:

> 'The offence of rape is one of the gravest offences against society and the human integrity of the victim … The circumstances which may be attendant on the commission of the offence of rape are multifarious and aggravating factors, when present, variable and often dissimilar in nature or in their combination. It is one of those offences where it would at least be difficult, or as the Supreme Court put it in the *Tiernan* case,

[109] Ibid at [255]–[256].
[110] [2007] IECCA 119.
[111] Ibid per Murray CJ delivering the judgment of the Court.

> inappropriate to lay down any general standardisation or tariff of penalties. Nonetheless the starting point for any Court when imposing sentence is, as so often stated, that of a substantial custodial sentence.'[112]

The Court emphasised the seriousness of the offence committed by the respondent. The offence was such that the Court considered that there were no circumstances relating either to the offence, or to the respondent himself, that would have justified the sentencing judge even considering any sentence other than a custodial one.

A Feminist Critique and Re-writing of *Tiernan*

In recent years, several feminist judgment projects have been undertaken in various jurisdictions in which the processes and outcomes of key cases have been re-imagined through a feminist lens (see Cowan, 2019: 51 and Cowan et al, 2017: 252). Such projects are a form of 'academic activism' which seeks to intervene in prevailing academic and political discourse on the law (McCandless et al, 2017: 4). In rewriting key judgments, legal scholars and practitioners put feminist theory, knowledge and critique into action, demonstrating how real-life cases could have been decided and/or reasoned differently, even within the bounds of the available law and evidence (McCandless et al, 2017: 5; see also Thompson, 2017: 50).

As part of the Northern/Irish Feminist Judgment Project (Enright et al, 2017), Kennefick and Fennell (2017) rewrote the decision in *Tiernan* as a guideline judgment. They employed O'Malley's notion of 'principled discretion',[113] setting out guidance as to the appropriate sentences for cases of rape (O'Malley, 2011: 5; see also Campbell, 2017: 484).

The Nature of the Rewritten Tiernan *Guidelines*

The rewritten guideline judgment begins with the following observation:

> 'The offence of rape is complex, value-laden and emotive. The wrongness of rape is manifold. Each victim experiences the offence on an individual basis. Rape sentencing is all too frequently influenced by stereotypical constructs of victims which can distort and even replace the true experience … [I]t is not the function of the criminal law to put words into the mouth of a person who has been raped or to seek to ascertain or replicate her wishes. The function of the law is to act as a conduit of justice whereby all such persons and society, are represented adequately and appropriately and the rights of the offender are protected and vindicated in accordance with [the principle of proportionality] … [T]he most effective means of achieving justice in cases of rape is through the issuance of sentencing guidelines' (Kennefick and Fennell, 2017: 485).

[112] Ibid.
[113] Discussed above.

The authors note that rather than presupposing the response of a victim of rape or simply assuming the offender's degree of culpability, the court must take account of the nuanced and wide-ranging effects of the particular offence on both the victim and society at large, while also taking account of the personal circumstances of the offender. For Kennefick and Fennell, sentencing guidelines for rape are required both to reaffirm societal values in terms of bodily integrity and sexual autonomy and to preserve public confidence in the judicial process through the appellate courts' establishment of general principles (2017: 485, 486).

The guidelines set out in the rewritten judgment comprise a system of sentencing ranges, with an indication of key mitigating and aggravating factors. As with sentencing guidelines issued or approved by the High Court of Justiciary on appeal in Scotland[114] and sentencing guidelines to be issued by the Sentencing Guidelines Information Committee in Ireland,[115] the guidelines are not binding; departure from them is permissible in exceptional circumstances as required in particular cases. The system proposed by Kennefick and Fennell is thus authoritative, in that the guidelines must be considered by judges, yet flexible, as they are not obliged to follow them where a different approach is justified by the facts of the case. Sentencing guidelines of this type ensure that undue disparity is reduced without enforcing what the authors describe as 'excessive standardisation' (Kennefick and Fennell, 2017: 486–87).

Kennefick and Fennell preface the guidelines with certain important observations regarding the relationship between the victim and the offender and the victim's prior sexual experience. The guidelines do not seek to pit the impact of 'stranger' rape against that of 'non-stranger' or 'acquaintance' rape. In principle, both stranger and non-stranger rape are put on an even footing in terms of assessing the relevant sentence range (Kennefick and Fennell, 2017: 490). With regard to the victim, his or her behaviour (including past sexual experience) is in no way relevant to the sentencing process (2017: 491).

Sentencing Methodology

The sentencing methodology proposed by Kennefick and Fennell in the rewritten guideline judgment comprises three steps (*cf People (DPP) v M*[116]). Step one involves the judge identifying the appropriate sentencing range to be applied, taking into account the gravity of the offence. At step two, the judge must adjust upwards the figure arrived at under step one if certain aggravating factors are present. Finally, at step three, the judge considers the offender's culpability and adjusts downwards the figure arrived at under step two if any mitigating factors are present (Kennefick and Fennell, 2017: 491–92).

[114] See Chapter 5.
[115] See above.
[116] *M* (n 7), discussed above.

Step One – The Sentencing Range

The sentencing guidelines set out by Kennefick and Fennell are similar to those issued by the New Zealand Court of Appeal[117] in that they establish a series of four bands, expressed in terms of imprisonment. Four bands are set out in the revised *Tiernan* judgment: zero to two years; three to seven years; eight to 14 years; and 15 years to life imprisonment (Kennefick and Fennell, 2017: 491–92).

In respect of band one (zero to two years), the guidelines state that while a non-custodial sentence is wholly exceptional, the court must not deprive itself of the possibility of identifying an exceptional case where a custodial sentence may not be appropriate. In respect of band two (three to seven years), the guidelines follow the corresponding guidelines in force in both England and Wales[118] and New Zealand[119] at the time of the commission of the offence in *Tiernan*. The guidelines state that the court should consider an approximate starting point of five years' imprisonment in respect of a single offence of rape on an adult victim by a single offender of good character who is convicted after trial.

The guidelines state that the range in band three (eight to 14 years), is appropriate (i) where the offender displays no realistic attitude or appropriate insight into the repellent and harmful nature of rape; (ii) where the offender uses a weapon to intimidate or injure the victim; and (iii) where the offender commits multiple counts of rape. Finally, the range in band four (15 years to life imprisonment), is appropriate where the offence is committed against a child victim or victims, or where the victim is subjected to abduction or prolonged detention by the offender (Kennefick and Fennell, 2017: 492).

Step Two – Uplift for Aggravating Factors

The guideline judgment includes a non-prescriptive list of aggravating factors, the presence of which will serve to increase the sentence arrived at under step one. Eight such factors are listed:

(1) premeditation or evidence of planning;
(2) the use of drugs, alcohol or other substances by the offender to facilitate the offence;
(3) the offender being aware that he is suffering from a venereal disease;
(4) the offender presents a high risk of re-offending;
(5) subjecting the victim to threats to prevent the incident from being reported;
(6) previous convictions for rape or other serious offences of a violent or sexual kind;
(7) the victim's personal circumstances including, for example, age, evident vulnerability, or disability; and

[117] See Chapter 7.
[118] See Chapter 4.
[119] See Chapter 7.

(8) the physical, psychological and/or emotional impact of the rape on the victim (Kennefick and Fennell, 2017: 492).

While the rewritten guideline judgment in *Tiernan* lists all eight factors as aggravating factors, they comprise a mixture of what in England and Wales are regarded as 'harm factors', 'culpability factors' and 'aggravating factors' under the Sentencing Council's current Definitive Guideline on Sexual Offences (Sentencing Council, 2013a: 10–11).[120] Thus, while under the proposed *Tiernan* guidelines, the fact that the rape is planned in advance, that drugs or alcohol are used by the offender to facilitate the offence and that the victim contracts a sexually transmitted infection as a result of the rape are all *aggravating* factors which serve to increase the sentence, in England and Wales these three factors are used to assess both the offender's *culpability* for the offence and the *harm* caused by it. In England and Wales, these factors (along with the victim's vulnerability and the physical, psychological and emotional impact on the victim) are not seen simply as aggravating factors, rather they are integral parts of assessing the seriousness of the offence itself.

To this extent, certain of the aggravating factors at step two in the guideline judgment could arguably be factored into step one in deciding the appropriate sentencing range. The rewritten judgment is, however, careful to avoid double counting: where a factor is an ingredient of the offence or is used to identify a sentencing range, it cannot also be an aggravating factor. Judges are directed to take all reasonable steps to ensure that double counting of any factor does not occur in sentencing the offender (Kennefick and Fennell, 2017: 493).

Step Three – Allowance for Mitigating Factors

Finally, the guideline judgment sets out a non-prescriptive list of mitigating factors, the presence of which can result in a downwards adjustment in the figure arrived at under step two. As with the operation of the Definitive Guideline on Sexual Offences in England and Wales,[121] the list of mitigating factors is brief. The first such factor is that the offender displays 'real and convincing remorse', that he cooperates fully with the authorities and demonstrates 'a manifest intention to seek to rehabilitate himself into society' (Kennefick and Fennell, 2017: 492).

The approach of the guideline judgment towards allowing a discount in sentence to reflect an offender's plea of guilty is more nuanced than traditional Irish sentencing practice, which has regarded a guilty plea as a mitigating factor.[122] In a statement that accords more with sentencing practice in Scotland and England and Wales than in Ireland, the guideline judgment suggests that the acceptance of a guilty plea in mitigation may be justified largely on the grounds of 'the efficient

[120] See Chapter 4.
[121] See Chapter 4.
[122] See below.

administration of justice in the public interest', rather than because the plea is an automatic indicator of the offender's remorse (Kennefick and Fennell, 2017: 492). The judgment continues:

> '[T]he assumption that the offender, on pleading guilty, is in some way saving the victim from additional suffering via testifying at trial shall not be accepted outright by the court, as the response of the victim is her own. One victim may wish to avoid a trial, another may wish to confront her attacker in a formal setting and give voice to her experience. It is for the sentencing judge to decide on the matter in light of the particular circumstances of the case' (ibid).

The second mitigating factor set out in the guideline judgment relates to the particular circumstances of the offender. The sentence may be adjusted downwards to reflect, for example, the offender's old age, youth, disability, or mental health issues. Judges are expressly given the power to depart from the prescribed sentencing range, determined at step one of the process, where a case 'presents exceptional and compelling circumstances' (Kennefick and Fennell, 2017: 493).

An application of the guidelines set out in the rewritten judgment to Tiernan's case results in a sentence of 21 years' imprisonment, rather than the sentence of 17 years imposed on appeal by the Supreme Court.[123] In particular, Kennefick and Fennell set a starting point of 18 years' imprisonment owing to the number of circumstances which go to the gravity of the offence (step one). The starting point is then increased to 22 years, given the offender's analogous previous convictions, which serve as aggravating factors (step two). Finally, at step three, a reduction in sentence of one year is permitted on the basis that the offender demonstrated some cooperation with the authorities from the point of investigation (Kennefick and Fennell, 2017: 493).

'Lenient', 'Ordinary', 'Severe' and 'Condign' Punishments – The Decision in *Drought*

In *People (DPP) v Drought (sub nom People (DPP) v D(W))*,[124] Charleton J sitting at first instance in the Central Criminal Court, undertook a thorough review of contemporary sentencing practice for rape. This was done not to establish sentencing guidelines but rather in an attempt to place the sentencing of the particular offender, who had raped the intoxicated victim after meeting her in a nightclub, 'within the parameters of the existing law and practice so that the disposal … can be regarded as being consistent with the penal policy of the Superior Courts in dealing with rape cases'.[125] To that end, Justice Charleton sought

[123] See above.
[124] [2007] IEHC 310; [2008] 1 IR 308.
[125] Ibid at [5].

to examine all previous relevant reported and unreported decisions of the superior courts; his Honour also conducted an analysis of the sentences imposed by the High Court in the preceding three years, between 2005 and 2007.[126] The result is an attempt to ascertain both the relevant sentencing principles and the parameters within which sentences for rape can be imposed, for the sake of 'consistency and predictability'.[127]

Justice Charleton prefaced his examination of the case law with certain comments redolent of the Supreme Court's observations in *Tiernan*:[128]

> 'Rape is an extremely serious offence … [It] constitutes a savage attack on the bodily and psychological integrity of a woman. It overrides her right to privacy in the most intimate area of human relationships. It discounts her personality by imposing a complete nullification of her existence as a sentient person who is entitled to choose where to place her affection … In rape, affection or sexual recreation is replaced by the opposites of violence and degradation.'[129]

His Honour analysed the relevant case law (a total of some 96 cases) in terms of the 'emerging pattern of sentencing bands'[130] and, to this end, grouped the decisions into four categories or bands: (i) lenient punishments;[131] (ii) ordinary punishments;[132] (iii) severe punishments;[133] and (iv) condign punishments.[134] The review of the case law disclosed that lenient punishment in the form of non-custodial disposals or suspended sentences is only contemplated where the circumstances of the offence are such as to be 'completely exceptional'.[135]

In the second 'band', 'ordinary punishment' tended to range from three to eight years' imprisonment, with the majority of these cases concluding with sentences of five to seven years.[136] Cases where sentences of eight years were imposed were characterised by high levels of violence, particularly serious effects on the victim, multiple offending and/or where the accused had previous convictions.[137] The case law indicated that where offenders pleaded guilty to rape in circumstances that involved no additional gratuitous humiliation or violence beyond those ordinarily involved in the offence, sentences tended towards five years' imprisonment.[138]

[126] Ibid.
[127] Ibid.
[128] *Tiernan* (n 12).
[129] *Drought* (n 124) at [6] and [7].
[130] Ibid at [37].
[131] Ibid at [14]–[25].
[132] Ibid at [26]–[36].
[133] Ibid at [37]–[41].
[134] Ibid at [42]–[48].
[135] Ibid at [24].
[136] Ibid at [28].
[137] Ibid at [29] and [36].
[138] Ibid at [36].

This figure accords with the 'starting point' of five years (with a range of four to seven years) for such cases of rape in England and Wales (Sentencing Council, 2013a: 10–11).[139] While, as we shall see in Chapter 7, this is lower than the 'starting point' of six to eight years' imprisonment for such instances of rape imposed by the courts in New Zealand following the decision of the Court of Appeal in *R v AM*,[140] it is 18 months longer than the so-called 'benchmark' sentence of three-and-a-half years' imprisonment for such offences in Scotland, as set by the Appeal Court in a Bench chaired by the Lord Justice General in *HMA v Shearer*[141] and later endorsed by a Bench chaired by the Lord Justice Clerk in *HMA v Cooperwhite*.[142] It is also two years longer than the three-year 'starting point' set by the Alberta Court of Appeal in *R v Sandercock*[143] which has long influenced sentencing practice for rape across Canada.[144] The practice of the Irish courts in imposing sentences of five years' imprisonment in such cases is to be commended, since the starting points set by the appellate courts in *Shearer*[145] and *Sandercock*[146] have been criticised as failing to adequately reflect modern societal attitudes towards the crime of rape (see, respectively, Brown, 2015a: 8 and O'Malley, 2013a: 661).[147]

Justice Charleton's analysis disclosed that 'severe punishment' (the third 'band') involved the imposition of sentences between nine and 14 years' imprisonment.[148] Sentences of 10 or 11 years appeared to be unusual unless the circumstances disclosed unusual levels of violence or premeditation.[149] Sentences towards the upper end of the band were imposed in cases involving gross levels of violation, humiliation and degradation of the victim; kidnapping and rape; and burglary and rape.[150] Finally, 'condign punishments' (the fourth band, comprising sentences of between 15 years and life imprisonment) were imposed in cases of gang rape or involving multiple incidents, multiple victims, or both.[151] Such cases often featured instances of rape committed against very young or very old victims; the infliction of severe and lasting psychological harm on the victims, particularly severe levels of violence and degradation (often committed over a period of years); abuse of positions of trust; and pursuit of campaigns of rape.[152] In the later case of *People (DPP) v Z*,[153] for example, the life sentence imposed on the appellant

[139] See the discussion in Chapter 4.
[140] [2010] 2 NZLR 750 at [90].
[141] 2003 SCCR 657, considered in Chapter 5.
[142] 2013 SCCR 461 at [19].
[143] 1985 ABCA 218; (1985) 22 CCC (3d) 79.
[144] See Chapter 5.
[145] *Shearer* (n 141).
[146] *Sandercock* (n 143).
[147] See Chapter 5.
[148] *Drought* (n 124) at [37].
[149] Ibid at [40].
[150] Ibid at [41].
[151] Ibid at [42].
[152] Ibid at [44] and [46]–[48].
[153] [2014] IECCA 13.

following his conviction on 14 counts of rape and child cruelty committed against his four daughters over a prolonged period was upheld on appeal.

Justice Charleton also discussed his findings regarding the typical aggravating and mitigating factors considered by the Irish courts.[154] With regard to aggravating factors, his Honour reported that the courts placed particular emphasis on the following: the harm caused to the victim; where there is 'a special violence', more than usual humiliation, or where the victim is subjected to additional and gratuitous sexual perversions; abuse of a position of trust; abuse of a particularly young or elderly victim; engaging in a campaign of rape (which demonstrated a 'particularly remorseless attitude … not necessarily mitigated by later claims of repentance'); gang rape; the issuing of threats; and the use of weapons.[155] These factors all accord with the guidance given by the Court of Appeal (Criminal Division) in *R v Billam and others*.[156]

With regard to mitigating factors, his Honour observed that the nature of rape is such as to tend towards a requirement for condign punishment.[157] As such and in common with sentencing guidance in England and Wales[158] and New Zealand,[159] mitigating factors were dealt with in short compass. The strongest mitigating factor in Irish sentencing practice was said to be an early admission of guilt, which may be evidence of contrition.[160] Additional mitigating factors include the offender's youth, mental illness, or his having been himself subjected to sexual abuse resulting in psychiatric disorder.[161]

Justice Charleton concluded by noting that provocation had no application to the offence of rape.[162] The conduct of the victim was irrelevant. In a passage that echoed the reasoning of the Court of Appeal (Criminal Division) in its guideline judgment in *Millberry*,[163] his Honour considered that it is only where there has been consent to sexual intercourse which is withdrawn during the act that anything involving the conduct of the victim can be regarded as relevant.[164] His Honour also stressed that, in addition to the above factors, an offender's background and previous convictions must all be taken into account in imposing sentence.[165]

The sentence of seven years' imprisonment (with the last 18 months suspended, subject to certain conditions) imposed by Charlton J in *Drought*[166] was appealed to the Court of Criminal Appeal. The Court's judgment was delivered *ex tempore*

[154] *Drought* (n 124) at [49]–[54].
[155] Ibid at [49].
[156] *Billam* (n 98) at 51, considered in Chapter 4.
[157] *Drought* (n 124) at [12].
[158] See Chapter 4.
[159] See Chapter 7.
[160] *Drought* (n 124) at [51].
[161] Ibid.
[162] Ibid at [52].
[163] *R v Millberry and others* [2003] 2 Cr App R (S) 31 at [14], considered in Chapter 4.
[164] *Drought* (n 124) at [52].
[165] Ibid at [54].
[166] Ibid at [57].

and neither endorsed nor criticised the analysis undertaken by Charlton J in the Central Criminal Court. Nevertheless, some seven-and-a-half months later, in delivering the judgment of the Court of Criminal Appeal in *People (DPP) v Keane*,[167] Murray CJ commended Justice Charlton's analysis in the following terms:

> 'The judgment did not purport to set standard sentences or tariffs but is a valuable reference point in ascertaining the wide variety of factors … which can influence sentencing in rape cases. The incidents of aggravation and mitigation of offences can be so variable that no Court should consider itself bound by precedent on a rigid basis and due weight should be given to considerations that at times can be unique to the features of a particular case.'[168]

Mr Justice Edwards of the Court of Appeal reports that the sentencing guidance provided by Justice Charlton in *Drought* was, and continues to be, regularly cited by counsel in appeals concerning sexual assaults, aggravated sexual assaults and related offences (Edwards, 2019: 47; see also Scott, 2017: 13–14).

'Ripples on a Lake' – Further Appellate Recognition of the Harm Caused by Rape

We have already seen how in *People (DPP) v Counihan (sub nom People (DPP) v C)*[169] the Court of Appeal re-affirmed its commitment to addressing questions of principle in sentencing by providing flexible sentencing guidance to judges. The decision in *Counihan* is also notable for certain observations made by the Court regarding the seriousness of sexual offences and, in particular, the effect such offences may have both on the victim and on the victim's family. The appellant in *Counihan* was convicted of historic sexual offences comprising two rapes and two sexual assaults. In disposing of the appeal, the Court made several general observations, which included the following:

> 'Rape is a very serious crime that calls for a substantial custodial sentence but there is not an absolute rule. The sentencing judge has discretion which must be exercised with respect for the general principle … This crime and other offences of sexual abuse cause suffering that is profound and long-lasting and is not confined to the victims themselves but extends outwards like ripples on a lake to partners and children of victims […] It often takes years for victims of abuse to report the crime and the investigation and trial are very traumatic experiences. Giving evidence and being cross-examined are extremely painful and distressing.'[170]

[167] *Keane* (n 110).
[168] Ibid at [80].
[169] *Counihan* (n 29), discussed above.
[170] Ibid at [8](i)–(iv).

As Leahy and Fitzgerald O'Reilly observe, the Irish courts are usually assertive about the need to be mindful of the harm inflicted by sexual violence, both upon victims and society (Leahy and Fitzgerald O'Reilly, 2018: 212; see also *People (DPP) v Walsh*[171]).

Marital and Relationship Rape

Neither the decision in *Tiernan*[172] nor *Drought*[173] specifically addressed the issue of sentencing marital or relationship rape. Indeed, the Supreme Court in *Tiernan* was unable to do so since it was only in 1990 that the 'marital rape exemption', whereby a husband could not be prosecuted for the rape of his wife, was abolished[174] (see Leahy, 2018: 423–27). Nevertheless, the observations of the Court in *Tiernan* that a victim's previous sexual experience can never be considered as a mitigating circumstance in any rape[175] and of Charleton J in *Drought* that '[t]he entitlement of a woman to refuse to consent to sexual intercourse is absolute since the presence of consent is what makes the act of sexual intercourse lawful',[176] could be construed as indicating that a prior or existing sexual relationship between the parties is *not* a mitigating factor. This approach is favoured by O'Malley, who considers that the same sentencing principles should apply irrespective of the relationship between the victim and the offender (O'Malley, 2006: 267).

Recent Reviews of Sentencing Practice

In 2012, a study on Irish rape sentencing was undertaken by the Judicial Researchers' Office, a group of solicitors, barristers and legal academics who provide professional legal support to the Irish judiciary (see Charleton and Scott, 2013: 15–18). The study found that lenient punishments for rape, defined as sentences of less than three years' imprisonment, were extremely rare, even where the accused had pleaded guilty at an early stage in the proceedings. The average sentence for rape was found to range between five and seven years' imprisonment. Exceptional factors existed in the few cases where lenient sentences were, in fact, imposed (O'Cathaoir, 2012).

O'Malley's 2013 review of sentencing practice for rape broadly corresponds to that of Charleton J in *Drought*[177] in identifying the ranges of sentence for the

[171] *Walsh* (n 75).
[172] *Tiernan* (n 12).
[173] *Drought* (124).
[174] See the Criminal Law (Rape) (Amendment) Act 1990, s 5.
[175] *Tiernan* (n 12) at 255.
[176] *Drought* (n 124) at [52].
[177] *Drought* (n 124).

offence and common aggravating and mitigating factors (O'Malley, 2013a: 648–58; see also the earlier analysis by O'Malley, 2006: 262–70). O'Malley (2013a: 658) also identifies evidence that the offender acted out of character and strong indications that he is unlikely to reoffend as additional factors that may justify treating a case as exceptional for sentencing purposes. O'Malley's latest review of the case law on rape sentencing again corresponds with earlier analyses (O'Malley, 2016: 367–73). O'Malley concludes his review with two additional observations: firstly, that an offender's mental illness or disability may mitigate the sentence to reflect reduced culpability and, secondly, that leniency may also be justified where an offender's amenability to rehabilitation in a community setting is likely to be more effective than a lengthy prison sentence in reducing the risk of re-offending (O'Malley, 2016: 373).

Rape Sentencing and the Guilty Plea Discount

While Irish judges had always taken account of the stage at which a guilty plea was entered in passing sentence (O'Malley, 2016: 165), there is now a statutory basis for doing so. Section 29(1) of the Criminal Justice Act 1999 ('the 1999 Act') provides that:

> 'In determining what sentence to pass on a person who has pleaded guilty to an offence, other than an offence for which the sentence is fixed by law, a court, *if it considers it appropriate to do so*, shall take into account: (a) the stage in the proceedings for the offence at which the person indicated an intention to plead guilty and (b) the circumstances in which this indication was given' (emphasis added).

As section 29 of the 1999 Act makes clear, the decision of whether to allow a discount, or reduction, in sentence is a discretionary one for the individual judge. This overturned suggestions in certain earlier decisions of the appellate courts that a discount in sentence must be given for a guilty plea *as a matter of principle* (see Campbell, 2017: 482). Section 29 does not preclude the imposition of the maximum sentence if the gravity of the offence warrants it, notwithstanding the accused's guilty plea (Leahy and Fitzgerald O'Reilly, 2018: 224–25 and *People (DPP) v McC*[178]).

In practice, the Irish courts almost inevitably allow a discount or reduction of some sort where a guilty plea has been entered (see O'Malley, 2016: 165 and 2013a: 559); however, Ireland adopts a less formal approach to guilty plea discounting than jurisdictions such as England and Wales. In particular, the Irish courts have never quantified the discount merited by a guilty plea (O'Malley, 2016: 164–65; 2013a: 558 and 2013b: 226). There is no 'standard' or 'sliding scale' of discount

[178] *McC* (n 76).

such as that used by the English courts (see Sentencing Council, 2017).[179] As the Court of Criminal Appeal observed in *People (DPP) v Daly*:[180]

> 'The Irish courts have no formal provision for the amount of adjustment merited by a guilty plea, preferring instead to uphold judicial discretion, to be exercised in light of the specific circumstances ... [T]here is no mathematical formula by which any such reduction may be arrived at [...]'.[181]

Sentencers are thus required to adopt a contextual approach in deciding upon the appropriate discount (if any) for a guilty plea (O'Malley, 2016: 166). The precise level of any such discount will be determined by the timing and circumstances of the offender's plea. In practice, the levels of discount typically allowed by the Irish courts tend to be similar to those recommended by the relevant English Definitive Guideline (Sentencing Council, 2017). The level of discount rarely exceeds a third for those who plead guilty at the first available opportunity (O'Malley, 2016: 165–166) and a discount in the region of one quarter is more typical (O'Malley, 2013a: 558).

Another factor that distinguishes this aspect of Irish sentencing practice is that, as seen in the decision in *People (DPP) v Tiernan*,[182] a guilty plea is treated by the Irish courts as a *mitigating* factor (Leahy and Fitzgerald O'Reilly, 2018: 224; O'Malley, 2016: 164; see also *People (DPP) v McC*[183] and *People (DPP) v Counihan*[184]). This is in stark contrast to practice in both England and Wales (Sentencing Council, 2017: 4; see also Maslen and Roberts, 2013: 127)[185] and in Scotland (see *Gemmell v HMA*[186]) where it is clear that an offender's remorse is *not* a proper justification for allowing a discount in sentence. In these jurisdictions, where there is convincing evidence of remorse then a sentencer may make allowance for it, as an aspect of mitigation, in deciding on the *headline* sentence (Brown, 2017a: 209–10). The Irish courts appear to regard a guilty plea as a mitigating factor on the grounds that it may indicate remorse and acceptance of responsibility for the harm caused, as well as sparing the victim the ordeal of giving evidence at trial (Leahy and Fitzgerald O'Reilly, 2018: 224; O'Malley, 2016: 162).

These views are at odds with contemporary academic and judicial thinking on the matter, with several commentators and judges having expressed the view that remorse is not a credible justification for allowing a discount in sentence (see Brown, 2017a: 209–10; Chasse, 2009: 57; Criminal Bar Association, 2016: 8; Darbyshire, 2000: 901; Field, 2002: 264–67; Leverick, 2004: 370; Rauxloh, 2012: 36–37; and Wasik, 2006: 146). Similarly, whilst the courts in both Scotland and

[179] See the discussion in Chapter 4.
[180] [2011] IECCA 104.
[181] Ibid at [100].
[182] *Tiernan* (n 12).
[183] *McC* (n 76) at 103.
[184] *Counihan* (n 29) at [5] and [8](v).
[185] See the discussion in Chapter 4.
[186] [2011] HCJAC 129; 2012 JC 223 at [51] per the Lord Justice Clerk (Gill). See the discussion in Chapter 5.

England and Wales traditionally regarded the notion of sparing victims from the ordeal of giving evidence as a reason for allowing discounts in sentence for guilty pleas, it is now regarded as an unconvincing justification.[187] In particular, some victims might prefer to give evidence at trial as it affords them the opportunity to be heard within the criminal justice system and it may lead to their learning more about the offence and the offender. Victims may also feel that, given the choice, they would rather undergo the pains of giving evidence if it means that the offender receives no discount and thus a longer sentence (see Ashworth, 2015: 181; Brown, 2017a: 207–8; Kennefick and Fennell, 2017: 492; and McConville and Marsh, 2016: 115).

Thus, an offender who pleads guilty to rape in the Republic of Ireland can, as in England and Wales, expect a discount in sentence. The extent of any such discount will depend on the timing of the offender's plea. Unlike in England, however, the rationale for such a discount in sentence is not purely 'utilitarian' in the sense of cost savings to the criminal justice system; rather, the Irish courts view a guilty plea as an aspect of mitigation.

[187] Compare, for example, *Du Plooy v HMA* 2005 1 JC 1 at [16] with *Gemmell* (n 185) at [45].

7

'Pragmatism and Individualisation' versus 'The Mandatory Minimums Algorithm'

Rape Sentencing in New Zealand and South Africa

Introduction

It is an unavoidable consequence of any attempt to structure sentencing discretion that it must necessarily involve circumscribing the powers of the sentencing judge, yet the exercise of judicial discretion is crucial if justice is to be done in the individual case (Brown, 2017a: 141; Duff, 2005: 1165; Easton and Piper, 2016: 37–38; Krasnostein, 2015: 164). In order to structure sentencing discretion effectively, decisions must be taken on the content of the sentencing guidance; on the source of the guidance; on the authority by which it is laid down; and on the style in which the guidance is formulated. Consideration must also be given to the mechanics of putting the sentencing guidance into practice (see Ashworth, 1998: 213 and Roberts, 2009: 230).

A comparison of sentencing law and practice in New Zealand and South Africa provides valuable insights into two very different ways of structuring judicial discretion in sentencing those convicted of rape. Although judges in both jurisdictions have traditionally enjoyed a very wide sentencing discretion, rape sentencing in New Zealand is governed by a guideline judgment from the Court of Appeal, while South Africa is unique amongst the common law jurisdictions examined in this work in having implemented a comprehensive scheme of mandatory and minimum sentences for rape.

Rape Sentencing in New Zealand

The Crime of Rape in New Zealand

In New Zealand, the crime of rape is defined in similar, albeit more restricted, terms to the offence in England and Wales, Scotland and the Republic of Ireland.

Sexual violation by rape comprises the penile penetration of the genitalia without consent[1] and carries a maximum sentence of 20 years' imprisonment.[2] There is a statutory presumption in favour of imprisonment for rape: an offender must be sentenced to imprisonment unless, having regard to the particular circumstances of both the offender and the offence, the court considers a custodial sentence inappropriate[3] (see Hall, 2014: 68 and 88–90). Other forms of non-consensual penetrative activity are criminalised as sexual violation by unlawful sexual connection.[4] This offence carries the same maximum penalty as rape[5] and the same statutory presumption in favour of imprisonment applies.[6]

Sentencing Practice, Guidance and Methodology in New Zealand

Judicial Discretion in Sentencing

The most significant feature of sentencing in New Zealand is the discretion vested in the sentencing judge (Hall, 2007a: 253; Mallett, 2015: 533–34; McGovern, 2014: 244; Oleson, 2017: 366, 374; Young and King, 2013: 211). The judge must weigh, usually intuitively, the various purposes of punishment; she must consider the circumstances of both the particular offence and the individual offender and then choose a disposal that does justice to the victim, the offender and the community alike (Hall, 2007b: 1; 2014: 5). The traditional, discretionary approach of the New Zealand courts towards sentencing is described by Richardson J in *Fisheries Inspector v Turner*:[7]

> 'It is only by allowing the sentencing authorities a wide discretion that they are enabled to take account of the innumerable factors affecting the nature of the offence, the circumstances of the offence and the circumstances of the offender, all of which should ordinarily be weighed in determining the appropriate sentence in the particular case.'[8]

The purpose of this discretion is not to allow individual judges to pursue their own sentencing preferences but to enable the judge to tailor the sentence to the facts of the case and to the offender's personal circumstances (Hall, 2014: 5; 2007a: 254; 2007b: 1). In so doing, the New Zealand judge, in common with his counterparts in England and Wales, will consider the seriousness of the offence having regard to the offender's culpability and the degree of harm caused by the offence with

[1] Crimes Act 1961, s 128(2).
[2] Ibid, s 128B(1).
[3] Ibid, s 128B(2) and (3).
[4] Ibid, s 128(3).
[5] Ibid, s128B(1).
[6] Ibid, s 128B(2) and (3).
[7] [1978] 2 NZLR 233.
[8] Ibid at 237.

reference to its impact on the victim (Hall, 2014: 152–53 and 2007a: 254, fn 32). The limits of the judge's sentencing discretion are constrained by the offence of which the offender is convicted and by the maximum penalty prescribed for that offence (Hall, 2014: 6 and 2007a: 253–54; Young and King, 2013: 202; 2011: 209–10; and 2010: 254), thereby ensuring sufficient flexibility to allow the judge to achieve individualised justice. As Hall explains:

> 'Sentencing is not a rational mechanical process; it is a human process and is subject to all the frailties of the human mind. A wide variety of factors, including the Judge's background, experience, social values, moral outlook, penal philosophy and views as to the merits or demerits of a particular penalty influence the sentencing decision' (Hall, 2007a: 254).

Despite the importance of individualised justice in New Zealand, sentencing should still be conducted on a principled and consistent basis (Hall, 2007a: 261). In developments that mirror practice in Scotland,[9] what Hall describes as the 'traditional pragmatic and individualised approach' by the New Zealand Court of Appeal to questions of sentence has, in recent years, given way to an increasing body of case law, both reported and unreported, on sentencing principles and practice (Hall, 2014: 8, 14–15 and 2007b: 5).

The Use of Guideline Judgments

Influenced by the practice of the Court of Appeal (Criminal Division) in England and Wales, in the late 1970s the New Zealand Court of Appeal began to issue guidance to sentencing judges in the form of guideline judgments, or 'principal appellate judgments' (French, 2015: 36; Panckhurst, 2008: 196; Young, 2008: 182; Young and Browning, 2008: 289; Young and King, 2011: 225). While the terms 'principal appellate judgments' and 'guideline judgments' were used interchangeably, 'guideline judgment' is now the preferred term (Hall, 2014: 18). As in other common law jurisdictions, including Scotland and the Republic of Ireland, guideline judgments in New Zealand are judicial narrative guidelines intended to give authoritative guidance to trial judges in certain areas of sentencing. They are judgments that go beyond the point raised in the particular appeal and which outline general principles of sentencing for a given offence (Hall, 2014: 12 and 2007b: 8). In issuing guideline judgments, the New Zealand Court of Appeal sought to facilitate the development of a measure of consistency in sentencing without undermining the importance of judicial discretion in the individual case (Hammond, 2007: 218; McGovern, 2014: 244–45; Tinsley, 2017: 531).

As is increasingly the case in Scotland, the development of such comprehensively drafted appellate decisions led to the establishment of a significant corpus of sentencing law (Young and King, 2010: 256). While, as was then the case in

[9] See Chapter 5.

England and Wales, there was no statutory basis for guideline judgments (Hall, 2007a: 262), they were characterised by the assumption that, as the Court of Appeal was later to explain in *R v AM*,[10] 'consistency would flow from a proper analysis of sentencing decisions and the reinforcement of existing sentencing patterns.'[11]

The New Zealand Court of Appeal continues to issue such guideline judgments. They have become increasingly sophisticated, evolving from the purely *descriptive* (setting ranges by reference to existing sentencing patterns) to the *prescriptive*, by setting norms (French, 2015: 40). Modern guideline judgments focus on specific offences or offence types, prescribing 'bands' of seriousness and setting the sentence range within each band, whilst also allowing room for departure from the guidelines (Mallett, 2015: 539; Young and King, 2013: 203, 211; 2011: 210; and 2010: 254). Such guideline judgments become the standard reference point for all future sentencing decisions in relation to that offence type (Hammond, 2007: 18; Young and King, 2010: 254).

Guideline judgments enable the formulation and dissemination of judicial sentencing policy by providing judges with a clear, integrated and detailed framework within which to assess the factors that influence the determination of the appropriate sentence (Hall, 2007a: 262). As with early guideline judgments in England and Wales[12] and guideline judgments currently issued by the appellate courts in both Scotland[13] and the Republic of Ireland,[14] New Zealand guideline judgments are expressed in narrative form. They provide an indication of how the Court of Appeal will deal with sentence appeals, whilst preserving the freedom of the sentencing judge to impose a different sentence should a particular case feature an unusual combination of factors (Hall, ibid 263; 2014: 14).

The status of New Zealand guideline judgments is akin to those of guideline judgments in Scotland and the Republic of Ireland: although they should be observed by trial courts, they are not to be slavishly applied and departure may be warranted by the facts of a particular case (French, 2015: 40; Hall, 2014: 15). For example, the decisions in *R v Pehi*[15] and *R v H*[16] both stated that the guideline judgment on sentencing rape that was then in force[17] was not to be applied in a formulaic or rigid manner. In *R v Taueki*,[18] a later guideline judgment on serious violent offending, the Court of Appeal explained:

> 'What we seek to achieve is consistency in the approach adopted by sentencing Judges, which should in turn lead to consistency in sentencing levels. This does not override

[10] [2010] NZCA 114; [2010] 2 NZLR 750.
[11] Ibid at [9].
[12] See the discussion in Chapter 4.
[13] See Chapter 5.
[14] See Chapter 6.
[15] [2007] BCL 58.
[16] (CA 488/05), Court of Appeal, 4 September 2006, unreported (cited in Hall, 2007a: 262, fn 65).
[17] Namely *R v A* [1994] 2 NZLR 129, discussed below.
[18] [2005] 3 NZLR 372.

> the discretion of sentencing Judges, but rather provides guidance in the manner of the exercise of that discretion.'[19]

Later in its judgment in *Taueki*,[20] the Court stressed that the sentencing judge is required to undertake 'a proper assessment of the seriousness of particular conduct and to pay regard to the circumstances of each case'.[21] The Court warned against using guideline judgments as 'a mechanical process of pigeonholing' and reiterated that 'a rigid or mathematical approach' was not appropriate[22] (see also Tinsley, 2017: 531–32). In the later decision in *R v D*,[23] the Court of Appeal cautioned that: '[m]echanical application [of guideline judgments] undermines judicial evaluation of the seriousness of the particular offending and the culpability of the offender, both of which are crucial parts of the sentencing process.'[24] In *R v Clotworthy*,[25] meanwhile, it was stated that:

> 'Within which category an individual case falls and where within the band applicable to that category, are matters of judgment depending on all the relevant circumstances of the case. While categories and bands are useful guides in the sentencing process, the question of what sentence is appropriate to the individual case is ultimately a matter of judgment on the basis of all the relevant factors. Care must be taken not to let categorisation result in too rigid or mathematical an approach.'[26]

The approach of the New Zealand Court of Appeal towards the use of guideline judgments accords with practice in both Scotland and the Republic of Ireland. In New Zealand, as in Scotland and Ireland, guideline judgments provide a structure for, but do not remove, judicial discretion;[27] they are intended to provide judges with broad guidance rather than seeking to impose any standardisation of penalty.[28] Sentencing is still seen by the New Zealand courts as an *evaluative* exercise, rather than a formulaic one.[29]

Guideline judgments have been issued by the New Zealand Court of Appeal in response to legislative change; concerns about consistency or other particular difficulties in relation to specific offences; or, as in the sentencing of rape,[30] as a means of responding to changes in societal values (French, 2015: 40, 43–44). As is the case in Scotland and Ireland, coverage of guideline judgments is essentially limited to serious crime, where the main question at the sentencing stage

[19] Ibid at [10].
[20] *Taueki* (n 18).
[21] Ibid at [16].
[22] Ibid.
[23] [2008] NZCA 267.
[24] Ibid at [43].
[25] (1998) 15 CRNZ 651.
[26] Ibid at 655.
[27] See *HMA v Graham* [2010] HCJAC 50; 2011 JC 1 at [21], considered in Chapter 5.
[28] See *People (DPP) v Ryan* [2014] IECCA 11 at 2.3, considered in Chapter 6.
[29] See *Nuku v R* [2012] NZCA 584; [2013] 2 NZLR 39 at [40]; *R v AM* (n 10) at [36] and [79]; and *R v Clifford* [2011] NZCA 360; [2012] 1 NZLR 23 at [57].
[30] See *R v AM* (n 10) at [1].

is usually the length of the prison term to be imposed on the offender (French, ibid 41; Goodall, 2014: 45; Mallett, 2015: 540–41; and Panckhurst, 2008: 200).

Sentencing Methodology in New Zealand – The Staged Approach

The development of guideline judgments has been associated with an increased emphasis on structured sentencing (French, 2015: 41).[31] Where the judge determines imprisonment to be the appropriate disposal, sentencing practice is based around a methodology first explained by the Court of Appeal in *R v Taueki*.[32] The methodology was refined by the Court of Appeal in *Hessell v R*.[33] The methodology was subsequently endorsed by the Supreme Court in *Hessell v R*[34] and later reiterated by the Court of Appeal in *R v Clifford*[35] (see generally Hall, 2014: 13 and 142–45 and McGovern, 2014: 245).

New Zealand sentencing methodology, as in the Republic of Ireland,[36] involves a staged approach. As a first step, the judge must identify a starting point sentence that appropriately reflects the intrinsic seriousness of the offence. The starting point thus takes into account aggravating and mitigating features of *the offending* but excludes mitigating and aggravating features relating to *the offender*.[37] As the Court of Appeal explained in *R v Mako*,[38] the starting point is a level of sentence that would be appropriate in a case of conviction after trial in the absence of any relevant mitigating or aggravating factors relating to the offender.[39] The second step involves evaluating the aggravating and mitigating factors personal to the *particular offender*: the starting point sentence is adjusted up or down to reflect these factors (Brook et al, 2016: 1202–03; Brown, 2019a: 60–61; French, 2015: 41–42; *R v AM*[40]). Thus, the actual sentence may be higher or lower than – or, occasionally, the same as – the starting point sentence (Hall, 2007a: 263–64).

The third step involves the application of an appropriate discount in sentence if the offender pleads guilty. While the Court of Appeal initially considered the application of a sentence discount as comprising part of the second step in the sentencing methodology (Hall, 2007a: 263–64; *R v AM*;[41] *R v Fatu*[42]), it refined its approach in *Hessell v R*[43] so that it formed a separate and distinct third step.[44]

[31] See also *R v AM*, ibid at [13].
[32] *Taueki* (n 18).
[33] [2009] NZCA 450; [2010] 2 NZLR 298.
[34] [2010] NZSC 135; [2011] 1 NZLR 607.
[35] [2011] NZCA 360; [2012] 1 NZLR 23 at [60].
[36] See Chapter 6.
[37] *Taueki* (n 18) at [8].
[38] [2000] 2 NZLR 170.
[39] Ibid at [34].
[40] *AM* (n 10) at [13] and [84].
[41] Ibid at [14].
[42] [2006] 2 NZLR 72 at [21].
[43] *Hessell* (n 33).
[44] Ibid at [14], approved by the Supreme Court in *Hessell* (n 34) at [73] and [74].

This third and final step is to be undertaken only after the sentencing judge has determined what sentence would have applied in the absence of the guilty plea, having taken into account all other personal mitigating and aggravating factors.[45] The approach of the New Zealand courts towards guilty plea discounting mirrors that of the Scottish[46] and Irish courts:[47] in all three jurisdictions the extent of any discount is a matter for the discretion of the sentencing judge (Hall, 2014: 385, *cf* Brown, 2017a: 198–203 and O'Malley, 2016: 165 respectively).

In *Hessell v R*,[48] the Supreme Court overruled an earlier guideline judgment of the Court of Appeal[49] and disapproved recourse to a sliding scale of discounts, affirming the discretionary nature of the process. The Supreme Court considered the Court of Appeal's sliding scale to be objectionable for two reasons: firstly, it was too heavily structured and involved an inappropriate departure from the duty placed on judges to evaluate 'the full circumstances of each individual case';[50] and secondly, it carried the unacceptable risk of pressuring innocent persons to plead guilty.[51] The Supreme Court held that any allowance for a guilty plea should be the result of the judge's evaluation of *all* the circumstances in which the plea is tendered.[52] The Court explained:

> 'The only way in which the many variable circumstances of individual cases which are relevant to a guilty plea can properly be identified is by requiring their evaluation by the sentencing judge and allowing that judge scope in light of the conclusion he or she reaches to give the most appropriate recognition of the guilty plea in fixing the sentence.'[53]

In contrast to the rigid, formalised scheme of sentence discounts (or plea-based sentence reductions) that operates in England and Wales under the Sentencing Council's Definitive Guideline (Sentencing Council, 2017),[54] the approach of the Supreme Court of New Zealand is, like that of the Appeal Court in Scotland, individualised. Arguably more principled than the mechanistic English approach, the approach of the Scottish and New Zealand courts involves focusing on the individual offender and the circumstances in which he tendered his guilty plea (Brown, 2017a: 237; Richardson, 2011: 127).

The levels of discount applied by the New Zealand courts are somewhat more restricted – one might say more equitable (see Brown, 2017a: 238) – than the levels routinely allowed in England and Wales. The closer the guilty plea is tendered to the trial date, the less reduction will be given. A guilty plea tendered at the earliest

[45] Ibid.
[46] See Chapter 5.
[47] See Chapter 6.
[48] *Hessell* (n 34).
[49] *Hessell* (n 33).
[50] *Hessell* (n 34) at [72].
[51] Ibid.
[52] Ibid at [74].
[53] Ibid at [62].
[54] See Chapter 4.

opportunity will generally attract a discount of between 20 and 25 per cent and should not exceed 25 per cent.[55] A guilty plea entered close to trial, meanwhile, may attract a discount in the region of 10 to 15 per cent (see Brook et al, 2016: 1203).

The Supreme Court in *Hessell*[56] referred to the standard rationales for allowing a discount in sentence for a guilty plea, including cost savings to the criminal justice system, reduction in the backlog of trials and the so-called 'social utility' of saving victims and witnesses from the ordeal of giving evidence. With regard to sexual offences in particular, the New Zealand courts have traditionally viewed saving victims from the anxiety and trauma of giving evidence at trial as a strong rationale for allowing an offender a discount in sentence for pleading guilty (see Hall, 2014: 388–89).

Following the staged approach to sentencing forces the judge to quantify the various decreases, increases and discounts. The combined effect of guideline judgments and the staged approach to sentencing is seen as striking a balance between consistency and individualised justice, whilst also providing transparency (French, 2015: 42; see also the decision of the Court of Appeal in *R v Fanguna*[57]). The Court of Appeal acknowledged in *R v AM*,[58] however, that heavily structured approaches to sentencing of this nature are not universally popular, with some critics maintaining that the staged approach reduces sentencing to a mathematical exercise and is wrong in principle.[59] Nevertheless, in *AM*, the Court of Appeal considered structured sentencing to have advantages in terms of consistency and transparency, noting also that the structured approach was 'well embedded' as the appropriate sentencing methodology in New Zealand.[60]

The Sentencing Act 2002 and the New Zealand Sentencing Council

The Sentencing Act 2002[61] was passed against a background of increasing public scrutiny and criticism of New Zealand's sentencing system (see Hall, 2007a: 258–59; Roberts, 2003; Young, 2008: 180–81; Young and Browning, 2008: 287–88; Young and King, 2011: 210–12 and 2010: 255–56). The 2002 Act represents the New Zealand legislature's most comprehensive attempt to influence sentencing practice through legislation (Panckhurst, 2008: 197; Young and King, 2011: 210).

[55] *Hessell* (n 34) at [75].
[56] Ibid at [45].
[57] [2009] NZCA 316 at [21].
[58] *AM* (n 10).
[59] Ibid at [15], *cf* the 'instinctive synthesis' approach to sentencing employed by the Australian and Scottish courts discussed in Chapter 5.
[60] Ibid.
[61] Hereinafter 'the 2002 Act'.

While not expressly stated in the legislation, the 2002 Act is arguably premised on a 'just deserts' approach to sentencing (Hall, 2007a: 259). As with sentencing practice in Scotland[62] and the Republic of Ireland,[63] proportionality is the foundation of sentencing in New Zealand: the sentence must be proportionate to the seriousness of the offence and also to the personal circumstances of the offender.

Section 7 of the 2002 Act contains a statement of the purposes for which a court may sentence an offender, expressed at a high level of generality. The purposes include, *inter alia*, providing for the interests of the victim; denunciation; deterrence; protection of the community; rehabilitation; and any combination thereof. The Act also contains, in section 8, a statement of mandatory principles that the court must take into account when sentencing an offender including, *inter alia*, the gravity of the offending and the offender's culpability; the seriousness of the offence; the 'general desirability' of consistency; and the notion of parsimony (or the principle of imposing the least restrictive outcome appropriate).

As well as statements of the purposes and principles of sentencing, the 2002 Act also includes, in section 9, a non-exhaustive list of aggravating and mitigating factors that judges must take into account 'to the extent that they are applicable' in a given case. These include particular cruelty in committing the offence; abuse of a position of trust and the vulnerability of the victim; and the offender's age, his diminished intellectual capacity, remorse and previous good character (see Brook et al, 2016: 1202; and French, 2015: 38–39). Section 9 comprises 'a crystallisation of sentencing practice' at the time the 2002 Act was passed (McGovern, 2014: 247).

The 2002 Act's purposes, principles and aggravating and mitigating factors mostly codify the current approach to sentencing by the New Zealand courts (Goodall, 2014: 45; Young and King, 2011: 212). These factors did not represent Parliament's view about any new sentencing policy but instead were, broadly, the factors most commonly relied upon by the courts when imposing sentence (French, 2015: 38; Hall, 2014: 461–62, 466 and 482; Panckhurst, 2008: 197; Young and King, 2011: 212; see also Roberts, 2003: 254–57; Young, 2008: 180–81; Young and Browning, 2008: 287; and Young and King, 2010: 255). As with the Scottish Sentencing Council's recent guideline on the *Principles and Purposes of Sentencing* (SSC, 2018a),[64] many of the sentencing principles listed in the 2002 Act are nothing more than statements of the self-evident (Mallett, 2015: 538). This led the New Zealand Court of Appeal in *R v Iona*[65] to note that it was 'not persuaded that the new legislation is other than [a] legislative enactment of the sort of factors which Judges have traditionally taken into account in determining appropriate sentences'.

[62] See Chapter 5.
[63] See Chapter 6.
[64] Discussed in Chapter 5.
[65] (CA 416/02), Court of Appeal, 27 March 2003, unreported (cited in Hall, 2014: 466).

The 2002 Act offers no guidance as to sentencing severity levels (Young and Browning, 2008: 288; Young and King, 2010: 256) nor does it specify the relative weight to be given to each factor (Tinsley, 2017: 532; Young and King, 2011: 212 and 2010: 255). The real significance of the provisions arguably lies in the clarity with which they are expressed to the courts and to the public (French, 2015: 38; Panckhurst, 2008: 197). For Roberts (2003: 256), however, the provisions of the 2002 Act represent a legislative recognition of accepted common law purposes and, in this sense, simply legislate the *status quo*. Judges have thus continued to make their own decisions about the weight of each statutory factor in light of the culpability of the particular offender and the seriousness of the individual case (Tinsley, 2017: 532).

Faced with a rapidly rising prison population through the early to mid-2000s, the New Zealand government asked the New Zealand Law Commission to consider whether improvements could be made to the country's sentencing and parole structures. In particular, in February 2006, the government asked the Commission to consider whether New Zealand should establish a sentencing council to provide judges with more guidance on appropriate types and levels of punishment (Mallett, 2015: 552; Panckhurst, 2008: 201; Young, 2008: 179; Young and King, 2011: 208–9 and 2010: 256). The Commission's subsequent report recommended the establishment of a sentencing council to draft sentencing guidelines (New Zealand Law Commission, 2006).

The government at the time accepted the Commission's recommendations and announced that it would introduce legislation to give effect to them (Young, 2008: 179). Ahead of the intended creation of the New Zealand Sentencing Council and to ensure that guidelines could be implemented as soon as possible, the government asked the Law Commission to prepare draft sentencing guidelines in collaboration with the judiciary. It was envisaged that these draft guidelines could be considered by the sentencing council once it was established (O'Malley, 2011: 126; Young and King, 2011: 209 and 2010: 259). This was achieved by creating a Sentencing Establishment Unit ('SEU') within the Law Commission, staffed by members of the Commission and four seconded judges (Panckhurst, 2008: 202–3; Priestley, 2009: 33; Young and King, 2011; Young and Browning, 2008: 294). The work of preparing the draft guidelines was undertaken in 2007 and 2008, with the SEU drawing extensively on the experience of the English Sentencing Guidelines Council in developing its own proposals (Young and King, 2011; Young, 2008: 186). Although a total of 59 sets of draft guidelines were prepared (Young and King, 2011: 213), including a draft guideline on sexual violation (New Zealand Law Commission, 2008), they were never made widely available due to their 'uncertain status' (Young and King, 2011: 209, fn 2 and 2010: 261, fn 21).

Although the Sentencing Council Act 2007 was enacted by Parliament, it was never implemented. Following a general election in November 2008, the succeeding administration indicated that it did not wish to proceed with the establishment of a sentencing council (Goodall, 2014: 21; Mallett, 2015: 552–53; Oleson, 2017: 370; Young and King, 2013: 203; 2011: 226; and 2010: 260).

In the absence of a sentencing council, the SEU's draft guidelines are held by the New Zealand Law Commission.[66] The Court of Appeal, however, developed a practice whereby it would draw on the SEU's draft guidelines in issuing its own guideline judgments when it considered it appropriate to do so (see O'Malley, 2011: 126; Young and King, 2011: 213, 221–22 and 2010: 260). This is precisely the route that the Court of Appeal followed in issuing revised sentencing guidelines for rape in *R v AM*.[67]

Sentencing Guidelines for Rape: The Decision in *R v AM*

While sentencing practice for the crime of rape was considered by the Court of Appeal in *R v Pawa*[68] and *R v Pui*[69] where general tariff guidance was provided, sentencing guidelines were first set out by the Court in *R v Clark*.[70] In *Clark* the Court cited with approval what was then the leading English guideline judgment in *R v Billam and others*[71] and followed the English Court of Appeal in setting a figure of five years' imprisonment as a starting point for a contested case.[72] *Clark* became accepted in subsequent cases as setting the New Zealand 'going rate' or 'tariff' for rape at five years (Hall, 2007b: 14 and 49).

When the statutory maximum penalty for rape in New Zealand was increased from 14 to 20 years' imprisonment,[73] the Court of Appeal reexamined the starting point sentence for rape in *R v A*.[74] The Court noted that additional indignities and the use of force had become 'a very marked feature of evidence relating to rape'[75] and that the five-year starting point in *Clark* had come to be seen by judges as being 'rather on the low side'.[76] The Court increased the starting point in a contested case to eight years' imprisonment[77] but observed that its judgment was not intended to fetter sentencing judges in assessing the gravity of particular cases. The Court stressed that almost everything would turn on the facts of the particular case and that it was part of the judicial responsibility to weigh those facts in arriving at the appropriate sentence.[78]

By 2010, the Court of Appeal considered that the guidance in *A* had, in some respects, been overtaken by emerging evidence about, and evolving social attitudes

[66] Personal communication with Mr Peter Adamson (Manager, Information Services) of the New Zealand Law Commission.
[67] *AM* (n 10).
[68] [1978] 2 NZLR 190.
[69] [1978] 2 NZLR 193.
[70] [1987] 1 NZLR 380.
[71] (1986) 8 Cr App R (S) 48, discussed in Chapter 4.
[72] *Clark* (n 70) at 383.
[73] By section 2 of the Crimes Amendment Act (No 3) 1993.
[74] *A* (n 17).
[75] Ibid at 131.
[76] Ibid.
[77] Ibid at 131–32.
[78] Ibid at 132.

to, rape.[79] The guidance in *A* also gave little assistance in cases where the culpability of the offender was particularly high.[80] Two further problems were identified with the judgment in *A*. Firstly, the courts had come to treat eight years' imprisonment as if it were the *minimum* available starting point, which the Court of Appeal had not intended. Secondly, sentencing outcomes tended to be closely clustered around the eight-year starting point with the result that sentencing for rape tended not to be closely calibrated to an offender's culpability.[81]

The Court of Appeal thus issued revised, integrated sentencing guidelines for sexual violation where rape is the lead offence, and for sexual violation where other unlawful sexual connection (such as digital penetration) is the lead offence, in *R v AM*.[82] The sentencing guidelines for rape apply to offences of sexual violation where the lead offence is rape, penile penetration of the mouth or anus, or violation involving objects.[83] Thus, a key feature of the guidelines set out in *AM* is the Court's equating of oral penile penetration with other forms of penetration, this being a significant departure from previous sentencing practice (Hall, 2014: 68, 96; see also McGovern, 2014: 246).

The Court explained that because sentencing practice in England and Wales is very similar to that in New Zealand, the sentencing guidelines it issued were influenced by the work of the English Sentencing Guidelines Council.[84] The Court also drew on the Sentencing Establishment Unit's draft sexual offence guideline, noting that it had been the subject of considerable consultation with interested parties and that it provided more information than would ordinarily be available to the Court in a guideline case.[85]

In remarks very similar to those of the English Court of Appeal in *R v Millberry and others*,[86] the Court of Appeal emphasised that its intention was to provide sentencing guidance[87] and stressed that it was not imposing a straitjacket on sentencing judges.[88] The Court also stated that it intended to provide direction in the manner of application of the requirements of the Sentencing Act 2002, to ensure properly graduated sentencing for rape and to avoid the previous clustering of sentences around the eight-year mark.[89] The Court began by discussing what it termed 'culpability assessment factors', setting out a non-exhaustive list of nine aggravating and two mitigating factors in sentencing rape.[90] The various factors, the Court observed, had been treated as relevant in domestic authorities

79 *AM* (n 10) at [1].
80 Ibid.
81 Ibid at [28].
82 *AM* (n 10).
83 Ibid at [5] and [65].
84 Ibid at [18]. The work of the SGC is discussed in Chapter 4.
85 Ibid at [20].
86 [2003] 2 Cr App R (S) 31, discussed in Chapter 4.
87 AM (n 10) at [29] and [88].
88 Ibid at [84], *cf* Millberry (n 86) at [13] and [34].
89 Ibid at [33], [35] and [88].
90 Ibid at [37]–[60].

and in the approaches taken by both the Sentencing Establishment Unit and the English Sentencing Guidelines Council.[91] The Court's reference in *AM* to the various culpability assessment factors as having featured in 'the United Kingdom guidelines [*sic*]',[92] however, failed to acknowledge the different approach to rape sentencing taken by the Scottish courts. It is thus a paradigmatic, and regrettable, example of 'the UK' really meaning 'England and Wales' in legal discourse (see generally Croall et al, 2010: 5–8; Garland, 1999: xiv; and McAra, 2008: 481).

The Court in *AM* prefaced its discussion of the various aggravating and mitigating factors with the following observation:

> '[I]t is trite but important to emphasise that what is required is an evaluation of all the circumstances. Listing relevant factors and setting out bands in the way we have done does not remove the need for judgement. A mechanistic approach is not appropriate.'[93]

With that caveat, the Court listed the following factors as aggravating an offence of rape:

- planning and premeditation;
- violence, issuing threats, intimidation, abduction, detention and home invasion;
- the vulnerability of the victim due to, for example, age or health;
- physical and psychological harm caused to the victim;
- rape committed by more than one offender acting in concert;
- the scale of the offending, repeated rape and associated degradation or indignities including recording or photographing the offence;
- breach of trust;
- hate crime; and
- the degree of violation, in the sense of the length of the assault and the amount of force used.[94]

The two factors listed as being capable of mitigating an offence were, first, a genuine mistaken belief as to consent[95] and, second, circumstances in which consensual sexual activity took place immediately before the offence.[96] The Court accepted that this latter consideration was 'difficult and controversial';[97] however, it was included as a mitigating factor on the basis that immediate prior consensual sexual activity may correlate with a lack of premeditation.[98] Later in its judgment,

[91] Ibid at [36].
[92] Ibid, see also [57].
[93] Ibid at [36].
[94] Ibid at [37]–[52].
[95] Ibid at [53].
[96] Ibid at [54]–[60].
[97] Ibid at [59].
[98] Ibid.

the Court also referred to the importance of an offender's youth, mental disability and prior good character as mitigating factors.[99] The culpability assessment factors thus represent intuitive judgements about what makes one instance of rape more serious than another. These judgements have developed over time through case law and reflect community attitudes to sexual violence (McGovern, 2014: 247).

Before setting out the relevant sentencing bands or ranges for rape, the Court dealt with two further important issues. Firstly, with regard to the sentencing of so-called 'relationship rape' (an issue which, as we have seen, has greatly exercised the Court of Appeal in England and Wales[100] and which, until recently, continued to cause divisions of judicial opinion in Scottish sentencing jurisprudence[101]), the Court was unequivocal:

> 'Culpability is not reduced by any sense of entitlement associated with a current or previous relationship. As this Court has said, there is no separate regime for sexual violation of a spouse or partner or those who have previously been in a relationship.'[102]

Although not cited by the Court in *AM*, the rationale for this approach was articulated by the New Zealand Court of Appeal as far back as 1987 in *R v N*.[103] As we have seen, in 1987 neither the English Court of Appeal nor the Scottish Appeal Court had considered the issue of sentencing relationship rape. The matter was not addressed in the English Court of Appeal's guideline judgment in *Billam*[104] and it would be another 12 months before the Court in *R v Berry*[105] held that a prior sexual relationship could serve to *mitigate* a sentence.[106] The Scottish Appeal Court was at that time some 12 years away from considering the issue, only to similarly determine, in *Ramage v HMA*,[107] that a prior sexual relationship between the parties could amount to a *mitigating* factor in sentencing rape.[108]

R v N[109] was a case in which the appellant raped his estranged wife at knife-point. What the New Zealand Court of Appeal said in *N* was this:

> 'We are firmly of the view that in cases of this nature no separate regime of sentencing is called for simply because the parties are married or have been in a continuing sexual relationship. To do so would deny to a woman in that position the rights over her body which are accorded to every other woman … [T]he sense of outrage and violation experienced by a woman in that position can be equally as severe.'[110]

[99] Ibid at [84].
[100] See Chapter 4.
[101] See Chapter 5.
[102] *AM* (n 10) at [61].
[103] [1987] 2 NZLR 268.
[104] *Billam* (n 71).
[105] (1988) 10 Cr App R (S) 13.
[106] See Chapter 4.
[107] 1999 SCCR 592.
[108] See Chapter 5.
[109] *N* (n 103).
[110] Ibid at 270. See also Hall, 2007b: 55–57.

Secondly, the Court in *AM* considered the issue of the extent to which sentencing for rape should be influenced by the views of the victim, particularly where the victim seeks a lenient disposal.[111] The Court noted that where sexual offending occurs within a family or social group, victims are often put under pressure not to involve the criminal justice system and that judges often treat victims' calls for leniency with caution, seeing them as likely to be the result of such illegitimate pressure.[112] On the other hand, the Court considered it difficult to see why a judge should ignore a claim by a victim that the harm suffered was minimal, at least where she is satisfied that such illegitimate pressure has not been brought to bear on the victim.[113] The Court concluded that no general rule could be set out and that judges would have to assess each case individually.[114]

Before it set out the sentencing guidelines, the Court emphasised the importance of judgement and judicial discretion in their application. It also stressed the importance of individualised justice in sentencing and of taking account of the effect on the victim:

> 'In considering the culpability of offending in a particular case, we emphasise that what is required is an evaluative exercise of judgment. We see judges as having a reasonable degree of latitude in this exercise … In assessing the gravity of offending judges must, of course, do this in a fact-specific way focusing on the culpability of the offender and the effect on the victim and, as a corollary, they must not reason by stereotype or seek to turn responsibility for the offending back on the victim, in terms of "she asked for it" or other excuses based on rape myths.'[115]

The Court's guidelines followed the same approach as previous guideline judgments such as *R v Taueki*[116] in establishing bands, expressed in terms of imprisonment, within which ranges of starting points were provided.[117] Four bands were set out for sexual violation where the lead offence is rape, penile penetration of the mouth or anus, or violation involving objects:

(i) rape band one: six to eight years' imprisonment;
(ii) rape band two: seven to 13 years' imprisonment;
(iii) rape band three: 12 to 18 years' imprisonment; and
(iv) rape band four: 16 to 20 years' imprisonment.[118]

Band one was described as being appropriate for offending at the lower end of the spectrum, where aggravating features are either not present or present only to a limited extent.[119] The range of six to eight years set by the Court for band

[111] *AM* (n 10) at [62]– [64].
[112] Ibid at [63].
[113] Ibid at [64].
[114] Ibid.
[115] Ibid at [79].
[116] *Taueki* (n 18).
[117] *AM* (n 10) at [88].
[118] Ibid at [90].
[119] Ibid at [93].

one offences is, however, a substantial term of imprisonment. Such high penalties reflect the importance of sexual autonomy, human dignity and bodily integrity, and the degree to which they are violated by the offence of rape[120] (see McGovern, 2014: 248).

Band two was said to be appropriate for cases where the scale of offending, levels of violence and premeditation are relatively moderate.[121] It applies to cases which involve a vulnerable victim, an offender acting in concert with others, or some additional violence.[122] *Band three* applies to offending accompanied by relatively serious aggravating features.[123] It is appropriate for offending which involves two or more of the factors increasing culpability to a high degree, or for offending which features more than three of those factors to a moderate degree.[124] The Court also stated that '[p]articularly cruel, callous or violent single episodes of offending involving rape' will fall into this band.[125]

Finally, *band four* applies to cases involving multiple offending over considerable periods of time, rather than single instances of rape.[126] The Court considered the paradigm example to be the repeated rape of one or more family members over a period of years. Gang rape, or multiple perpetrator rape, was also said to be an offence which is likely to fall within this band.[127]

In describing the types of rape that come within the various bands, the Court provided illustrations by reference to several dozen earlier cases, usually decided at first instance, along with brief summaries of the facts.[128] These illustrations were made possible due to the practice in New Zealand of transcribing sentencing decisions for most sentences imposed at first instance (see Young and King, 2013: 216).

The Court recognised that cases would arise which were so unusual, in the sense of their featuring a combination of mitigating factors and perhaps a comparatively low level of harm, that the judge would require to set a starting point outside of the guidelines, below the bottom of band one.[129] Where a judge departed from the guidelines in this way, the Court stated that reasons should be given for the departure.[130] The Court also stressed that the bands set out ranges of starting points (*not* final sentences) which were to be adjusted up or down to reflect circumstances personal to the offender.[131] Judges were directed not to

[120] See the discussion in Chapter 2.
[121] *AM* (n 10) at [98].
[122] Ibid.
[123] Ibid at [105].
[124] Ibid.
[125] Ibid.
[126] Ibid at [108].
[127] Ibid at [109].
[128] Ibid at [93]–[112].
[129] Ibid at [83].
[130] Ibid.
[131] Ibid at [84]. See above.

diminish the importance of mitigating factors such as youth, mental disability and prior good character.[132]

An Assessment of the *AM* Guidelines

The sentencing guidelines in *AM*[133] are criticised by Mathias (2010) who considers the grouping of bands of sexual offending based on the physical details of the offence as comprising a 'grotesque' level of analysis. Mathias's main objection to the guidelines, however, is that they fetter judicial discretion: while he accepts that the guidelines are 'honest endeavours to promote uniformity [*sic*] in sentencing', he considers that they are based on the underlying assumption that judges are unable to exercise their sentencing discretion judicially.

Although the illustrations of the types of rape that come within the various bands set by the Court in *AM*[134] make for difficult (and, in some cases, extremely harrowing) reading, they nevertheless serve a useful purpose in illustrating, in narrative form, the application of the guidelines themselves (O'Malley, 2013a: 661; see also Terblanche, 2010: 1284 and 2016: 146). More importantly, however, Mathias's criticism is based on a flawed understanding of the nature of the Court's guidelines. Mathias appears to focus purely on the four rape bands; he arguably overlooks the repeated statements of the Court throughout the decision in *AM* which stress that the guidelines are provided only to guide judges in imposing sentence;[135] emphasise that the rape bands set out ranges of starting points and *not* final sentences;[136] stress the need for judicial evaluation of all the circumstances in the particular case; the importance of judgement; the degree of latitude afforded to judges in their application and the Court's statements which highlight the fact that a mechanistic approach towards the application of the guidelines is inappropriate.[137]

The two mitigating culpability assessment factors set out by the Court in *AM* (namely a genuine mistaken belief as to consent[138] and prior consensual sexual activity immediately before the offence[139]) are criticised by McGovern (2014). While the Court included prior consensual sexual activity as a mitigating factor on the basis that 'there *may* be a correlation with lack of premeditation',[140] McGovern considers it 'plainly wrong' for the Court to have done so when examined in light of the violation of the victim's sexual autonomy, human dignity and

[132] Ibid.
[133] *AM* (n 10).
[134] Ibid at [93]–[112].
[135] Ibid at [29], [35], [84] and [88].
[136] Ibid at [84].
[137] Ibid at [36] and [79].
[138] Ibid at [53].
[139] Ibid at [54]–[60].
[140] Ibid at [58], emphasis added.

bodily integrity. McGovern argues that consensual sexual activity before a rape occurs does not reduce the level of intrusion into the victim's interests, so this factor has no bearing on offence seriousness. For McGovern, including prior consensual sexual activity as a mitigating factor undermines an individual's right to say no to any sexual activity at any time (McGovern, 2014: 70; see also Chalton, 2015: 24). In the Republic of Ireland, however, the courts adopt the same position as the New Zealand Court of Appeal in regarding consensual sexual activity immediately prior to the offence as a mitigating factor (see O'Malley, 2016: 373 and the decision in *People (DPP) v Keogh*[141]).

McGovern also questions the Court's position that prior consensual sexual activity can serve as a mitigating factor since it may indicate a lack of premeditation on the part of the offender. She explains:

> '[P]remeditation is already recognised as an aggravating factor in its own right and lack of premeditation should be treated simply as the absence of an aggravating factor, not as a mitigating factor. Additionally, prior consensual sexual activity may signal that the offending involved a breach of trust, an aggravating factor. For that reason it is not logical to treat prior consensual sexual activity as a mitigating factor' (McGovern, 2014: 70).

Although McGovern (2014: 70) suggests that offence seriousness would be assessed more accurately if prior consensual sexual activity was removed as a culpability factor, her criticism of this aspect of the judgment in *AM*, like that of Mathias (2010), arguably pays insufficient regard to the inherent flexibility of the guidelines. In particular, McGovern appears to overlook what the Court in *AM* described as 'the evaluative nature of the sentencing process'.[142] The Court was clear that prior consensual sexual activity *may* correlate with a lack of premeditation[143] and so equally it may not do so, depending on the facts and circumstances of the particular case. As the Court itself emphasised, an 'evaluative exercise of judgment' is required.[144] The judge must evaluate all the circumstances of the case and the sentencing guidance is not to be applied in a mechanistic way.[145] The sentencing judge will assess the gravity of the offence in a fact-specific way, focusing on the culpability of the offender and the effect on the victim.[146] Any consensual sexual activity that took place between the parties prior to the rape may, or may not, feature in the judge's assessment of culpability and harm in imposing a proportionate sentence.

The decision in *AM* is thus an example of the Court of Appeal seeking to achieve what Sir Grant Hammond, a former judge of the New Zealand Court of Appeal, describes as 'reasonable regularity' in sentencing (Hammond, 2007: 233).

[141] *Ex tempore*, Court of Criminal Appeal, 17 July 2009 (cited in O'Malley, 2016: 373).
[142] *AM* (n 10) at [81].
[143] Ibid at [58].
[144] Ibid at [79].
[145] Ibid at [36].
[146] Ibid at [79].

The most practicable way to reach this ideal, Hammond suggests, is through structured, but not inflexible, guidance, coupled with a decent width of appellate review. Similarly, O'Malley commends the approach of the Court in combining narrative guidance on the differentiation of offences falling into the same broad legal category with concrete indications of appropriate starting points and sentence ranges (2011: 126). For O'Malley, if one assumes a reasonable level of compliance on the part of sentencing judges and a reasonable level of vigilance on the part of the Court of Appeal, the approach should produce a fair degree of consistency in sentencing whilst leaving sufficient room for the exercise of judicial discretion. This is borne out by contemporary sentencing practice for rape in New Zealand, where the guidelines in *AM* have been consistently applied, both by the High Court and by the Court of Appeal (see Hall, 2014: 82).

Rape Sentencing in South Africa

The Crime of Rape in South Africa

Rape in South Africa was defined at common law as unlawful, intentional sexual intercourse with a woman without her consent, with sexual intercourse being defined as vaginal penetration by a penis (Burchell, 2005: 162). Following a lengthy period of law reform commencing in 1996 with an investigation by the South African Law Reform Commission (SALRC, 1997; see also Artz and Combrinck, 2003: 80–90), the Criminal Law (Sexual Offences and Related Matters) Amendment Act 32 of 2007[147] came into force towards the end of 2007. The 2007 Act comprised a codification, or at least a consolidation, of sexual crimes under South African law (Kemp et al, 2018: 350). It repealed the common law of rape,[148] replacing it with an expanded, gender-neutral, statutory offence of rape that encompasses a number of penetrative acts.

Section 3 of the 2007 Act provides that: 'Any person ("A") who unlawfully and intentionally commits an act of sexual penetration with a complainant ("B"), without the consent of B, is guilty of the offence of rape.' In terms of section 1 of the 2007 Act, 'sexual penetration' is defined as including any act that causes penetration, to any extent whatsoever, by:

(a) the genital organs of one person into or beyond the genital organs, anus, or mouth of another person;
(b) any other part of the body of one person or any object, including any part of the body of an animal, into or beyond the genital organs or anus of another person; or
(c) the genital organs of an animal, into or beyond the mouth of another person.

147 Hereinafter 'the 2007 Act'.
148 See s 68(1)(b) of the 2007 Act which repeals various common law crimes, including rape.

A significant feature of the definition of sexual penetration is that it relates to an act that 'causes penetration'. The gender of the accused is not restricted and a woman may be guilty of rape if, for example, she causes the penetration of another woman's genital organs either by using any part of her own body, or by using an object. This, as Kemp et al (2018: 366) observe, is 'a monumental departure from the previous common law position'. In particular, it has had a substantial impact on the number of offenders subject to the mandatory and minimum sentences for rape discussed later in this chapter (Terblanche, 2016: 63). Section 1 of the 2007 Act also defines 'genital organs' as including the whole or part of the male or female genital organs, thus making the offence gender-neutral (see generally Kemp et al, 2018: 359–68).

Section 4 of the 2007 Act introduces a new offence of 'compelled rape', making it an offence for a person to force another person to commit rape. In terms of section 4, the accused must be responsible for causing the sexual penetration to occur. The accused must be both the factual and legal cause of the sexual penetration before (s)he is liable for the crime of compelled rape (see Kemp et al, 2018: 368–69).

A 'Dual Sentencing System': An Overview of South African Sentencing Practice

Two different but parallel approaches towards sentencing currently operate in South Africa. Judicial discretion has traditionally been the hallmark of South African sentencing practice, with the judge's discretion determining the complete creation of the sentence. Operating alongside the discretionary approach, however, is a wide-ranging scheme of mandatory and minimum custodial sentences that apply to many of the most serious offences, including rape (Terblanche, 2011: 261). Thus, in contrast to the other common law jurisdictions examined thus far, South Africa operates what Terblanche terms 'a dual sentencing system' (2011: 262).

Judicial Discretion and 'The Triad of *Zinn*': The Traditional Approach to Sentencing in South Africa

The Importance of Judicial Discretion

As in other common law jurisdictions, judges in South Africa have traditionally enjoyed a wide sentencing discretion (Baehr, 2008: 227–28; Roth, 2008: 157–58; Spies, 2016: 393; Terblanche, 2017: 4; 2016: 131 and 140–41; 2013a: 95; 2011: 261; and 1997: 173; Terblanche and Mackenzie, 2008: 403; Terblanche and Roberts, 2005: 189; van der Merwe, 2005: 7; van Zyl Smit, 2002: 90–91). Indeed, judicial discretion has been described as 'a cornerstone of [the South African] sentencing tradition' (Viljoen Commission, 1976: para. 5.1.4.1.3). Judges traditionally resisted interference with their sentencing discretion, regarding it as a fundamental aspect of judicial independence (Sloth-Nielsen and Ehlers, 2005a: 15; 2005b: 1; Terblanche, 2006: 2).

In discussing the importance of the judge's sentencing discretion, Smalberger JA noted in *S v Toms; S v Bruce*[149] '[t]hat courts should, as far as possible, have an unfettered discretion in relation to sentence is a cherished principle which calls for constant recognition'.[150] For Justice Smalberger, such discretion 'permits of balance and fair sentencing which is the hallmark of enlightened criminal justice. The second and somewhat related principle, is that of individualisation of punishment'.[151] Individualised punishment had earlier been affirmed in *S v Scheepers*[152] as a key principle in South African law: judges were directed not to lose sight of the offender's personal circumstances, including 'sociological circumstances, experience of punishment and potential for rehabilitation'.[153]

Thus, the South African courts have traditionally followed the same approach as the courts in Scotland,[154] the Republic of Ireland[155] and New Zealand[156] in focusing on the attainment of individualised justice. The courts in all four jurisdictions have traditionally ensured that the sentence is tailored to fit both the offence and the circumstances of the particular offender. This process of individualisation in sentencing cannot take place without judicial discretion (Terblanche, 2016: 135, 165).

The 'Triad of Zinn'

The factors to which the judge must have regard in imposing sentence were set out by the then Appellate Division of the Supreme Court of South Africa in *S v Zinn*.[157] In what was to become a much-quoted dictum in South African sentencing jurisprudence, Rumpff JA held that in imposing sentence, '[w]hat has to be considered is the triad consisting of the crime, the offender and the interests of society'.[158] Arguably, there was nothing novel about Justice Rumpff's 'sentencing triad' since it merely reflected judicial practice, as opposed to introducing a new line of thinking on sentencing. The importance of the dictum lay in the fact that it was the first time that the relevant factors had been articulated in an appellate judgment (see Terblanche, 2016: 153–54). Nevertheless, the *Zinn* triad was to become the foundation for sentencing in South Africa (Terblanche, 1997: 173).

149 (1990) (2) SA 802 (A).
150 Ibid at 806H–I.
151 Ibid at 806I.
152 1977 (2) SA 155.
153 Ibid at 158G–H (translation from Afrikaans by Terblanche, 2016: 135, fn 79).
154 See Chapter 5.
155 See Chapter 6.
156 See above.
157 1969 (2) SA 537.
158 Ibid at 540G–H.

Although Justice Rumpff's dictum has come to be seen as somewhat trite (Terblanche, 2016: 153; 2013a: 96; and 2011: 263), it is still routinely applied by the South African courts (see van der Merwe, 2015: 415). In *S v M*,[159] for example, the Constitutional Court described the *Zinn* triad both as 'the paradigm from which to proceed' when embarking on the task of passing sentence and as the 'sentencing north star'.[160] In *DPP Kwazulu-Natal v P*,[161] meanwhile, the Supreme Court of Appeal stated that '[t]he so-called traditional approach to sentencing required (and still does) the sentencing court to consider the "triad"'.[162] In *S v Mudau (sub nom S v SMM)*,[163] the Court noted that the *Zinn* dictum remains the leading authority on sentencing methodology and that it 'epitomises the very essence of a balanced, effective sentence which meets all the sentencing objectives'.[164]

The principles set out in *Zinn* are commended by Terblanche and Roberts (2005: 198–99) as they allow the court to make an accurate assessment of the seriousness of the offence, to take the personal circumstances of the offender into consideration and to have regard to the interests of society (see also Kemp et al, 2018: 40–41 and Terblanche, 2008a: 123). It is the task of the sentencing judge to balance the three factors forming the *Zinn* triad in arriving at the final sentence. Although the notion of 'balance' is routinely invoked by courts throughout the common law world as a shorthand way of describing the sentencing task (see, eg, Cooke, 1987: 57; Mackenzie, 2005: 14–15; Nicholson, 1992: 177; O'Malley, 2003: 134; and Taylor, 1993: 129), this is not 'balance' in the ordinary sense of the word since the seriousness of the offence may completely outweigh any mitigating factors. In such circumstances, this cannot amount to 'balance' since the scales would be heavily weighed against the offender (see Brown, 2017a: 139 and Terblanche, 2016: 161).

This more pragmatic view of the balancing exercise involved in the *Zinn* triad was later adopted by Rumpff himself, by this time Chief Justice, in *S v Holder*.[165] Here, his Honour stated that in the case of serious crimes, whatever their nature, the punishment component in the triad must be given priority.[166] Similarly, in the later decision in *S v De Kock*,[167] van der Merwe J acknowledged that recourse to the *Zinn* triad did not involve an exercise in balancing in the usual sense of the word. In the course of his judgment, Justice van der Merwe stressed that the three factors of the *Zinn* triad must be considered in conjunction with one another and that each should be *afforded a certain weight* depending on the facts of the individual case.[168] This approach, in which *the correct amount of weight* is attached to

159 [2007] ZACC 18; 2007 (2) SACR 539 (CC).
160 Ibid at [10].
161 2006 (1) SACR 243 (SCA).
162 Ibid at [13].
163 [2013] ZASCA 56; 2013 (2) SACR 292 (SCA).
164 Ibid at [14].
165 1979 (2) SA 70 (A).
166 Ibid at 81A.
167 1997 (2) SACR 171 (T).
168 Ibid at 197g–h.

each factor, is a more accurate description of the task facing the sentencing judge. In the case of particularly serious crimes, including rape, the court will often afford greater weight to the aggravating features of the offence than to the offender's personal circumstances (see Terblanche, 2016: 161, 167 and 210).

A series of appellate decisions demonstrate that discretion is key to the judicial balancing exercise inherent in the *Zinn* triad. As Holmes JA noted in his judgment in *S v Rabie*,[169] for example, 'the degree of emphasis of any relevant factor is ordinarily a matter falling within the exercise of judicial discretion'.[170] In *S v Banda*,[171] it was acknowledged that the elements of the *Zinn* triad 'contain an equilibrium and a tension' which means that the judge should counterbalance them to ensure that one element is not unduly accentuated at the expense or exclusion of another.[172] Meanwhile, in *S v Nkambule*,[173] in a passage echoing the observations of Rumpff CJ in *Holder*,[174] it was noted both that society's interests are often given a higher priority in the case of violent crimes[175] and that its abhorrence of such crimes should also be reflected in the sentence.[176] Finally, in *S v Dzukuda and others*,[177] Ackermann J of the Constitutional Court explained that the decision as to the weight to give to each element in the triad, 'calls for the exercise of a normative judgment, almost invariably referred to as a "discretion", for which no precise formula exists'.[178] Justice Ackermann proceeded to acknowledge that the exercise of this discretion 'could lead different sentencing courts, on exactly the same facts and scrupulously applying their minds to the correct sentencing principles applicable, to reach different conclusions'.[179]

As Terblanche (2016: 163–64) explains, the modern approach to determining the seriousness of an offence is contained in the South African Law Commission's report on sentencing (South African Law Commission, 2000: 36). Similar to the focus of the current system of English sentencing guidelines,[180] the South African approach involves the court considering both the *harm* caused by the offence and the *culpability* of the offender (see *S v Dodo*[181]). As with contemporary sentencing practice in the other common law jurisdictions examined in this book, sentencing in South Africa is thus founded upon the principle of proportionality: the sentence must be proportionate both to the gravity of the offence and to the personal circumstances of the offender (Terblanche, 2016: 12; 182–83; 193–94; *cf* Terblanche and Roberts, 2005: 199).

169 1975 (4) SA 855 (A).
170 Ibid at 864F–G.
171 1991 (2) SA 352 (B).
172 Ibid at 355.
173 1993 (1) SACR 136 (A).
174 *Holder* (n 165).
175 Ibid at 145c–d.
176 Ibid at 147h.
177 [2000] ZACC 16; 2000 (2) SACR 443 (CC).
178 Ibid at [35].
179 Ibid.
180 See Chapter 4.
181 [2001] ZACC 16; 2001 (1) SACR 594 (CC) at [37].

South African Sentencing Methodology

The sentencing methodology employed by South African judges is explained by Terblanche in terms redolent of the 'instinctive synthesis' approach used in its pure form by judges in Scotland and Australia[182] and in a somewhat diluted form by judges in the Republic of Ireland:[183]

> 'Normally, in the course of the trial … the sentencing officer gets a feel for the punishment he *instinctively considers appropriate in the case*, considering all the circumstances as a whole. The sentencing officer then proceeds to justify this sentence, basing it on the basic principles of sentencing and on all those facts which, objectively speaking, act to aggravate or mitigate the punishment. During this exercise in logic the sentencing officer will *check his instinct* and may make minor adjustments to the sentence' (Terblanche, 2016: 133, emphasis added; see also Terblanche, 2011: 271 and 2007: 118).

While in the leading case of *S v De Kock*[184] van der Merwe J did not specifically conceptualise sentencing in terms of an instinctive synthesis, he did nevertheless stress the importance, firstly, of the judge using her experience, objectivity and integrity in deciding upon sentence[185] and, secondly, of the judge seeking to balance the various purposes of punishment on the basis of the facts of the individual case.[186] Both these aspects are, in fact, key elements in sentencing by way of instinctive synthesis (see Brown, 2017a: 29–33; Freiberg, 2016: 427; Hewton, 2010: 80; Krasnostein, 2015: 36–40; and Krasnostein and Freiberg, 2014: 18). The methodology used by South African judges in arriving at sentence (at least under the traditional, discretionary-based model of sentencing) thus comprises an instinctive synthesis of the various aspects involved in the punitive process. Unlike the staged approach employed by the courts in the Republic of Ireland[187] and New Zealand,[188] the traditional model of sentencing in South Africa accords with that in Scotland.[189] As with the methodology employed by Scottish judges, the South African approach involves a single process of reasoning in which the judge identifies all the factors that are relevant to the sentence. The judge evaluates their significance and then makes a value judgement as to what is the appropriate sentence given all the factors in the case, each circumstance being afforded such weight as it deserves in combination with all other relevant circumstances.

In common with jurisdictions such as Scotland and the Republic of Ireland, sentencing by way of the South African 'instinctive synthesis' is not entirely unconstrained: the judge's discretion is guided by principles laid down by the

[182] See Chapter 5.
[183] See Chapter 6.
[184] *De Kock* (n 167).
[185] Ibid at 182g.
[186] Ibid at 192e.
[187] See Chapter 6.
[188] See above.
[189] See Chapter 5.

appellate courts. Terblanche (2016: 164) explains that in time, judges develop their own tariffs, or points of departure, for the sentences imposed for specific offences. As with the operation of what O'Malley terms 'principled discretion' in the Republic of Ireland (O'Malley, 2011: 5; 2001: 135),[190] the operation of any such tariff will be assisted by appellate review and by appellate judgments (Terblanche, 2016: 164).

Guideline Judgments

There is a tradition of the South African courts, both in general and in specific parts of the country, developing guidelines for the sentencing of certain offences. Guidelines were introduced in the late 1990s and early 2000s for drug offences, drink driving offences and stock theft (Terblanche, 2003a: 874–75). These guidelines resembled the traditional form of guideline judgment introduced by the English Court of Appeal[191] (see Terblanche, 2016: 144– 45). They have the same status as guideline judgments in Scotland,[192] the Republic of Ireland[193] and New Zealand[194] in that they are intended only to *guide*, not remove, judicial sentencing discretion. In *S v Serabo*,[195] for example, it was made clear that, despite the relevant guideline judgment having served to increase penalties for drink driving offences, the sentence in each case must still be determined on an individual basis:

> 'It is objectionable if the increased sentence is imposed arbitrarily in every case because it is now the standard sentence, without reference to the facts and circumstances of the case and without individuating the sentence by taking into account the personal circumstances of the particular offender. The norm should be no more than a point of departure. The sentencing officer must still exercise his discretion judicially in order to arrive at a sentence which is just, balanced, compassionate and appropriate, due regard being had to [all the factors] which lie at the root of criminal punishment. If he does so, he will frequently find himself departing from the norm.'[196]

It remains within the powers of the South African courts to issue guideline judgments for specific offences, should the need arise (Terblanche, 2016: 145). At present, however, unlike the courts in Scotland, the Republic of Ireland and New Zealand, the South African courts do not make use of guideline judgments as a method of aiding judicial discretion in sentencing (see Terblanche, 2011: 275).

[190] See Chapter 6.
[191] See Chapter 4.
[192] See Chapter 5.
[193] See Chapter 6.
[194] See above.
[195] 2002 (1) SACR 391 (E).
[196] Ibid at 397.

The Criminal Law Amendment Act 105 of 1997: Mandatory and Minimum Sentences for Rape

An 'Undesirable Intrusion' – The Traditional Judicial View of Mandatory and Minimum Sentences

The importance of judicial sentencing discretion and the view that judges are uniquely positioned to impose appropriate sentences meant that mandatory and minimum sentences were traditionally unpopular in South Africa. In *S v Gibson*,[197] for example, Holmes JA opined that a mandatory sentence 'unduly puts all the emphasis on the punitive and deterrent factors of sentence and precludes the traditional consideration of subjective factors relating to the convicted person'.[198] Similarly, the Commission of Inquiry into the Penal System ('the Viljoen Commission'), which reported two years after the decision in *Gibson*, emphasised the sophistication of the sentencing process. The Commission highlighted the ability of the courts to develop principles that accommodate the various purposes of sentencing; it stressed the importance of the *Zinn* triad;[199] and objected to the use of mandatory sentences (Viljoen Commission, 1976: paras 5.1.3.33–34 and 5.1.4.1.2–7; see also Brown, 2017a: 139 and van Zyl Smit, 2002: 91). In the later decision in *S v Toms; S v Bruce*,[200] Corbett CJ observed that:

> '[T]he imposition of a mandatory minimum prison sentence has always been regarded as an undesirable intrusion by the Legislature upon the jurisdiction of the courts to determine the punishment to be meted out to persons convicted of statutory offences and as a kind of enactment that is calculated in certain instances to produce grave injustice.'[201]

These traditional criticisms of mandatory sentences are based on two closely related considerations. Mandatory sentencing makes individualisation of punishment impossible. In turn, this leads to punishment which is unreasonable or disproportionate (Terblanche, 2016: 48; see also Brown, 2017a: 69–72).

Despite the misgivings of the South African judiciary, minimum sentences were common during the 1970s; however, they fell out of favour through the 1980s and for most of the 1990s (Terblanche, 2016: 49). Yet, as South Africa experienced rising levels of violent crime, including murder and sexual assault,[202] in late 1997 the South African Parliament passed legislation introducing mandatory

[197] 1974 (4) SA 478 (A).
[198] Ibid at 482A–B.
[199] See above.
[200] *S v Toms; S v Bruce* (n 149).
[201] Ibid at 822C–D.
[202] On the prevalence of rape in South Africa and the presence of a 'rape culture', see Anderson, 2000; Deane, 2018: 87–92; Jewkes and Abrahams, 2002; Jewkes and Sikweyiya, 2013; Jewkes et al, 2011; 2010; 2006; 2005; and 2002; Kapp, 2004; Pitcher and Bowley, 2002; Rumney and van der Bijl, 2009; van der Bijl and Rumney, 2010; Wojcicki, 2002; Wood, 2005; Wood and Jewkes, 1997 and Wood et al, 2007.

and minimum sentences for specified offences, including rape. The legislation was passed with the intention of reducing levels of serious violent and sexual crime (see Roth, 2008: 155; Sloth-Nielsen and Ehlers, 2005a: 15; Terblanche, 2018: 28 and 2001: 14–15; and Terblanche and Mackenzie, 2008: 406–8).

The Mandatory and Minimum Sentence Provisions for Rape

The provisions setting out mandatory and minimum sentences for rape are found in section 51 of the Criminal Law Amendment Act 105 of 1997,[203] colloquially referred to as 'the minimum sentences Act' or 'the minimum sentences legislation'. The 1997 Act came into force on 1 May 1998. Section 51 prescribes various mandatory or minimum terms of imprisonment for a variety of serious offences, the offences themselves (including rape) being set out in Schedule 2 to the 1997 Act. The 1997 Act was originally intended as a short-term measure. In terms of section 53, the Act would cease to have effect on 30 April 2000; however, South Africa's President repeatedly extended its operation. Section 53 was eventually repealed[204] and the minimum sentence scheme is now in place until such time as the 1997 Act itself is repealed (see Cameron, 2017: 11–12; Spies, 2016: 393; Terblanche, 2016: 50–51; and Terblanche and Mackenzie, 2008: 410).

As the 1997 Act prescribes which sentences to impose, it amounts to a substantial departure from the traditional discretionary-based approach to sentencing in South Africa. In examining the operation of the minimum sentences legislation in the leading case of *S v Malgas*,[205] the Supreme Court of Appeal noted that the legislature had aimed at ensuring a severe, standardised and consistent response from the courts to the commission of serious crimes such as rape. When considering the appropriate sentence, the emphasis was shifted to the objective gravity of the type of crime and the public's need for effective sanctions against it.[206] In the later decision in *S v Kimberley*,[207] however, the Court held that as the 1997 Act prescribes minimum sentences and thus eliminates the usual discretion of the court to impose a sentence which fits the facts and circumstances of the individual case, the statutory provisions will usually be construed 'in such a way that the penal discretion remains intact as far as possible'[208] (see Terblanche, 2016: 52).

The statutory provisions are convoluted and their poor drafting has been the subject of extensive academic criticism (see Baehr, 2008: 224–25;

[203] Hereinafter 'the 1997 Act'. For a full discussion of the background to the passing of the 1997 Act, see Baehr, 2008: 213–25; Sloth-Nielsen and Ehlers, 2005b: 1–5; and van Zyl Smit, 2002.

[204] By the Criminal Law (Sentencing) Amendment Act 38 of 2007.

[205] [2001] ZASCA 30; 2001 (1) SACR 469 (SCA).

[206] Ibid at [8].

[207] [2005] ZASCA 78; 2005 (2) SACR 663 (SCA).

[208] Ibid at [13].

Terblanche, 2016: 51; 90; 2003b: 195, 220; and 2001: 7–8; and Terblanche and Mackenzie, 2008: 410). Section 51(1) of the 1997 Act provides that:

> 'Notwithstanding any other law but subject to [subsection] (3) … a regional court or a High Court shall sentence a person it has convicted of an offence referred to in Part I of Schedule 2 to imprisonment for life.'

The offences listed in Part I of Schedule 2 of the 1997 Act include rape, but *only* with respect to the situations specifically described (so-called 'Part I rape' – see Baehr, 2008: 215 and Spies, 2016: 394). Part I rapes which attract *a mandatory sentence of life imprisonment* comprise the following:

- repeated rape of the same victim;
- multiple perpetrator rape (or 'gang-rape');
- rape committed by an offender who has been convicted of two or more offences of rape but who has not yet been sentenced in respect of those convictions;
- rape committed by an offender who is HIV positive;
- rape of a victim aged under 16;
- rape of a victim who is physically disabled and particularly vulnerable;
- rape of a victim who is mentally disabled; and
- rape involving the infliction of grievous bodily harm.[209]

The mandatory sentence of life imprisonment applies also to convictions for compelled rape committed in, broadly, the same circumstances. If an offence of rape, or compelled rape, is committed in any other circumstances (so-called 'Part III rape' – see Baehr, 2008: 215 and Spies, 2016: 394) then section 51(2) of the 1997 Act applies and certain *minimum terms of imprisonment* are prescribed. The minimum term of imprisonment depends on whether the offender has previous convictions for rape and, if so, the number of those convictions. A conviction for so-called Part III rape results in:

- 10 years' imprisonment for an offender who has never previously been convicted of rape or compelled rape;
- 15 years' imprisonment for an offender who has one previous conviction for rape or compelled rape; and
- 20 years' imprisonment for an offender who has two or more previous convictions for rape or compelled rape.[210]

Thus, if a rape does *not* feature any of the circumstances that lead to the mandatory sentence of life imprisonment under section 51(1), the offender will nevertheless be subject to a minimum term of imprisonment under section 51(2) of either 10, 15 or 20 years depending on his offending history (Terblanche, 2016: 68, 73).

[209] Part I of Schedule 2 to the 1997 Act.
[210] Ibid, Part III, Sch 2.

As Baehr (2008: 226) observes, the statutory differences between Part I rape and Part III rape are relatively arbitrary and disproportionate: raping a victim twice rather than once, or raping a 16-year-old rather than a 15-year-old, could result in a difference in sentence of anywhere between perhaps 20 and 50 years, depending on the age of the offender.

Baehr further criticises the statutory provisions as both over-inclusive and under-inclusive. The system has aggravating factors built into what Baehr (2008: 240) describes as 'the mandatory minimums algorithm'. A life sentence is prescribed where any of the factors in Part I of Schedule 2 of the 1997 Act are present. If just one of these criteria is met then a mandatory sentence of life imprisonment applies; however, the circumstances in which a life sentence must be imposed are not *necessarily* the same aggravating factors that would ordinarily justify life imprisonment. Furthermore, the legislation focuses only on some aggravating factors whilst many others (including the use of a weapon, kidnapping and filming or photographing the offence) have been disregarded (Baehr, 2008: 226–27 and 240–41; see also Terblanche, 2016: 85).

It is important to note that the legislation prescribes *minimum* sentences for Part III rape. In *S v Kolea*,[211] the Supreme Court of Appeal held that section 51(2) of the 1997 Act does not prevent the court from imposing longer sentences, up to life imprisonment. Nevertheless, in respect of both the mandatory life sentence under section 51(1) of the 1997 Act and the mandatory minimum sentences under section 51(2), a so-called 'departure' or 'escape' clause exists under section 51(3).

'Substantial and Compelling Circumstances' – The Departure Test

The departure clause under section 51(3) of the 1997 Act allows the court to impose a lesser sentence if it is satisfied that 'substantial and compelling circumstances' exist which justify the imposition of a lesser sentence. As van Zyl Smit (2002: 100) explains, the words 'substantial and compelling' are not terms of art in South African criminal law. While their legislative history is somewhat obscure, it seems that they may have been drawn from the sentencing guidelines operating in the US State of Minnesota which provide for a departure test in the same terms (van Zyl Smit, 2002: 100; see also Sloth-Nielsen and Ehlers, 2005b: 6; Terblanche, 2006: 30; and Terblanche and Roberts, 2005: 192).

What Constitutes 'Substantial and Compelling Circumstances'? The Decision in Malgas

The leading case on the operation of the departure test is the decision of the Supreme Court of Appeal in *S v Malgas*.[212] In *Malgas*, a successful appeal against

[211] 2013 (1) SACR 409 (SCA) at [17].
[212] *Malgas* (n 205). The Court summarised the key points of its judgment at [25].

the mandatory sentence of life imprisonment following a conviction for murder, it was held that 'substantial and compelling circumstances' is a composite, and not a disjunctive, test.[213] Writing for the Court, Marais JA explained:

> 'That [the legislature] has refrained from giving … guidance [as to what constitutes "substantial and compelling circumstances"] is significant. It signals that it has deliberately and advisedly left it to the courts to decide in the final analysis whether the circumstances of any particular case call for a departure from the prescribed sentence. In doing so, they are required to regard the prescribed sentences as being *generally appropriate* for crimes of the kind specified and enjoined not to depart from them unless they are satisfied that there is weighty justification for doing so.'[214]

The Court in *Malgas* confirmed that the prescribed sentences under section 51 of the 1997 Act are the points of departure. The court no longer has 'a clean slate on which to inscribe whatever sentence it [thinks] fit'.[215] Rather, the court is required to approach the question of sentence 'conscious of the fact that the legislature has ordained life imprisonment or the particular prescribed period of imprisonment as the sentence which should *ordinarily* be imposed for the commission of the listed crimes in the specified circumstances'.[216]

In light of these considerations, it was held that the prescribed sentences should not be departed from 'lightly' or for 'flimsy reasons which could not withstand scrutiny'.[217] In particular, the Court noted that '[s]peculative hypotheses favourable to the offender, maudlin sympathy, aversion to imprisoning first offenders, personal doubts as to the efficacy of the policy implicit in the … legislation and like considerations' would not qualify as substantial and compelling circumstances.[218] There must be 'truly convincing reasons for a different response'[219] before the court can depart from imposing a prescribed sentence.

The Court also made it clear, however, that sentencing judges should not hesitate to depart from imposing a prescribed sentence if this is warranted by the circumstances of the particular case. The Court noted that section 51(3) of the 1997 Act '… vests the sentencing court with the power, indeed the obligation, to consider whether the particular circumstances of the case require a different sentence to be imposed'.[220] The Court proceeded to note that a prescribed sentence *must* be departed from if the court is satisfied that substantial and compelling circumstances exist which justify its doing so.[221] Judges, the Court noted, are a good deal more free to depart from the prescribed sentences than had been supposed in some previously decided cases.[222]

[213] Ibid at [19].
[214] Ibid at [18], emphasis per original.
[215] Ibid at [8].
[216] Ibid, emphasis per original. See also the Court's observations at [20] and [25B].
[217] Ibid at [9].
[218] Ibid.
[219] Ibid at [8] and [25C].
[220] Ibid at [14].
[221] Ibid.
[222] Ibid at [25].

The Court acknowledged that part of the process for sentencing offences such as rape involves the judge considering what an appropriate sentence would have been in the absence of the minimum sentences legislation.[223] In particular, this involves judges using past sentencing patterns as a 'provisional standard' or 'starting point' for comparison when deciding whether a prescribed sentence is to be regarded as unjust.[224] The Court continued:

> 'To attempt to deny a court the right to have any regard whatsoever to past sentencing patterns when deciding whether a prescribed sentence is in the circumstances of a particular case manifestly unjust is tantamount to expecting someone who has not been allowed to see the colour blue to appreciate and gauge the extent to which the colour dark blue differs from it. As long as it is appreciated that the mere existence of *some* discrepancy between them cannot be the sole criterion and that something more than that is needed to justify departure, no great harm will be done. What that something more must be it is not possible to express in precise, accurate and all-embracing language.'[225]

The Court held that if a sentencing judge decides to depart from the prescribed sentence and impose a lesser sentence, she must nevertheless take account of the fact that offences such as rape have been singled out for severe punishment.[226] The sentence to be imposed in lieu of the prescribed sentence 'should be assessed paying due regard to the bench mark which the legislature has provided'.[227] This is an important statement for, as Terblanche (2016: 87) observes, even if the judge departs from the prescribed sentence, the 1997 Act continues to have an impact on the sentence imposed. As later explained by the Supreme Court of Appeal in *S v Abrahams*[228] and by the Constitutional Court in *Centre for Child Law v Minister for Justice and others*,[229] even if the prescribed sentence does not have to be imposed due to the presence of substantial and compelling circumstances, the minimum sentences legislation nevertheless has a weighting effect leading to the imposition of consistently heavier sentences.

The Court in *Malgas* also confirmed the importance of the traditional sentencing considerations[230] in determining whether a departure is called for. The Court should weigh all the factors traditionally taken into consideration when assessing sentence.[231] All factors relating to the offence and the offender are relevant; the essential question is whether any, or some, or all of them amount to substantial and compelling circumstances within the contemplation of the legislation.[232]

[223] Ibid at [21].
[224] Ibid.
[225] Ibid at [21] and [22], emphasis per original.
[226] Ibid at [25J].
[227] Ibid.
[228] 2002 (1) SACR 116 (SCA) at [25].
[229] 2009 (2) SACR 477 (CC) at [17].
[230] See above.
[231] *Malgas* (n 205) at [9] and [25F].
[232] See the later decision in *S v Nel* [2007] ZASCA 51 at [19].

While the Court in *Malgas* did not refer directly to the *Zinn* triad,[233] in the later decision in *S v M*[234] the Constitutional Court interpreted *Malgas* as approving judicial recourse to the triad of the crime, the offender and the interests of society[235] (see Terblanche, 2016: 78, fn 299).

On the issue of departure, the Court in *Malgas* concluded by holding that the sentencing judge must depart from a prescribed sentence in circumstances where to impose it would be unjust. The Court explained:

> '[The power to depart] plainly was given to the courts in recognition of the easily foreseeable injustices which could result from obliging them to pass the specified sentences come what may … The greater the sense of unease a court feels about the imposition of a prescribed sentence, the greater its anxiety will be that it may be perpetrating an injustice. Once a court reaches the point where unease has hardened into a conviction that an injustice will be done, that can only be because it is satisfied that the circumstances of the particular case render the prescribed sentence unjust or, as some might prefer to put it, disproportionate to the crime, the criminal and the legitimate needs of society. If that is the result of a consideration of the circumstances the court is entitled to characterise them as substantial and compelling and such as to justify the imposition of a lesser sentence.'[236]

Kubista (2005: 81) suggests that this amounts to the construction of a 'hybrid sentencing scheme'. Judges are entitled to use techniques from pre-minimum sentencing practices to depart from the legislatively prescribed sentences in appropriate cases. A study by the South African Law Commission undertaken some three years after the introduction of the minimum sentences legislation found that judges do, in fact, find 'substantial and compelling circumstances' to justify departure from the prescribed sentences in the majority of cases (Paschke and Sherwin, 2000: 9, cited in Baehr, 2008: 228; see also Terblanche, 2003b: 219–20). As one advocate interviewed for the study explained:

> 'In a situation where the minimum is specified to be 15 years, in most instances it is possible to find substantial and compelling circumstances. Hence judges and magistrates feel that they have to impose less than 15 years, because one should only impose 15 years where there are no substantial and compelling circumstances … so the minimum is in effect operating as a maximum' (Paschke and Sherwin, 2000: 55–56).

The Continued Focus on Proportionality – The Decision in Vilakazi

In the years following *Malgas*[237] it became apparent both that certain prosecutors had interpreted the decision incorrectly, taking the view that the prescribed

[233] See above.
[234] *M* (n 159).
[235] Ibid at [10].
[236] Malgas (n 205) at [8] and [22].
[237] *Malgas* (n 205).

sentences required to be imposed as the norm, and that certain courts were not applying the principles correctly.[238] Some seven-and-a-half years after it issued its decision in *Malgas*, the Supreme Court of Appeal revisited the principles governing the departure test in *S v Vilakazi*.[239]

The Court in *Vilakazi* emphasised the continued importance of proportionality in sentencing, making it clear that the principle of proportionality applies not only to sentences imposed through the traditional, discretionary-based model of South African sentencing practice, but also to sentences imposed under the minimum sentences legislation. The Court reiterated, by reference to *Malgas*, that any circumstances that would render a prescribed sentence *disproportionate to the offence* would justify a court in departing from imposing the prescribed sentence and in imposing a lesser one.[240] By reference to the decision of the Constitutional Court in *S v Dodo*,[241] the Court noted that punishment must always be proportionate to the deserts of the particular offender.[242] The Court concluded:

> '[T]he essence of *Malgas* and of *Dodo* is that *disproportionate sentences are not to be imposed and that courts are not vehicles for injustice* … [A] court is not compelled to perpetrate injustice by imposing a sentence that is disproportionate to the particular offence. Whether a sentence is proportionate cannot be determined in the abstract, but only upon a consideration of all material circumstances of the particular case, though bearing in mind what the legislature has ordained … It is enough for the [prescribed] sentence to be departed from that it would be unjust to impose it.'[243]

As the High Court later noted in *S v Mqikela*,[244] in considering all the material circumstances of the particular case, the judge is required to undertake a balancing exercise. The judge must weigh and balance all factors relevant to the nature and seriousness of the crime and all relevant personal and other circumstances relating to the offender which could have a bearing on the seriousness of the offence and the offender's culpability.[245] If the result of this exercise shows that a lesser sentence than that prescribed by the minimum sentences legislation would be appropriate, then the judge is 'not only justified but bound to impose the lesser sentence'.[246] Thus, although not specifically referred to by the courts in either *Vilakazi* or *Mqikela*, sentencing judges must still have regard to the *Zinn*[247] triad of the crime, the offender and the interests of society when sentencing rape under the mandatory and minimum sentence provisions.

[238] *S v Vilakazi* [2008] ZASCA 87; 2009 (1) SACR 552 (SCA) at [16].
[239] Ibid.
[240] Ibid at [14]–[16].
[241] *Dodo* (n 181).
[242] *Vilakazi* (n 238) at [3], citing *Dodo* (n 181) at [38].
[243] Ibid at [18] and [20], emphasis added.
[244] 2010 (S) SACR 589 (ECG) at [3].
[245] On the notion of sentencing as a balancing exercise, see above.
[246] *Mqikela* (n 244) at [3].
[247] *Zinn* (n 157).

Restating the Importance of Judicial Sentencing Discretion – The Decision in Bailey

The most recent decision of the Supreme Court of Appeal to consider questions of principle in the application of the minimum sentences legislation is *S v Bailey (sub nom S v PB).*[248] In this case, the appellant pleaded guilty to a charge of having raped his 12-year-old daughter. The sentencing judge found no substantial and compelling circumstances to be present and imposed the mandatory sentence of life imprisonment. On appeal, it was submitted firstly that the appellant's remorse and prospects for rehabilitation amounted to substantial and compelling circumstances such as to warrant the imposition of a lesser sentence and secondly that the sentence of life imprisonment was 'unreasonable and out of kilter with the sentences imposed for similar offences by [the] court'.[249]

In delivering the judgment of the Court, Bosielo JA suggested that the term 'substantial and compelling circumstances' was so 'elastic' that it could accommodate 'even ordinary mitigating circumstances'.[250] All the Court was prepared to say on the matter was that the departure test 'involves a value judgment on the part the sentencing court'.[251] It was not persuaded that the appellant's circumstances met the threshold of substantial and compelling circumstances in terms of the legislation.[252] With regard to the issue of whether the life sentence was inconsistent with sentences imposed for comparable offences, Justice Bosielo stated, by reference to the decision in *S v D*,[253] that decided cases on sentence 'provide guidelines, not straightjackets [*sic – read 'straitjackets'*]'.[254] Justice Bosielo then reiterated the view, long held among South African judges, that every case should be dealt with on its own facts, that no two cases are exactly alike and that every case is unique.[255] His Honour explained:

> 'Our everyday experience in the criminal courts proves that … no two cases present exactly the same factual matrix. To compound the problem further, it is hard to imagine two accused persons who have exactly the same personal circumstances. Further still, in a case involving rape, for instance, it is unthinkable that two different complainants in two different cases would manifest the same physical, emotional or behavioural problems after the rape. Evidently, these are important matters which must be considered in the determination of an appropriate sentence as they have a direct bearing on what an appropriate sentence should be. It follows … that the sentence in such matters will be different because of the variation in personal circumstances of the accused, the nature and gravity of the offence and all other factors germane to sentencing … *[I]t remains an established principle of our criminal law that sentencing discretion lies pre-eminently*

248 [2012] ZASCA 154; 2013 (2) SACR 533 (SCA).
249 Ibid at [3].
250 Ibid at [21].
251 Ibid.
252 Ibid at [24].
253 1995 (1) SACR 259 (A) at 260 per Van den Heever JA.
254 *Bailey* (n 248) at [17].
255 See the discussion above.

> *in the sentencing court and must be exercised judiciously and in line with established and valid principles governing sentencing* as enunciated in a long line of cases which includes *S v Zinn* … *S v Rabie* … [and] *S v Malgas*.'[256]

This passage from the judgment of Justice Bosielo is key to understanding how South African judges sentence those convicted of rape and other serious offences under the mandatory and minimum sentences legislation. The dicta of Justice Bosielo makes it clear that the *legal category* of an offence specified in the legislation, such as a 'Part I' rape or a 'Part III' rape, will not, *in and of itself*, determine whether the requisite prescribed sentence will be imposed on the particular offender. In this regard, South African judges must still have regard to the whole facts and circumstances of the case and should not simply 'read off the machine', as the High Court put it in *S v Moganedisa*.[257] This is well illustrated, albeit in a different context, by Tombs and Jagger (2006) in their study of how Scottish judges arrive at their decisions to impose custodial sentences. Whilst mandatory and minimum sentences for rape do not operate in Scotland,[258] the authors' findings on the importance that judges attach to the offender *as an individual* are nonetheless apposite:

> '[T]he individualized notions of justice embedded in forms of legal argument mean that some offences have an ambiguous status within discourse … [O]ffenders themselves (as individuals) do not fit neatly into the limited number of categories discursively available: they are only ever approximations of these categories … [W]hen making their decisions, sentencers consider not only the severity and nature of the offence, but also the characteristics of the offender … [This] opens up a space for judgment. The attributes of offenders and their offences can be endlessly reconfigured to legitimate sentencers' claims that the "punishment fits the crime"' (Tombs and Jagger, 2006: 806–7; see also Brown, 2017a: 96–97 and Millie et al, 2007: 254).

As the Supreme Court of Appeal noted in *S v Jimenez*,[259] every case is unique: each offender is different and the circumstances of each crime will vary (see also Terblanche, 2017: 26–27). In delivering the judgment of the Supreme Court of Appeal in *S v Mudau (sub nom S v SMM)*,[260] Majiedt JA observed that: 'it is trite that each case must be decided on its own merits. It is also self-evident that sentence must always be individualised, for punishment must always fit the crime, the criminal and the circumstances of the case'.[261] Thus, for the South African judge sentencing an offender convicted of rape, the key considerations remain, firstly, the triad comprising the seriousness of the crime, the personal circumstances of the offender and the interests of society as set out in *S v Zinn*[262] and,

[256] *Bailey* (n 248) at [18] and [19] (emphasis added and citations omitted).
[257] [2013] ZAGPPHC 238; 2014 (1) SACR 53 (GNP) at [9].
[258] See Chapter 5.
[259] [2003] ZASCA 2; 2003 (1) SACR 507 (SCA) at [6].
[260] *Mudau* (n 163).
[261] Ibid at [13].
[262] *Zinn* (n 157) at 540G–H.

secondly, the duty to impose a proportionate sentence as emphasised by the Supreme Court of Appeal in *S v Vilakazi*.[263] South African judges simply will not impose sentences that are disproportionate and unjust, even if prescribed by the legislature (see Terblanche, 2003b: 219–20).

In its decision in *S v Mabuza*,[264] the Supreme Court of Appeal characterised the mandatory and minimum sentences set by the 1997 Act as a 'benchmark',[265] while in *S v Tuswa*,[266] the Kwazulu-Natal High Court referred to them as a 'starting point'.[267] If, having undertaken the requisite balancing exercise as described in *S v Mqikela*,[268] the sentencing judge does decide that the 'benchmark' or 'starting point' of a prescribed sentence should be departed from (and she should not hesitate from doing so if warranted by the facts and circumstances of the individual case[269]) then she must nevertheless take account of the observation of the Court in *Malgas*[270] that rape has been singled out for severe punishment by the legislature.

In sum, despite the mandatory and minimum sentences for rape set out in the 1997 Act, the actual sentencing practice of South African judges mirrors that of judges in other common law jurisdictions where the legislature has sought to limit judicial sentencing discretion. In sentencing rape, South African judges endeavour to sentence according to values that privilege their own professional knowledge and experience *as judges*, rather than the policy goals of politicians (see generally Brown, 2017a: 97, 226 and Tombs, 2008: 97). This invariably results in a degree of variance in the sentencing of those convicted of rape in South Africa (see Terblanche, 2016: 82 and *S v Mabaso*[271]). Nevertheless, by privileging their own professional knowledge and experience in this manner, the South African judiciary ensures that offenders are treated as whole persons and not, as Tonry (1996: 20) vividly describes, as two-dimensional 'crime-and-criminal-history amalgams'.

'Sentencing Cliffs', False Perceptions of Leniency and the 'Worst Category' Test – Systemic Problems with Prescribed Sentences for Rape

Terblanche (2016: 51) demonstrates, by reference to several appellate decisions, the way in which the minimum sentences legislation has been subject

[263] *Vilakazi* (n 238) at [3], [18] and [20].
[264] [2007] ZASCA 110; [2007] SCA 110 (RSA).
[265] Ibid at [20].
[266] 2013 (2) SACR 269
[267] Ibid at [63].
[268] *Mqikela* (n 244) at [3].
[269] See *Malgas* (n 205) at [14] and [25].
[270] Ibid at [25J].
[271] 2014 (1) SACR 299 at [11]–[25].

to scathing criticism by the South African judiciary. In *S v Vilakazi*,[272] for example, the Supreme Court of Appeal noted that the 1997 Act 'purports to cover the field of serious crime in no more than a handful of blunt paragraphs'.[273] In *S v Sukwazi*,[274] the 1997 Act was said to be an 'ill-conceived and badly drafted' piece of legislation[275] while in *S v Vuma*[276] it was described as 'the most invasive piece of legislation enacted since the advent of the democratic South Africa'.[277] In delivering the majority judgment in *S v Opperman*,[278] meanwhile, Heher JA described the sanctions provided by the 1997 Act as 'draconian'.[279] Most recently, in delivering an address at the University of the Western Cape, Justice Edwin Cameron of the Constitutional Court of South Africa described the mandatory sentencing laws as having 'plagued [South Africa] for the past 20 years' (Cameron, 2017: 3); his Honour also criticised the system of mandatory and minimum sentences as 'pernicious, misguided and futile' (Cameron, 2017: 33).

While mandatory and minimum sentence schemes have, in recent times, been criticised as constraining judicial sentencing discretion too tightly, producing the injustice of treating differently situated offenders similarly (see Brown, 2017a: 69–72; Freiberg, 2016: 428; and Krasnostein, 2015: 227), the core difficulty presented by such regimes was identified by Smalberger JA of the then Appellate Division of the Supreme Court of South Africa in *S v Toms; S v Bruce*,[280] some 17 years before mandatory and minimum sentences for rape were introduced in South Africa:

> 'A mandatory sentence … reduces the Court's normal sentencing function to the level of a rubber stamp. It negates the ideal of individualisation. The morally just and the morally reprehensible are treated alike. Extenuating and aggravating factors both count for nothing. No consideration, no matter how valid or compelling, can affect the question of sentence.'[281]

The setting of mandatory and minimum sentences for rape in particular have presented further problems for the South African courts. These issues comprise the failure of the legislation to adequately reflect an offender's culpability through the creation of 'sentencing cliffs'; a false perception of leniency towards rapists when the mandatory sentences are departed from; and the position whereby, to avoid the imposition of disproportionate sentences, judges have felt obliged to compare individual cases to a hypothetical standard of the so-called 'worst category' of rape.

[272] *Vilakazi* (n 238).
[273] Ibid at [11].
[274] 2002 (1) SACR 619 (N).
[275] Ibid at 623.
[276] 2003 (1) SACR 597 (W).
[277] Ibid at 599c.
[278] 2010 (2) SACR 248 (SCA).
[279] Ibid at [40]. See also *S v Mofokeng* 1999 (1) SACR 502 (W) at 525, per Stegmann J.
[280] *S v Toms; S v Bruce* (n 149).
[281] Ibid at 806H–807B. See also Botha JA at 831B who described mandatory sentences as 'wholly repugnant'.

Proportionality and the Creation of 'Sentencing Cliffs'

The severity with which the South African courts view rape – 'a crime of almost indescribable gravity' (Terblanche, 2014: 109) – is not in doubt.[282] In *S v Vilakazi*,[283] for example, rape was described as 'a repulsive crime … an invasion of the most private and intimate zone of a woman [which] strikes at the core of her personhood and dignity'. In *S v Chapman*,[284] the Court made specific reference to the 'humiliating, degrading and brutal invasion of the privacy, the dignity and the person of the victim'. In *S v Mudau (sub nom S v SMM)*,[285] meanwhile, the Court stated that:

> '[R]ape is undeniably a degrading, humiliating and brutal invasion of a person's most intimate, private space. The very act itself, even absent any accompanying violent assault inflicted by the perpetrator, is a violent and traumatic infringement of a person's fundamental right to be free from all forms of violence and not to be treated in a cruel, inhumane or degrading way.'[286]

Nevertheless, the 1997 Act prescribes life imprisonment for rape in many circumstances where a life sentence would never have been considered prior to the minimum sentences legislation. Prior to the minimum sentences Act, the median sentence for rape in the regional courts was seven-and-a-half years' imprisonment whilst the median sentence in the High Courts, where the most serious offences are tried, was 17-and-a-half years (see Baehr, 2008: 227).

Terblanche (2017: 26; 2013b: 118) criticises the legislature for introducing, through the 1997 Act, what he terms 'sentencing cliffs': a standard of 10 years' imprisonment under certain conditions, but another standard which is potentially at least five times as severe under only slightly different conditions. There is no internal logic to the way in which the 1997 Act categorises rape scenarios, or to the terms of imprisonment it prescribes (Baehr, 2008: 238–39; Terblanche, 2016: 91; van der Merwe, 2013: 411). While proportionate sentencing is more easily achievable in respect of Part III rapes, where judges have the latitude to impose a sentence above or below the mandatory minimum (Baehr, 2008: 233–34), it is difficult to see how mandatory life sentences for Part I rapes can ever be regarded as proportionate (Terblanche, 2017: 26–27; 2016: 85; 2001: 5).

The presence of Terblanche's 'sentencing cliffs' (the absence of any gradation to reflect increasing levels of severity between 10 years' imprisonment for a first offender convicted of Part III rape and life imprisonment for an offender convicted of Part I rape) is completely alien to traditional sentencing philosophy and practice in South Africa. This absence of gradation does not accord with anything resembling the approach that the courts normally follow in determining

[282] *Pace* Hoffman-Wanderer, 2008, Kubista, 2005 and Spies, 2016, considered below.
[283] *Vilakazi* (n 238) at [1].
[284] 1997 (3) SA 341 (SCA) at 345A–B.
[285] *Mudau* (n 163).
[286] At [17].

the appropriateness of a sentence (Terblanche, 2016: 85–86; 2013b: 118–19; Terblanche and Mackenzie, 2008: 408). Disproportionate sentences result from the 'all-or-nothing' structure of the 1997 Act (Baehr, 2008: 241).

The Supreme Court of Appeal considered the issue in *S v Vilakazi*:[287]

> 'What is striking about [the] regime is the absence of any gradation between 10 years' imprisonment and life imprisonment. The minimum sentence of 10 years' imprisonment progresses immediately to the maximum sentence that our law allows once any of the aggravating features is present, irrespective of how many of those features are present, irrespective of the degree in which the feature is present and irrespective of whether the convicted person is a first or repeat offender. On the face of it a first-offending 18-year-old boy who rapes his 15-year-old girlfriend on one occasion must receive the same sentence as a recidivist serial rapist who repeatedly gang-rapes and beats senseless a disabled victim whom he consciously infects with HIV. The 18-year-old boy who rapes his 15-year-old girlfriend must also receive the same sentence as the adult recidivist who rapes an infant. The offender who imprisons and rapes his victim repeatedly every day for a week is considered to be no more culpable than one who rapes his victim twice within ten minutes.'[288]

The 1997 Act thus places a much greater emphasis on criminal acts than on an offender's biographical and social narratives (Aas, 2005: 110). The mandatory sentence of life imprisonment for Part I rape focuses on the *harmfulness* of the offence but ignores completely the offender's *culpability*. Yet, as evidenced by the sentencing practice of the courts in other common law jurisdictions and, indeed, by the frequent recourse of the South African courts to the departure clause under section 51(3) of the 1997 Act, the sentencing judge must have regard to both harm *and* culpability in gauging the seriousness of an offence if a proportionate sentence is to be imposed (see also von Hirsch, 2017: 23 and 1993: 29 and Fox, 1994: 498). The sentencing judge must not impose a sentence that offends against the proportionality requirement[289] and so the prescription of life imprisonment for instances of rape which may very well feature certain important mitigating factors means that differentiation becomes possible only through the court departing from the prescribed sentence (Terblanche, 2016: 87).

Departures from the Mandatory Sentences and Perceived Leniency

Baehr (2008: 215) explains that while severe penalties for rape may appear attractive, symbolically establishing the seriousness of the offence and perhaps even changing societal norms, extremely harsh mandatory minimum sentences have, paradoxically, resulted in a perception of leniency towards the offence. As we have seen, judges continue to sentence proportionately, departing from imposing the

[287] *Vilakazi* (n 238).
[288] Ibid at [13].
[289] *Dodo* (n 181) at [40].

prescribed sentences by finding 'substantial and compelling circumstances'. In the case of Part I rapes, the minimum sentence of life imprisonment is effectively a maximum sentence. Since every departure is necessarily downwards, every such sentencing judgment must focus on factors that justify a lesser sentence, rather than on the factors that make rape a particularly serious crime.

Thus, Baehr considers that to impose a proportionate sentence, judges are frequently compelled to effectively 'make excuses for offenders' convicted of Part I rapes, thereby creating an illusion of greater leniency for sexual assault (Baehr, 2008: 215, 229, 233 and 239; see also Hoffman-Wanderer, 2008: 233–35). For Baehr, whilst the actual sentence imposed by the judge will be proportionate to the gravity of the offence or, at the very least, will comprise a genuine attempt to impose such a proportionate sentence, her written opinion and reasoning may be (or may appear to be) 'deeply destructive' (2008: 237). In order to bring the case within the ambit of 'substantial and compelling circumstances', thereby achieving a proportionate sentence, the judge is compelled by the terms of the 1997 Act to 'play down' certain aspects of the rape in question (see van Zyl Smit, 2002: 103–4).

The decision in *S v Jansen*,[290] one of the first reported decisions involving rape under the minimum sentences legislation, illustrates these difficulties. *Jansen* was decided some two years before the Supreme Court of Appeal issued its decision in *Malgas*.[291] Without the benefit of appellate guidance on the application of the departure test, the sentencing judge carefully interpreted the words 'substantial and compelling' and concluded that judges had a limited but significant power to depart from the mandatory sentence of life imprisonment. As van Zyl Smit (2002: 103) suggests, this was a clear attempt to find an appropriate *via media*. Rather than the mandatory life sentence, the judge imposed a sentence of 18 years' imprisonment – a severe sentence by the standards that applied before the introduction of the mandatory and minimum sentence provisions. Nevertheless, the sentence was widely criticised by pressure groups and the media; in particular, the sentencing judge was criticised for stressing, in an inappropriate way, aspects of the crime that made it relatively 'less heinous'. Van Zyl Smit explains:

> '[T]he legislation has placed the judiciary at a disadvantage. Prior to [the 1997 Act] a sentence of 18 years' imprisonment … accompanied by some stern words from the bench, would have drawn widespread public approval. To impose the same sentence now judges have to explain why the crime is relatively not so serious. In so doing they run the risk of being perceived as being soft on crime … [and as] too lenient and out of touch' (2002: 104; see also Baehr, 2008: 239).

Thus, the ceiling for what is an acceptable sentence for rape has been raised and raised considerably. As Terblanche and Mackenzie (2008: 411–12) argue, in many ways the minimum sentences legislation has institutionalised bad sentencing practices.

[290] 1999 (2) SA 368 (C).
[291] *Malgas* (n 205).

The 'Worst Category' Test in Rape Cases

The focus on proportionate sentencing under the minimum sentences legislation has led to the courts informally 'grading' offences (van der Merwe, 2005: 8, 295) by developing the concept of the 'worst category' of rape. Since, in their endeavour to impose proportionate sentences, the courts have indicated that a rape must be one of the most serious manifestations of the offence to merit a life sentence, judges are constantly placed in the invidious position of having to justify sentences less than life imprisonment in all but the most serious cases (Baehr, 2008: 234). The appellate courts have often reasoned that a particular case could not be classified as falling within 'the worst category of rape', both in allowing appeals against the mandatory sentence of life imprisonment for Part I rapes and in allowing appeals against sentence by the prosecution.

For example, in *S v Abrahams*,[292] a sentence of seven years' imprisonment imposed on a father for raping his 14-year-old daughter was increased on appeal to 12 years. In the course of its judgment, the Supreme Court of Appeal noted that:

> '[T]his is not one of the worst cases of rape. That is not to say that rape can ever be condoned. But some rapes are worse than others and the life sentence ordained by the Legislature should be reserved for cases devoid of substantial factors compelling the conclusion that such a sentence is inappropriate and unjust.'[293]

In *S v Mudau (sub nom S v SMM)*,[294] while the Supreme Court of Appeal acknowledged the seriousness of rape,[295] it considered it a 'self-evident truth (albeit somewhat contentious)' that there are 'categories of severity of rape'.[296] In *S v Mahomotsa*,[297] meanwhile, in a successful appeal by the State against concurrent sentences of six and 10 years' imprisonment imposed on the respondent following his conviction for the repeated rape of two 15-year-old victims, the Supreme Court of Appeal increased the sentences to eight and 12 years, noting that:

> 'The rapes that we are concerned with here, though very serious, cannot be classified as falling within the worst category of rape. Although what appeared to be a firearm was used to threaten the complainant in the first count and a knife in the second, no serious violence was perpetrated against them. Except for a bruise to the second complainant's genitalia no subsequently visible injuries were inflicted on them … [T]hey do not suffer from any after-effects following their ordeals … These factors need to be taken into account in the process of considering whether substantial and compelling circumstances are present justifying a departure from the prescribed sentence.'[298]

[292] *Abrahams* (n 228).
[293] Ibid at [29].
[294] *Mudau* (n 163).
[295] Ibid at [17]. See n 286, above.
[296] Ibid at [18].
[297] [2002] ZASCA 64; 2002 (2) SACR 435 (SCA).
[298] Ibid at [17]. See also *Rammoko v Director of Public Prosecutions* [2002] ZASCA 138; 2003 (1) SACR 200 (SCA) at [12]; *S v Nkomo* 2007 (2) SACR 198 (SCA) (compare the dissenting judgment of

The appellate courts' focus on the so-called 'worst category' of rape has been much criticised (Terblanche, 2016: 85). For commentators such as Amanda Spies (2016: 389–90) and Rebecca Chennells (2009: 33–35), it amounts to judicial acceptance of commonly held rape myths and stereotypes that ultimately reinforce violent behaviour towards women. Spies (2016: 394–404) considers that the reasons given by judges for justifying downward departures from the prescribed sentences frequently correlate with rape myths and stereotypes, including a focus on physical injuries (or the absence thereof) sustained by the victim and a lack of understanding of the violation associated with rape.

Similarly, both Nicole Kubista (2005: 81) and Yonina Hoffman-Wanderer (2008: 231) consider that the courts' focus on the so-called 'worst category' of rape develops a jurisprudence that minimises the inherent violence of the offence. Kubista (2005: 82–83) suggests that the appellate courts have created 'a continuum of rape' and have imported what she considers to be 'a false benchmark standard' of violent rape into the sentencing process, with any case that does not meet the benchmark being one in which the judge will depart from the prescribed sentence. Kubista also maintains that the decision in *Mahomotsa*[299] creates a false distinction between rape and rape that causes physical injury (2005: 83–86). She explains:

> 'The implications of creating a rape continuum where crimes are measured against a hypothetical "worst" case scenario corrals rape, without further aggravating circumstances, to the lower end of the spectrum. Moreover, the use of the dichotomy of physically violent and non-physically violent rape perpetuates the idea that rape, in and of itself, is not violent' (2005: 86; see also Baehr, 2008: 229 and 235; Chennells, 2009: 27–29; and Hoffman-Wanderer, 2008: 231–32).

Such criticism of the South African courts' routine departure from the mandatory sentence of life imprisonment for Part I rape fails to recognise the importance of proportionality and of individualised justice.[300] It is the structure of the legislation itself, rather than supposedly inconsistent and inappropriate recourse to the departure clause by sentencing judges, that is responsible for false perceptions of leniency in rape sentencing (Terblanche, 2013b: 118).[301] Nevertheless, the Court's focus in *Mahomotsa* on the absence of physical injury sustained by the victims is troublesome. In emphasising the absence of such injuries, it is at least arguable that the Supreme Court of Appeal followed the same course as the Supreme Court of Ireland in *People (DPP) v Tiernan*[302] in distinguishing between 'types' of rape and ranking them, with so-called 'forcible rape' at the apex. Parallels can also be

Theron AJA with the majority judgment delivered by Lewis JA); and *S v Zamla* [2018] ZAWCHC 130 (compare the dissenting judgment of Binns-Ward J with the judgments of Nuku and Papier JJ).

[299] *Mahomotsa* (n 297).

[300] See above.

[301] See above.

[302] [1988] IR 250 discussed in Chapter 6.

drawn with the sentencing practice of the Scottish courts, where cases of so-called 'non-forcible rape', often involving intoxicated or unconscious victims, generally attract far lower sentences than cases involving the use of force.[303] Thus, as in the Republic of Ireland and Scotland, the decision in *Mahomotsa* suggests the operation of a *de facto* hierarchy of rape in the South African courts.

The legislature later amended the departure clause under section 51(3) of the 1997 Act by adding a new section 51(3)(*a*A).[304] The amendment added a list of circumstances which do *not* constitute 'substantial and compelling circumstances' for the purpose of the departure test. The circumstances include the complainant's previous sexual history; an apparent lack of physical injury to the complainant; and any relationship between the accused and the complainant prior to the offence being committed. In amending the departure clause in this way, the legislature sought to challenge certain rape myths,[305] including the belief that if the offender and the victim previously had a sexual relationship then the rape was somehow less serious (see Hoffman-Wanderer, 2008: 239). In so doing, the legislature brought the sentencing of so-called 'relationship rape' in South Africa into line with practice in jurisdictions such as England and Wales[306] and New Zealand.[307]

The amendments to the departure clause were considered by Plasket J of the Eastern Cape High Court in *S v Nkawu*,[308] a case involving the abduction and anal rape of a 10-year-old girl by a 21-year-old offender. As the victim was aged under 16, this constituted a Part I rape with a mandatory sentence of life imprisonment in the absence of substantial and compelling circumstances. Counsel for the accused submitted that substantial and compelling circumstances were indeed present due to the *cumulative effect* of the absence of any serious or permanent physical injuries sustained by the victim; the fact that the victim suffered no extraordinary psychological trauma; the accused's comparative youth; and the fact that he provided financial support for his family. The prosecution, meanwhile, argued that the Court was not permitted to take account of the absence of serious injury at all since, in terms of 51(3)(*a*A) of the 1997 Act, an apparent lack of physical injury to the complainant is not to be regarded as a substantial and compelling circumstance.

In delivering his sentencing judgment, Justice Plasket began by noting the seriousness of rape,[309] observing that, as a general rule, a rape will be progressively more serious the younger the victim.[310] In rejecting the prosecution's submission,

[303] See Chapter 5.
[304] By virtue of the Criminal Law (Sentencing) Amendment Act 38 of 2007.
[305] See Chapter 2.
[306] See Chapter 4.
[307] See the discussion of the decision in *R v AM* (n 10) above.
[308] [2009] ZAECGHC 21; 2009 (2) SACR 402 (ECG).
[309] Ibid at [9].
[310] Ibid at [10].

his Honour held that a literal interpretation of section 51(3)(*a*A), to the effect that a sentencing judge may not have regard to the victim's apparent lack of physical injury at all, would be unconstitutional: it would amount to Parliament directing judges to ignore factors that are relevant to sentence and thus to impose sentences which are consequently unjust.[311] Justice Plasket considered that the problem could be overcome by interpreting the provisions of 51(3)(*a*A) – previous sexual history, apparent lack of physical injury and any prior relationship – to mean that any one factor *on its own* may not be regarded as a substantial and compelling circumstance; however, each factor may be considered along with other factors *cumulatively* to amount to substantial and compelling circumstances justifying a departure from the prescribed sentence.[312] On this interpretation, Justice Plasket held that he was not precluded from considering the fact that the victim suffered injuries that were neither serious nor permanent, in addition to the other facts and circumstances of the case, in arriving at a just and proportionate sentence – in this case, one of 20 years' imprisonment.[313]

Justice Plasket's decision in *Nkawu* is commended by Terblanche (2016: 86; 2013b: 112) as comprising a careful assessment of the competing issues and of resulting in the correct interpretation of section 51(3)(*a*A) of the 1997 Act (*cf* Spies, 2016: 396–99). Indeed, Justice Plasket's interpretation of section 51(3)(*a*A) was subsequently approved by the Supreme Court of Appeal in *S v Mudau (sub nom S v SMM)*[314] where the sentence of life imprisonment imposed on the appellant for raping his 13-year-old niece was quashed and replaced with a sentence of 15 years' imprisonment. The Court in *Mudau* considered that the offence 'was not the most severe form of rape';[315] in particular, it noted the appellant's prospects for rehabilitation,[316] the absence of further violence and the apparent absence of psychological trauma or physical injuries suffered by the victim.[317]

Terblanche reports, however, that in cases which feature one or more of the circumstances listed in section 51(3)(*a*A) there is a tendency for the South African courts to look no further than the statutory provisions in imposing life imprisonment. Rather than interpreting the legislation in the same way as the courts in *Nkawu*[318] and *Mudau*,[319] judges often simply declare that the victim's absence of injuries will not amount to substantial and compelling circumstances justifying departure from the prescribed sentence (Terblanche, 2016: 86; see also Le Roux-Kemp, 2016: 359–61). This, clearly, has the potential to result in unjust and disproportionate sentences.

[311] Ibid at [15].
[312] Ibid at [16].
[313] Ibid at [16] and [20].
[314] *Mudau* (n 163) at [26].
[315] Ibid at [25].
[316] Ibid at [24].
[317] Ibid at [25] and [26].
[318] *Nkawu* (n 308).
[319] *Mudau* (n 163).

Guideline Judgments versus Mandatory and Minimum Sentences

It is widely accepted that the system of mandatory and minimum sentences for rape and other serious offences in South Africa has failed to achieve its goal of reducing violent crime and has led to substantial increases in the prison population (Baehr, 2008: 229; Brown, 2017a: 71; Cameron, 2017; Mujuzi, 2008: 3–4; Phelps, 2013: 227–28; Roth, 2008: 163–64; Sloth-Nielsen and Ehlers, 2005a: 16 and 2005b: 8–12; Terblanche, 2016: 90–91; 2003b: 219; and 2001: 14–15). Terblanche and Mackenzie (2008: 413–14) note that while mandatory sentencing schemes are 'rarely a good idea', they are at their most 'acceptable' (if the term can, in fact, be used in this context) when they fit rationally with the rest of a jurisdiction's sentencing scheme and with the basic penal philosophy of the jurisdiction in question. Perhaps the key problem with the minimum sentences legislation as it operates in South Africa, however, is that the legislature sought to graft the scheme on to a sentencing system which, traditionally, prioritised a wide judicial discretion.

Mandatory and minimum sentences were, and continue to be, anathema to South African judges: they continue to impose individually crafted sentences by recourse to the *Zinn* triad[320] and by applying the statutory departure, or escape, clause. As Marais JA noted in delivering the judgment of the Supreme Court of Appeal in *S v Malgas*:[321]

> 'Judicial hostility to legislative prescriptions which strip courts of their sentencing discretion is hardly surprising. Given the infinite variety of circumstances which attend the commission of crimes, who are better placed than the courts, which experience daily the complexities of imposing sentences which are as just as human fallibility can make them, to understand the arbitrariness and potential unjustness of such edicts? Sentencing has rightly been described as "a lonely and onerous task". For those who must shoulder that responsibility in society's name, to have to impose a statutorily decreed sentence which is manifestly unjust in the particular circumstances of the case is a monstrous thing.'[322]

In short, when considering how to structure judicial sentencing discretion, the South African system of mandatory and minimum sentences is an excellent example 'of how things should not be done' (Terblanche and Mackenzie, 2008: 405). Stephan Terblanche, the leading commentator on South African sentencing law and practice, has repeatedly called for the scheme to be abolished (see Terblanche, 2016: 91 and 2003b: 220).

Baehr (2008: 244) notes that whilst severe penalties for rape may symbolically establish the serious nature of the offence, 'not all sexual offenses are the same and

[320] *Zinn* (n 157). See above.
[321] *Malgas* (n 205).
[322] Ibid at [1], citing Hogarth, 1971: 5.

judges do not take kindly to a binary system that does not allow them to provide a range of sentences for a range of offenses'. She suggests that the entire mandatory and minimum sentence scheme should be replaced with a form of sentencing guideline comprising a graduated, rather than a bifurcated, scale. The guideline would seek to create a more appropriate range of sentences between 10 years and life imprisonment. In this way, Baehr argues, fairness, proportionality and certainty in sentencing would all be improved (2008: 240–43).

Baehr's model comprises two stages, or steps. She suggests starting at a base level (a benchmark or starting point) of 10 years' imprisonment and then increasing sentence severity for each additional aggravating factor. Having completed this first step, the sentencing judge would then be required, as a second step, to examine whether any 'substantial and compelling circumstances' exist to justify either an increase or decrease in sentence, should the sentence arrived at using the first step be disproportionate to the particular offence. In this manner, Baehr argues, judicial sentencing discretion would focus on the offender's culpability – on the aspects of the offence that actually render it blameworthy – rather than on stereotypical preconceptions and rape myths that justify a more lenient sentence (Baehr, 2008: 24–42).

Other commentators have suggested that comprehensive sentencing reform could be achieved in South Africa through the issuing of guideline judgments, either from the Supreme Court of Appeal or from a sentencing council or commission (see Sloth-Nielsen and Ehlers, 2005b: 17 and Terblanche, 2008b and 2003a: 881–82). The model proposed by Baehr would continue to prioritise incapacitation and punishment for serious sex crimes. As judges would no longer be constantly forced into a position of defending reductions in sentence, the revised model would, Baehr suggests, allow judges to resume their role of imposing proportionate sentences for rape: sentences that are severe, but fair (Baehr, 2008: 243).

One issue which Baehr omits from her model is the question of whether an offender should be allowed a reduction, or a discount, in sentence to reflect his plea of guilty. The South African sentencing jurisprudence on guilty plea discounts is far less developed than in other common law jurisdictions such as England and Wales and Scotland where the courts have grappled with the issue, often in considerable detail, for many years.[323] In South Africa, a guilty plea in and of itself tends to be viewed by judges as a neutral factor (Terblanche, 2016: 230). Although the South African courts often note that an accused has pleaded guilty simply because of the strength of the case against him,[324] a guilty plea will sometimes be accepted as an indication of remorse[325] (Terblanche 2016: 230). Thus, as in the Republic of Ireland,[326] a guilty plea will occasionally be regarded as a mitigating factor.

[323] See Chapters 4 and 5 respectively.

[324] See, eg, *S v Michele* [2009] ZASCA 116 at [7] and *S v Piater* [2012] ZAGPPHC 366 at [39]–[40].

[325] See, eg, *S v Chipape* [2009] ZAGPPHC 174 at [17].

[326] See Chapter 6.

Baehr's model could be amended to follow the practice of the New Zealand courts[327] by including consideration of an offender's guilty plea as a distinct third step. The preferable course, however, would be to include consideration of the guilty plea as part of the second step, the issue for the sentencing judge being whether the plea was a 'substantial and compelling circumstance' such as to warrant a reduction in sentence. The questions of whether a guilty plea would in any given case warrant a reduction in sentence and, if so, the extent of any such reduction would be matters for the discretion of the sentencing judge, having regard to the individual offender and the circumstances in which he tendered his plea. This approach would be consistent with practice in jurisdictions such as Scotland and the Republic of Ireland.[328]

There is much to commend Baehr's model of a graduated scale for rape sentencing and it is certainly a marked improvement over the rigidity of the 'mandatory minimums algorithm' (Baehr, 2008: 240) set out in the 1997 Act. Yet, in order to allow judges to exercise fully informed judgment, navigating their way through the facts and the aggravating and mitigating circumstances of a particular case, to arrive at a proportionate sentence – in short, to achieve O'Malley's notion of 'principled discretion' (O'Malley, 2011: 5, 2001: 135)[329] – the necessarily wide judicial sentencing discretion must be exercised in accordance with settled principles.

South African sentencing practice for rape is in urgent need of reform and there are clear lessons to be learned from the approach of the Court of Appeal in New Zealand. In New Zealand, judicial discretion in rape sentencing is not structured by means of an ill-conceived, badly drafted,[330] pernicious, misguided, futile[331] and draconian[332] system of mandatory and minimum sentences; a system which is 'wholly repugnant'[333] to the country's legal and judicial traditions and culture. Rather, the sentencing discretion of New Zealand judges is structured in such cases by a non-binding guideline judgment containing various statements of principle from the Court of Appeal.[334]

In delivering the judgment of the Supreme Court of Appeal in *S v Mudau (sub nom S v SMM)*,[335] Majiedt JA made the following observations regarding the sentencing of rape:

> 'It is … important to remind ourselves that sentencing should always be considered and passed dispassionately, objectively and upon a careful consideration of all relevant factors. Public sentiment cannot be ignored, but it can never be permitted to displace

[327] See *Hessell v R* (n 33) at [14] and *Hessell v R* (n 34) at [73] and [74], discussed above.
[328] See Chapters 5 and 6 respectively.
[329] See Chapter 6.
[330] See *S v Sukwazi* (n 274).
[331] See Cameron, 2017: 33.
[332] See *S v Opperman* (n 278).
[333] See *S v Toms; S v Bruce* (n 149) per Botha JA at 831B.
[334] See above.
[335] *Mudau* (n 163).

> the careful judgment and fine balancing that is involved at arriving at an appropriate sentence. Courts must therefore always strive to arrive at a sentence which is just and fair to both the victim and the perpetrator, has regard to the nature of the crime and takes account of the interests of society.'[336]

It is through the issuing of an appropriate guideline judgment from the Supreme Court of Appeal – sentencing guidance crafted *by* judges, *for* judges – that principled discretion in the sentencing of rape can best be achieved in South Africa. Following the decision of the New Zealand Court of Appeal in *R v AM*,[337] the guideline judgment should comprise narrative guidance on the differentiation of particular instances of rape falling into distinct categories, with concrete indications of appropriate starting points and sentence ranges, *not* final sentences (see O'Malley, 2011: 126). Such guidelines should be provided, however, only to guide judges in sentencing rape.[338] The need remains for judicial evaluation of all the circumstances of the particular case by recourse to the *Zinn* triad.[339] A mechanistic application of any guideline issued by the Supreme Court of Appeal – reading 'off the machine'[340] – is not appropriate.[341]

[336] Ibid at [13].
[337] *R v AM* (n 10).
[338] Ibid at [29], [35], [84] and [88].
[339] *Zinn* (n 157). See above.
[340] See *S v Moganedisa* (n 257).
[341] *R v AM* (n 10) at [36] and [79].

8

Principled Discretion in Rape Sentencing

> 'An appeal court *should* say, "Listen. If you rape someone here, in this country, the starting point's so many years. If it's a really bad rape, it'll be much higher. If there are some mitigating features then it may be a bit less". But we're *not* getting that spelled out. You couldn't tell me what the going sentence for rape is at the moment … It is *very, very hard* to get guidance because many of the sentences that are right aren't appealed … In truth, the best you can say is that there is a *right range*. For consistency purposes, you need the senior judges for the time being who are in post to set the tariff, to tell you where in the band you should be going. *That's* what you need. That's a system of *law*. And that's what sentencing is – it's part of a system of law' (Judge, emphasis *per* original).

The above quote is taken from an interview with an experienced Scottish judge, conducted as part of this author's doctoral research into judicial decision-making in sentencing at the University of Edinburgh (Brown, 2014).[1] It neatly summarises the problem with contemporary sentencing practice for the crime of rape in Scotland and in certain other 'non-guideline' jurisdictions which have eschewed prescriptive, numerical sentencing guidelines and in which judges have traditionally enjoyed considerable discretion in sentencing. On this judge's account and the account presented in this book there is a clear need for sentencing guidelines for rape. As Campbell (2017: 484) notes, guidelines are a statement to judges in future sentencing contexts, but also to the community and to victims. Properly drafted sentencing guidelines for rape will also recognise the experience of rape victims and acknowledge the harms caused by the offence.

Current Issues and the Need to Structure Discretion in Rape Sentencing

Through an in-depth analysis of sentencing practice, this book has sought to highlight certain historic and contemporary problems in rape sentencing. In the UK, the courts have moved away from their traditional position of regarding

[1] Later published, in an expanded form, as *Criminal Sentencing as Practical Wisdom* (Brown, 2017a).

relationship or acquaintance rape as somehow less serious than stranger rape. The English Court of Appeal recognised the seriousness of relationship rape in December 2002 in *R v Millberry and others*,[2] a decision which went a considerable way towards breaking from past sentencing practice in which stranger rape was perceived by the courts as the paradigm of 'real' rape.[3] In Scotland, however, it took until October 2015, with the decision in *HMA v SSK*,[4] for the Appeal Court to acknowledge that a rapist's culpability is not reduced by any sense of entitlement associated with a current or previous relationship.[5] The New Zealand courts have long recognised that relationship rape is no less traumatic, and therefore no less serious, than stranger rape.[6] The principle was first articulated by the New Zealand Court of Appeal in 1987 in its judgment in *R v N*[7] and was reiterated by the Court in its guideline judgment in *R v AM*.[8] In the Republic of Ireland, while there is no specific appellate guidance on the issue, the decision of the Supreme Court in *People (DPP) v Tiernan*[9] has been interpreted as indicating that a prior or existing sexual relationship between the parties is not a mitigating factor in sentencing (see O'Malley, 2006: 267).[10]

This study has highlighted the importance of the courts recognising the particular harm caused by offenders using mobile and online technologies to record or photograph acts of sexual assault.[11] By reference to the research literature, recent empirical studies and case law, it has been shown that the psychological effects on victims who are filmed or photographed in this way can be profound. In England and Wales, recording a rape in this way is listed as a culpability factor in the Sexual Offences Definitive Guideline (Sentencing Council, 2013a: 10) and is thus seen as being inextricably linked to the seriousness of the offence itself.[12] In Scotland, the Appeal Court held in *HMA v CH*[13] that recording images of sexual offending constitutes a very serious aggravation of the offence in question.[14] In New Zealand, meanwhile, the guideline judgment in *R v AM*[15] recognises the recording or photographing of an offence as conduct that further degrades the victim, increasing the offender's culpability.[16] It is imperative that offenders' use of mobile phones to record or photograph acts of rape and sexual assault is adequately recognised in sentencing guidelines as a serious aggravating factor.

[2] [2003] 2 Cr App R (S) 31 at [9].
[3] See Chapter 4.
[4] [2015] HCJAC 114; 2016 SCCR 74 at [27].
[5] See Chapter 5.
[6] See Chapter 7.
[7] [1987] 2 NZLR 268 at 270.
[8] [2010] NZCA 114; [2010] 2 NZLR 750 at [61].
[9] *People (DPP) v Tiernan* [1988] IR 250.
[10] See Chapter 6.
[11] See Chapter 3.
[12] Ibid.
[13] [2017] HCJAC 82; 2017 SCCR 587.
[14] See Chapter 3.
[15] *AM* (n 8).
[16] Ibid at [47]. See Chapter 3.

Perhaps the key issue in contemporary sentencing practice for rape, at least in Scotland and Canada, is the disproportionally low starting points used by the courts in these jurisdictions. In Scotland, following the decision in in *HMA v Shearer*,[17] the starting point for sentencing so-called 'non-forcible' rape (cases featuring no particular aggravating or mitigating features), or, as the Lord Justice Clerk described it in in *HMA v Cooperwhite*,[18] 'the benchmark',[19] is currently three-and-a-half years' imprisonment. This is a figure far below the starting points set by either the appellate courts or by the bodies which promulgate sentencing guidelines in other common law jurisdictions.[20]

In England and Wales, for example, the equivalent starting point sentence was initially set at five years' imprisonment by the Court of Appeal in in *R v Billam and others*.[21] The subsequent guideline judgment in *Millberry*[22] retained this starting point while also setting a general starting point of eight years where certain aggravating factors were present. These starting points were, in turn, retained by the Sentencing Guidelines Council's Definitive Guideline on the Sexual Offences Act 2003 (SGC, 2007a), although the relevant sentencing ranges were set by the SGC at between four and eight years' imprisonment and six and 11 years' imprisonment respectively (SGC, 2007a 25).[23] Most recently, as a result of the Sentencing Council's Sexual Offences Definitive Guideline, starting points for rape sentencing have been set at five years' imprisonment (with a range of four to seven years) in cases of lesser culpability and at seven years' imprisonment (with a range of six to nine years) in cases of greater culpability (Sentencing Council, 2013a: 11).[24]

The equivalent starting points in New Zealand were set by the Court of Appeal in *R v AM*[25] at between six and eight years' imprisonment ('band one') for offending at the lower end of the spectrum, where aggravating features are either not present or present only to a limited extent[26] and seven to 13 years' imprisonment ('band two') in cases where the scale of offending, levels of violence and premeditation are relatively moderate.[27] While no such sentencing guidelines currently exist in the Republic of Ireland, the analysis of sentencing practice for rape in the Irish courts undertaken by Charleton J in *People (DPP) v Drought (sub nom People (DPP) v D(W)*[28]) indicates that 'ordinary punishment' in the majority of cases tends to comprise sentences of between five and seven years' imprisonment.[29]

[17] 2003 SCCR 657.
[18] [2013] HCJAC 88; 2013 SCCR 461.
[19] Ibid at [19].
[20] See Chapter 5.
[21] (1986) 8 Cr App R (S) 48. See Chapter 4.
[22] *Millberry* (n 2). See Chapter 4.
[23] See Chapter 4.
[24] Ibid.
[25] *AM* (n 8).
[26] Ibid at [93].
[27] Ibid at [98]. See Chapter 7.
[28] [2007] IEHC 310; [2008] 1 IR 308.
[29] Ibid at [28].

Most recently, O'Malley's review of Irish sentencing practice for rape broadly corresponds to that of Justice Charleton in *Drought* in identifying the ranges of sentence for the offence and common aggravating and mitigating factors (see O'Malley, 2016: 367–73).[30]

This study has shown that the current Scottish starting point in rape sentencing of three-and-a-half years' imprisonment is most closely aligned with sentencing practice in many Canadian provinces and territories. The decision of the Alberta Court of Appeal in *R v Sandercock*[31] set a starting point of three years' imprisonment for what it described as 'major sexual assault',[32] including vaginal rape and forced oral and anal penetration.[33] Despite being decided over 30 years ago, *Sandercock* remains one of the leading cases on sentencing for sexual offending in Canada and has influenced sentencing practice for sexual assault across the country.

Neither the Canadian starting point sentence of three years' imprisonment nor the Scottish benchmark of three-and-a-half years reflect current societal attitudes towards the crime of rape (see Brown, 2015a: 8; O'Malley, 2013a: 661; and the decision of the Ontario Court of Appeal in *R v Glassford*[34]). In particular, sentences at, or around, the starting point or benchmark level are frequently imposed in these jurisdictions in cases involving the rape of intoxicated or incapable victims.[35] Starting points, or benchmarks, of between three and three-and-a-half years' imprisonment reflect neither offenders' culpability nor the harm caused by all rapes, whether physical harm or, more particularly, the psychological harm sustained by victims.[36] Most common law jurisdictions adopt higher starting points and so, in short, the Scottish and Canadian benchmarks or starting points do not adequately reflect the seriousness of rape.

The need for sentencing guidelines for sentencing rape is clear, yet a key issue is the form that such sentencing guidelines should take. In considering the source of sentencing guidance, its style and the authority by which it should be promulgated, the traditions and legal culture of the jurisdiction will be a significant factor (Ashworth, 1998: 215–16; Freed, 1992: 1683; Padfield, 2013: 32; Roberts, 2009: 232). O'Malley (2013b: 227) explains:

> '[W]hen deciding upon the optimal structuring mechanism, regard must be had to particular jurisdictional characteristics, the receptiveness of the judiciary and the bar to the proposed reforms, the likely levels of compliance and the extent to which the existing system might be developed and refined in order to generate more consistency of approach, if not more consistency of outcome' (see also see Ashworth, 1998: 213 and Roberts, 2009: 230).

[30] See Chapter 6.
[31] 1985 ABCA 218; (1985) 22 CCC (3d) 79.
[32] Ibid at [17].
[33] Ibid at [13].
[34] [1988] OJ No 359, 42 CCC (3d) 259 at 265.
[35] See Chapter 5.
[36] See Chapter 2.

This book has reviewed three principal ways of structuring judicial discretion in rape sentencing: firstly, mandatory and minimum sentences set by the legislature; secondly, formal sentencing guidelines issued by a sentencing council; and thirdly, guideline judgments issued by the appellate courts.

Mandatory and Minimum Sentences

Through an analysis of sentencing practice for rape in South Africa, in particular the operation of the Criminal Law Amendment Act 105 of 1997 (the so-called 'minimum sentences Act'), it has been demonstrated that mandatory and minimum sentences frequently result in injustice.[37] Such schemes are based on the nomenclature of crimes, rather than on the seriousness of individual acts (Aas, 2005: 20). They constrain judicial sentencing discretion too tightly and, as the Supreme Court of Appeal acknowledged in *S v Vilakazi*,[38] produce the injustice of treating differently situated offenders similarly (see also Freiberg, 2016: 428; Krasnostein, 2015: 227; and O'Malley, 2008: 11). Mandatory and minimum sentence regimes seek to transform sentencing into a formal and standardised process: individualised justice is usurped by punitive uniformity (Brown, 2017a: 72; Mallett, 2015: 546).

Despite the introduction of mandatory sentences of life imprisonment for certain forms of rape and lengthy minimum custodial terms for others (sanctions described by a majority of the Supreme Court of Appeal in *S v Opperman*[39] as 'draconian'[40]), the minimum sentences Act has, paradoxically, resulted in public and media perception that many sentences for rape are unduly lenient. In seeking to impose proportionate sentences for rape, South African judges frequently apply the statutory departure, or 'escape', clause in the Act whereby a lesser sentence may be imposed if the court is satisfied that 'substantial and compelling circumstances' exist. In order to bring a case within the ambit of 'substantial and compelling circumstances', judges are compelled by the terms of the Act to 'play down' certain aspects of the rape in question.

Judicial recourse to the departure clause also illustrates one of the key shortcomings of mandatory and minimum sentencing regimes. The minimum sentences Act is regarded by the South African courts as 'wholly repugnant'[41] to the country's legal and judicial traditions and culture. As the Supreme Court of Appeal stated in *Vilakazi*,[42] the courts are not 'vehicles for injustice'[43] and so, in imposing proportionate sentences, South African judges continue to sentence according to

[37] See Chapter 7.
[38] [2008] ZASCA 87; 2009 (1) SACR 552 (SCA) at [13] (see Chapter 7).
[39] 2010 (2) SACR 248 (SCA).
[40] Ibid at [40].
[41] *S v Toms; S v Bruce* (1990) (2) SA 802 (A), per Botha JA at 831B.
[42] *Vilakazi* (n 38).
[43] Ibid at [18].

values that privilege their own professional knowledge and experience *as judges*, rather than the policy goals of politicians. In sum, the South African minimum sentences legislation is an example of how *not* to structure judicial sentencing discretion (see Terblanche and Mackenzie, 2008: 405).

Sentencing Council Guidelines

With respect to formal guidelines issued by sentencing councils, this study has shown that, despite being established in 2015, the Scottish Sentencing Council ('SSC'), an advisory body, has been slow to issue guidelines for approval by the High Court.[44] The sole guideline issued by the SSC at the time of writing, on the *Principles and Purposes of Sentencing* (SSC, 2018a), simply reflects pre-existing sentencing law and is of very little practical value, at least to judges and the legal profession. Indeed, many of the principles and purposes set out in the SSC's guideline are nothing more than statements of the self-evident. This study has also noted recent developments in the Republic of Ireland where, in July 2019, the Oireachtas passed the Judicial Council Bill, which provides for the creation of a Sentencing Guidelines and Information Committee ('SGIC').[45] The SGIC has yet to be established but, like the SSC, it too will be an advisory body. As with sentencing guidelines issued by the SSC in Scotland, any guidelines issued by the SGIC and subsequently adopted by the Judicial Council will not be presumptively binding. Irish judges will be under a duty simply to have regard to any such guidelines.

It is, however, in England and Wales that we see the most sophisticated structuring of judicial sentencing discretion through guidelines. In *R v Thelwall*,[46] the Court of Appeal made it clear that, rather than case law, guidelines issued by the Sentencing Council are now the basis of the English sentencing system.[47] Since 1 April 2014, sentencing for rape has been governed by the Sentencing Council's Sexual Offences Definitive Guideline (Sentencing Council, 2013a). Guidelines issued by the Sentencing Council, including its Definitive Guideline on Sexual Offences, structure the decision-making process by creating what one former member of the Council describes as an 'algorithm' (Roberts, 2011: 1011). Judges must follow a nine-step decision-making process in sentencing rape. This comprises a detailed, structured and prescriptive sentencing methodology (Roberts, 2012b: 283), with its key aim being the achievement of consistency in sentencing. Within the common law world, such algorithmic guidelines remain exceptional (O'Malley, 2013b: 219). Indeed, England and Wales is the only jurisdiction outside the United States to implement a detailed, national system of presumptively binding

[44] See Chapter 5.
[45] See Chapter 6.
[46] [2016] EWCA Crim 1755.
[47] Ibid at [22].

sentencing guidelines containing specific sentence ranges (Ashworth and Roberts, 2013: 1–2; Roberts and Ashworth, 2016: 310, fn 3; Wiles, 2015: xi).

Unlike the draconian penalties for rape set out in the South African minimum sentences Act, the range of sentences prescribed by the Definitive Guideline are, in the main, proportionate to the gravity of the offence. The Definitive Guideline's recognition that there is a baseline of harm in all cases of rape and, particularly, its focus on harm and culpability in sentencing (with, importantly, 'harm' incorporating psychological harm to the victim) are, generally, commendable; however, this approach does appear to marginalise the influence of personal mitigation (see Cooper, 2013).

Leading academic commentators in England have lauded the Sentencing Council's system of algorithmic guidelines as an ideal model and as an exemplar for other jurisdictions to follow, or at least consider, before introducing their own schemes to structure judicial sentencing discretion (Ashworth and Roberts, 2013: 11; Roberts, 2012a: 320, 343 and 2012b: 267– 68, 281 and 283; Roberts and Ashworth, 2016: 334; and Roberts and Rafferty, 2011: 688). While commentators in certain other jurisdictions have called for the introduction of sentencing guidelines similar to the English model (see, eg, Mosonyi, 2017; Roberts and Pei, 2016; and Roberts et al, 2011), the present system of English guidelines has not been enthusiastically embraced by all academic commentators, by the legal profession, or by certain judges.

The format of the Sentencing Council's guidelines and the Council's Sexual Offences Definitive Guideline (Sentencing Council, 2013a) in particular, is seen as too mechanistic and restrictive (Thomas, 2013). The guidelines have been criticised as an artificial method of calculating sentence which, in many cases, arguably hinders the judge's ability to do justice in sentencing sexual offences (Harris and Gerry, 2013). Cooper (2013) argues that the guidelines focus on offence severity and offender culpability at the expense of personal mitigation. For Cooper the focus on aggravating factors at the expense of mitigation clearly affects the ability of judges to respond to the characteristics of the individual offender. The public finds the multi-step approach of the guidelines difficult, if not impossible, to follow (Bottoms, 2018; Harris and Gerry, 2013; Secret Barrister, 2019). The guidelines are regarded as less easy to apply and more difficult to use than the guidelines issued by the Council's predecessor, the Sentencing Guidelines Council (Padfield, 2013). There is also a perception among practitioners that, since the creation of the Sentencing Guidelines Council in 2004 and the structured and prescriptive sentencing methodology it introduced, sentencing in England and Wales has become a 'box ticking exercise'. Rather than being helpful signposts to a fair and proportionate disposal, judges may use the guidelines simply as 'fireproofing' against any subsequent appeal against sentence (Cooper, 2008: 279–80).

The current English system of prescriptive, heavily structured, numerical and presumptively binding sentencing guidelines is inimical to the traditional, discretionary-based approach to sentencing in jurisdictions such as South Africa,[48]

[48] See Chapter 7.

New Zealand,[49] the Republic of Ireland[50] and Scotland.[51] In these jurisdictions, the courts have traditionally focused on the imposition of proportionate sentences, rather than achieving consistency or uniformity in sentencing. Although in Scotland, the Appeal Court has recently approved judicial recourse to the English sentencing guidelines as a form of 'cross-check', the extent to which judges routinely 'proof' their sentences in this way is questionable, with even the Appeal Court itself apparently eschewing this approach.[52]

In short, the algorithmic English sentencing guidelines are anathema to sentencing systems that prioritise judicial discretion to achieve individualised justice. Indeed, recent empirical research involving interviews with 25 Scottish judges found that while the overwhelming majority of respondents welcomed sentencing *guidance* from the Appeal Court, systems of algorithmic, prescriptive and presumptively binding sentencing guidelines which promote a rule-based rationality over practical experience did not find favour (Brown, 2017a: 171–75). Similar findings are reported in earlier empirical studies with Scottish judges (see Millie et al, 2007: 251 and Tombs: 2004: 35, 43). For these reasons, it would not be appropriate for the appellate courts in jurisdictions such as Scotland and the Republic of Ireland to adopt, even in a modified form, the sentencing guidelines for rape set out in the Sentencing Council's Definitive Guideline (Sentencing Council, 2013a).

Guideline Judgments

Guideline judgments are the third method of structuring judicial discretion in rape sentencing explored in this study. They comprise judgments of the appellate courts which go beyond the facts of the particular case before the court by articulating sentencing principles (Freiberg, 2014: 977–78). Guideline judgments may, for example, consider the importance of aggravating and mitigating factors; they may discuss the relevance of different sanctions to the particular offence; and they may suggest appropriate sentencing ranges. The principal objective of the appellate courts in issuing such guideline judgments has been to structure and to guide judicial sentencing discretion, rather than restricting or abolishing it (Brown, 2017a: 155–56). Guideline judgments also promote transparency in the judicial decision-making process and can result in increased public confidence in the criminal justice system (Krasnostein, 2015: 163).

[49] Ibid.
[50] See Chapter 6.
[51] See Chapter 5.
[52] Ibid.

This study has examined the use of guideline judgments for rape sentencing issued by the Court of Appeal (Criminal Division) and used by the courts in England and Wales in the first and second phases of the development of English sentencing guidelines between January 1982[53] and May 2007.[54] The system has since changed dramatically and, as the Court noted in *R v Thelwall*,[55] now proceeds on the basis not of case law but on the Sentencing Council's algorithmic guidelines. Such judicial self-regulation through the issuing of guideline judgments, however, offered an excellent basis for the development of principles that are highly sensitive to the practical problems of sentencing judges (Ashworth, 2009: 254). As Ashworth (2001: 74) observes, English guideline judgments demonstrate that sentencing guidance can be fashioned in a judge-friendly way, based on experience, to shape discretion without unduly constraining it.

The increasing use of guideline judgments by the appellate courts in both Scotland and the Republic of Ireland has been considered although, at the time of writing, both jurisdictions await a specific guideline judgment in respect of sentencing rape.[56] While rape sentencing in South Africa remains governed by the Criminal Law Amendment Act 105 of 1997, the study has highlighted the many problems caused by the minimum sentences legislation. The use of guideline judgments by the South African courts in respect of certain offences in the late 1990s and early 2000s has been noted and Baehr's suggestion of replacing the mandatory and minimum sentence scheme with a form of sentencing guideline comprising a graduated, rather than a bifurcated, scale has been considered (see Baehr, 2008).[57]

Finally, this study has examined the most comprehensive modern guideline judgment on rape sentencing: the decision of the New Zealand Court of Appeal in *R v AM*.[58] In issuing such detailed and practical guidance on rape sentencing, the New Zealand Court of Appeal regulates the courts' sentencing practices within the boundaries set by the legislature (Ashworth, 2009: 243). The guideline judgment in *AM* assists in guiding judicial decision-making in an area in which sensitive, individual calculations are required. Judges are thus provided with a framework within which they can locate the individual case, without being deprived of the discretion to deal differently with a case which has unusual features (Ashworth, 2009: 243; Cooper, 2008: 278). Comprehensive guideline judgments such as *AM*, constructed by judges for judges, allow sentencers to retain sufficient flexibility to

[53] See *R v Roberts and Roberts* (1982) 4 Cr App R (S) 8 considered in Chapter 4.

[54] On 14 May 2007, the Sentencing Guidelines Council's Definitive on the Sexual Offences Act 2003 (SGC, 2007a) came into force. The guideline judgment in *R v Millberry and others* [2003] 2 Cr App R (S) 31 was used by the English courts between December 2002 and May 2007. For a full discussion, see Chapter 4.

[55] *Thelwall* (n 46) at [22].

[56] See the discussions in Chapters 5 and 6 respectively.

[57] See Chapter 7.

[58] *AM* (n 8), discussed in Chapter 7.

keep justice to the fore, while injecting enough consistency to make sentencing outcomes more predictable (Ashworth, 2009: 244; Brown, 2017a: 157; O'Donnell, 2012: 257; O'Malley, 2013b: 231).

In particular, such guideline judgments allow judges to retain sufficient discretion to take each case on its merits and to impose an appropriate sentence that takes account of all the circumstances of the offence and of the offender. The guidelines are not rules of universal application. They can be departed from if, given the particular facts and circumstances, justice so demands (Brown, 2017a: 167–68). As O'Malley (2016: 19–20) explains:

> 'It may be a cliché, but it also happens to be true, that guidelines are not tramlines. They are intended to guide rather than determine the sentences to be imposed by trial judges in specific cases. Allowance must always be made for exceptional circumstances, whether relating to the offence or the offender, that may call for a sentence more lenient or severe than the norm posited by any applicable guideline … What [sentencing judges] must avoid doing is applying a guideline rigidly or automatically, without regard to any particular factors that may justify upward or downward departures from the recommended ranges.'

'Principled Discretion' in Sentencing Rape

This study has shown that the issuing of guideline judgments is key to achieving what O'Malley (2011: 5) terms 'principled discretion'.[59] This is a method of structuring sentencing discretion that ensures procedural fairness, equality and adherence to the rule of law by permitting judges to retain a high level of discretion, while ensuring that this discretion is exercised in accordance with settled principles. Individualised justice remains possible because the *principles* operate at a higher level of generality than *rules* and are sufficiently flexible to permit departure and variation when the particular circumstances of a case so demand (O'Malley, 2013a: 533; 2001: 135).

Principled discretion thus results in *informed* judgment (O'Malley, 2011: 5), with the principles laid down by the appellate courts guiding judges in navigating their way through the facts of the particular case to arrive at a proportionate sentence (O'Malley, 2013a: 533). The result is a sentencing discretion that is underpinned by principles, rather than hemmed in by rules (O'Donnell, 2012: 256; see also Brown, 2017a: 168–71). As O'Malley (2013b: 234) observes, it is possible for modern sentencing systems to survive without (algorithmic) guidelines, but not without sentencing guidance. For jurisdictions which have not implemented systems of detailed, prescriptive and algorithmic sentencing guidelines, judicial discretion in sentencing rape can best be guided by principled discretion, through the issuing of guideline judgments.

[59] See the discussion in Chapter 6.

Towards Sentencing Guidelines for Rape

> 'Sentencing … is founded upon two premises that are in perennial conflict: individualized justice and consistency. The first holds that courts should impose sentences that are just and appropriate according to all of the circumstances of each particular case. The second holds that similarly situated offenders should receive similar sentencing outcomes. The result is an ambivalent jurisprudence that challenges sentencers as they attempt to meet the conflicting demands of each premise' (Krasnostein and Freiberg, 2013: 265).

This book has considered a variety of differing approaches towards structuring judicial discretion in sentencing rape. While a system of mandatory and minimum sentences operates in South Africa, the very different approaches to the use of sentencing guidelines in, on the one hand, England and Wales and, on the other, jurisdictions such as Scotland, Ireland and New Zealand can be seen as a dichotomy between two different methods of judicial decision-making in sentencing. The English approach is system-orientated, abstract and objective, while the approaches of the Scottish, Irish and New Zealand courts are more case-orientated, concrete and intuitive (see Aas, 2005: 26 and Brown, 2017a: 157).

Lessons from Non-Guideline Jurisdictions

In continuing the example set in Scotland by the High Court of Justiciary on appeal with its 'internationalism of jurisprudence' (Lord Gill, 2016: 18)[60] appellate courts should, in drafting guideline judgments, make full use of comparative material from other jurisdictions. This study's international review of case law in various non-guideline jurisdictions and its critique of the English system of algorithmic guidelines, highlights the key requirements of a guideline judgment on sentencing rape. From the review of Scottish sentencing methodology and practice, we see that what is required is a set of guidelines that provides a structure for, but which does not remove, judicial discretion.[61] The guidelines must assist judges in exercising their discretion, rather than being 'straitjacket[s] from which they cannot escape'.[62] The guidelines are not to be interpreted and applied in a mechanistic way.[63] Whilst the guidelines will assist judges in imposing proportionate sentences, the decision as to the appropriate sentence in the individual case lies with the sentencing judge alone.[64]

From the review of sentencing practice in the Republic of Ireland, we again see the importance of a wide judicial discretion in the application of sentencing

[60] See Chapter 5.
[61] *HMA v Graham* [2010] HCJAC 50; 2011 JC 1 at [21].
[62] Ibid at [22].
[63] *Neill v HMA* [2014] HCJAC 67 at [11].
[64] *Jakovlev v HMA* [2011] HCJAC 90; 2012 JC 120 at [11].

guidelines.[65] Any range of penalties provides broad guidance to judges but does not seek to impose any form of standardisation of penalty.[66] In New Zealand, meanwhile, it has been shown that the most significant feature of sentencing is the discretion vested in the sentencing judge.[67] While the New Zealand courts benefit from guideline judgments, the appellate courts have made it clear that such guidelines are not to be slavishly applied; that rigid or mathematical approaches to sentencing are not appropriate; and that departure from sentencing guidelines may be warranted by the facts of a particular case.[68]

Finally, the review of the traditional approach of the South African courts towards sentencing also demonstrates the importance of judicial sentencing discretion and individualised justice.[69] In particular, in imposing proportionate sentences, the South African courts have long had recourse to the so-called 'triad of *Zinn*', considering the crime, the offender and the interests of society.[70]

Understanding the Offence

While establishing sentencing guidelines can be useful in eliminating unwarranted disparities in sentences, such guidelines are only truly beneficial when judges are able to understand the nature of the offence to which they apply (Nightingale, 1991: 89). It is for this reason that a guideline judgment for rape must begin by properly situating the offence. The relevant appellate court must explain the wrongness of rape[71] (see, eg, the judgment of Charleton J in *People (DPP) v Drought (sub nom People (DPP) v D(W)))*.[72] The typical effects of rape on the victim, both physical and psychological, must be acknowledged.[73] As the New Zealand Court of Appeal stated in *R v AM*,[74] judges must be directed to assess the gravity of offending in a fact-specific way, focusing on the culpability of the offender and the effect on the victim (see also Harris and Gerry, 2013: 241–42). As a corollary, any guideline judgment ought to be clear that judges must not reason by stereotype or seek to turn responsibility for the offending back on the victim, in terms of excuses based on rape myths[75] (see also Kennefick and Fennell, 2017: 485). No distinction for

[65] *People (DPP) v Casey and Casey* [2018] IECA 121 at [49]; *People (DPP) v Fitzgibbon* [2014] IECCA 12 at para 8.11.

[66] *People (DPP) v Ryan* [2014] IECCA 11 at para 2.3.

[67] *Fisheries Inspector v Turner* [1978] 2 NZLR 233 at 237.

[68] *R v Clotworthy* (1998) 15 CRNZ 651; *R v Taueki* [2005] 3 NZLR 372 at [10] and [16]; *R v H* (CA 488/05), Court of Appeal, 4 September 2006; *R v Pehi* [2007] BCL 58; *R v D* [2008] NZCA 267 at [43]; *AM* (n 8) at [10], [29], [79], [84] and [88].

[69] *S v Toms; S v Bruce* (1990) (2) SA 802 (A) at 806H–I; *S v Scheepers* 1977 (2) SA 155 at 158G–H.

[70] *S v Zinn* 1969 (2) SA 537 at 540G–H; *S v Rabie* 1975 (4) SA 855 (A) at 864F–G; *S v De Kock* 1997 (2) SACR 171 (T) at 197g–h.

[71] See Chapter 2.

[72] [2007] IEHC 310; [2008] 1 IR 308 at [6] and [7].

[73] See Chapter 2.

[74] *AM* (n 8) at [79].

[75] Ibid.

sentencing purposes should necessarily be made between vaginal, anal and oral rape (*R v AM*;[76] *HMA v AB*;[77] Hall, 2014: 68, 96; Rook and Ward, 2016: 39). Any guideline judgment must also be clear that the same sentencing regime applies to so-called 'relationship', 'acquaintance', or marital rape, as to 'stranger' rape.[78]

A victim statement provides the sentencing judge with an account of how the particular victim has been affected physically, psychologically and financially by the offence. By considering Bottoms' (2010) work on victim participation in the criminal process, it has been shown why such statements are particularly important in sentencing rape. Victim statements provide an individualised, victim-orientated, appreciative description of how the offence has impacted on the victim, completing the picture of the offence and assisting the judge in the task of imposing a proportionate sentence that fully reflects the harm caused and the offender's culpability. Any guideline judgment should follow the practice of the Court of Appeal (Criminal Division), as set out in *R v Ismail*,[79] in stating that victim statements should routinely be obtained in cases of rape and made available to the sentencing judge.

The Nature of the Guidelines

While this book argues for reform of rape sentencing in non-guideline jurisdictions, sentencing reform measures are likely to succeed only if they leave adequate scope for the continued exercise of judicial discretion where it is needed. As Sir Igor Judge (as he then was) observed in an address delivered at Lincoln's Inn in October 2007:

> 'You can have your guidelines. You can have the endless – is it now 17, or maybe more? – factors which the judge is under a statutory obligation to address. In the end you may be able to sentence a piece of paper by a process which you can colourably describe as scientific. But sentencing a fellow human being is indeed an art, a human skill, a skill in humanity, not a science and it is this skill and its application, that is embodied in the possibly pompous sounding phrase, "judicial discretion"' (Judge, 2007: 1).

Sentencing reform measures must be respectful of judicial skills and wisdom (see Brown, 2017a). Such measures must also demonstrate due recognition of the integrity with which judges customarily discharge their obligations (O'Malley, 2013b: 229). Properly drafted guideline judgments meet the three requirements of respecting judicial discretion, judicial skills and wisdom, and judicial integrity. In issuing guideline judgments, the relevant appellate court acts as a forum of principle, as well as a decision-making tribunal (O'Malley, 2011).

[76] Ibid at [5] and [65].
[77] [2015] HCJAC 106; 2016 SCCR 47 at [11] and [12].
[78] See *AM* (n 8) at [61].
[79] [2005] 2 Cr App R (S) 88, considered in Chapter 2.

An important feature of guideline judgments such as the decision of the New Zealand Court of Appeal in *R v AM*[80] is that, rather than presenting the lower courts with a stark table of numbers, a grid, or a sentencing matrix, the appellate guidance is narrative and has the familiar form of an appellate court judgment (Ashworth, 2009: 243). Sentencing involves judges engaging in the trained application of reasons of law to individual cases. This is more likely to be achieved from a set of narrative guidelines than from numerical guidelines (Bottoms, 1998: 70), particularly in jurisdictions committed to maintaining a healthy level of judicial discretion (Brown, 2017a: 157; O'Malley, 2011: 13).

The Format of the Guidelines

The precise format of any guideline judgment on sentencing for rape will depend on the sentencing methodology in the jurisdiction in question. We have seen that in Scotland, for example, judges have traditionally sentenced by way of 'instinctive synthesis', aggregating and assessing all factors bearing on a sentencing decision in a single, global process of reasoning. Indeed, two successive Lords Justice General (Lords Gill and Carloway) specifically approved the instinctive synthesis sentencing methodology in a series of appellate decisions beginning with *Gemmell v HMA*[81] and concluding, most recently, with *Wilson v Shanks*.[82] The recent draft guideline by the Scottish Sentencing Council on *The Sentencing Process* (SSC, 2019a), which was going through its public consultation at the time of writing, is unlikely to result in major changes to Scottish sentencing methodology, at least amongst experienced judges.[83] Thus, in imposing sentence, Scottish judges identify all relevant factors; however, rather than ascribing a particular weight to individual mitigating and aggravating factors, the Scottish judge simply arrives at an end sentence representing her own intuitive synthesis.

In both the Republic of Ireland and New Zealand, however, the courts follow a tiered, or staged, approach to sentencing. We have seen that in Ireland, this process comprises two stages.[84] The first stage of the process requires the judge to locate the particular offence on the overall scale of gravity to identify a presumptively appropriate, or 'headline', sentence. Aggravating circumstances of the particular offence are factored into this first stage of the sentencing process. The second stage, meanwhile, involves consideration of the offender's personal circumstances. It is at the second stage that the judge applies any mitigation to the headline sentence

[80] *AM* (n 8).

[81] [2011] HCJAC 129; 2012 JC 223.

[82] [2018] HCJAC 50; 2019 JC 1. See also *Ferguson v HMA* [2014] HCJAC 19; 2014 SCCR 244 and the discussion in Chapter 5.

[83] See Chapter 5.

[84] See Chapter 6.

to reach the final sentence, including any reduction in sentence to reflect the offender's guilty plea.[85]

Sentencing guideline judgments in Ireland serve to provide the judge with some assistance in undertaking the first stage of the process by identifying the presumptively appropriate penalty or range of penalties. Thereafter, the judge is still required, in terms of the second stage, to give credit for any mitigating factors. As O'Malley (2016: 74) explains, even when courts use guideline judgments, the two-tiered approach to sentencing remains intact, albeit that the judge will make her decision at both stages by recourse to a form of 'instinctive synthesis' involving professional experience, intuition and subjective judgment.

In New Zealand, meanwhile, the courts employ a three-stage approach.[86] The first step similarly involves the judge identifying a starting point, taking into account the aggravating and mitigating features of *the offending* but excluding mitigating and aggravating features relating to *the offender*. The second step involves evaluating the aggravating and mitigating factors personal to the *particular offender*. The starting point sentence is then adjusted up or down to reflect these factors. The third step involves the judge allowing an appropriate reduction in sentence if the offender pleads guilty.[87]

Despite differences in judicial sentencing methodology, the decision of the New Zealand Court of Appeal in *R v AM*[88] is the most informative, detailed and considered guideline judgment on sentencing rape. The decision in *AM* was influenced by the work of the Sentencing Guidelines Council in England and Wales and drew on the draft sexual offence guideline prepared by the New Zealand Sentencing Establishment Unit ('SEU'). The SEU's draft guideline was itself the subject of extensive consultation with criminal justice stakeholders.[89] It behoves the appellate courts in other common law and non-guideline jurisdictions to study the decision in *AM* with a view either to adopting the guidelines, or to implementing a modified version of them.

The *AM* guidelines have been fully considered in Chapter 7[90] where it was shown that the Court of Appeal prefaced its guidelines with the following observation:

> '[I]t is trite but important to emphasise that what is required is an evaluation of all the circumstances. Listing relevant factors and setting out bands in the way we have done does not remove the need for judgment. A mechanistic approach is not appropriate.'[91]

[85] See *People (DPP) v M* [1994] 3 IR 306; *People (DPP) v O'B* [2015] IECA 255; and *People (DPP) v Molloy (Raymond)* [2018] IECA 37.

[86] See Chapter 7.

[87] See *R v Taueki* [2005] 3 NZLR 372; *Hessell v R* [2010] NZSC 135; [2011] 1 NZLR 607 and *R v Clifford* [2011] NZCA 360; [2012] 1 NZLR 23.

[88] *AM* (n 8).

[89] See the discussion in Chapter 7.

[90] Ibid.

[91] *AM* (n 8) at [36].

To recap, the Court in *AM* listed the following 'culpability assessment factors' as aggravating an offence of rape:

- planning and premeditation;
- violence, issuing threats, intimidation, abduction, detention and home invasion;
- the vulnerability of the victim due to, for example, age or health;
- physical and psychological harm caused to the victim;
- rape committed by more than one offender acting in concert;
- the scale of the offending, repeated rape and associated degradation or indignities including recording or photographing the offence;
- breach of trust;
- hate crime; and
- the degree of violation, in the sense of the length of the assault and the amount of force used.[92]

The two factors stated as being capable of mitigating an offence were, first, a genuine mistaken belief as to consent[93] and, second, circumstances in which consensual sexual activity took place immediately before the offence.[94] The Court also referred to the importance of an offender's youth, mental disability and prior good character as mitigating factors[95]

The Court's guidelines established four bands, expressed in terms of imprisonment, within which ranges of starting points were provided:

(i) *Rape band one*: six to eight years' imprisonment. This band is appropriate for offending at the lower end of the spectrum, where aggravating features are either absent, or present only to a limited extent.[96]
(ii) *Rape band two*: seven to 13 years' imprisonment. This band is appropriate for cases where the scale of offending, levels of violence and premeditation are relatively moderate. It applies to cases which involve a vulnerable victim, an offender acting in concert with others, or some additional violence.[97]
(iii) *Rape band three*: 12 to 18 years' imprisonment. This band applies to offending accompanied by relatively serious aggravating features. It is appropriate for offending which involves two or more of the factors increasing culpability to a high degree, or for offending which features more than three of those factors to a moderate degree.[98] Particularly cruel, callous or violent single episodes of rape will fall into this band.[99]

[92] Ibid at [37]–[52].
[93] Ibid at [53].
[94] Ibid at [54]–[60].
[95] Ibid at [84].
[96] Ibid at [90] and [93].
[97] Ibid at [90] and [98].
[98] Ibid at [90] and [105].
[99] Ibid.

(iv) *Rape band four*: 16 to 20 years' imprisonment. This band applies to cases involving multiple offending over considerable periods of time, rather than single instances of rape. Historic sexual abuse involving the repeated rape of one or more family members over a period of years is the paradigm example of such offending. Multiple perpetrator rape is also likely to fall within this band.[100]

It is important to appreciate, however, that cases will arise which are so unusual, in the sense of their featuring a combination of mitigating factors and perhaps a comparatively low level of harm, that the judge will require to set a starting point outside of the guidelines, below the bottom of band one.[101] Such cases include, for example, the decisions of the Court of Appeal (Criminal Division) in *R v Charles and others*[102] and *R v B*[103] considered in Chapter 4[104] and the decision of Lady Scott sitting at Glasgow High Court in *HMA v Cieslak*[105] considered in Chapter 5.[106] In these three cases, the facts and circumstances were such as to warrant suspended sentences, a conditional discharge, and an absolute discharge respectively. Where a judge departs from the guidelines in this way, reasons should be given for the departure.[107]

Finally, the Court in *AM* stressed the importance of judgement and flexibility in the application of the guidelines. The bands *do not* set final sentences. They set out *ranges of starting points*, which are to be adjusted up or down to reflect the circumstances personal to the offender.[108] The Court was clear that the guidelines were not designed to 'impose a straitjacket on sentencing judges'[109] and that they provided only guidance for sentencers.[110] In particular, it emphasised that applying the guidelines involves 'an evaluative exercise of judgment' by the sentencing judge.[111]

The *AM* guidelines provide structured, but not inflexible, guidance. They harness the advantages of structured and self-reflective decision-making, while preserving flexibility of outcomes within broadly set boundaries (Du Bois-Pedain, 2017: 396). In particular, the *AM* guidelines combine narrative guidance on the differentiation of types of rape with concrete indications of appropriate sentence ranges. They produce a fair degree of consistency in rape sentencing whilst, importantly, leaving sufficient room for the exercise of judicial discretion (see O'Malley, 2011: 126). The guidelines result in individualised, person-responsive

[100] Ibid at [90] and [108]–[109].
[101] Ibid at [83].
[102] [2012] 1 Cr App R (S) 74.
[103] [2011] EWCA Crim 165.
[104] See pp 99–100.
[105] Glasgow High Court, 17 March 2017, unreported.
[106] See p 154.
[107] *AM* (n 8) at [83].
[108] Ibid at [84].
[109] Ibid.
[110] Ibid at [29] and [88].
[111] Ibid at [79].

sentencing (Du Bois-Pedain, 2017: 395, 431) and are thus eminently suitable for use in other common law jurisdictions.

Rape Sentencing and the Guilty Plea Discount

The issue of the guilty plea discount – or plea-based sentence reductions – is particularly problematic in sentencing rape: various tensions surround the practice in such serious and morally repugnant cases. On one view, a significant discount in sentence may be warranted for an offender's guilty plea as the victim and other witnesses will be spared the often distressing ordeal of having to give evidence at trial (see Brown, 2017a: 206–10; Leverick, 2014: 339–40; 2013: 259–60; 2012: 234; 2008a: 45; and 2004: 370; McConville and Marsh, 2014: 221–29; and O'Malley, 2009: 877–78). Against this, however, some victims might wish to go through the ordeal of giving evidence as it gives them the opportunity to be heard within the criminal justice system (Brown, 2017a: 208; Leverick, 2004: 373), or because it may lead to their learning more about the offence and the offender (Brown, 2017a: 208; Sanders et al, 2010: 494–95). Victims may also feel that, given the choice, they would rather undergo the pains of giving evidence if it means that the offender receives no discount and thus a longer sentence (Ashworth, 2015: 181; Brown, 2017a: 208; Henham, 2012: 157; Dawes et al, 2011: 19; and Fenwick, 1997: 327).

The harm caused by rape, the generally high levels of offender culpability and the possibility that the allowance of substantial sentence discounts may cause the sentencing decisions of the criminal courts to lose credibility, thus eroding the authority of the courts generally,[112] all indicate that the judge's discretion to allow a discount should be exercised sparingly.[113] As Leverick acknowledges, it is close to impossible to find a way to balance the competing public interest concerns in applying guilty plea discounts in cases of rape (Leverick, 2013: 264). Following the decisions in *Gemmell*[114] and *Murray v HMA*,[115] judges in Scotland have more discretion in the application of guilty plea discounts than their counterparts in England and Wales, where practice is governed by the guideline issued by the Sentencing Council (Sentencing Council, 2017). The decisions of the Court of Appeal (Criminal Division) in *R v Wilson*[116] and *R v Caley*[117] make it clear that those who plead guilty to morally reprehensible crimes such as rape are entitled to credit for their guilty pleas in the same way as any other offender.

One option for reform that could be incorporated into any guideline judgment on rape sentencing would be for the relevant appellate court to 'cap' the maximum

[112] See the observations of Lord Justice Clerk Gill in *Gemmell* (n 81) at [74].
[113] Ibid at [77].
[114] *Gemmell* (n 81).
[115] [2013] HCJAC 3; 2013 SCCR 88.
[116] [2012] 2 Cr App R (S) 77.
[117] [2013] 2 Cr App R (S) 47.

permissible discount for the offence at a lower level than the one third that is routinely granted for a plea tendered at the first opportunity in England and Wales. A maximum discount of 10 per cent might be sufficient to provide a small incentive for an accused to plead guilty (Brown, 2017a: 233–40; see also Ashworth, 1983: 314; Ashworth and Zedner, 2008: 47; JUSTICE, 1993: 11; and Mack and Roach Anleu, 1997: 142). Capping the discount in this way would also have the advantage of addressing the issue of public confidence discussed by Lord Justice Clerk Gill in *Gemmell*,[118] allowing the judge to assess a proportionate sentence reduction in light of the specific circumstances of the individual case.

Concluding Observations

In advocating reform of rape sentencing in non-guideline jurisdictions (jurisdictions which have traditionally eschewed numerical, prescriptive and presumptively binding sentencing guidelines), this study has demonstrated that certain aspects of contemporary sentencing practice in such jurisdictions, in particular in Scotland and Canada, do not reflect modern societal attitudes to the offence. There is a need for the appellate courts in these jurisdictions to issue sentencing guidelines that take account of emerging evidence about the nature of rape and of evolving social attitudes to the offence.

This study has presented a thorough analysis of the development of sentencing guidance for the offence in various common law jurisdictions. It is suggested that the most effective way of implementing sentencing guidance that remains compatible with the traditional, discretionary-based systems of sentencing in non-guideline jurisdictions is for the appellate courts to adopt the guidelines issued by the New Zealand Court of Appeal in *R v AM*.[119] By issuing a guideline judgment in the same, or similar, terms as the decision in *AM*, the appellate courts would ensure that those who commit rape receive sentences proportionate to the gravity of the offence; an offence that amounts to a gross attack on the victim's human dignity, sexual autonomy and bodily integrity.

[118] *Gemmell* (n 81) at [74], see Chapter 5.
[119] *AM* (n 8).

BIBLIOGRAPHY

Aas, KF (2005), *Sentencing in the Age of Information: From Faust to Macintosh* (London, The Glasshouse Press).

Allen, R (2016), *The Sentencing Council for England and Wales: Brake or Accelerator on the Use of Prison?* (London, Transform Justice).

Anderson, MJ (2000), 'Rape in South Africa' 1 *The Georgetown Journal of Gender and the Law* 789–821.

Antoniou, A K and Akrivos, D (2017), *The Rise of Extreme Porn – Legal and Criminological Perspectives on Extreme Pornography in England and Wales* (Basingstoke, Palgrave Macmillan).

Archard, D (2007), 'The Wrong of Rape' 57(228) *The Philosophical Quarterly* 374–93.

Armstrong, CL, Hull, K and Saunders, L (2015), 'Victimized on Plain Sites' 4(2) *Digital Journalism* 247–65.

Artz, L and Combrinck, H (2003), '"A Wall of Words": Redefining the Offence of Rape in South African Law' *Acta Juridica*, pp 72–91.

Ashworth, A (2015), *Sentencing and Criminal Justice* (6th edn) (Cambridge, Cambridge University Press).

Ashworth, A (2013a), *Why Sentencing Matters*, Roger Hood Annual Public Lecture Series, 23 May 2013, University of Oxford. Available at: http://podcasts.ox.ac.uk/people/andrew-ashworth (accessed 1 September 2019).

Ashworth, A (2013b), 'The Struggle for Supremacy in Sentencing' in Ashworth, A and Roberts, JV (eds), *Sentencing Guidelines – Exploring the English Model* (Oxford, Oxford University Press).

Ashworth, A (2012), 'Departures from the Sentencing Guidelines' *Criminal Law Review*, pp 81–96.

Ashworth, A (2010), 'Coroners and Justice Act 2009: Sentencing Guidelines and the Sentencing Council' *Criminal Law Review*, pp 389–401.

Ashworth, A (2009), 'Techniques for Reducing Sentence Disparity' in von Hirsch, A, Ashworth, A and Roberts, J (eds), *Principled Sentencing – Readings on Theory and Policy* (3rd edn) (Oxford, Hart Publishing).

Ashworth, A (2008), 'English Sentencing Guidelines in their Public and Political Context' in Freiberg, A and Gelb, K (eds), *Penal Populism, Sentencing Councils and Sentencing Policy* (Cullompton, Willan Publishing).

Ashworth, A (2006), 'The Sentencing Guideline System in England and Wales' 19(1) *South African Journal of Criminal Justice* 1–22.

Ashworth, A (2005), *Sentencing and Criminal Justice* (4th edn) (Cambridge, Cambridge University Press).

Ashworth, A (2004), 'Criminal Justice Act 2003 – Criminal Justice Reform: Principles, Human Rights and Public Protection' *Criminal Law Review*, pp. 516–532.

Ashworth, A (2001), 'The Decline of English Sentencing and Other Stories' in Tonry, M and Frase, RS (eds), *Sentencing and Sanctions in Western Countries* (Oxford, Oxford University Press).

Ashworth, A (2000), *Sentencing and Criminal Justice* (3rd edn) (London, Butterworths LexisNexis).

Ashworth, A (1998), 'Structuring Sentencing Discretion' in von Hirsch, A and Ashworth, A (eds), *Principled Sentencing – Readings on Theory and Policy* (2nd edn) (Oxford, Hart Publishing).

Ashworth, A (1993), 'Victim Impact Statements and Sentencing' *Criminal Law Review*, 498–509.

Ashworth, A (1987), 'Disentangling Disparity' in Pennington, DC and Lloyd-Bostock, S (eds), *The Psychology of Sentencing – Approaches to Consistency and Disparity* (Oxford, Centre for Socio-Legal Studies).

Ashworth, A (1983), *Sentencing and Penal Policy* (London, Weidenfeld and Nicolson).

Ashworth, A, Genders, E, Mansfield, G, Peay, J and Player, E (1984), *Sentencing in the Crown Court*, Occasional Paper Number 10, Centre for Criminological Research, Oxford, University of Oxford.

Ashworth, A and Ormerod, D (2013), 'Obituary: Dr David Thomas QC (1938–2013)' *Criminal Law Review*, pp. 945–946.

Ashworth, A and Padfield, N (2015), 'Editorial – Five Years of the Sentencing Council' *Criminal Law Review*, pp. 657–658.

Ashworth, A and Player, E (2005), 'Criminal Justice Act 2003: The Sentencing Provisions' *Modern Law Review*, Vol. 68(5), pp. 822–838.

Ashworth, A and Roberts, JV (2017), 'Sentencing' in Liebling, A, Maruna, S and McAra, L (eds), *The Oxford Handbook of Criminology* (6th edn) (Oxford, Oxford University Press).

Ashworth, A and Roberts, JV (2013), 'The Origins and Nature of the Sentencing Guidelines in England and Wales' in Ashworth, A and Roberts, JV (eds), *Sentencing Guidelines – Exploring the English Model* (Oxford, Oxford University Press).

Ashworth, A and Roberts, JV (2012), 'Sentencing: Theory, Principle, and Practice' in Maguire, M, Morgan, R and Reiner, R (eds), *The Oxford Handbook of Criminology* (5th edn) (Oxford, Oxford University Press).

Ashworth, A and Zedner, L (2008), 'Defending the Criminal Law: Reflections on the Changing Character of Crime, Procedure, and Sanctions' 2 *Criminal Law and Philosophy* 21–51.

Avegno, J, Mills, TJ and Mills, LD (2009), 'Sexual Assault Victims in the Emergency Department: Analysis by Demographic and Event Characteristics' 37(3) *The Journal of Emergency Medicine* 328–34.

Bacik, I (2002a), 'Women and the Criminal Justice System' in O'Mahony, P (ed), *Criminal Justice in Ireland* (Dublin, Institute of Public Administration).

Bacik, I (2002b), 'The Practice of Sentencing in the Irish Courts' in O'Mahony, P (ed), *Criminal Justice in Ireland* (Dublin, Institute of Public Administration).

Baehr, KS (2008), 'Mandatory Minimums Making Minimal Difference: Ten Years of Sentencing Sex Offenders in South Africa' 20(1) *Yale Journal of Law & Feminism* 213–46.

Bagaric, M, Alexander, T and Edney, R (2018), *Sentencing in Australia* (6th edn) (Sydney, Thomson Reuters).

Baird, V (2013), 'Response to Consultation' in Sentencing Council for England and Wales, *Sexual Offences – Response to Consultation*, London, Sentencing Council.

Banks, R (2015), *Banks on Sentence – Vol. I* (10th edn) (Etchingham, Robert Banks).

Banks, R (2003), *Banks on Sentencing* (London, Butterworths).

Bassindale, C and Rahuf, A (2014), 'The Genital Examination' in Dalton, M (ed), *Forensic Gynaecology* (Cambridge, Cambridge University Press).

Bates, S (2017), 'Revenge Porn and Mental Health: A Qualitative Analysis of the Mental Health Effects of Revenge Porn on Female Survivors' 12(1) *Feminist Criminology* 22–42.

Bates, S (2015), *"Stripped": An Analysis of Revenge Porn Victims' Lives After Victimization* (MA Thesis, Burnaby, Simon Fraser University).

Ben-David, S and Silfen, P (1993), 'Rape Death and Resurrection: Male Reaction After Disclosure of the Secret of Being a Rape Victim' 12 *Medicine and Law* 181–89.

Benedet, J (2019), 'Sentencing for Sexual Offences Against Children and Youth: Mandatory Minimums, Proportionality and Unintended Consequences' 44(2) *Queen's Law Journal* 284–314.

Benedet, J and Grant, I (2010), 'Sexual Assault of Women with Mental Disabilities – A Canadian Perspective' in McGlynn, C and Munro, VE (eds), *Rethinking Rape Law – International and Comparative Perspectives* (Abingdon, Routledge).

Bennice, JA, Resick, PA and Mechanic, M (2003), 'The Relative Effects of Intimate Partner Physical and Sexual Violence on Post-Traumatic Stress Disorder Symptomatology' 18(1) *Violence and Victims* 87–94.

Bergen, RK (1996), *Wife Rape: Understanding the Response of Survivors and Service Providers* (London, Sage).

Bijleveld, CCJH, Weerman, FM, Looije, D and Hendriks, J (2007), 'Group Sex Offending by Juveniles – Coercive Sex as a Group Activity' 4(1) *European Journal of Criminology* 5–31.

Bloom, S (2014), 'No Vengeance For "Revenge Porn" Victims: Unravelling Why This Latest Female-Centric Intimate-Partner Offense Is Still Legal, And Why We Should Criminalize It' 42 *Fordham Urban Law Journal* 233–89.

Bluett-Boyd, N, Fileborn, B, Quadara, A and Moore, S (2013), *The Role of Emerging Communication Technologies in Experiences of Sexual Violence: A New Legal Frontier?* (Australian Government Research Report No 23) (Melbourne, Australian Institute of Family Studies).

Bohner, G, Eyssel, F, Pina, A, Siebler, F and Viki, GT (2009), 'Rape Myth Acceptance: Cognitive, Affective and Behavioural Effects of Beliefs that Blame the Victim and Exonerate the Perpetrator' in Horvath, MAH and Brown, J (eds), *Rape – Challenging Contemporary Thinking* (Cullompton, Willan).

Bottoms, A (2018), *The Sentencing Council in 2017 – A Report on Research to Advise on How the Sentencing Council Can Best Exercise Its Statutory Functions* (Cambridge, University of Cambridge Institute of Criminology).

Bottoms, A (2010), 'The "Duty to Understand": What Consequences for Victim Participation?' in Bottoms, A. and Roberts, JV (eds), *Hearing the Victim – Adversarial Justice, Crime Victims and the State* (Abingdon, Willan Publishing).

Bottoms, A (1998), 'Five Puzzles in von Hirsch's Theory of Punishment' in Ashworth, A and Wasik, M (eds), *Fundamentals of Sentencing Theory* (Oxford, Oxford University Press).

Bownes, IT, O'Gorman, EC and Sayers, A (1991), 'Assault Characteristics and Posttraumatic Stress Disorder in Rape Victims' 83 *Acta Psychiatrica Scandinavica*, 27–30.

Bowyer, L and Dalton, ME (1997), 'Female Victims of Rape and their Genital Injuries' 104 *British Journal of Obstetrics and Gynaecology* 617–20.

Brew-Graves, E and Morgan, L (2015), 'Injuries and Allegations of Oral Rape: A Retrospective Review of Patients Presenting to a London Sexual Assault Referral Centre' 34 *Journal of Forensic and Legal Medicine* 155–58.

Brook, CA, Fiannaca, Justice B, Harvey, Judge D, and Marcus, P (2016), 'A Comparative Look at Plea Bargaining in Australia, Canada, England, New Zealand, and the United States' 57(4) *William & Mary Law Review* 1147–224.

Brooker, C and Tocque, K (2016), 'Mental Health Risk Factors in Sexual Assault: What Should Sexual Assault Referral Centre Staff Be Aware Of?' 40 *Journal of Forensic and Legal Medicine* 28–33.

Brooks, T (2012), *Punishment* (Abingdon, Routledge).

Brooks, T (2011), 'Punishment: Political, Not Moral' 14(3) *New Criminal Law Review: An International and Interdisciplinary Journal* 427–38.

Brooks-Hay, O, Burman, M, and Bradley, L (2019), *Justice Journeys – Informing Policy and Practice Through Lived Experiences of Victim-Survivors of Rape and Serious Sexual Assault* (Glasgow, Scottish Centre for Crime and Justice Research).

Brown, Sheriff AN (2015), *Greens Annotated Acts – Sexual Offences (Scotland) Act 2009* (2nd edn) (Edinburgh, W Green).

Brown, Sheriff AN (2010), *Criminal Evidence and Procedure* (3rd edn) (Edinburgh, Avizandum Publishing).

Brown, G (2019a), 'Four Models of Judicial Reasoning in Sentencing' 3 *Irish Judicial Studies Journal* 55–73.

Brown, G (2019b), 'How Not to Make a Mountain Out of a Molehill – Appellate Guidance on Guilty Plea Discounting in Road Traffic Cases' 157 *Criminal Law Bulletin* 2–5.

Brown, G (2018a), 'Amending a Statutory Charge to a Common Law Offence and the Operation of Section 96 – The Decision in *Ronald v HM Advocate*' 154 *Criminal Law Bulletin* 3–6.

Brown, G (2018b), 'Rape of A Young Child, Undue Leniency, and the Filming of Sexual Offences as an Aggravating Factor in Sentencing – the Crown Sentence Appeal in *HM Advocate v CH*' 151 *Criminal Law Bulletin* 2–7.

Brown, G (2018c), 'The Sentencing Range for Rape – The Decision in *JGC v HM Advocate*' 151 *Criminal Law Bulletin* 7–8.

Brown, G (2018d), 'Some Observations on the Scottish Sentencing Council's Guideline on the "Principles and Purposes of Sentencing"' 156 *Criminal Law Bulletin* 6–7.

Brown, G (2017a), *Criminal Sentencing as Practical Wisdom* (Oxford, Hart Publishing).

Brown, G (2017b), 'Rape of a 14-year-old Intoxicated Complainer by 17-year-old – Application of the Guidance in *Smart* and *McCormick*' 150 *Criminal Law Bulletin* 7–8.

Brown, G (2017c), 'Absolute Discharge for Rape of a Young Child – Some Observations on the Decision in *HM Advocate v Cieslak*' 147 *Criminal Law Bulletin* 1–4.

Brown, G (2017d), 'Guilty Plea Discounting and the Overruling of the Sheriff Appeal Court's First Guideline Judgment – The Decision in *Saini v PF* 150 *Dundee*' *Criminal Law Bulletin* 3–6.

Brown, G (2016a), 'Rape – Court's Reiteration that there is Neither a Minimum Nor A Maximum Sentence for the Offence' 140 *Criminal Law Bulletin* 7–8.

Brown, G (2016b), 'Sentencing Guidance for Rape: The Crown Sentence Appeals in *K* and *B*' 139 *Criminal Law Bulletin* 2–7.

Brown, G (2015a), 'Rape of Intoxicated Complainer – Appellant's Belief that Complainer Consented' 135 *Criminal Law Bulletin* 7–8.

Brown, G (2015b), 'Supply of Heroin – Reference to English Sentencing Guidelines Disapproved' 134 *Criminal Law Bulletin* 6–7.

Brown, G (2015c), 'The Proper Use of English Sentencing Guidelines and Further Observations on the Guilty Plea Discount – *Geddes v HM Advocate* [2015] HCJAC 43' 136 *Criminal Law Bulletin* 3–6.

Brown, G (2014), *Practical Wisdom? A Reconstruction of the Sentencing Task* (PhD Thesis, Edinburgh, University of Edinburgh).

Brown, G (2013), 'Sentence Discounting in England and Scotland – Some Observations on the Use of Comparative Authority in Sentence Appeals' *Criminal Law Review* 674–77.

Brown, G (2010), 'New Guidelines for Sentencing in Cases Involving Child Pornography' 106 *Criminal Law Bulletin* 2–5.

Brown, J M and Horvath, MAH (2009), 'Do You Believe Her and Is It Rape?' in Horvath, MAH and Brown, J (eds), *Rape – Challenging Contemporary Thinking* (Cullompton, Willan).

Brudner, A (2009), *Punishment and Freedom – A Liberal Theory of Penal Justice* (Oxford, Oxford University Press).

Bullock, CM and Beckson, M (2011), 'Male Victims of Sexual Assault: Phenomenology, Psychology, Physiology' 39(2) *The Journal of the American Academy of Psychiatry and the Law* 197–205.

Burchell, J (2005), *Principles of Criminal Law* (3rd edn) (Cape Town, Juta).

Burt, MR (1980), 'Cultural Myths and Supports for Rape' 38(2) *Journal of Personality and Social Psychology* 217–230.

Bussani, M and Mattei, U (2012), 'Diapositives Versus Movies – The Inner Dynamics of the Law and its Comparative Account' in Bussani, M and Mattei, U (eds), *The Cambridge Companion to Comparative Law* (Cambridge, Cambridge University Press).

Butler, J (2007), 'Torture and the Ethics of Photography' 25 *Environment and Planning D: Society and Space* 951–66.

Cahillane, L (2013), 'Need for Sentencing Guidelines in Ireland?' 23(1) *Irish Criminal Law Journal* 11–15.

Cameron, Justice E (2017), 'Imprisoning the Nation: Minimum Sentences in South Africa' Dean's Distinguished Lecture, 19 October 2017, University of the Western Cape Faculty of Law, Cape Town.

Campbell, L (2017), 'Commentary on *DPP v Tiernan*' in Enright, M, McCandless, J and O'Donoghue, A (eds), *Northern/Irish Feminist Judgments – Judges' Troubles and the Gendered Politics of Identity* (Oxford, Hart Publishing).

Campbell, L (2008), 'Reconstituting Sentencing Policy in the Republic of Ireland' 59(3) *Northern Ireland Legal Quarterly* 291–303.

Campbell, L, Ashworth, A, and Redmayne, M (2019), *The Criminal Process* (5th edn) (Oxford, Oxford University Press).

Carline, A, Palmer, E, Burton, M, Kyd, S and Jooman, P (2018), *Assessing the Implementation of the Sentencing Council's Sexual Offences Definitive Guideline*, London, Sentencing Council.

Carloway, Lord (2016), 'Imprisonment in Scotland: Towards a Penological Post-Modernism?' Address delivered at the Scottish Universities Insight Institute, 15 March 2016, Dovecot Studios, Edinburgh.

Carloway, Lord (2014), 'The Purpose of Sentencing – From Beccaria to the OLR and Beyond' 2014 Howard League Scotland Drummond Hunter Memorial Lecture, 22 October 2014, Playfair Library, University of Edinburgh, Edinburgh.

Carloway, Lord (2013), 'Sentencing: Beyond Punishment and Deterrence' 2013 Sacro Lecture, 5 November 2013, Playfair Library, University of Edinburgh, Edinburgh.

Carney, Mr Justice P (2002), 'The Central Criminal Court: A View from the Bench' in O'Mahony, P (ed), *Criminal Justice in Ireland* (Dublin, Institute of Public Administration).

Cattaneo, C, Gibelli, D and Ruspa, M (2014), 'Sexual Abuse' in Madea, B (ed), *Handbook of Forensic Medicine* (Chichester, Wiley-Blackwell).

Cecil, AL (2014), 'Taking Back the Internet: Imposing Civil Liability on Interactive Computer Services in an Attempt to Provide an Adequate Remedy to Victims of Nonconsensual Pornography' 71 *Washington & Lee Law Review* 2513–556.

Chalmers, J (2019), 'Sexual Offences in Scotland' in Rook, P and Ward, R, *Rook and Ward on Sexual Offences Law & Practice – Supplement to the Fifth Edition* (London, Sweet & Maxwell).

Chalmers, J (2010), *The New Law of Sexual Offences in Scotland – Supplement I to Volume II of Gordon's Criminal Law* (Edinburgh, W Green).

Chalmers, J (2004), 'Distress as Corroboration of *Mens Rea*' 23 *Scots Law Times* 141–45.

Chalmers, J, Duff, P, Leverick, F and Melvin, Y (2007a), *An Evaluation of the High Court Reforms Arising from the Criminal Procedure (Amendment) (Scotland) Act 2004*, Edinburgh, Scottish Executive Social Research.

Chalmers, J, Duff, P and Leverick, F (2007b), 'Victim Impact Statements: Can Work, Do Work (For Those Who Bother to Make Them)' *Criminal Law Review* 360–79.

Chalmers, J, Duff, P and Leverick, F (2007c), 'The Pilot Victim Statement Scheme in Scotland' *Scots Law Times (News)* 103–7.

Chalmers, J and Leverick, F (2017), *The Criminal Law of Scotland* (4th edn), Vol. II (Edinburgh, W Green).

Chalton, A (2015), 'Rape Myths and Invisible Crime: The Use of Actuarial Tools to Predict Sexual Recidivism' 2 *Public Interest Law Journal of New Zealand* 19–52.

Chambers, JC, Horvath, MAH and Kelly, L (2013), 'Reconstructing and Sequencing Behaviours in Multiple Perpetrator Rape' 19(3) *Psychology, Crime & Law* 253–75.

Chambers, JC, Horvath, MAH and Kelly, L (2010), 'A Typology of Multiple-Perpetrator Rape' 37(10) *Criminal Justice and Behavior* 1114–139.

Charleton, the Hon Mr Justice and Scott, L (2013), *Throw Away the Key: Public and Judicial Approaches to Sentencing – Towards Reconciliation*. The 2013 Martin Tansey Memorial Lecture, Dublin, Association for Criminal Justice Research and Development.

Chasse, K (2009), 'Plea Bargaining Is Sentencing' 14(1) *Canadian Criminal Law Review* 55–77.

Chennells, R (2009), 'Sentencing: The *Real Rape* Myth' 82 *Agenda* (Gender and the Legal System) 23–38.

Childs, M (2001), 'Review Article – Sexual Autonomy and the Law' 64(2) *Modern Law Review* 309–23.

Christie, MGA (ed) (2005), *Supplement to The Criminal Law of Scotland* (3rd edn) (Edinburgh, W Green).

Christie, MGA (ed) (2001), *The Criminal Law of Scotland* (3rd edn), Vol II (Edinburgh, W Green).

Citron, DK and Franks, MA (2014), 'Criminalizing Revenge Porn' 49 *Wake Forest Law Review* 345–91.

Clarke, A, Moran-Ellis, J and Sleny, J (2002), *Attitudes to Date Rape and Relationship Rape*, Department of Sociology, Guilford, University of Surrey.

Clay-Warner, J and McMahon-Howard, J (2009), 'Rape Reporting: "Classic Rape" and the Behavior of Law' 24(6) *Violence and Victims* 723–43.

Cohen-Lask, M (2016), 'Unbalancing the Burden of Proof' 113(8) *Law Society Gazette* 9.

Cole, J, Logan, TK and Shannon, L (2005), 'Intimate Sexual Victimization Among Women with Protective Orders: Types and Associations of Physical and Mental Health Problems' 20(6) *Violence and Victims* 695–715.

Cole, D and Roberts, JV (2018), 'What's the Point of Pleading Guilty?' 44 *Criminal Reports* 44–58.

Conaghan, J (2019), 'The Essence of Rape' 39(1) *Oxford Journal of Legal Studies* 151–82.

Connell, R (1987), *Gender and Power: Society, the Person and Sexual Politics* (Cambridge, Polity Press).

Connop, V and Petrak, J (2004), 'The Impact of Sexual Assault on Heterosexual Couples' 19(1) *Sexual and Relationship Therapy* 29–38.

Conway, V, Daly, Y and Schweppe, J (2010), *Irish Criminal Justice: Theory, Process and Procedure* (Dublin, Clarus Press).

Cooke, Judge RK (1987), 'The Practical Problems of the Sentencer' in Pennington, DC and Lloyd-Bostock, S (eds), *The Psychology of Sentencing – Approaches to Consistency and Disparity* (Oxford, Centre for Socio-Legal Studies).

Cooper, J (2013), 'Nothing Personal – The Impact of Personal Mitigation at Sentencing Since Creation of the Council' in Ashworth, A and Roberts, JV (eds), *Sentencing Guidelines – Exploring the English Model* (Oxford, Oxford University Press).

Cooper, J (2008), 'The Sentencing Guidelines Council – A Practical Perspective' 4 *Criminal Law Review* 277–86.

Cowan, S. (2019), 'Sense and Sensibilities: A Feminist Critique of Legal Interventions Against Sexual Violence' 23(1) *Edinburgh Law Review* 22–51.

Cowan, S (2010), 'All Change or Business as Usual? Reforming the Law of Rape in Scotland' in McGlynn, C and Munro, VE (eds), *Rethinking Rape Law – International and Comparative Perspectives* (Abingdon, Routledge).

Cowan, S and Hunt, AC (2008), *Mason's Forensic Medicine for Lawyers* (5th edn) (Haywards Heath, Tottel Publishing).

Cowan, S, Kennedy, C and Munro, V (2017), 'Scottish Feminist Judgments Project' 482 *SCOLAG* 252–54.

Coxell, A, King, M, Mezey, G and Gordon, D (1999), 'Lifetime Prevalence, Characteristics, and Associated Problems of Non-consensual Sex in Men: Cross Sectional Survey' 318 *British Medical Journal* 846–50.

Craig, E (2018), *Putting Trials on Trial – Sexual Assault and the Failure of the Legal Profession* (Montreal & Kingston, McGill-Queen's University Press).

Crane, J (2013), 'Interpretation of Non-Genital Injuries in Sexual Assault' 27 *Best Practice & Research Clinical Obstetrics and Gynaecology* 103–11.

Criminal Bar Association of England and Wales (2016), 'A Sentencing Council Consultation Response: On the Reduction in Sentence for a Guilty Plea Guidelines' 2 *Current Sentencing Practice News* 7–9.

Croall, H, Mooney, G and Munro, M (2010), 'Criminal Justice in Contemporary Scotland: Themes, Issues and Questions' in Croall, H, Mooney, G and Munro, M (eds), *Criminal Justice in Scotland* (Abingdon, Willan Publishing).

Cubie, A (2016), *Scots Criminal Law* (4th edn) (Haywards Heath, Bloomsbury Professional).

Cybulska, B (2014a), 'Aftercare: Genitourinary Medicine Issues' in Dalton, M (ed), *Forensic Gynaecology* (Cambridge, Cambridge University Press).

Cybulska, B (2014b), 'Medical Aspects of Sexual Assault' in Rook, P and Ward, R, *Rook and Ward on Sexual Offences Law & Practice – First Supplement to the Fourth Edition* (London, Sweet & Maxwell).

da Silva, T, Woodhams, J and Harkins, L (2014), 'Heterogeneity Within Multiple Perpetrator Rapes: A National Comparison of Lone, Duo, and 3+ Perpetrator Rapes' 26(6) *Sexual Abuse* 503–22.

da Silva, T, Harkins, L and Woodhams, J (2013), 'Multiple Perpetrator Rape – An International Phenomenon' in Horvath, MAH and Woodhams, J (eds), *Handbook on the Study of Multiple Perpetrator Rape – A Multidisciplinary Response to an International Problem* (Abingdon, Routledge).

Dahl, S (1989), 'Acute Response to Rape – A PTSD Variant' 80 *Acta Psychiatrica Scandinavica*, Issue Supplement s 355, 56–62.

Darbyshire, P (2000), 'The Mischief of Plea Bargaining and Sentencing Rewards' *Criminal Law Review* 895–910.

Daly, K (2014), 'Reconceptualizing Sexual Victimization and Justice' in Vanfraechem, I, Pemberton, A, and Mukwiza Ndahinda, F (eds), *Justice for Victims – Perspectives on Rights, Transition and Reconciliation* (Abingdon, Routledge).

Davey, E (2014), 'Sentence Structure' 108(5) *Gazette of the Law Society of Ireland* 30–33.

Davies, M (2002), 'Male Sexual Assault Victims: A Selective Review of the Literature and Implications for Support Services' 7 *Aggression and Violent Behavior* 203–14.

Davies, M and Rogers, P (2006), 'Perceptions of Male Victims in Depicted Sexual Assaults: A Review of the Literature' 11 *Aggression and Violent Behavior* 367–77.

Davies, M, Takala, J-P, and Tyrer, J (2002), 'Sentencing Burglars in England and Finland: A Pilot Study' in Tata, C and Hutton, N (eds), *Sentencing and Society – International Perspectives* (Aldershot, Ashgate).

Dawes, W, Harvey, P, McIntosh, B, Nunney, F and Phillips, A (2011), *Attitudes to Guilty Plea Sentence Reductions (Sentencing Council Research Series 02/11)*, London, Sentencing Council.

DeKeseredy, WS, Muzzatti, SL and Donnermeyer, JF (2014), 'Mad Men in Bib Overalls: Media's Horrification and Pornification of Rural Culture' 22(2) *Critical Criminology* 179–97.

DeKeseredy, WS and Schwartz, MD (2016), 'Thinking Sociologically About Image-Based Sexual Abuse: The Contribution of Male Peer Support Theory' 2(4) *Sexualization, Media & Society* 1–8.

Deane, T (2018), 'Sexual Violence and the Limits of Laws' Powers to Alter Behaviour: The Case of South Africa' 19(2) *Journal of International Women's Studies* 84–103.

Densley, JA, Davis, A and Mason, N (2013), 'Girls and Gangs – Preventing Multiple Perpetrator Rape' in Horvath, MAH and Woodhams, J (eds), *Handbook on the Study of Multiple Perpetrator Rape – A Multidisciplinary Response to an International Problem* (Abingdon, Routledge).

Dingwall, G (2008), 'Deserting Desert? Locating the Present Role of Retributivism in the Sentencing of Adult Offenders' 47(4) *The Howard Journal* 400–10.

Doak, J (2008), *Victims' Rights, Human Rights and Criminal Justice – Reconceiving the Role of Third Parties* (Oxford, Hart Publishing).

Doak, J, Henham, R, and Mitchell, B (2009), 'Victims and the Sentencing Process: Developing Participatory Rights?' 29(4) *Legal Studies* 651–77.

Dodge, A (2016), 'Digitizing Rape Culture: Online Sexual Violence and the Power of the Digital Photograph' 12(1) *Crime Media Culture* 65–82.

Dodge, A and Spencer, DC (2017), 'Online Sexual Violence, Child Pornography or Something Else Entirely? Police Responses to Non-Consensual Intimate Image Sharing among Youth' *Social & Legal Studies*, DOI: 10.1177/0964663917724866.

Dorrian, Lady (2019), 'Scottish Sentencing Council – Development of Guidelines on Sexual Offences' (Letter to Humza Yousaf MSP, Cabinet Secretary for Justice, 13 May 2019). Available at: www.scottishsentencingcouncil.org.uk/media/1969/20190509-letter-from-ljc-to-cab-sec-re-sexual-offences.pdf (accessed 1 September 2019).

Dorrian, Lady (2017), *Reducing the Use of Imprisonment in Sentencing and Penal Decision-Making: A European Conference*, 8 June 2017, Surgeons' Hall, Edinburgh.

Du Bois-Pedain, A (2017), 'In Defence of Substantial Sentencing Discretion' 28 *Criminal Law Forum* 391–435.

Du Mont, J, Miller, K-L, and Myhr, TL (2003), 'The Role of "Real Rape" and "Real Victim" Stereotypes in the Police Reporting Practices of Sexually Assaulted Women' 9(4) *Violence Against Women* 466–86.

Dubber, MD (2006), 'Comparative Criminal Law' in Reimann, M and Zimmerman, R (eds), *The Oxford Handbook of Comparative Law* (New York, Oxford University Press).

Duff, RA (2005), 'Guidance and Guidelines' 105 *Columbia Law Review* 1162–89.

Duncan, AGM (1992), *Green's Glossary of Scottish Legal Terms* (3rd edn) (Edinburgh, W Green).

Easton, S (2011), 'Criminalising the Possession of Extreme Pornography: Sword or Shield?' 75(5) *Journal of Criminal Law* 391–413.

Easton, S and Piper, C (2016), *Sentencing and Punishment – The Quest for Justice* (4th edn) (Oxford, Oxford University Press).

Edwards, I (2013), 'Victims, Sentencing Guidelines, and the Sentencing Council' in Ashworth, A and Roberts, JV (eds), *Sentencing Guidelines – Exploring the English Model* (Oxford, Oxford University Press).

Edwards, I (2004), 'An Ambiguous Participant – The Crime Victim and Criminal Justice Decision-Making' 44(6) *British Journal of Criminology* 967–82.

Edwards, Mr Justice J (2019), 'Sentencing Methodology – Towards Improved Reasoning in Sentencing' 3 *Irish Judicial Studies Journal* 40–54.

Elliott, DM, Mok, DS and Briere, J (2004), 'Adult Sexual Assault: Prevalence, Symptomatology, and Sex Differences in the General Population' 17(3) *Journal of Traumatic Stress* 203–11.

Ellison, L and Munro, VE (2010), 'Jury Deliberation and Complainant Credibility in Rape Trials' in McGlynn, C and Munro, VE (eds), *Rethinking Rape Law – International and Comparative Perspectives* (Abingdon, Routledge).

Ellison, L and Munro, VE (2009a), 'Reacting to Rape: Exploring Mock Jurors' Assessments of Complainant Credibility' 49(2) *British Journal of Criminology* 202–19.

Ellison, L and Munro, VE (2009b), 'Of 'Normal Sex' and 'Real Rape': Exploring the Use of Socio-Sexual Scripts in (Mock) Jury Deliberation' 18(3) *Social & Legal Studies* 291–312.

Enright, M, McCandless, J and O'Donoghue, A (2017), *Northern/Irish Feminist Judgments – Judges' Troubles and the Gendered Politics of Identity* (Oxford, Hart Publishing).

Erez, E (2000), 'Integrating a Victim Perspective in Criminal Justice Through Victim Impact Statements' in Crawford, A and Goodey, J (eds), *Integrating a Victim Perspective within Criminal Justice – International Debates* (Aldershot, Ashgate).

Erez, E (1999), 'Who's Afraid of the Big Bad Victim? Victim Impact Statements as Victim Empowerment *and* Enhancement of Justice' *Criminal Law Review* 545–56.

Erez, E and Rogers, L (1999), 'Victim Impact Statements and Sentencing Outcomes and Processes – The Perspectives of Legal Professionals' 39(2) *British Journal of Criminology*, 216–39.

Estrich, S (1986), 'Rape' 95(6) *The Yale Law Journal* 1087–184.

Fairbairn, J, Bivens, R and Dawson, M (2013), *Sexual Violence and Social Media: Building a Framework for Prevention* (Ottawa, Crime Prevention Ottawa).

Fairbairn, J and Spencer, D (2017), 'Virtualized Violence and Anonymous Juries: Unpacking Steubenville's "Big Red" Sexual Assault Case and the Role of Social Media' *Feminist Criminology*, DOI: 10.1177/1557085116687032.

Feinberg, J (1984), *Harm to Others* (New York, Oxford University Press).

Fenwick, H (1997), 'Procedural 'Rights' of Victims of Crime: Public or Private Ordering of the Criminal Justice Process?' 60(3) *Modern Law Review* 317–33.

Fenwick, H (1992), 'Marital Rights or Partial Immunity' *New Law Journal* 831–32 and 870–71.

Ferguson, PR (2008), 'Reforming Rape and Other Sexual Offences' 12(2) *Edinburgh Law Review* 302–7.

Ferguson, PR (1993), 'Controversial Aspects of the Law of Rape: An Anglo-Scottish Comparison' in Hunter, RF (ed), *Justice and Crime – Essays in Honour of The Right Honourable The Lord Emslie* (Edinburgh, T & T Clark).

Ferguson, PR and McDiarmid, C (2014), *Scots Criminal Law – A Critical Analysis* (2nd edn) (Edinburgh, Edinburgh University Press).

Ferguson, PR and Raitt, FE (2006), 'Reforming the Scots Law of Rape: Redefining the Offence' 10(2) *Edinburgh Law Review* 185–208.

Field, D (2002), 'Plead Early and Convincingly to Avoid Disappointment' 14(2) *Bond Law Review* 251–84.

Finch, E and Munro, VE (2007), 'The Demon Drink and the Demonized Woman: Socio-Sexual Stereotypes and Responsibility Attribution in Rape Trials Involving Intoxicants' 16(4) *Social & Legal Studies* 591–614.

Finch, E and Munro, VE (2005), 'Juror Stereotypes and Blame Attribution in Rape Cases Involving Intoxicants' 45 *British Journal of Criminology* 25–38.

Finkelhor, D and Yllo, K (1985), *License to Rape: Sexual Abuse of Wives* (New York, The Free Press).

Firmin, C (2013), 'Busting the "Gang-Rape" Myth – Girls' Victimisation and Agency in Gang-Associated Sexual Violence' in Horvath, MAH and Woodhams, J (eds), *Handbook on the Study of Multiple Perpetrator Rape – A Multidisciplinary Response to an International Problem* (Abingdon, Routledge).

Flanagan, C (2019), 'Speech by Mr Charles Flanagan T.D. on the Judicial Council Bill 2017' 4 July 2019. Available at: www.justice.ie/en/JELR/Pages/SP19000183 (accessed 1 September 2019).

Foster, S (2010), 'Possession of Extreme Pornographic Images, Public Protection and Human 15(1) Rights' *Coventry Law Journal* 21–27.

Fox, R (1994), 'The Meaning of Proportionality in Sentencing' 19 *Melbourne Law Review* 489 511.
Foy, J (2018), 'Proportionality in Sentence Appeals: Towards a Guiding Principle of Appellate Review' 23(1) *Canadian Criminal Law Review* 77–95.
Franklin, K (2013), 'Masculinity, Status, and Power – Implicit Messages in Western Media Discourse on High-Profile Cases of Multiple Perpetrator Rape' in Horvath, MAH and Woodhams, J (eds), *Handbook on the Study of Multiple Perpetrator Rape – A Multidisciplinary Response to an International Problem* (Abingdon, Routledge).
Franklin, K (2004), 'Enacting Masculinity: Antigay Violence and Group Rape as Participatory Theater' *Sexuality Research & Social Policy*, Vol. 1(2), pp. 25–40.
Freed, D (1992), 'Federal Sentencing in the Wake of Guidelines: Unacceptable Limits on the Discretion of Sentencers' 101(8) *Yale Law Journal* 1681–754.
Freer, E (2019), *A Practitioner's Guide to Ancillary Orders in Criminal Courts* (Haywards Heath, Bloomsbury Professional).
Freiberg, A (2016), 'The Road Well Traveled in Australia: Ignoring the Past, Condemning the Future' 45(1) *Crime and Justice* 419–57.
Freiberg, A (2014), *Fox & Freiberg's Sentencing – State and Federal Law in Victoria* (3rd edn) (Pyrmont, Thomson Reuters).
Freiberg, A (2002), 'What's it Worth? A Cross-Jurisdictional Comparison of Sentence Severity' in Tata, C and Hutton, N (eds), *Sentencing and Society – International Perspectives* (Aldershot, Ashgate).
French, Justice C (2015), "The Role of the Judge in Sentencing: From Port-Soaked Reactionary to Latte Liberal' – The New Zealand Law Foundation Ethel Benjamin Commemorative Address 2015' 33(1) *Otago Law Review* 33–47.
Gallagher, C (2018), 'Appeal Judges Set Down Sentencing Guidelines for Burglary and Robbery' *The Irish Times*, 1 May 2018. Available at: www.irishtimes.com/news/crime-and-law/appeal-judges-set-down-sentencing-guidelines-for-burglary-and-robbery-1.3479375 (accessed 1 September 2019).
Gane, C (1992), *Sexual Offences* (Edinburgh, Butterworths).
Gardner, J (2018), 'The Opposite of Rape' 38(1) *Oxford Journal of Legal Studies* 48–70.
Gardner, J (2017), 'Reasonable Reactions to the Wrongness of Rape' 29 *The Denning Law Journal* 3–16.
Gardner, J (2012), 'In Defence of *Offences and Defences*' 4 *Jerusalem Review of Legal Studies* 110–28.
Gardner, J (2007a), 'Preface' in Gardner, J, *Offences and Defences – Selected Essays in the Philosophy of Criminal Law* (Oxford, Oxford University Press).
Gardner, J (2007b), 'The Wrongness of Rape' in Gardner, J, *Offences and Defences – Selected Essays in the Philosophy of Criminal Law* (Oxford, Oxford University Press).
Gardner, J (2007c), 'Reply to Critics' in Gardner, J, *Offences and Defences – Selected Essays in the Philosophy of Criminal Law* (Oxford, Oxford University Press).
Gardner, J and Shute, S (2000), 'The Wrongness of Rape' in Horder, J (ed), *Oxford Essays in Jurisprudence – Fourth Series* (Oxford, Oxford University Press).
Garland, D (1999), 'Preface' in Duff, P and Hutton, N (eds), *Criminal Justice in Scotland* (Aldershot, Dartmouth).
Gerry, F (2011a), 'Rape is Rape and Sentencing is Hard' 175(22) *Criminal Law & Justice Weekly* 314.
Gerry, F (2011b), 'Judges Mete Out Some Sex Ed' 175(30) *Criminal Law & Justice Weekly* 454.
Gerry, F and Sjölin, C (2012), 'A Matter of Perception' *Counsel*, May 26–27.
Gill, Lord (2016), *The Scottish Legal System – What Next?*, The Judicial Institute for Scotland Lecture, Edinburgh, Parliament Hall, 14 July 2016.
Gillespie, AA (2010), 'Sentences for Offences Relating to Indecent Photographs' 74(6) *Journal of Criminal Law* 510–15.
Girardin, B, Faugno, D K, and Howitt, J (2003), 'Adult Sexual Assaults: Practical Management' in Payne-James, J, Busuttil, A and Smock, W (eds), *Forensic Medicine: Clinical and Pathological Aspects* (London, Greenwich Medical Media).
Godden, NM (2013), *Seeking Justice for Victim-survivors: Unconventional Legal Responses to Rape*, Durham theses, Durham University. Available at: Durham E-Theses Online: http://etheses.dur.ac.uk/6379/ (accessed 1 September 2019).

Godden, N M (2009), *Rape and the Civil Law: An Alternative Route to Justice*, Durham theses, Durham University. Available at: Durham E-Theses Online: http://etheses.dur.ac.uk/252/ (accessed 1 September 2019).

Goodall, W (2014), *Sentencing Consistency in the New Zealand District Courts* (PhD thesis, Wellington, Victoria University of Wellington).

Gordon, Sir GH (2017), 'Commentary to *Gubinas and Radavicius v HM Advocate* 2017 SCCR 463' *Scottish Criminal Case Reports* 484.

Gordon, Sir GH (2003), 'Commentary to *HM Advocate v Shearer* 2003 SCCR 657' *Scottish Criminal Case Reports* 663.

Gotell, L (2010), 'Canadian Sexual Assault Law – Neoliberalism and the Erosion of Feminist-Inspired Law Reforms' in McGlynn, C and Munro, VE (eds), *Rethinking Rape Law – International and Comparative Perspectives* (Abingdon, Routledge).

Graham, R (2006), 'Male Rape and the Careful Construction of the Male Victim' 15(2) *Social & Legal Studies* 187–208.

Grande, E (2012), 'Comparative Criminal Justice' in Bussani, M and Mattei, U (eds), *The Cambridge Companion to Comparative Law* (Cambridge, Cambridge University Press).

Grubb, A and Turner, E. (2012), 'Attribution of Blame in Rape Cases: A Review of the Impact of Rape Myth Acceptance, Gender Role Conformity and Substance Use on Victim Blaming' 17 *Aggression and Violent Behaviour* 443–52.

Guilfoyle, E (2019), 'Before Sentencing Guidelines, We Need Sentencing Information' *Irish Legal News*, 12 June 2019. Available at: www.irishlegal.com/article/dr-eoin-guilfoyle-before-sentencing-guidelines-we-need-sentencing-information (accessed 1 September 2019).

Hall, G (2014), *Sentencing Law and Practice* (3rd edn) (Wellington, LexisNexis New Zealand).

Hall, G (2007a), 'Sentencing' in Tolmie, J and Brookbanks, W (eds), *Criminal Justice in New Zealand* (Wellington, LexisNexis New Zealand).

Hall, G (2007b), *Sentencing: 2007 Reforms in Context* (Wellington, LexisNexis New Zealand).

Hall, M (2010), *Victims and Policy Making – A Comparative Perspective* (Abingdon, Willan Publishing).

Hall, M (2009), *Victims of Crime – Policy and Practice in Criminal Justice* (Abingdon, Willan Publishing).

Hall, J A and Moore, C B T (2008), 'Drug Facilitated Sexual Assault – A Review' 15 *Journal of Forensic and Legal Medicine* 291–97.

Hammond, The Hon Justice G (2007), 'Sentencing: Intuitive Synthesis or Structured Discretion?' *New Zealand Law Review* 211–34.

Hampton, J (1999), 'Defining Wrong and Defining Rape' in Burgess-Jackson, K (ed), *A Most Detestable Crime: New Philosophical Essays on Rape* (New York, Oxford University Press).

Harris, L (2017), 'Commentary to *R v Thelwall* [2017] Crim L R 240' *Criminal Law Review*, 242–43.

Harris, L (2016), 'Commentary to *Attorney General's Reference (Nos 49 and 50 of 2015) (R v Bakht)* [2016] Crim L R 72' *Criminal Law Review*, 73.

Harris, R (2016), 'Could the Guilty Plea Write Out the Role of the Defence?' 160 *Solicitors' Journal* 15.

Harris, L (2015a), 'Commentary to *R v DJ* [2015] Crim L R 650' *Criminal Law Review*, 653–54.

Harris, L (2015b), 'Commentary to *R v DO* [2015] Crim L R 379' *Criminal Law Review*, 379–80.

Harris, L (2015c), 'Commentary to *Attorney General's Reference (No 7 of 2015) (R v F)* [2015] Crim L R 827' *Criminal Law Review* 828–29.

Harris, L (2015d), 'Aggravation and Mitigation: Have We Lost Our Way?' *Sentencing News*, Issue 1, 7–9.

Harris, L (2013), 'The New Sentencing Council Sexual Offences Definitive Guideline' 177(52) *Criminal Law & Justice Weekly* 847–48.

Harris, L and Gerry, F (2013), 'A Behaviour-Based Approach to Sentencing for Sexual Offences' 177(15) *Criminal Law & Justice Weekly* 239–42.

Hauffe, S and Porter, L (2009), 'An Interpersonal Comparison of Lone and Group Rape Offences' 15(5) *Psychology, Crime & Law* 469–91.

Heger, AH (2000), 'Sexual Violence' in Mason, JK and Purdue, BN (eds), *The Pathology of Trauma* (3rd edn) (London, Arnold).

Heidensohn, F and Gelsthorpe, L (2007), 'Gender and Crime' in Maguire, M, Morgan, R and Reiner, R (eds), *The Oxford Handbook of Criminology* (4th edn) (Oxford, Oxford University Press).

Henham, R (2012), *Sentencing and the Legitimacy of Trial Justice* (Abingdon, Routledge).
Henham, R (1995), 'Sentencing Policy and the Role of the Court of Appeal' 34(3) *The Howard Journal* 218–27.
Henham, R (1994), 'Attorney-General's References and Sentencing Policy' *Criminal Law Review*, 499–512.
Henry, N and Powell, A (2016a), 'Sexual Violence in the Digital Age: The Scope and Limits of Criminal Law' 25(4) *Social & Legal Studies* 397–418.
Henry, N and Powell, A (2016b), 'Technology-Facilitated Sexual Violence: A Literature Review of Empirical Research' *Trauma, Violence & Abuse* 1–14.
Henry, N and Powell, A (2015a), 'Embodied Harms: Gender, Shame, and Technology-Facilitated Sexual Violence' 21(6) *Violence Against Women* 758–79.
Henry, N and Powell, A (2015b), 'Beyond the "Sext": Technology-Facilitated Sexual Violence and Harassment Against Adult Women' 48(1) *The Australian and New Zealand Journal of Criminology* 104–18.
Henry, N and Powell, A (2014), 'The Dark Side of the Virtual World – Towards a Digital Sexual Ethics' in Henry, N and Powell, A (eds), *Preventing Sexual Violence – Interdisciplinary Approaches to Overcoming a Rape Culture* (Basingstoke, Palgrave Macmillan).
Henry, N, Powell, A and Flynn, A (2017), *Not Just 'Revenge Pornography': Australians' Experiences of Image-Based Abuse – A Summary Report* (Melbourne: RMIT University).
Hewton, T (2010), 'Instinctive Synthesis, Structured Reasoning, and Punishment Guidelines: Judicial Discretion in the Modern Sentencing Process' 31(1) *The Adelaide Law Review* 79–93.
Hilden, M, Schei, B and Sidenius, K (2005), 'Genitoanal Injury in Adult Female Victims of Sexual Assault' 154 *Forensic Science International* 200–5.
Hillman, RJ, Tomlinson, D, McMillan, A, French, PD and Harris JRW (1990), 'Sexual Assault of Men: A Series' 66 *Genitourinary Medicine* 247–50.
HM Crown Prosecution Service Inspectorate (2007), *Without Consent – A Report on the Joint Review of the Investigation and Prosecution of Rape Offences*, London, Her Majesty's Inspectorate of Constabulary.
Hodge, Lord (2016), *Upholding the Rule of Law: How We Preserve Judicial Independence in the United Kingdom*, Address to the Lincoln's Inn Denning Society, 7 November 2016.
Hodgson, J (2000), 'Comparing Legal Cultures: The Comparativist as Participant Observer' in Nelken, D (ed), *Contrasting Criminal Justice – Getting from Here to There* (Aldershot, Ashgate).
Hoffman-Wanderer, Y (2008), 'Sentencing and Management of Sexual Offenders' in Artz, L and Smythe, D (eds), *Should We Consent? Rape Law Reform in South Africa* (Cape Town, Juta).
Hogarth, J (1971), *Sentencing as a Human Process* (Toronto, University of Toronto Press).
Holmes, MM, Resnick, HS, Kilpatrick, DG and Best, CL (1996), 'Rape-related Pregnancy: Estimates and Descriptive Characteristics from a National Sample of Women' 175 *American Journal of Obstetrics and Gynecology* 320–24.
Homans, G C (1984), 'Review of *A Treatise on Social Theory: Vol. 1, The Methodology of Social Theory* by W G Runciman' 13 *Theory and Society* 137–40.
Home Office (2001), *Making Punishments Work – Report of a Review of the Sentencing Framework for England and Wales*, London, Home Office.
Horvath, MAH and Brown, J (2009), 'Setting the Scene: Introduction to Understanding Rape' in Horvath, MAH and Brown, J (eds), *Rape – Challenging Contemporary Thinking* (Cullompton, Willan).
Horvath, MAH and Brown, J (2007), 'Alcohol as Drug of Choice: Is Drug-Assisted Rape a Misnomer?' 13(5) *Psychology, Crime & Law* 417–29.
Horvath, MAH and Gray, JM (2013), 'Multiple Perpetrator Rape in the Courtroom' in Horvath, MAH and Woodhams, J (eds), *Handbook on the Study of Multiple Perpetrator Rape – A Multidisciplinary Response to an International Problem* (Abingdon, Routledge).
Horvath, MAH and Kelly, L (2009), 'Multiple Perpetrator Rape: Naming an Offence and Initial Research Findings' 15(1) *Journal of Sexual Aggression* 83–96.

Hough, M, Jacobson, J and Millie, A (2003), *The Decision to Imprison – Sentencing and the Prison Population* (London, Prison Reform Trust).

Hoyle, C (2012), 'Victims, The Criminal Process, and Restorative Justice' in Maguire, M, Morgan, R and Reiner, R (eds), *The Oxford Handbook of Criminology* (5th edn) (Oxford, Oxford University Press).

Huckle, P L (1995), 'Male Rape Victims Referred to a Forensic Psychiatric Service' 35(3) *Journal of Interpersonal Violence* 187–92.

Hume, D (1797), *Commentaries on the Law of Scotland, Respecting Crimes (with a Supplement by Benjamin Robert Bell, Esq.)*, Vol I (1986 Reprint) (Edinburgh, Law Society of Scotland).

Hunter, J (2016), 'Rape Law, Past Wrongs and Legal Fictions: Telling Law's Story with Integrity' in Hunter, J, Roberts, P, Young, S N M, and Dixon, D (eds), *The Integrity of Criminal Process – From Theory Into Practice* (Oxford, Hart).

Hutton, N (2013), 'The Definitive Guideline on Assault Offences – The Performance of Justice' in Ashworth, A and Roberts, J V (eds), *Sentencing Guidelines – Exploring the English Model* (Oxford, Oxford University Press).

Hutton, N (2008), 'The Sentencing Commission for Scotland' in Freiberg, A and Gelb, K (eds), *Penal Populism, Sentencing Councils and Sentencing Policy* (Cullompton, Willan Publishing).

Hutton, N (1999), 'Sentencing in Scotland' in Duff, P and Hutton, N (eds), *Criminal Justice in Scotland* (Aldershot, Dartmouth).

Hutton, N and Tata, C (2010), 'A Sentencing Exception? Changing Sentencing Policy in Scotland' 22(4) *Federal Sentencing Reporter* 272–78.

Ingemann-Hansen, O, Sabroe, S, Brink, O, Knudsen, M, and Charles, AV (2009), 'Characteristics of Victims and Assaults of Sexual Violence – Improving Inquiries and Prevention' 16 *Journal of Forensic and Legal Medicine* 182–88.

Inspectorate of Prosecution in Scotland (2017), 'Thematic Review of the Investigation and Prosecution of Sexual Crimes' (Glasgow, Inspectorate of Prosecution in Scotland).

Jacobson, J and Hough, M (2007), *Mitigation: The Role of Personal Factors in Sentencing* (London, Prison Reform Trust).

Jewkes, R and Abrahams, N (2002), 'The Epidemiology of Rape and Sexual Coercion in South Africa: An Overview' 55 *Social Science & Medicine* 1231–44.

Jewkes, R, Sikweyiya, Y, Morrell, R, and Dunkle, K (2011), 'Gender Inequitable Masculinity and Sexual Entitlement in Rape Perpetration South Africa: Findings of a Cross-Sectional Study' 6(12) *Plos One* 1–11.

Jewkes, R, Sikweyiya, Y, Morrell, R, and Dunkle, K (2010), 'Why, When and How Men Rape' 34 *South Africa Crime Quarterly* (December) 23–31.

Jewkes, R, Dunkle, K, Koss, MP, Levin, JB, Nduna, M, Jama, N, and Sikweyiya, Y (2006), 'Rape Perpetration by Young, Rural South African Men: Prevalence, Patterns and Risk Factors' 63 *Social Science & Medicine* 2949–961.

Jewkes, R, Penn-Kekana, L, and Rose-Junius, H (2005), '"If They Rape Me, I Can't Blame Them": Reflections on Gender in the Social Context of Child Rape in South Africa and Namibia' 61 *Social Science & Medicine* 1809–20.

Jewkes, R, Levin, J, Mbananga, N and Bradshaw, D (2002), 'Rape of Girls in South Africa' 359 *The Lancet* 319–20.

Jewkes, R and Sikweyiya, Y (2013), 'Streamlining – Understanding Gang Rape in South Africa' in Horvath, MAH and Woodhams, J (eds), *Handbook on the Study of Multiple Perpetrator Rape – A Multidisciplinary Response to an International Problem* (Abingdon, Routledge).

Jina, R and Thomas, L S (2013), 'Health Consequences of Sexual Violence Against Women' 27 *Best Practice & Research Clinical Obstetrics and Gynaecology* 15–26.

Jones, TH (1989), 'Marital Rape' *Scots Law Times (News)*, 279–82.

Jones, TH and Taggart, I (2015), *Criminal Law* (6th edn) (Edinburgh, W Green).

Jones, JS, Wynn, BN, Kroeze, B, Dunnuck, C and Rossman, L (2004), 'Comparison of Sexual Assaults by Strangers Versus Known Assailants in a Community-Based Population' 22 *American Journal of Emergency Medicine* 454–59.

Jordan, J (2008), *Serial Survivors – Women's Narratives of Surviving Rape* (Sydney, The Federation Press).

Judge, Lord (2015), 'The Sentencing Decision' in Judge, I, *The Safest Shield – Lectures, Speeches and Essays* (Oxford, Hart Publishing).

Judge, Lord (2014a), 'Publication Review – *Sentencing Guidelines: Exploring the English Model*' 130 *The Law Quarterly Review* 678–81.

Judge, Sir I (2014b), 'Dr David Thomas QC' 178(26) *Criminal Law and Justice Weekly* 395.

Judge, Sir I (2009), 'David Thomas' in Walston, C, Bottoms, A, Eisner, M, and Lösel, F (eds), *Challenging Crime – A Portrait of the Cambridge Institute of Criminology* (London, Third Millennium Publishing).

Judge, Sir I (2007), 'Current Sentencing Issues' address delivered at Lincoln's Inn, 29 October 2007, London.

JUSTICE (1993), *Negotiated Justice – A Closer Look at the Implications of Plea Bargains* (London, JUSTICE).

Kalichman, SC, Benotsch, E, Rompa, D, Gore-Felton, C, Austin, J, Luke, W, DiFonzo, K, Buckles, J, Kyomugisha, F and Simpson, D (2001), 'Unwanted Sexual Experiences and Sexual Risks in Gay and Bisexual Men: Associations Among Revictimization, Substance Use, and Psychiatric Symptoms' 38(1) *The Journal of Sex Research* 1–9.

Kapp, C (2004), 'Rape on Trial in South Africa' 367 *The Lancet* 718–19.

Kelly, D (1993), *Criminal Sentences* (Edinburgh, T&T Clark).

Kelly, L (2013), 'Foreword' in Horvath, MAH and Woodhams, J (eds), *Handbook on the Study of Multiple Perpetrator Rape – A Multidisciplinary Response to an International Problem* (Abingdon, Routledge).

Kelly, L (2008), 'Contradictions and Paradoxes: International Patterns of, and Responses to, Reported Rape Cases' in Letherby, G, Williams, K, Birch, P and Cain, M (eds), *Sex as Crime?* (Cullompton, Willan).

Kemp, G, Walker, S, Palmer, R, Badqwa, D, Gevers, C, Leslie, B, and Steynberg, A (2018), *Criminal Law in South Africa* (3rd edn) (Cape Town, Oxford University Press).

Kennefick, L and Fennell, C (2017), '*The People (at the Suit of the Director of Public Prosecutions) v Edward Tiernan*' in Enright, M, McCandless, J and O'Donoghue, A (eds), *Northern/Irish Feminist Judgments – Judges' Troubles and the Gendered Politics of Identity* (Oxford, Hart Publishing).

Kerr, E, Cottee, C, Chowdhury, R, Jawad, R and Welch, J (2003), 'The Haven: A Pilot Referral Centre in London for Cases of Serious Sexual Assault' 110 *British Journal of Obstetrics and Gynaecology* 267–71.

Kift, S (1995), 'That All Rape is Rape Even if Not by a Stranger' 4(1) *Griffith Law Review* 60–111.

Kilcommins, S, Leahy, S, Moore Walsh, K and Spain, E (2018), *The Victim in the Irish Criminal Process* (Manchester, Manchester University Press).

Kilcommins, S, O'Donnell, I, O'Sullivan, E and Vaughan, B (2004), *Crime, Punishment and the Search for Order in Ireland* (Dublin, Institute of Public Administration).

Kilpatrick, DG, Saunders, BE, Veronen, LJ, Best, CL and Von, JM (1987), 'Criminal Victimization: Lifetime Prevalence, Reporting to Police, and Psychological Impact' 33(4) *Crime & Delinquency* 479–89.

Kimerling, R, Rellini, A, Kelly, V, Judson, PL and Learman, LA (2002), 'Gender Differences in Victim and Crime Characteristics of Sexual Assaults' 17(5) *Journal of Interpersonal Violence* 526–32.

King, M B (1990), 'Male Rape – Victims Need Sensitive Management' 301 *British Medical Journal*1345–46.

King, M, Coxell, A and Mezey, G (2000), 'The Prevalence and Characteristics of Male Sexual Assault' in Mezey, GC and King, MB (eds), *Male Victims of Sexual Assault* (2nd edn) (Oxford, Oxford University Press).

Knight, B (1992), *Legal Aspects of Medical Practice* (5th edn) (Edinburgh, Churchill Livingstone).

Koffman, L (2006), 'The Rise and Fall of Proportionality: The Failure of the Criminal Justice Act 1991' *Criminal Law Review*, 281–99.

Koss, MP, Goodman, LA, Browne, A, Fitzgerald, LF, Keita, GP and Russo, NF (1994), *No Safe Haven: Male Violence Against Women at Home, at Work, and in the Community* (Washington, American Psychological Association).

Krasnostein, S (2015), *Pursuing Consistency – The Effect of Different Reforms on Unjustified Disparity in Individualised Sentencing Frameworks* (PhD thesis, Melbourne, Monash University).

Krasnostein, S and Freiberg, A (2014), 'Sentencing Guideline Schemes Across the United States and Beyond' in *Oxford Handbooks Online: Criminology and Criminal Justice* (Oxford, Oxford University Press).

Krasnostein, S and Freiberg, A (2013), 'Pursuing Consistency in an Individualistic Sentencing Framework: If You Know Where You're Going, How Do You Know When You've Got There?' *Law and Contemporary Problems*, No 1, 265–88.

Kubista, NJ (2005), '"Substantial and Compelling Circumstances": Sentencing of Rapists Under the Mandatory Minimum Sentencing Scheme' 18(1) *South African Journal of Criminal Justice* 77–86.

Lacey, N (1998), 'Unspeakable Subjects, Impossible Rights: Sexuality, Integrity and Criminal Law' in Lacey, N, *Unspeakable Subjects – Feminist Essays in Legal and Social Theory* (Oxford, Hart Publishing).

Lacey, N and Wells, C (1998), *Reconstructing Criminal Law – Text and Materials* (2nd edn) (London, Butterworths).

Lambine, M (2013), 'Numbers Matter – Characteristic Differences Between Lone, Duo and 3+ Group Rapes' in Horvath, MAH and Woodhams, J (eds), *Handbook on the Study of Multiple Perpetrator Rape – A Multidisciplinary Response to an International Problem* (Abingdon, Routledge).

Larcombe, W (2011), 'Falling Rape Conviction Rates: (Some) Feminist Aims and Measures for Rape Law' 19 *Feminist Legal Studies* 27–45.

Larsen, M and Hilden, M (2016), 'Male Victims of Sexual Assault: 10 Years' Experience from a Danish Assault Center' 43 *Journal of Forensic and Legal Medicine* 8–11.

Lavi, S (2011), 'Justice, Plurality, and Criminal Law: A Review of Alan Brudner's *Punishment and Freedom: A Liberal Theory of Penal Law*' 14(3) *New Criminal Law Review: An International and Interdisciplinary Journal* 439–48.

Le Roux-Kemp, A (2016), 'Criminal Procedure and Sentencing' *Annual Survey of South African Law – 2014* 316–63 (Claremont, Juta).

Leahy, S (2019), 'Sexual Offences Law in Ireland – Countering Gendered Stereotypes in Adjudications of Consent in Rape Trials' in Black, L and Dunne, P (eds), *Law and Gender in Modern Ireland – Critique and Reform* (Oxford, Hart Publishing).

Leahy, S (2018), 'Section 5 of the Criminal Law (Rape) (Amendment) Act 1990' in Rackley, E and Auchmuty, R (eds), *Women's Legal Landmarks – Celebrating the History of Women and Law in the UK and Ireland* (Oxford, Hart Publishing).

Leahy, S (2014), 'Bad Laws or Bad Attitudes? Assessing the Impact of Societal Attitudes Upon the Conviction Rate for Rape in Ireland' 14(1) *Irish Journal of Applied Social Studies* 18–29.

Leahy, S and Fitzgerald O'Reilly, M (2018), *Sexual Offending in Ireland – Laws, Procedures and Punishment* (Dublin, Clarus Press).

Lees, S (2002), *Carnal Knowledge – Rape on Trial* (London, The Women's Press).

Leverick, F (2014), 'Sentence Discounting for Guilty Pleas: An Argument for Certainty Over Discretion' *Criminal Law Review*, 338–49.

Leverick, F (2013), 'The Rise and Fall of the Sentence Discount' 38 *Scots Law Times (News)*, 259–64.

Leverick, F (2012), 'Sentence Discounting for Guilty Pleas: A Question of Guidelines' 16(2) *Edinburgh Law Review* 233–38.

Leverick, F (2008a), 'Sentencing Following a Guilty Plea: *Spence v HM Advocate* and *Leonard v Houston*' *Scots Law Times (News)*, 43–7.

Leverick, F (2008b), 'Sentencing Guidelines under Section 118(7): *Lin v HM Advocate* and *Spence v HM Advocate*' 12(2) *Edinburgh Law Review* 307–12.

Leverick, F (2004), 'Tensions and Balances, Costs and Rewards: the Sentence Discount in Scotland' 8 *Edinburgh Law Review* 360–88.

Leveson, Lord Justice (2013a), *The Parmoor Lecture – Achieving Consistency in Sentencing*, London, 24 October 2013.

Leveson, Lord Justice (2013b), 'Foreword' in Sentencing Council for England and Wales, *Sexual Offences – Response to Consultation*, London, Sentencing Council.

Light, D and Monk-Turner, A (2009), 'Circumstances Surrounding Male Sexual Assault and Rape – Findings from the National Violence Against Women Survey' 24(11) *Journal of Interpersonal Violence* 1849–58.

Lindsay, M, Booth, JM, Messing, JT and Thaller, J (2016), 'Experiences of Online Harassment Among Emerging Adults: Emotional Reactions and the Mediating Role of Fear' 31(19) *Journal of Interpersonal Violence* 3174–95.

Lodrick, Z and Hosier, K (2014), 'Aftercare: Psychological Issues' in Dalton, M (ed), *Forensic Gynaecology* (Cambridge, Cambridge University Press).

Lothian, A (2004), 'On Sentencing' 49(2) *Journal of the Law Society of Scotland* 44–45.

Lovett, J and Horvath, MAH (2009), 'Alcohol and Drugs in Rape and Sexual Assault' in Horvath, MAH and Brown, J (eds), *Rape – Challenging Contemporary Thinking* (Cullompton, Willan).

Lovegrove, A (2010), 'The Sentencing Council, the Public's Sense of Justice and Personal Mitigation' *Criminal Law Review*, 906–23.

MacDonald, DR (1989), 'Marital Rape' *Juridical Review*, 208–10.

Mack, K and Roach Anleu, S (1997), 'Sentence Discount for a Guilty Plea: Time for a New Look' 1(2) *Flinders Journal of Law Reform* 123–43.

Mackenzie, G (2005), *How Judges Sentence* (Sydney, The Federation Press).

Mackenzie, G (2001), *A Question of Balance: A Study of Judicial Methodology, Perceptions and Attitudes in Sentencing* (PhD Thesis, Sydney, University of New South Wales).

Maguire, N (2016), 'Sentencing' in Healy, D, Hamilton, C, Daly, Y and Butler, M (eds), *The Routledge Handbook of Irish Criminology* (Abingdon, Routledge).

Maguire, N (2012), 'Consistency in Sentencing' 2 *Judicial Studies Institute Journal* 14–54.

Maguire, N (2008), *Sentencing in Ireland: An Exploration of the Views, Rationales and Sentencing Practices of District and Circuit Court Judges* (PhD Thesis, Dublin, Trinity College).

Maguire, W, Goodall, E and Moore, T (2009), 'Injury in Adult Female Sexual Assault Complainants and Related Factors' 142 *European Journal of Obstetrics & Gynecology and Reproductive Biology* 149–53.

Mallett, S J (2015), 'Judicial Discretion in Sentencing: A Justice System that is No Longer Just?' 46(2) *Victoria University of Wellington Law Review* 533–71.

Manson, A (2001), *The Law of Sentencing* (Toronto, Irwin Law).

Manson, A, Healy, P, Trotter, G, Roberts, J and Ives, D (2016), *Sentencing and Penal Policy in Canada – Cases, Materials and Commentary* (3rd edn) (Toronto, Emond Montgomery Publications).

Martin, EK, Taft, CT, and Resick, PA (2007), 'A Review of Marital Rape' 12 *Aggression and Violent Behaviour* 329–47.

Martín Alcoff, L (2018), *Rape and Resistance* (Cambridge, Polity Press).

Maslen, H (2015), 'Penitence and Persistence: How Should Sentencing Factors Interact?' in Roberts, JV (ed), *Exploring Sentencing Practice in England and Wales* (Basingstoke, Palgrave Macmillan).

Maslen, H and Roberts, JV (2013), 'Remorse and Sentencing – An Analysis of Sentencing Guidelines and Sentencing Practice' in Ashworth, A and Roberts, JV (eds), *Sentencing Guidelines – Exploring the English Model* (Oxford, Oxford University Press).

Mason, F (2014), 'Psychological Effects of Rape and Serious Sexual Assault' in Rook, P and Ward, R, *Rook and Ward on Sexual Offences Law & Practice – First Supplement to the Fourth Edition* (London, Sweet & Maxwell).

Mason, F (2013), 'Response to Consultation' in Sentencing Council for England and Wales, *Sexual Offences – Response to Consultation*, London, Sentencing Council.

Mason, F and Lodrick, Z (2013), 'Psychological Consequences of Sexual Assault' 27(1) *Best Practice & Research – Clinical Obstetrics and Gynaecology* 27–37.

Mason, F and Murphy, P (2016), 'Psychological Effects of Rape and Serious Sexual Assault' in Rook, P and Ward, R, *Rook and Ward on Sexual Offences Law & Practice* (5th edn) (London, Sweet & Maxwell).

Mathias, D (2010), 'Judging or Calculating?' *Criminal Law Casebook – Developments in Leading Appellate Courts*, Web Log. Available at: http://nzcriminallaw.blogspot.co.uk/2010_12_01_archive.html (accessed 1 September 2019).

Maw, A, Womersley, G, and O'Sullivan, M (2008), 'The Psycho-Social Impact of Rape and its Implications for Expert Evidence in Rape Trials' in Artz, L and Smythe, D (eds), *Should We Consent? – Rape Law Reform in South Africa* (Cape Town, Juta).

McAra, L (2008), 'Crime, Criminology and Criminal Justice in Scotland' 5(4) *European Journal of Criminology* 481–504.

McCall-Hosenfeld, JS, Freund, KM, and Liebschutz, JM (2009), 'Factors Associated with Sexual Assault and Time to Presentation' 48 *Preventative Medicine* 593–95.

McCandless, J, Enright, M and O'Donoghue, A (2017), 'Introduction: Troubling Judgment' in Enright, M, McCandless, J and O'Donoghue, A (eds), *Northern/Irish Feminist Judgments – Judges' Troubles and the Gendered Politics of Identity* (Oxford, Hart Publishing).

McClellan, Justice P (2012), 'Sentencing in the 21st Century'. Paper presented at the Crown Prosecutors' Conference, 10 April 2012, Pokolbin, Hunter Valley.

McLean, I A (2013), 'The Male Victim of Sexual Assault' 27 *Best Practice & Research Clinical Obstetrics and Gynaecology* 39–46.

McLean, IA, Balding, V and White, C (2005), 'Further Aspects of Male-on-Male Rape and Sexual Assault in Greater Manchester' 45(3) *Medicine, Science and the Law* 1–8.

McLean, IA, Balding, V and White, C (2004), 'Forensic Medical Aspects of Male-on-Male Rape and Sexual Assault in Greater Manchester' 44(2) *Medicine, Science and the Law* 165–69.

McLean, I, Roberts, SA, White, C, and Paul, S (2011), 'Female Genital Injuries Resulting from Consensual and Non-Consensual Vaginal Intercourse' 204 *Forensic Science International* 27–33.

McConville, M and Marsh, L (2016), 'Factory Farming and State-Induced Guilty Pleas' in Hunter, J, Roberts, P, Young, SNM and Dixon, D (eds), *The Integrity of Criminal Process – From Theory into Practice* (Oxford, Hart Publishing).

McConville, M and Marsh, L (2014), *Criminal Judges – Legitimacy, Courts and State-Induced Guilty Pleas in Britain* (Cheltenham, Edward Elgar).

McFarlane, J, Malecha, A, and Watson, K (2005a), 'Intimate Partner Sexual Assault Against Women: Frequency, Health Consequences, and Treatment Outcomes' 105 *Obstetrics and Gynecology* 99.

McFarlane, J, Malecha, A and Gist, J (2005b), 'Intimate Partner Sexual Assault Against Women and Associated Victim Substance Use, Suicidality, and Risk Factors for Femicide' 26 *Issues in Mental Health Nursing* 953–67.

McGlynn, C (2011), 'Feminism, Rape and the Search for Justice' 31(4) *Oxford Journal of Legal Studies* 825–42.

McGlynn, C (2010a), 'Feminist Activism and Rape Law Reform in England and Wales – A Sisyphean Struggle?' in McGlynn, C and Munro, V E (eds), *Rethinking Rape Law – International and Comparative Perspectives* (Abingdon, Routledge).

McGlynn, C (2010b), 'Marginalizing Feminism? Debating Extreme Pornography Laws in Public and Policy Discourse' in Boyle, K (ed), *Everyday Pornography* (Abingdon, Routledge).

McGlynn, C and Munro, VE (2010), 'Rethinking Rape Law: An Introduction' in McGlynn, C and Munro, VE (eds), *Rethinking Rape Law – International and Comparative Perspectives* (Abingdon, Routledge).

McGlynn, C and Rackley, E (2017a), 'Image-Based Sexual Abuse' *Oxford Journal of Legal Studies* 1–28.

McGlynn, C and Rackley, E (2017b), 'More than "Revenge Porn": Image-Based Sexual Abuse and the Reform of Irish Law' 14 *Irish Probation Journal* 38–51.

McGlynn, C and Rackley, E (2016), 'Not "revenge porn", but abuse: let's call it image-based sexual abuse' *Inherently Human* (the GLAD [Gender and Law at Durham] Blog, Durham Law School, Durham University). Available at: https://inherentlyhuman.wordpress.com/2016/02/15/not-revenge-porn-but-abuse-lets-call-it-image-based-sexual-abuse/ (accessed 1 September 2019).

McGlynn, C and Rackley, E (2015a), 'New law on "revenge porn" is "unlikely" to tackle hackers distributing intimate images' *Holyrood Magazine*. Available at: www.holyrood.com/articles/comment/new-law-revenge-porn-unlikely-tackle-hackers-distributing-intimate-images (accessed 1 September 2019).

McGlynn, C and Rackley, E (2015b), *Abusive Behaviour and Sexual Harm (Scotland) Bill – Written submission from Professor Clare McGlynn (Durham University) and Professor Erika Rackley (University of Birmingham)* (ABSH 3) (Edinburgh, Scottish Parliament). Available at: www.parliament.scot/S4_JusticeCommittee/Inquiries/ABSH3._McGlynn_and_Rackley.pdf (accessed 1 September 2019).

McGlynn, C and Rackley, E (2009), 'Criminalising Extreme Pornography: A Lost Opportunity' *Criminal Law Review*, 245–60.

McGlynn, C and Rackley, E (2007), 'Striking a Balance: Arguments for the Criminal Regulation of Extreme Pornography' *Criminal Law Review* 677–90.

McGlynn, C, Rackley, E, and Houghton, R (2017), 'Beyond "Revenge Porn": The Continuum of Image-Based Sexual Abuse' 25(1) *Feminist Legal Studies* 25–46.

McGlynn, C, Westmarland, N, and Godden, N (2012), '"I Just Wanted Him to Hear Me": Sexual Violence and the Possibilities of Restorative Justice' 39(2) *Journal of Law and Society* 213–40.

McGovern, D (2014), 'Assessing Offence Seriousness at Sentencing: New Zealand's Guideline Judgment for Sexual Violation' 26(2) *New Zealand Universities Law Review* 243–72.

McGregor, J (2005), *Is it Rape? On Acquaintance Rape and Taking Women's Consent Seriously* (Aldershot, Ashgate).

McMillan, L and White, D (2015), '"Silly Girls" and "Nice Young Lads": Vilification and Vindication in the Perceptions of Medico-Legal Practitioners in Rape Cases' 10(3) *Feminist Criminology* 279–98.

McPherson, R (2013), 'The Rise of Agreed Narratives in Scottish Criminal Procedure' 2 *Juridical Review* 141–56.

Mezey, G and King, M (2000), 'Treatment of Male Victims of Sexual Assault' in Mezey, G C and King, MB (eds), *Male Victims of Sexual Assault* (2nd edn) (Oxford, Oxford University Press).

Mezey, G and King, M (1989), 'The Effects of Sexual Assault on Men: A Survey of 22 Victims' 19 *Psychological Medicine* 205–9.

Miller, K (2014), 'Relational Caring: The Use of the Victim Impact Statements by Sexually Assaulted Women' 29(5) *Violence and Victims* 797–813.

Millie, A, Tombs, J, and Hough, M (2007), 'Borderline Sentencing: A Comparison of Sentencers' Decision Making in England and Wales, and Scotland' 7(3) *Criminology and Criminal Justice* 243–67.

Ministry of Justice, Home Office, and the Office for National Statistics (2013), *An Overview of Sexual Offending in England and Wales – Statistics Bulletin* (London, Ministry of Justice, Home Office, and the Office for National Statistics).

Möller, AT, Bäckström, T, Söndergaard, HP, and Helström, L (2014), 'Identifying Risk Factors for PTSD in Women Seeking Medical Help After Rape' 9(10) *Plos One* 1–9.

Möller, AS, Bäckström, T, Söndergaard, HP, and Helström, L (2012), 'Patterns of Injury and Reported Violence Depending on Relationship to Assailant in Female Swedish Sexual Assault Victims' 27(16) *Journal of Interpersonal Violence* 3131– 48.

Moloney, T (2016), 'Notification and Notification Orders' in Rook, P and Ward, R, *Rook and Ward on Sexual Offences Law & Practice* (5th edn) (London, Sweet & Maxwell).

Moody, S (1995), 'Images of Women: Sentencing in Sexual Assault Cases in Scotland' in Bridgeman, J and Millns, S (eds), *Law and Body Politics – Regulating the Female Body* (Aldershot, Dartmouth).

Morgan, L, Brittain, B and Welch, J (2012), 'Multiple Perpetrator Sexual Assault: How Does It Differ from Assault by a Single Perpetrator?' 27(12) *Journal of Interpersonal Violence* 2415–436.

Mosonyi, S (2017), 'Sentencing Guidelines for Canada: A Re-Evaluation' 22(3) *Canadian Criminal Law Review* 275–95.

Moxon, D (1988), *Sentencing Practice in the Crown Court*, Home Office Research Study 103 (Home Office Research and Planning Unit Report), London, Her Majesty's Stationery Office.

Mujuzi, J S (2008), 'The Prospect of Rehabilitation as a "Substantial and Compelling" Circumstance to Avoid Imposing Life Imprisonment in South Africa: A Comment on *S v Nkomo*' 21(1) *South African Journal of Criminal Justice* 1–21.

Müller, K and van der Merwe, A (2006), 'Recognising the Victim in the Sentencing Phase: The Use of Victim Impact Statements in Court' 22(4) *South African Journal on Human Rights* 647–63.

Munro, M (2016), 'Victims in Scotland: A Review' in Croall, H, Mooney, G and Munro, M (eds), *Crime, Justice and Society in Scotland* (Abingdon, Routledge).

Munro, VR (2014), 'Sexual Autonomy' in Dubber, MD and Hörnle, T (eds), *The Oxford Handbook of Criminal Law* (Oxford, Oxford University Press).

Munro, VE and Kelly, L (2009), 'A Vicious Cycle? Attrition and Conviction Patterns in Contemporary Rape Cases in England and Wales' in Horvath, MAH and Brown, J (eds), *Rape – Challenging Contemporary Thinking* (Cullompton, Willan).

Najdowski, CJ and Ullman, SE (2011), 'The Effects of Revictimization on Coping and Depression in Female Sexual Assault Victims' 24(2) *Journal of Traumatic Stress* 218–21.

Nardello, R, Compagno, A, Argo, A, Zerbo, S, Procaccianti, P and Mangano, S (2013), 'Sexual Abuse – Current Medico-legal, Forensic and Psychiatric Aspects' in Beran, R G (ed), *Legal and Forensic Medicine* (Heidelberg, Springer-Verlag).

Nelken, D (2017), 'Rethinking Comparative Criminal Justice' in Liebling, A, Maruna, S and McAra, L (eds), *The Oxford Handbook of Criminology* (6th edn) (Oxford, Oxford University Press).

Nelken, D (2012), 'Comparing Criminal Justice' in Maguire, M, Morgan, R and Reiner, R (eds), *The Oxford Handbook of Criminology* (5th edn) (Oxford, Oxford University Press).

Nelken, D (2009), 'Comparative Criminal Justice – Beyond Ethnocentrism and Relativism' 6(4) *European Journal of Criminology* 291–311.

Nelken, D (2007), 'Comparative Law and Comparative Legal Studies' in Örücü, E and Nelken, D (eds), *Comparative Law – A Handbook* (Oxford, Hart Publishing).

Nelken, D (2002), 'Comparative Sociology of Law' in Banakar, R and Travers, M (eds), *An Introduction to Law and Social Theory* (Oxford, Hart Publishing).

Nelken, D (2000), 'Just Comparing' in Nelken, D (ed), *Contrasting Criminal Justice – Getting from Here to There* (Aldershot, Ashgate).

Nelken, D (1995), 'Disclosing/Invoking Legal Culture: An Introduction' 4(4) *Social & Legal Studies* 435–52.

Nesvold, H, Worm, A, Vala, U and Agnarsdóttir, G (2005), 'Different Nordic Facilities for Victims of Sexual Assault: A Comparative Study' 84 *Acta Obstetricia et Gynecologica Scandinavica* 177–83.

New Zealand Law Commission (2008), *Draft Sentencing Guideline – Sexual Violation*, New Zealand Law Commission Sentencing Establishment Unit, Wellington, New Zealand Law Commission.

New Zealand Law Commission (2006), *Sentencing Guidelines and Parole Reform* (Report No 94), Wellington, New Zealand Law Commission.

Nicholls, C, Mitchell, M, Simpson, I, Webster, S and Hester, M (2012), *Attitudes to Sentencing Sexual Offences (Sentencing Council Research Series 01/12)*, London, Sentencing Council.

Nicholson, CGB (1992), *Sentencing – Law and Practice in Scotland* (2nd edn) (Edinburgh, W Green).

Nicholson, CGB (1981), *The Law and Practice of Sentencing in Scotland* (Edinburgh, W Green).

Nightingale, ML (1991), 'Judicial Attitudes and Differential Treatment: Native Women in Sexual Assault Cases' 23(1) *Ottawa Law Review* 71–98.

O'Cathaoir, K (2012), *Recent Rape Sentencing Analysis: The WD Case & Beyond*, Dublin, Judicial Researchers' Office.

O'Donnell, I (2012), 'Publication Review – *Sentencing: Towards a Coherent System* (Thomas O'Malley)' 47 *Irish Jurist* 255–57.

O'Flaherty, H (2002), 'Punishment and the Popular Mind: How Much is Enough?' in O'Mahony, P (ed), *Criminal Justice in Ireland* (Dublin, Institute of Public Administration).

O'Malley, T (2018), 'The Allocation of Criminal Jurisdiction – Again'. Paper presented at the Seminar on Court Reform, 17 January 2018, School of Law, NUI Galway, Galway.

O'Malley, T (2017), 'Judgment and Calculation in the Selection of Sentence' 28 *Criminal Law Forum* 361–89.
O'Malley, T (2016), *Sentencing Law and Practice* (3rd edn) (Dublin, Round Hall).
O'Malley, T (2014), 'A Quiet Revolution Occurred this Month: Sentencing Guidelines were Introduced' *The Irish Times*, 31 March 2014. Available at: www.irishtimes.com/news/crime-and-law/a-quiet-revolution-occurred-this-month-sentencing-guidelines-were-introduced-1.1741707 (accessed 1 September 2019).
O'Malley, T (2013a), *Sexual Offences* (2nd edn) (Dublin, Round Hall).
O'Malley, T (2013b), 'Living Without Guidelines' in Ashworth, A and Roberts, JV (eds), *Sentencing Guidelines – Exploring the English Model* (Oxford, Oxford University Press).
O'Malley, T (2011), *Sentencing – Towards a Coherent System* (Dublin, Round Hall).
O'Malley, T (2009), *The Criminal Process* (Dublin, Round Hall).
O'Malley, T (2008), 'Principles of Sentencing: Towards a European Conversation' 23 January 2008, Leiden University, Leiden.
O'Malley, T (2006), *Sentencing Law and Practice* (2nd edn) (Dublin, Round Hall).
O'Malley, T (2003), 'Sentencing Values and Sentencing Structures' 3(1) *Judicial Studies Institute Journal* 130–55.
O'Malley, T (2001), 'Principled Discretion: Towards the Development of a Sentencing Canon' 7(3) *The Bar Review* 135–39; 156–59.
O'Malley, T (1995), *Sexual Offences – Law, Policy and Punishment* (Dublin, Round Hall).
O'Malley, T (1994), 'Resisting the Temptation of Elegance: Sentencing Discretion Re-affirmed' 4(1) *Irish Criminal Law Journal* 1–30.
Office for National Statistics (2018), *Sexual Offences in England and Wales: Year Ending March 2017*, Office for National Statistics, Newport.
Oleson, J C (2017), 'Sentencing Theories, Practices, and Trends' in Deckert, A and Sarre, R (eds), *The Palgrave Handbook of Australian and New Zealand Criminology, Crime and Justice* (Cham, Palgrave Macmillan).
Ormerod, D (2013), 'Editorial – Sentencing Council Consultation on Sexual Offences' *Criminal Law Review*, 181–83.
Ormerod, D, Perry, D, and Murphy, P (2018), *Blackstone's Criminal Practice 2018* (Oxford, Oxford University Press).
Orr, N (2007), '*Du Plooy* Deployed' 21 *Scots Law Times (News)* 143–50.
Örücü, E (2007a), 'Developing Comparative Law' in Örücü, E and Nelken, D (eds), *Comparative Law – A Handbook* (Oxford, Hart Publishing).
Örücü, E (2007b), 'Comparative Law in Practice: The Courts and the Legislator' in Örücü, E and Nelken, D (eds), *Comparative Law – A Handbook* (Oxford, Hart Publishing).
Padfield, N (2019), 'Sentencing Mentally Ill Offenders' *Criminal Law Review*, 653–55.
Padfield, N (2016a), 'Reflections on Sentencing in England and Wales' in Kapardis, A and Farrington, DP (eds), *The Psychology of Crime, Policing and Courts* (Abingdon, Routledge).
Padfield, N (2016b), 'Editorial – Guidelines Galore' *Criminal Law Review*, 301–2.
Padfield, N (2013), 'Exploring the Success of Sentencing Guidelines' in Ashworth, A and Roberts, JV (eds), *Sentencing Guidelines – Exploring the English Model* (Oxford, Oxford University Press).
Padfield, N (2011), 'Intoxication as a Sentencing Factor: Mitigation or Aggravation?' in Roberts, JV (ed), *Mitigation and Aggravation at Sentencing* (Cambridge, Cambridge University Press).
Palmer, CT (1988), 'Twelve Reasons Why Rape Is Not Sexually Motivated: A Skeptical Examination' 25(4) *The Journal of Sex Research* 512–30.
Panckhurst, Justice G (2008), 'A Sentencing Council: Enlightened or Folly?' 14 *Canterbury Law Review* 191–205.
Paschke, R and Sherwin, H (2000), *Quantitative Research Report on Sentencing* (Pretoria, South African Law Commission).
Payne-James, J and Beh, P (2011), 'Adult Sexual Assault' in Gall, J and Payne-James, J (eds), *Current Practice in Forensic Medicine* (Chichester, Wiley-Blackwell).

Payne-James, J, Jones, R, Karch, SB, and Manlove, J (2011), *Simpson's Forensic Medicine* (13th edn) (London, Hodder Arnold).

Pennington, R and Birthisel, J (2016), 'When New Media Make News: Framing Technology and Sexual Assault in the Steubenville Rape Case' 18(11) *New Media & Society* 2435–451.

Peterson, ZD, Voller, EK, Polusny, MA and Murdoch, M (2011), 'Prevalence and Consequences of Adult Sexual Assault of Men: Review of Empirical Findings and State of the Literature' 31 *Clinical Psychology Review* 1–24.

Petrak, J, Doyle, A, Williams, L, Buchan, L, and Forster, G (1997), 'The Psychological Impact of Sexual Assault: A Study of Female Attenders of a Sexual Health Psychology Service' 12(4) *Sexual and Marital Therapy* 339–45.

Phelps, K (2013), 'Sentencing' 26(2) *South African Journal of Criminal Justice* 224–34.

Picton, Judge M (2016), 'Sexual Harm Prevention Orders and Sexual Risk Orders' in Rook, P and Ward, R, *Rook and Ward on Sexual Offences Law & Practice* (5th edn) (London, Sweet & Maxwell).

Piegsa, K (2014), 'Aftercare: Emergency Contraception' in Dalton, M (ed), *Forensic Gynaecology* (Cambridge, Cambridge University Press).

Pina-Sánchez, J (2015), 'Defining and Measuring Consistency in Sentencing' in Roberts, JV (ed), *Exploring Sentencing Practice in England and Wales* (Basingstoke, Palgrave Macmillan).

Pitcher, GJ and Bowley, DMG (2002), 'Infant Rape in South Africa' 359 *The Lancet* 274 – 75.

Player, E (2012), 'Sentencing Women: Towards Gender Equality' in Zedner, L and Roberts, JV (eds), *Principles and Values in Criminal Law and Criminal Justice: Essays in Honour of Andrew Ashworth* (Oxford, Oxford University Press).

Porter, LE and Alison, LJ (2006), 'Examining Group Rape: A Descriptive Analysis of Offender and Victim Behaviour' 3(3) *European Journal of Criminology* 357–81.

Powell, A (2015), 'Seeking Rape Justice: Formal and Informal Responses to Sexual Violence Through Technosocial Counter-Publics' 19(4) *Theoretical Criminology* 571–88.

Powell, A (2010), 'Configuring Consent: Emerging Technologies, Unauthorised Sexual Images and Sexual Assault' 43(1) *The Australian and New Zealand Journal of Criminology* 76–90.

Powell, A (2009), 'New Technologies, Unauthorised Visual Images and Sexual Assault' *ACSSA Aware*, No. 23 (Nov), 6–12.

Powell, A and Henry, N (2017a), *Sexual Violence in a Digital Age* (Basingstoke, Palgrave Macmillan).

Powell, A and Henry, N (2017b), 'Sexual Violence and Harassment in the Digital Era' in Deckert, A and Sarre, R (eds), *The Palgrave Handbook of Australian and New Zealand Criminology, Crime and Justice* (Cham, Palgrave Macmillan).

Powell, A and Henry, N (2016a), 'Technology-Facilitated Sexual Violence Victimization: Results From an Online Survey of Australian Adults' *Journal of Interpersonal Violence* (October 2016), 1–29.

Powell, A and Henry, N (2016b), 'Policing Technology-Facilitated Sexual Violence Against Adult Victims: Police and Service Sector Perspectives' *Policing and Society*, DOI: 10.1080/10439463.2016.1154964.

Powell, A and Henry, N (2015), *Digital Harassment and Abuse of Adult Australians: A Summary Report* (Melbourne, RMIT University).

Powell, A and Henry, N (2014a), 'Blurred Lines? Responding to "Sexting" and Gender-Based Violence Among Young People' 39(2) *Children Australia* 119–24.

Powell, A and Henry, N (2014b), 'Framing Sexual Violence Prevention – What Does it Mean to Challenge a Rape Culture?' in Henry, N and Powell, A (eds), *Preventing Sexual Violence – Interdisciplinary Approaches to Overcoming a Rape Culture* (Basingstoke, Palgrave Macmillan).

Powell, A, Henry, N, and Flynn, A (2018a), 'Image-Based Sexual Abuse' in DeKeseredy, WS and Dragiewicz, M (eds), *The Routledge Handbook of Critical Criminology* (2nd edn) (Abingdon, Routledge).

Powell, A, Stratton, G and Cameron R (2018b), *Digital Criminology – Crime and Justice in Digital Society* (Abingdon, Routledge).

Priestley, Justice J (2009), *Chipping Away at the Judicial Arm? – Harkness Henry Lecture, 2009* (Hamilton, University of Waikato).

Rackley, E and McGlynn, C (2013), 'Prosecuting the Possession of Extreme Pornography: A Misunderstood and Mis-used Law' *Criminal Law Review*, 400–5.

Ranyard, R, Hebenton, B, and Pease, K (1994), 'An Analysis of a Guideline Case as Applied to the Offence of Rape' 33(3) *The Howard Journal* 203–17.

Ratner, PA, Johnson, JL, Shoveller, JA, Chan, K, Martindale, SL, Schilder, AJ, Botnick, M R and Hogg, RS (2003), 'Non-consensual Sex Experienced by Men Who Have Sex with Men: Prevalence and Association with Mental Health' 49 *Patient Education and Counselling* 67–74.

Rauxloh, R (2012), *Plea Bargaining in National and International Law* (Abingdon, Routledge).

Reed, Lord (2015), *Triremes and Steamships: Scholars, Judges, and the Use of the Past*, The Scrymgeour Lecture, Dundee, University of Dundee, 30 October 2015.

Reeves, I, Jawad, R and Welch, J (2004), 'Risk of Undiagnosed Infection in Men Attending a Sexual Assault Referral Centre' 80 *Sexually Transmitted Infections* 524–25.

Rentoul, L and Appleboom, N (1997), 'Understanding the Psychological Impact of Rape and Serious Sexual Assault of Men: A Literature Review' 4 *Journal of Psychiatric and Mental Health Nursing* 267–74.

Resnick, HS, Veronen, LJ, Saunders, B, Kilpatrick, DG, and Cornelison, V (1989), *Assessment of PTSD in a Subset of Rape Victims at 12 to 36 Months Post-Assault*, Unpublished manuscript.

Richardson, J (2011), 'A "Just" Outcome: Losing Sight of the Purpose of Criminal Procedure' *Journal of Commonwealth Criminal Law* 105–31.

Richardson, PJ (2018), *Archbold – Criminal Pleading, Evidence and Practice* (London, Sweet & Maxwell).

Richardson, DR and Hammock, GS (1991), 'Alcohol and Acquaintance Rape' in Parrot, A and Bechhofer, L (eds), *Acquaintance Rape – The Hidden Crime* (New York: John Wiley & Sons).

Riggs, N, Houry, D, Long, G, Markovchick, V, and Feldhaus, K M (2000), 'Analysis of 1,076 Cases of Sexual Assault' 35(4) *Annals of Emergency Medicine* 358–62.

Ripstein, A (2006), 'Beyond the Harm Principle' 34(3) *Philosophy & Public Affairs* 215–45.

Roberts, JV (2019), 'The Evolution of Sentencing Guidelines in Minnesota and England and Wales' 48(1) *Crime and Justice* 187–253.

Roberts, JV (2013), 'Sentencing Guidelines in England and Wales: Recent Developments and Emerging Issues' 76(1) *Law and Contemporary Problems* 1–25.

Roberts, JV (2012a), 'Structuring Sentencing in Canada, England and Wales: A Tale of Two Jurisdictions' 23 *Criminal Law Forum* 319–45.

Roberts, JV (2012b), 'Structured Sentencing: Lessons from England and Wales for Common Law Jurisdictions' 14(3) *Punishment & Society* 267–88.

Roberts, JV (2011), 'Sentencing Guidelines and Judicial Discretion – Evolution of the Duty of Courts to Comply in England and Wales' 51(6) *British Journal of Criminology* 997–1013.

Roberts, JV (2010), 'First-Offender Sentencing Discounts: Exploring the Justifications' in Roberts, J V and von Hirsch, A (eds), *Previous Convictions at Sentencing – Theoretical and Applied Perspectives* (Oxford, Hart Publishing).

Roberts, JV (2009), 'Structuring Sentencing Discretion' in von Hirsch, A, Ashworth, A and Roberts, J (eds), *Principled Sentencing – Readings on Theory and Policy* (3rd edn) (Oxford, Hart Publishing).

Roberts, JV (2003), 'Sentencing Reform in New Zealand: An Analysis of the Sentencing Act 2002' 36(3) *Australian & New Zealand Journal of Criminology* 249–71.

Roberts, JV and Ashworth, A (2016), 'The Evolution of Sentencing Policy and Practice in England and Wales, 2003 – 2015' 45(1) *Crime and Justice* 307–58.

Roberts, JV and Azmeh, U (2019), 'Cleansing the Augean Stables: A Commentary on the Law Commission's Sentencing Code for England and Wales' *Criminal Law Review*, 694–705.

Roberts, JV, Azmeh, U, and Tripathi, K (2011), 'Structured Sentencing in England and Wales: Recent Developments and Lessons for India' 23(1) *National Law School of India Review* 27–45.

Roberts, JV and Baker, E (2008), 'Sentencing Structure and Reform in Common Law Jurisdictions' in Shoham, SG, Beck, O and Kett, M (eds), *International Handbook of Penology and Criminal Justice* (Boca Raton, CRC Press).

Roberts, JV, Doob, AN, and Marinos, V (with the assistance of La Prairie, C, Cole, D, and Perry, T) (2000), *Judicial Attitudes to Conditional Terms of Imprisonment: Results of a National Survey*, Report 2000-10e, Ottawa, Department of Justice.

Roberts, JV and Erez, E (2010), 'Communication at Sentencing: The Expressive Function of Victim Impact Statements' in Bottoms, A and Roberts, JV (eds), *Hearing the Victim – Adversarial Justice, Crime Victims and the State* (Abingdon, Willan Publishing).

Roberts, JV and Erez, E (2004), 'Communication in Sentencing: Exploring the Expressive Function of Victim Impact Statements' 10 *International Review of Victimology* 223–44.

Roberts, JV and Hough, M (2015), 'Empirical Sentencing Research: Options and Opportunities' in Roberts, JV (ed), *Exploring Sentencing Practice in England and Wales* (Basingstoke, Palgrave Macmillan).

Roberts, JV and Pei, W (2016), 'Structuring Judicial Discretion in China: Exploring the 2014 Sentencing Guidelines' 27(1) *Criminal Law Forum* 3–33.

Roberts, JV and Rafferty, A (2011), 'Sentencing Guidelines in England and Wales: Exploring the New Format' 9 *Criminal Law Review* 681–89.

Robertshaw, P (1994), 'Sentencing Rapists: First Tier Courts in 1991–92' *Criminal Law Review*, 343–45.

Rodger of Earlsferry, Lord (2010), 'Foreword' in Chalmers, J, Leverick, F and Farmer, L (eds), *Essays in Criminal Law in Honour of Sir Gerald Gordon* (Edinburgh, Edinburgh University Press).

Rogers, DJ (2009), 'Adult Sexual Offences' in McLay, WDS (ed), *Clinical Forensic Medicine* (3rd edn) (Cambridge, Cambridge University Press).

Rogers, D and McBride, BM (2011), 'Sexual Assault Examination' in Stark, MM (ed), *Clinical Forensic Medicine – A Physician's Guide* (3rd edn) (New York, Humana Press).

Rogers, D and Newton, M (2005), 'Sexual Assault Examination' in Stark, MM (ed), *Clinical Forensic Medicine – A Physician's Guide* (2nd edn) (Totowa, Humana Press).

Rook, P and Ward, R (2019), *Rook and Ward on Sexual Offences Law and Practice – Supplement to the Fifth Edition* (London, Sweet and Maxwell).

Rook, P and Ward, R (2016), *Rook and Ward on Sexual Offences Law and Practice* (5th edn) (London, Sweet and Maxwell).

Rook, P and Ward, R (2014), *Rook and Ward on Sexual Offences Law and Practice – First Supplement to the Fourth Edition* (London, Sweet and Maxwell).

Rook, P and Ward, R (2010), *Rook and Ward on Sexual Offences Law and Practice* (4th edn) (London, Sweet and Maxwell).

Rook, P and Ward, R (2008), *Rook and Ward on Sexual Offences Law and Practice – First Supplement to the Third Edition* (London, Sweet and Maxwell).

Rook, P and Ward, R (2004), *Rook and Ward on Sexual Offences Law and Practice* (3rd edn) (London, Sweet and Maxwell).

Ross, M and Chalmers, J (2015), *Walker and Walker – The Law of Evidence in Scotland* (4th edn) (Haywards Heath, Bloomsbury Professional).

Roth, SM (2008), 'South African Mandatory Minimum Sentencing: Reform Required' 17(1) *Minnesota Journal of International Law* 155–82.

Rothbaum, BO, Foa, EB, Riggs, DS, Murdock, T, and Walsh, W (1992), 'A Prospective Examination of Post-Traumatic Stress Disorder in Rape Victims' 5(3) *Journal of Traumatic Stress* 455–75.

Ruby, CC, Chan, GJ, Hasan, NR, and Enenajor, A (2017), *Sentencing* (9th edn) (Toronto, LexisNexis Canada).

Rumney, PNS (2003), 'Progress at a Price: The Construction of Non-Stranger Rape in the *Millberry* Sentencing Guidelines' 66(6) *Modern Law Review* 870–84.

Rumney, PNS (1999), 'When Rape Isn't Rape: Court of Appeal Sentencing Practice in Cases of Marital and Relationship Rape' 19 *Oxford Journal of Legal Studies* 243–69.

Rumney, PNS and van der Bijl, C (2010), 'Rape, Attitudes, and Law Enforcement in South Africa' 13(4) *New Criminal Law Review* 826–40.

Runciman, WG (1983), *A Treatise on Social Theory: Volume 1, The Methodology of Social Theory* (Cambridge, Cambridge University Press).

Russell, DEH (1982), *Rape in Marriage* (New York, Macmillan).

Sachs-Ericsson, N, Kendall-Tackett, KA, Sheffler, J, Arce, D, Rushing, NC and Corsentino, E (2014), 'The Influence of Prior Rape on the Psychological and Physical Health Functioning of Older Adults' 18(6) *Aging & Mental Health* 717–30.

Sandberg, S and Ugelvik, T (2017), 'Why Do Offenders Tape Their Crimes? Crime and Punishment in the Age of the Selfie' 57 *British Journal of Criminology* 1023–40.

Sanders, A, Young, R and Burton, M (2010), *Criminal Justice* (4th edn) (Oxford, Oxford University Press).

Sanders, A, Hoyle, C, Morgan, R and Cape, E (2001), 'Victim Impact Statements: Don't Work, Can't Work' *Criminal Law Review* 447–58.

Sangiovanni, A (2017), 'Rights and Interests in Ripstein's Kant' in Kisilevsky, S and Stone, MJ (eds), *Freedom and Force – Essays on Kant's Legal Philosophy* (Oxford, Hart Publishing).

Satish, M (2017), *Discretion, Discrimination and the Rule of Law – Reforming Rape Sentencing in India* (Cambridge, Cambridge University Press).

Scott, J (2018), 'When Crime No Longer Pays' 63(10) *Journal of the Law Society of Scotland* 12–14.

Scott, L (2017), 'Developments in Irish Sentencing' 1 *Irish Judicial Studies Journal* 1–14.

Scott, ME (2005), 'Redefined Rape and the Difficulties of Proof' 11 *Scots Law Times (News)* 65–69.

Scottish Law Commission (2007), *Report on Rape and Other Sexual Offences (Scottish Law Commission Report No 209)* (Edinburgh, Her Majesty's Stationery Office).

Scottish Sentencing Council (2019a), *The Sentencing Process – Draft Sentencing Guideline* (Edinburgh, Scottish Sentencing Council).

Scottish Sentencing Council (2019b), *The Sentencing Process – Consultation Paper* (Edinburgh, Scottish Sentencing Council).

Scottish Sentencing Council (2018a), *Principles and Purposes of Sentencing – Sentencing Guideline* (Edinburgh, Scottish Sentencing Council).

Scottish Sentencing Council (2018b), 'Scotland's First Sentencing Guideline Approved by High Court of Justiciary'. Available at: www.scottishsentencingcouncil.org.uk/news-and-media/news/first-sentencing-guideline-approved-by-high-court/ (last accessed 1 September 2019).

Scottish Sentencing Council (2018c), *Scottish Sentencing Council Business Plan 2018–2021* (Edinburgh, Scottish Sentencing Council).

Secret Barrister (2019), *Stories of the Law and How It's Broken* (London, Picador).

Selfe, D (2012), 'Sentencing for Rape of a Child under Thirteen' 207 *Criminal Lawyer* 3–5.

Selfe, D (2011), 'Sentencing for the Rape of a Child under Thirteen Years of Age' 204 *Criminal Lawyer* 5–6.

Sentencing Advisory Panel (2002), *Advice to the Court of Appeal – 9. Rape* (London, Sentencing Advisory Panel Secretariat).

Sentencing Commission for Scotland (2006), *The Scope to Improve Consistency in Sentencing* (Edinburgh, Sentencing Commission for Scotland).

Sentencing Council for England and Wales (2019), *Sentencing Offenders with Mental Health Conditions or Disorders: Draft Guideline* (London, Sentencing Council).

Sentencing Council for England and Wales (2017), *Reduction in Sentence for a Guilty Plea Definitive Guideline* (London, Sentencing Council).

Sentencing Council for England and Wales (2016), *Reduction in Sentence for a Guilty Plea Guideline – Consultation* (London, Sentencing Council).

Sentencing Council for England and Wales (2013a), *Sexual Offences Definitive Guideline* (London, Sentencing Council).

Sentencing Council for England and Wales (2013b), *Sexual Offences – Response to Consultation* (London, Sentencing Council).

Sentencing Council for England and Wales (2012), *Sexual Offences Guideline Consultation* (London, Sentencing Council).

Sentencing Council for England and Wales (2011), *Assault – Definitive Guideline* (London, Sentencing Council).

Sentencing Guidelines Council (2008), *Assault and other Offences against the Person – Definitive Guideline* (London, Sentencing Guidelines Secretariat).

Sentencing Guidelines Council (2007a), *Sexual Offences Act 2003 – Definitive Guideline* (London, Sentencing Guidelines Secretariat).

Sentencing Guidelines Council (2007b), *Reduction in Sentence for a Guilty Plea – Definitive Guideline (Revised 2007)* (London, Sentencing Guidelines Secretariat).

Sentencing Guidelines Council (2007c), *Dangerous Offenders: Guide for Sentencers and Practitioners* (London, Sentencing Guidelines Secretariat).

Sentencing Guidelines Council (2006a), *Overarching Principles: Domestic Violence*, Definitive Guideline (London, Sentencing Guidelines Secretariat).

Sentencing Guidelines Council (2006b), *Robbery – Definitive Guideline* (London, Sentencing Guidelines Secretariat).

Shapland, J and Hall, M (2010), 'Victims at Court: Necessary Accessories or Principal Players at Centre Stage?' in Bottoms, A and Roberts, JV (eds), *Hearing the Victim – Adversarial Justice, Crime Victims and the State* (Abingdon, Willan Publishing).

Shaw, A (2014), 'The Power to Increase Sentence *Ex Proprio Motu* on Appeal' 18(2) *Edinburgh Law Review* 265–70.

Shead, Sheriff C (2017), 'The Decision in *Gubinas (Justinas) v HM Advocate*' *Scottish Criminal Law*, 825–27.

Shead, Sheriff C (2013), 'The Decision in *Murray v HM Advocate*' *Scottish Criminal Law*, 93–95.

Shead, Sheriff C (2008), 'The Power of the Appeal Court to Increase Sentences: Time for Reform?' *Scottish Criminal Law*, 413–15.

Shepherd, R (2003), *Simpson's Forensic Medicine* (12th edn) (London, Hodder Arnold).

Shiels, R (1992), 'Marital Rape: A Sentencing Dilemma' 37 *Journal of the Law Society of Scotland*, 363–66.

Shiels, R, Bradley, I, Brown, AN, and Ferguson, PW (2015), *Greens Annotated Acts – Criminal Procedure (Scotland) Act 1995* (14th edn) (Edinburgh, W Green).

Sills, S, Pickens, C, Beach, K, Jones, L, Calder-Dawe, O, Benton-Greig, P and Gavey, N (2016), 'Rape Culture and Social Media: Young Critics and a Feminist Counterpublic' 16(6) *Feminist Media Studies* 935–51.

Sloth-Nielsen, J and Ehlers, L (2005a), 'Assessing the Impact – Mandatory and Minimum Sentences in South Africa' *South Africa Crime Quarterly*, No 14 (December), 15–22.

Sloth-Nielsen, J and Ehlers, L (2005b), 'A Pyrrhic Victory? Mandatory and Minimum Sentences in South Africa' Institute for Security Studies Paper 111 (Pretoria, Institute for Security Studies).

Smith, O and Skinner, T (2017), 'How Rape Myths are Used and Challenged in Rape and Sexual Assault Trials' 26(4) *Social and Legal Studies* 441–66.

Solley, S (2002), 'The Role of the Advocate' in McConville, M and Wilson, G (eds), *The Handbook of The Criminal Justice Process* (Oxford, Oxford University Press).

South African Law Commission (2000), *Sentencing (A New Sentencing Framework) – Report No 82* (Pretoria, South African Law Commission).

South African Law Reform Commission (1997), *Sexual Offences Against Children Project 108 Issue Paper 10* (Pretoria, South African Law Reform Commission).

Spies, A (2016), 'Perpetuating Harm: The Sentencing of Rape Offenders under South African Law' 133(2) *South African Law Journal* 389–408.

Stanbury, M (2016), 'Reduction in Sentence for a Guilty Plea: Comments on the Proposed Reforms' *Current Sentencing Practice – News*, Issue 1, 6–7.

Stanton–Ife, J (2010), 'Horrific Crime' in Duff, RA, Farmer, L, Marshall, SE, Renzo, M and Tadros, V (eds), *The Boundaries of the Criminal Law* (Oxford, Oxford University Press).

Statman, D (2012), 'Gardner on the Wrongness of Rape' 4 *Jerusalem Review of Legal Studies* 105–9.

Stermac, L, Del Bove, G and Addison, M (2004), 'Stranger and Acquaintance Sexual Assault of Adult Males' 19(8) *Journal of Interpersonal Violence* 901–15.

Stermac, L, Del Bove, G and Addison, M (2001), 'Violence, Injury, and Presentation Patterns in Spousal Sexual Assaults' 7(11) *Violence Against Women* 1218–33.

Stermac, L, Du Mont, JA and Kalemba, V (1995), 'Comparison of Sexual Assaults by Strangers and Known Assailants in an Urban Population of Women' 153 *Canadian Medical Association Journal* 1089–94.

Stern, Baroness V (2010), *The Stern Review – A Report by Baroness Vivien Stern CBE of an Independent Review into How Rape Complaints are Handled by Public Authorities in England and Wales*, London, Government Equalities Office/Home Office.

Stewart, AL (1997), *The Scottish Criminal Courts in Action* (2nd edn) (Edinburgh, Butterworths).

Stewart, MW, Dobbin, SA, and Gatowski, SI (1996), '"Real Rapes' and 'Real Victims": The Shared Reliance on Common Cultural Definitions of Rape' 4(2) *Feminist Legal Studies* 159–77.

Stormo, KJ, Lang, AR, and Stritzke, WGK (1997), 'Attitudes about Acquaintance Rape: The Role of Alcohol and Individual Differences' 27(4) *Journal of Applied Social Psychology* 279–305.

Sugar, NF, Fine, DN, and Eckert, LO (2004), 'Physical Injury After Sexual Assault: Findings of a Large Case Series' 190 *American Journal of Obstetrics and Gynecology* 71–76.

Tarling, R (2006), 'Sentencing Practice in Magistrates' Courts Revisited' 45 *Howard Journal of Criminal Justice* 29–41.

Tata, C (2013), 'The Struggle for Sentencing Reform – Will the English Sentencing Guidelines Model Spread?' in Ashworth, A and Roberts, JV (eds), *Sentencing Guidelines – Exploring the English Model* (Oxford, Oxford University Press).

Tata, C (2010), 'Sentencing and Penal Decision-Making: Is Scotland Losing its Distinctive Character?' in Croall, H, Mooney, G and Munro, M (eds), *Criminal Justice in Scotland* (Abingdon, Willan Publishing).

Tata, C (2002), 'So What Does "and Society" Mean?' in Tata, C and Hutton, N (eds), *Sentencing and Society – International Perspectives* (Aldershot, Ashgate).

Taylor, Lord (1993), 'Judges and Sentencing' 38(4) *Journal of the Law Society of Scotland* 129–31.

Temkin, J (2002), *Rape and the Legal Process* (2nd edn) (Oxford, Oxford University Press).

Temkin, J and Ashworth, A (2004), 'The Sexual Offences Act 2003: (1) Rape, Sexual Assaults and the Problems of Consent' *Criminal Law Review*, 328–46.

Temkin, J, Gray, JM, and Barret, J (2018), 'Different Functions of Rape Myth Use in Court: Findings from a Trial Observation Study' 13(2) *Feminist Criminology* 205–26.

Temkin, J and Krahé, B (2008), *Sexual Assault and the Justice Gap: A Question of Attitude* (Oxford, Hart Publishing).

Temple, JR, Weston, R, Rodriguez, BF, and Marshall, LL (2007), 'Differing Effects of Partner and Non-partner Sexual Assault on Women's Health' 13(3) *Violence Against Women*, 285–97.

Terblanche, SS (2017), 'Twenty Years of Constitutional Court Judgments: What Lessons are there about Sentencing?' 20 *Potchefstroom Electronic Law Journal* 1–37.

Terblanche, SS (2016), *A Guide to Sentencing in South Africa* (3rd edn) (Durban, LexisNexis).

Terblanche, SS (2014), 'Sentencing' 27(1) *South African Journal of Criminal Justice* 104–16.

Terblanche, SS (2013a), 'Judgements on Sentencing: Leaving a Lasting Legacy' 76(1) *The Journal of Contemporary Roman-Dutch Law* 95–106.

Terblanche, SS (2013b), 'Sentencing' 26(1) *South African Journal of Criminal Justice* 105–21.

Terblanche, SS (2011), 'The Discretionary Effect of Mitigating and Aggravating Factors: A South African Case Study' in Roberts, JV (ed), *Mitigation and Aggravation at Sentencing* (Cambridge, Cambridge University Press).

Terblanche, SS (2010), 'Annual Survey of South African Law 2010 – Sentencing' (Pretoria, The Centre for Business Law of the University of South Africa).

Terblanche, SS (2008a), 'Sentencing' 21(1) *South African Journal of Criminal Justice* 119–34.

Terblanche, SS (2008b), 'A Sentencing Council in South Africa' in Freiberg, A and Gelb, K (eds), *Penal Populism, Sentencing Councils and Sentencing Policy* (Cullompton, Willan Publishing).

Terblanche, SS (2007), *A Guide to Sentencing in South Africa* (2nd edn) (Durban, LexisNexis).

Terblanche, SS (2006), 'Rape Sentencing with the Aid of Sentencing Guidelines' 39(1) *The Comparative and International Law Journal of South Africa* 1–38.

Terblanche, SS (2003a), 'Sentencing Guidelines for South Africa: Lessons from Elsewhere' 120(4) *South African Law Journal* 858–82.

Terblanche, SS (2003b), 'Mandatory and Minimum Sentences: Considering S.51 of the Criminal Law Amendment Act 1997' *Acta Juridica*, 194–220.

Terblanche, SS (2001), 'Aspects of Minimum Sentence Legislation: Judicial Comment and the Courts' Jurisdiction' 14(1) *South African Journal of Criminal Justice* 1–19.

Terblanche, SS (1997), 'Sentencing in South Africa' in Tonry, M and Hatlestad, K (eds), *Sentencing Reform in Overcrowded Times* (New York, Oxford University Press).

Terblanche, SS and Mackenzie, G (2008), 'Mandatory Sentences in South Africa: Lessons for Australia?' 41(3) *The Australian and New Zealand Journal of Criminology* 402–20.

Terblanche, SS and Roberts, JV (2005), 'Sentencing in South Africa: Lacking in Principle but Delivering Justice?' 18(2) *South African Journal of Criminal Justice* 187–202.

Tewksbury, R (2007), 'Effects of Sexual Assaults on Men: Physical, Mental and Sexual Consequences' 6(1) *International Journal of Men's Health* 22–35.

Thomas, DA (2013), 'Case Comment – *R v Karam (Mawawe Ibrahim) – Rape – Sentencing Guideline – Discretion of Judge – Victim Impact*' *Criminal Law Review*, 998–1000.

Thomas, DA (2012), 'Case Comment – Sentencing – *R v Wilson* – Guilty Plea in Face of Overwhelming Evidence' *Criminal Law Review*, 560–62.

Thomas, DA (2011), 'Case Comment – *Re Attorney General's Reference (Nos 73, 75 and 3 of 2010)*: Sentencing – Rape – Rape of Victim by Burglar Breaking into Victim's Home' *Criminal Law Review*, 580–84.

Thomas, DA (2008), 'Sentencing: Rape of Child – Sexual Offences Act 2003 s. 5 – Definitive Guideline' *Criminal Law Review*, 155–60.

Thomas, DA (2003), 'Sentencing Rape – Sentencing Guidelines' *Criminal Law Review*, 207–09.

Thomas, DA (2002), 'The Sentencing Process' in McConville, M and Wilson, G (eds), *The Handbook of The Criminal Justice Process* (Oxford, Oxford University Press).

Thomas, DA (1988), 'Rape by Person with Previous Settled Relationship with Victim – Relevance to Sentence' *Criminal Law Review*, 325–26.

Thomas, DA (1987), 'Sentencing: Some Current Questions' in Pennington, D C and Lloyd-Bostock, S (eds), *The Psychology of Sentencing – Approaches to Consistency and Disparity* (Oxford, Centre for Socio-Legal Studies).

Thomas, DA (1986), 'Rape – Sentencing Guidelines' *Criminal Law Review* 347–49.

Thomas, DA (1979), *Principles of Sentencing – The Sentencing Policy of the Court of Appeal Criminal Division* (2nd edn) (London, Heinemann).

Thompson, MS (2017), 'Doing Feminist Judgments' in Enright, M, McCandless, J and O'Donoghue, A (eds), *Northern/Irish Feminist Judgments – Judges' Troubles and the Gendered Politics of Identity* (Oxford, Hart Publishing).

Tickell, A (2015), 'Judge: victim "condoned" and "acquiesced" in her rape' Rape Crisis Scotland blog,. Available at: www.rapecrisisscotland.org.uk/blog/judge-victim-condoned-and-acquiesced-in-her-rape/ (accessed 1 September 2019).

Tinsley, Y (2017), 'Commentary on *R v Taueki* – Sentencing Guidelines for Domestic Violence: The Missing Factors' in McDonald, E, Powell, R, Stephens, M, and Hunter, R (eds), *Feminist Judgments of Aotearoa New Zealand – Te Rino: A Two-Stranded Rope* (Oxford, Hart Publishing).

Tombs, J (2008), 'Telling Sentencing Stories' in Carlen, P (ed), *Imaginary Penalities* (Cullompton, Willan Publishing).

Tombs, J (2004), *A Unique Punishment – Sentencing and the Prison Population in Scotland* (Edinburgh, Scottish Consortium on Crime & Criminal Justice).

Tombs, J and Jagger, E (2006), 'Denying Responsibility – Sentencers' Accounts of their Decisions to Imprison' 46(65) *British Journal of Criminology* 803–21.

Tonry, M (2002), 'Foreword' in Tata, C and Hutton, N (eds), *Sentencing and Society – International Perspectives* (Aldershot, Ashgate).

Tonry, M (1996), *Sentencing Matters* (New York, Oxford University Press).

Treacy, Lord Justice (2016), 'Letter to the Editor' *Criminal Law Review*, 489–90.

Treacy, Lord Justice (2014), 'Letter to the Editor: Section 125 of the Coroners and Justice Act 2009 and Sentencing Guidelines' *Criminal Law Review*, 298–99.

Treacy, Lord Justice (2013), 'Foreword' in Sentencing Council for England and Wales, *Sexual Offences – Response to Consultation*, London, Sentencing Council.

Ullman, SE (2013), 'Multiple Perpetrator Rape Victimization – How it Differs and Why it Matters' in Horvath, MAH and Woodhams, J (eds), *Handbook on the Study of Multiple Perpetrator Rape – A Multidisciplinary Response to an International Problem* (Abingdon, Routledge).

Ullman, SE (2007), 'Comparing Gang and Individual Rapes in a Community Sample of Urban Women' 22(1) *Violence and Victims* 43–51.

Ullman, SE and Siegel, JM (1993), 'Victim-Offender Relationship and Sexual Assault' 8(2) *Violence and Victims* 121–34.

van der Bijl, C and Rumney, PNS (2009), 'Attitudes, Rape and Law Reform in South Africa' 73(5) *The Journal of Criminal Law* 414 –29.

van der Merwe, A (2015), 'Sentencing' 28(3) *South African Journal of Criminal Justice* 415–29.

van der Merwe, A (2013), 'Sentencing' 26(3) *South African Journal of Criminal Justice* 399–418.

van der Merwe, A (2008), 'Addressing Victims' Harm: The Role of Impact Reports' 30 *Thomas Jefferson Law Review* 391 406.

van der Merwe, A (2005), *Aspects of the Sentencing Process in Child Sexual Abuse Cases* (PhD Thesis, Grahamstown, Rhodes University).

van der Merwe, A and Skelton, A (2015), '"Victims" Mitigating Views in Sentencing Decisions: A Comparative Analysis' 35(2) *Oxford Journal of Legal Studies* 355–72.

van Zyl Smit, D (2002), 'Mandatory Sentences: A Conundrum for the New South Africa?' in Tata, C and Hutton, N (eds), *Sentencing and Society – International Perspectives* (Aldershot, Ashgate).

Vearnals, S and Campbell, T (2001), 'Male Victims of Male Sexual Assault: A Review of Psychological Consequences and Treatment' 16(3) *Sexual Relationship Therapy* 279–86.

Viljoen Commission (1976), *Report of the Commission of Inquiry into the Penal System of the Republic of South Africa*, RP 78 (Pretoria, Government Printer).

von Hirsch, A (2017), *Deserved Criminal Sentences – An Overview* (Oxford, Hart Publishing).

von Hirsch, A (2009), 'Proportionate Sentences: A Desert Perspective' in von Hirsch, A, Ashworth, A and Roberts, J (eds), *Principled Sentencing – Readings on Theory and Policy* (3rd edn) (Oxford, Hart Publishing).

von Hirsch, A (1993), *Censure and Sanctions* (Oxford, Clarendon Press).

von Hirsch, A and Ashworth, A (2005), *Proportionate Sentencing – Exploring the Principles* (Oxford, Oxford University Press).

von Hirsch, A, Ashworth, A and Jareborg, N (2005), 'Gauging Crime Seriousness: A 'Living Standard' Conception of Criminal Harm' in von Hirsch, A and Ashworth, A, *Proportionate Sentencing – Exploring the Principles* (Oxford, Oxford University Press).

von Hirsch, A and Jareborg, N (1991), 'Gauging Criminal Harm: A Living-standard Analysis' 11(1) *Oxford Journal of Legal Studies* 1–38.

von Hirsch, A and Roberts, J V (2004), 'Legislating Sentencing Principles: The Provisions of the Criminal Justice Act 2003 Relating to Sentencing Purposes and the Role of Previous Convictions' *Criminal Law Review*, 639 – 52.

Walker, G (2015), 'The (In)Significance of Genital Injury in Rape and Sexual Assault' 34 *Journal of Forensic and Legal Medicine* 173–78.

Walker, J, Archer, J and Davies, M (2005a), 'Effects of Rape on Men: A Descriptive Analysis' 34(1) *Archives of Sexual Behavior* 69–80.

Walker, J, Archer, J and Davies, M (2005b), 'Effects of Male Rape on Psychological Functioning' 44 *British Journal of Clinical Psychology* 445–51.

Wall, IF (2014), 'The Examination: Injuries' in Dalton, M (ed), *Forensic Gynaecology* (Cambridge, Cambridge University Press).

Walston, C, Bottoms, A, Eisner, M, and Lösel, F (2009), *Challenging Crime – A Portrait of the Cambridge Institute of Criminology* (London, Third Millennium Publishing).

Warner, K (2005), 'Sexual Offending: Victim, Gender and Sentencing Dilemmas' in Chappell, D and Wilson, P (eds), *Issues in Australian Crime and Criminal Justice* (Chatswood, LexisNexis Butterworths Australia).

Warner, K (2002), 'Sentencing Sexual Offenders in the UK and Australia' in Tata, C and Hutton, N (eds), *Sentencing and Society – International Perspectives* (Aldershot, Ashgate).

Warner, K (2000), 'Sentencing in Cases of Marital Rape: Towards Changing the Male Imagination' 20(4) *Legal Studies* 592–611.

Warner, K (1998), 'Sentencing for Rape' in Easteal, P (ed), *Balancing the Scales – Rape, Law Reform and Australian Culture* (Sydney, The Federation Press).

Wasik, M (2014), *A Practical Approach to Sentencing* (5th edn) (Oxford, Oxford University Press).

Wasik, M (2008), 'Sentencing Guidelines in England and Wales – State of the Art?' *Criminal Law Review* 253–63.

Wasik, M (2006), 'Publication Review – *Sentencing: Law and Practice* (Thomas O'Malley)' 41 *Irish Jurist* 146–47.

Wasik, M (2003), 'Sentencing Guidelines – Past, Present and Future' 56 *Current Legal Problems* 239–64.

Wasik, M (2001), *Emmins on Sentencing* (4th edn) (London, Blackstone Press).

Watt, B (2014), 'The Story of Rape: Wrongdoing and the Emotional Imagination' 26 *The Denning Law Journal* 46–61.

Weitzdörfer, J, Shiroshita, Y and Padfield, N (2018), 'Sentencing and Punishment in Japan and England: A Comparative Discussion' in Liu, J and Miyazawa, S (eds), *Crime and Justice in Contemporary Japan* (Cham, Springer International).

Welch, J and Mason, F (2007), 'Clinical Review – Rape and Sexual Assault' 334 *British Medical Journal* 1154– 58.

Wellman, A, Reddington, F and Clark, K (2017), 'What's Trending? #Sexual Assault: An Exploratory Study of Social Media Coverage of Teen Sexual Assaults' 18(1) *Criminology, Criminal Justice, Law & Society* 88–105.

Wells, C and Quick, O (2010), *Lacey, Wells and Quick – Reconstructing Criminal Law – Text and Materials* (Cambridge, Cambridge University Press).

Welsh, Sheriff T (2011), 'Commentary to *Petrie v HM Advocate*, 2011 SCL 424, *Scottish Criminal Law*, 427–29.

Welsh, Sheriff T (2010), 'Commentary to *HM Advocate v Graham*, 2010 SCL 789' *Scottish Criminal Law*, 808–10.

Wertheimer, A (2003), *Consent to Sexual Relations* (Cambridge, Cambridge University Press).

White, C (2019), 'Medical Evidence: Adults' in Rook, P and Ward, R, *Rook and Ward on Sexual Offences Law & Practice – Supplement to the Fifth Edition* (London, Sweet & Maxwell).

White, C (2016), 'Medical Evidence: Adults' in Rook, P and Ward, R, *Rook and Ward on Sexual Offences Law & Practice* (5th edn) (London, Sweet & Maxwell).

White, C (2013), 'Genital Injuries in Adults' 27(1) *Best Practice & Research – Clinical Obstetrics and Gynaecology* 113–30.

White, D and McMillan, L (2018), 'Statutory Response to Sexual Violence – Where Doubt is Always Considered Reasonable' in Lombard, N (ed), *The Routledge Handbook of Gender and Violence* (Abingdon, Routledge).

Whittington, R and Wykes, T (2000), 'The Psychopathology of Violence' in Mason, J K and Purdue, B N (eds), *The Pathology of Trauma* (3rd edn) (London, Arnold).

Whitwell, H, Thorne, K, Kolar, A, Harvey, P, Butler, B and Riddell, A (2015), 'Sexual Assaults' in Whitwell, H, Thorne, K, Kolar, A and Harvey, P (eds), *Mason's Forensic Medicine for Lawyers* (6th edn) (Haywards Heath, Bloomsbury Professional).

Wiles, P (2015), 'Foreword' in Roberts, JV (ed), *Exploring Sentencing Practice in England and Wales* (Basingstoke, Palgrave Macmillan).

Williams, LS (1984), 'The Classic Rape: When Do Victims Report?' 31(4) *Social Problems*, 459–67.

Wojcicki, JM (2002), '"She Drank His Money": Survival Sex and the Problem of Violence in Taverns in Gauteng Province, South Africa' 16(3) *Medical Anthropology Quarterly* 267–93.

Wood, K (2005), 'Contextualizing Group Rape in Post-Apartheid South Africa' 7(4) *Culture, Health & Sexuality* 303–17.

Wood, K and Jewkes, R (1997), 'Violence, Rape and Sexual Coercion: Everyday Love in a South African Township' 5(2) *Gender and Development* 41–6.

Wood, K, Lambert, H, and Jewkes, R (2007), '"Showing Roughness in a Beautiful Way": Talk about Love, Coercion, and Rape in South African Youth Sexual Culture' 21(3) *Medical Anthropology Quarterly* 277–300.

Woodhams, J (2013), 'Offender Aggression and Violence in Multiple Perpetrator Rape' in Horvath, MAH and Woodhams, J (eds), *Handbook on the Study of Multiple Perpetrator Rape – A Multidisciplinary Response to an International Problem* (Abingdon, Routledge).

Woodhams, J and Cooke, C (2013), 'Suspect Aggression and Victim Resistance in Multiple Perpetrator Rapes' 42 *Archives of Sexual Behaviour* 1509–16.

Woodhams, J, Cooke, C, Harkins, L and da Silva, T (2012), 'Leadership in Multiple Perpetrator Stranger Rape' 27(4) *Journal of Interpersonal Violence* 728–52.

Woodhams, J and Horvath, MAH (2013), 'Introduction' in Horvath, MAH and Woodhams, J (eds), *Handbook on the Study of Multiple Perpetrator Rape – A Multidisciplinary Response to an International Problem* (Abingdon, Routledge).

Woodlock, D (2017), 'The Abuse of Technology in Domestic Violence and Stalking' 23(5) *Violence Against Women* 584–602.

Wright, S (2019), 'Disclosing Private Sexual Images' in Rook, P and Ward, R, *Rook and Ward on Sexual Offences Law & Practice – Supplement to the Fifth Edition* (London, Sweet & Maxwell).

Wyatt, J, Squires, T, Norfolk, G and Payne-James, J (2011), *The Oxford Handbook of Forensic Medicine* (Oxford, Oxford University Press).

Yar, M (2012), 'Crime, Media and the Will-to-Representation: Reconsidering Relationships in the New Media Age' 8(3) *Crime Media Culture* 245–60.

Young, W (2008), 'Sentencing Reform in New Zealand: A Proposal to Establish a Sentencing Council' in Freiberg, A and Gelb, K (eds), *Penal Populism, Sentencing Councils and Sentencing Policy* (Cullompton, Willan Publishing).

Young, W and Browning, C (2008), 'New Zealand's Sentencing Council' *Criminal Law Review* 287–98.

Young, W and King, A (2013), 'The Origins and Evolution of Sentencing Guidelines – A Comparison of England and Wales and New Zealand' in Ashworth, A and Roberts, JV (eds), *Sentencing Guidelines – Exploring the English Model* (Oxford, Oxford University Press).

Young, W and King, A (2011), 'Addressing Problematic Sentencing Factors in the Development of Guidelines' in Roberts, JV (ed), *Mitigation and Aggravation at Sentencing* (Cambridge, Cambridge University Press).

Young, W and King, A (2010), 'Sentencing Practice and Guidance in New Zealand' 22(4) *Federal Sentencing Reporter* 254–61.

Zilkens, RR, Phillips, MA, Kelly, MC, Mukhtar, SA, Semmens, JB, and Smith, DA (2016), 'Non-Fatal Strangulation in Sexual Assault: A Study of Clinical and Assault Characteristics Highlighting the Role of Intimate Partner Violence' 43 *Journal of Forensic and Legal Medicine* 1–7.

INDEX